THE ROLE OF MULTILATERAL ENVIRONMENTAL AGREEMENTS

The environment suffers enormously during armed conflicts and, despite the increasing awareness of the pressing need to protect the planet, devastating environmental damage can occur legally at times of war. This book suggests that – apart from the protection offered under law of armed conflict – environmental treaties or multilateral agreements (MEAs) can complement and strengthen environmental protection when war occurs.

Previous research has focused on the protection offered under the law of armed conflict (in particular international humanitarian law) and customary international environmental law concerning wartime environmental damage, or whether environmental treaties remain applicable at times of armed conflict. This book, however, is the first in-depth scholarly examination of how environmental treaties can apply in wartime and how they can contribute to the protection of the environment in relation to armed conflict. It also offers an updated study of environmental protection under the law of armed conflict, including the latest developments in the International Law Commission's work on this underexplored topic.

Volume 76 in the series Studies in International Law

Studies in International Law

Recent titles in this series

Complicity in International Criminal Law
Marina Aksenova

Arctic Law and Governance: The Role of China and Finland
Edited by Timo Koivurova, Qin Tianbao, Tapio Nykänen and Sébastien Duyck

States, the Law and Access to Refugee Protection: Fortresses and Fairness
Edited by Maria O'Sullivan and Dallal Stevens

Revisiting the Concept of Defence in the Jus ad Bellum: The Dual Face of Defence
Johanna Friman

The International Legal Protection of Persons in Humanitarian Crises
Dug Cubie

The International Committee of the Red Cross and its Mandate to Protect and Assist: Law and Practice
Christy Shucksmith

The Impact of Investment Treaty Law on Host States: Enabling Good Governance
Mavluda Sattorova

Allocating International Responsibility Between Member States and International Organisations
Nikolaos Voulgaris

Predictability and Flexibility in the Law of Maritime Delimitation, 2nd edition
Yoshifumi Tanaka

Feminist Engagement with International Criminal Law: Norm Transfer, Complementarity, Rape and Consent
Eithne Dowds

Asylum Control and Access to Protection: Admission, Readmission and Human Rights
Mariagiulia Giuffré

Intertemporal Linguistics in International Law: Beyond Contemporaneous and Evolutionary Treaty Interpretation
Julian Wyatt

The Responsibility to Protect and the Failures of the United Nations Security Council
P M Butchard

For a complete list of titles in this series, see www.bloomsburyprofessional.com/uk/series/studies-in-international-law

The Role of Multilateral Environmental Agreements

A Reconciliatory Approach to Environmental Protection in Armed Conflict

Britta Sjöstedt

•HART•
OXFORD • LONDON • NEW YORK • NEW DELHI • SYDNEY

HART PUBLISHING

Bloomsbury Publishing Plc

Kemp House, Chawley Park, Cumnor Hill, Oxford, OX2 9PH, UK

1385 Broadway, New York, NY 10018, USA

HART PUBLISHING, the Hart/Stag logo, BLOOMSBURY and the Diana logo are trademarks of Bloomsbury Publishing Plc

First published in Great Britain 2020

A catalogue record for this book is available from the British Library.

Library of Congress Cataloging-in-Publication data

Library of Congress Control Number: 2020930520

ISBN: HB: 978-1-50992-253-6
ePDF: 978-1-50992-255-0
ePub: 978-1-50992-254-3

Typeset by Compuscript Ltd, Shannon
Printed and bound in Great Britain by CPI Group (UK) Ltd, Croydon CR0 4YY

MIX
Paper from responsible sources
FSC® C013604
FSC www.fsc.org

To find out more about our authors and books visit www.hartpublishing.co.uk. Here you will find extracts, author information, details of forthcoming events and the option to sign up for our newsletters.

Contents

Abbreviations

CITES	Convention for International Trade in Endangered Species
CNDP	National Congress for the Defence of the People
COP	Conference of the Parties
DRC	Democratic Republic of the Congo
ECHR	European Convention on Human Rights
ENMOD	Convention on the Prohibition of Military or Any Other Hostile Use of Environmental Modification Techniques
EUTM	European Training Mission
FAO	UN Food and Agricultural Organization
FODESA	Sahelian Areas Development Fund Programme
GEF	Global Environment Facility
ICCPR	International Covenant on Civil and Political Rights
ICCWC	International Consortium on Combating Wildlife Crime
ICRC	International Committee of the Red Cross
ICTY	International Criminal Tribunal for the former Yugoslavia
IEA	International Environmental Agreements
IFAD	International Fund for Agricultural Development
IIHL Manual	Manual on the Law of Non-International Armed Conflict
ILPI	International Law and Policy Institute
INTERPOL	International Criminal Police Organization
IUCN	International Union for Conservation of Nature and Natural Resources
LRTAP	Convention on Long-Range Transboundary Air Pollution
OSPAR	Convention for the Protection of the Marine Environment of the North-East Atlantic
M23	March 23 Movement
MEA	Multilateral Environmental Agreement

MINUSMA	Multidimensional Integrated Stabilization Mission in Mali
MONUC	United Nations Organization Mission in the DRC
MONUSCO	United Nations Organization Stabilization Mission in the DRC
NATO	North Atlantic Treaty Organization
UN	United Nations
UNCHR	United Nations High Commissioner for Refugees
UNCHS	United Nations Human Settlements Programme
UNCLOS	United Nations Convention on the Law of the Sea
UNDP	United Nations Development Programme
UNEP	United Nations Environmental Programme
UNESCO	United Nations Educational, Scientific and Cultural Organization
UNPROFOR	United Nations Protection Force
VCLT	Vienna Convention on the Law of Treaties
WH	World Heritage Committee
WTO	World Trade Organization
WWF	World Wide Fund for Nature

Table of International Treaties, Resolutions, Decisions, etc

International Treaties

Resolutions and Decisions from UN Bodies

UNESCO Decisions

UN General Assembly Resolutions

UN Security Council Resolutions

Judgments of the International Court of Justice

Other Cases

1

Setting the Scene

I. INTRODUCTION

THIS BOOK EXAMINES how environmental treaties, also referred to as multilateral environmental agreements (MEAs), can add to the protection of the environment during armed conflicts of international and non-international character. The examination also covers the immediate aftermath of armed conflicts, ie, the blurry transition phase between armed conflict and peace (post-conflict).[1] I argue that MEAs can apply both in peacetime and wartime, as well as in international and non-international armed conflicts to strengthen environmental protection in all times, albeit to a degree adjusted to the circumstances.

The analysis will encompass the law of armed conflict and international environmental law – both treaty-based as well as customary law – in order to provide a broad description of the existing mechanisms under international law to address wartime environmental damage. Most of the previous research addressing the issue of environmental protection during war has focused on the application of the law of armed conflict (also referred to as the international humanitarian law or laws of war),[2] which is the body of international law specially designed to deal with situations of armed conflict. The law of armed conflict does not prioritise the environment and the environmental protection under this regime has been criticised for permitting substantial environmental damage despite the serious consequences.

Previous research has also explored how the application of international environmental law having customary law status can improve environmental

[1] This phase is included because of the difficulty in establishing a clear boundary between the state of armed conflict and the state of peace. For further reading, see C Stahn, '"*Jus ad bellum*", "*jus in bello*" … "*jus post bellum*"? – Rethinking the Conception of the Law of Armed Force' (2006) 17 *European Journal of International Law* 921; D Fleck, '*Jus Post Bellum* as Partly Independent Legal Framework' in C Stahn, JS Easterday and J Iverson (eds), *Jus Post Bellum: Mapping the Normative Foundations* (Oxford University Press, 2014).

[2] International humanitarian law was introduced through the adoption of the Geneva Conventions in 1949. It has a more narrow scope than the laws of war and the law of armed conflict, which not only cover the conduct of war, but also the law of neutrality and the law of occupation. Throughout this book, I use the term 'the law of armed conflict' as being a broader and more updated term than the other two.

protection during armed conflicts. However, what is missing in the scholarly analysis is the application of MEAs in times of war. What has been examined in previous research on this topic is the question of *whether* MEAs continue to apply during armed conflicts.[3] Whereas little attention has been directed on *how* these apply in an armed conflict context. There are different presumptions regarding MEAs' ability to provide environmental protection in such a context: either they are criticised for the vague formulations in their provisions and seen as unable to add any substantial protection,[4] or they are viewed as having promising potential because they contain detailed rules specifically dealing with the environment.[5] There is little explanation, however, on how such rules may substantially add to the protection.

Overall, there is a knowledge gap on how MEAs may contribute to protect the environment in relation to armed conflict because the environmental treaties' potential in this context has not been explored. I claim that it is a missed opportunity for improving environmental protection during armed conflicts, in particular, because these treaties use innovative strategies to fulfil the treaty objectives that differ from treaties in other legal areas, such as the law of armed conflict. For instance, MEAs establish whole treaty systems in which the treaty bodies are able to launch projects and programmes to advance the treaty objectives. In many cases, these initiatives are focused on supporting institutionally weak states that are unable to fulfil their obligations under MEAs, which could include those affected by armed conflicts.[6] In addition to the law of armed conflict and customary international environmental law, the study of MEAs may offer new paths to protect the environment during wartime. MEAs addressing specific environmental problems and operating in a broader international structure can strengthen environmental protection, both normatively as well as operationally.

[3] S Vöneky, 'Peacetime Environmental Law as a Basis of State Responsibility for Environmental Damage Caused by War' in JE Austin and CE Bruch (eds), *The Environmental Consequences of War* (Cambridge University Press, 2000); S Vöneky, 'A New Shield for the Environment: Peacetime Treaties as Legal Restraints of Wartime Damage' (2000) 9 *Review of European, Comparative & International Environmental Law* 20; K Bannelier-Christakis, 'International Law Commission and Protection of the Environment in Times of Armed Conflict: A Possibility for Adjudication?' (2013) 20 *Journal of International Cooperation Studies* 129; A Loets, 'An Old Debate Revisited: Applicability of Environmental Treaties in Times of International Armed Conflict Pursuant to the International Law Commission's "Draft Articles on the Effects of Armed Conflict on Treaties"' (2012) 21 *Review of European, Comparative & International Environmental Law* 127.

[4] A Leibler, 'Deliberate Wartime Environmental Damage' (1992) 23 *California Western International Law Journal* 67, 80–81; A-L Bunker, 'Protection of the Environment During Armed Conflict: One Gulf, Two Wars' (2004) 13 *Review of European, Comparative & International Environmental Law* 201, 211. Bunker notes that MEAs protecting particular areas of environmental significance may be able to sustain some protection – defined areas can be avoided and protected in situations of armed conflict.

[5] M Bothe et al, 'International Law Protecting the Environment During Armed Conflict: Gaps and Opportunities' (2010) 92 *International Review of the Red Cross* 569; Loets (n 3).

[6] E Louka, *International Environmental Law: Fairness, Effectiveness, and World Order*, 1st edn (Cambridge University Press, 2006) 29.

II. SCOPE OF THE BOOK

Wartime environmental protection is located at the intersection of several legal areas, but mainly it concerns the law of armed conflict and international environmental law.[7] Therefore, this book studies norms (rules and principles) under both in order to analyse the ability of contemporary international law to deal with the issue. The book will (A) analyse the ability of the law of armed conflict to protect the environment adopting an evolutionary approach when interpreting its norms; and (B) assess how the application of environmental treaties could advance the protection under the law of armed conflict. Throughout this book, I argue that rules and principles of international environmental law should continue to apply in wartime. My arguments are based on the understanding that international law is a single albeit diversified legal system striving for coherence.[8] The idea of coherence is inherent in the concept of a legal system, in the sense that the rules must be understood as having a normative meaning and be coordinated to function together.[9] International environmental law addresses complex problems that often permeate various areas of international law, such as the rights of future generations, the need to protect ecosystems and endangered species as well as prevent irreparable environmental damage. Therefore, these values protected under international environmental law must remain protected even when applying other areas of international law. To this end, many MEAs have incorporated provisions that allow for consideration of other concerns, such as human rights, sustainable development, or international trade.[10] This enables the adoption of what I refer to as a 'reconciliatory approach'. Such an approach opens up for the harmonisation of the obligations of international environmental law and the law of armed conflict, which also contributes to achieving coherence in the international legal system.

Regarding part A, I argue that the existing provisions under the law of armed conflict should be interpreted in the light of customary international environmental law. This corpus of law has developed new concepts and principles on the basis of new scientific discoveries when assessing and preventing environmental damage that also need to be taken into account in wartime. As wartime

[7] Other areas of international law are also of interest, such as human rights law (in particular considering its reproaching of the environment), international criminal law and even trade law. However, these legal areas fall outside this study.

[8] This perception is supported by the Study Group of the International Law Commission on the Topic of Fragmentation of International Law. The Study Group was examining the alleged fragmentation of international law. See International Law Commission, 'Fragmentation of International Law: Difficulties Arising from the Diversification and Expansion of International Law'. Report of the Study Group of the International Law Commission, UN Doc A/CN.4/L.702, 18 July 2006, para 14(1) (Report of the Study Group).

[9] CE Alchourrón and E Bulygin, *Normative Systems* (Springer, 1971) 3.

[10] See, for instance, A Boyle, 'Relationship between International Environmental Law and Other Branches of International Law' in D Bodansky, J Brunnée and E Hey (eds), *Oxford Handbook of International Environmental Law* (Oxford University Press, 2007) 145.

environmental protection falls under the scope of both the law of armed conflict and international environmental law, normative tensions between the two legal frameworks may arise. In such a case, the law of armed conflict applies as the *lex specialis* during armed conflicts and prevails over an incompatible environmental (peacetime) rule. Nevertheless, peacetime law continues to have a normative influence during armed conflicts. The law of armed conflict and international environmental law may therefore become a challenging marriage of two distinct legal areas striving towards different aims. In particular, there is no uniform practice on how to apply the *lex specialis* rule, as I will discuss in chapter six.

In regard to part B, I will scrutinise how the application of MEAs can contribute to safeguarding the environment in war-torn states. As there are over 1,300 MEAs,[11] I have restricted the focus of this study to the Convention Concerning the Protection of the World Cultural and Natural Heritage[12] (World Heritage Convention), and the Convention on Wetlands of International Importance, and Especially the Waterfowl Habitat[13] (Ramsar Convention). Both conventions provide protection for environmental areas that are of interest to the international community. The World Heritage Convention, negotiated under the United Nations Educational, Scientific and Cultural Organization (UNESCO),[14] protects both natural and cultural world heritage sites of outstanding value to humankind. The Ramsar Convention protects wetlands of international significance. The conventions permit their state parties to nominate sites to be protected under the conventions through inscription on certain lists: the World Heritage List and the List of Wetlands of International Importance (Ramsar List). The designation of protected environmental areas is an important tool for nature conservation at an international level.[15] The safeguarding of internationally important environmental areas, as identified under the Ramsar Convention and the World Heritage Convention, contributes to preserve endangered species, sensitive ecosystems, and prevent biodiversity loss. Therefore, ensuring the protection of these areas can advance environmental protection in relation to armed conflict. This is of particular importance

[11] The International Environmental Agreements (IEA) Database project includes over 1,300 MEAs, over 2,200 BEAs, 250 other environmental agreements. See the website of the IEA Database project, available at: iea.uoregon.edu.

[12] Convention Concerning the Protection of the World Cultural and Natural Heritage (adopted 23 November 1972, entered into force 15 December 1979) 1037 UNTS 151 (World Heritage Convention).

[13] Convention on Wetlands of International Importance Especially as Waterfowl Habitat (adopted 2 February 1971, entered into force 21 December 1975) 996 UNTS 245 (Ramsar Convention).

[14] The World Heritage Convention was adopted at the General Conference of United Nations Educational, Scientific and Cultural Organization (UNESCO). Thus, UNESCO and the operation of the World Heritage Convention are intertwined.

[15] R Tarasofsky, 'Protecting Specifically Important Areas During International Armed Conflict: A Critique of the IUCN Draft Convention on the Prohibition of Hostile Military Activities in Protected Areas' in JE Austin and CE Bruch (eds), *The Environmental Consequences of War* (Cambridge University Press, 2000).

because protected areas are often exposed during armed conflicts since they can offer hiding places, shelter, nutrition, firewood and revenues for armed groups, as well as for those displaced persons fleeing the hostilities.[16] Thus, the area-based protection mechanisms under the World Heritage Convention and the Ramsar Convention could provide standards on how states should behave in relation to these protected sites during and after armed conflicts. In addition, new developments under international law strive to ensure that areas of major ecological importance also remain protected in wartime as will be discussed in chapter four.

The final chapter will include a normative analysis by generalising some of the findings from the case studies in B and linking these with the theoretical framework outline in A. Thus, the A- and B-part complement each other in order to determine the role of MEAs during and in the aftermath of armed conflicts by the adoption of the reconciliatory approach. The main contribution of this book is to show the possibilities of how MEAs and the law of armed conflict can support each other using different strategies to improve environmental protection in relation to armed conflict.

III. WHY READ THIS BOOK?

The destructive nature of armed conflict can cause large-scale damage within a short time period: an entire ecosystem that has taken decades or even centuries to create can be destroyed in one single attack, having implications for a larger region or even on a global scale. The exact consequences of much environmental damage remain uncertain. However, increasing knowledge shows that ecosystems are interconnected and the state of them can affect other ecosystems and accelerate environmental problems. As human life is dependent on a healthy environment, its destruction can have long-term effects on public health,[17] affecting both present and future generations.[18] Much of this damage is lawful under the law of armed conflict. However, new discoveries on how ecosystems connect and are interdependent on each other puts this legality into question, in particular given the new threats of climate change, biodiversity loss and environmental degradation.

International environmental law has developed as a response to tackle and prevent complex global environmental problems and risks.[19] Safeguarding

[16] International Law and Policy Institute (ILPI) 2014, 'Protection of the Natural Environment in Armed Conflict: An Empirical Study', ILPI, Report 12/2014, 6.

[17] J Jacoby, 'Introduction' in JE Austin and CE Bruch (eds), *The Environmental Consequences of War* (Cambridge University Press, 2000) 379.

[18] JE Austin and CE Bruch, 'Introduction' in JE Austin and CE Bruch (eds), *The Environmental Consequences of War* (Cambridge University Press, 2000) 5.

[19] D Bodansky, *The Art and Craft of International Environmental Law* (Harvard University Press, 2010) 32–33.

the environment mainly functions on the premise to take preventative and precautionary measures in order to manage the uncertain and sometimes irreversible environmental damage.[20] For that reason, international environmental law advances new legal requirements, including the principle of prevention, the concept of common but differentiated responsibility, and the principle of cooperation to establish a holistic and long-term environmental protection for present and future generations.[21] The principles enable approaches that take into account the particularities of the environmental problems, which are coupled with uncertainty with regard to their effects.[22]

The principle of prevention establishes a standard for states to act with due diligence in order to prevent and minimise the potential risks of transboundary harm and for harm occurring outside a state's jurisdiction. The principle of prevention also implies a requirement for states to assess their obligations under the principle continuously in order to keep up-to-date with advancements in scientific knowledge.[23] The introduction of the ecosystem approach stresses the need to provide a holistic protection of ecological processes as such and not solely the protection of certain species. The approach opts for protection of the complex interaction between different animals, plants and micro-organisms and their non-living environment.[24] The principle of cooperation encourages states to collaborate to address environmental problems, which could include exchanging information and notifying and consulting states on activities that may have harmful effects on their environment.[25] The concept of common but differentiated responsibility entails that states shall cooperate to protect and restore the environment, but it acknowledges that states have contributed differently to the global environmental degradation. It also looks at the differences in the ability of states to prevent, reduce and control environmental threats – where the more developed states must carry most of the burden in environmental actions and have a responsibility to support developing states by financial and technological means.[26]

In warfare, environmental harm can take place lawfully if it serves to achieve successful military operations. This is because the law of armed conflict is considered to apply as the *lex specialis* law in wartime. The *lex specialis* rule entails that specialised law takes precedence over incompatible rules of law that

[20] P-M Dupuy and JE Viñuales, *International Environmental Law*, 2nd edn (Cambridge University Press, 2018) 61–62.

[21] P Sands et al, *Principles of International Environmental Law*, 4th edn (Cambridge University Press, 2018) 211.

[22] Bodansky (n 19) 200–02.

[23] P Birnie, A Boyle and C Redgwell, *International Law & the Environment* (Oxford University Press, 2009) 143.

[24] See Article 2(6) in the Convention on Biological Diversity (Biodiversity Convention). See also Dupuy and Viñuales (n 20) 205.

[25] Dupuy and Viñuales (n 20) 74.

[26] U Beyerlin and T Marauhn, *International Environmental Law* (Hart Publishing, 2011) 63–64.

are regarded as more general. Consequently, in a war context, the law of armed conflict enables exceptions or derogations from the law created for peacetime, including international environmental law, which is considered as more general in such a context. The law of armed conflict seeks to avoid unnecessary suffering among combatants and to minimise harm to civilians and civilian objects, but permits proportional collateral damage caused to secure a military advantage, even it involves serious environmental impacts. Nevertheless, peacetime rules continue to apply alongside the law of armed conflict.

Given that the law of armed conflict and international environmental law have different characteristics, origins, functions and objectives, they may be able to complement each other to address wartime environmental damage. The law of armed conflict operates on the basis of the known information and predictable effects assessed from the current situation. International environmental law, on the other hand, aims to achieve long-lasting environmental protection by ensuring preventative measures, not only for the present but also for the future generations, which is not acknowledged as a concern under the law of armed conflict. As these legal areas are construed in distinctive ways, it can be a challenge for international lawyers specialised in one of the disciplines to fully comprehend the dynamics of the other.

Environmental concerns have not had much influence on the rules regulating warfare. The environment has mainly received protection under the law of armed conflict, as far as it may adversely affect the civilian population based on the foreseeable harm of planned attacks. However, more recent instruments of the law of armed conflict have recognised the need to protect the environment as such. In the 1977 Additional Protocol I to the 1949 Geneva Conventions[27] (Protocol I), the environment was offered special protection. In addition, the environment receives protection under the general rules of the law of armed conflict as a civilian object as long it does not provide any military contribution. However, there is no consensus on how to deal with the environment, because the negotiators of the law of armed conflict instruments have intentionally left much discretion to the law-applier (in this case the party to an armed conflict) with regard to the environmentally related rules. As a result, legal scholars often describe the existing environmental protection provided under the law of armed conflict as being weak, vague and even inadequate.[28] Thus, I argue that

[27] Protocol Additional to the Geneva Conventions of 12 August 1949, and Relating to the Protection of Victims of International Armed Conflicts (adopted 8 June 1977, entered into force 7 December 1978) 1125 UNTS 3 (Protocol I).

[28] For further reading, see Bothe et al (n 5); Y Dinstein, 'Protection of the Environment in International Armed Conflict' (2001) 5 *Max Plank Yearbook of United Nations Law* 523–46; R Falk, 'Evaluating the Adequacy of Existing International Law Standards' in JE Austin and CE Bruch (eds), *The Environmental Consequences of War* (Cambridge University Press, 2000); W Verwey, 'Protection of the Environment in Times of Armed Conflict: In Search of a New Legal Perspective' (1995) 8 *Leiden Journal of International Law* 7; S Simonds, 'Conventional Warfare and Environmental Protection: A Proposal for International Legal Reform' (1992) 29 *Stanford Journal of International Law* 165; Vöneky, 'Peacetime Environmental Law' (n 3) 190–93; K Hulme, 'Taking Care to Protect

the discretion of the law-applier, as well as the vagueness in the rules, can be narrowed with the assistance of customary international environmental law and environmental treaties.

Similar to the law of armed conflict, a wide discretion is provided to the law-applier (the state party) under the MEAs. However, in this case it can be an advantage for environmental protection when applying the treaties during armed conflicts because it provides for adjustable and context-based measures. The treaty bodies in place for most MEAs can advise the law-applier and thus narrow the discretion. The rising environmental awareness of states, international organisations, non-governmental organisations and individuals has spurred the expansion of international environmental law, which has not been reflected in the law of armed conflict. Nevertheless, by narrowing the discretion of the law-applier under the law of armed conflict with the requirements of international environmental law, the protection of the environment during armed conflicts can better cohere with a contemporary view of the environment.

In addition, the law of armed conflict only deals with environmental damage that is the result of warfare. Other environmental issues related to armed conflict are not addressed under the legal framework because these are often connected with the knock-on effects resulting from the institutional collapse that is commonly experienced in war-torn states. The application of international environmental law offers recourse to respond to such issues by using the strategies available under MEAs, which can apply during armed conflicts as well as in post-conflict situations.

During armed conflicts, there are many problems in ensuring compliance with the rules of the law of armed conflict to protect civilians and prevent unnecessary suffering. The expectations of complying with MEAs in wartime must be realistically estimated and environmental protection measures have to be adjusted to the realities of the conflict accordingly. Therefore, it is mainly the tools and mechanisms available under the treaties that are studied, as observed in the case studies, and not necessarily the level of protection that can be offered. In the examination of the World Heritage Convention and the Ramsar Convention, I study the treaty provisions, as well as the activities undertaken by their treaty bodies in the application of the conventions. The treaty bodies may employ assistance to their state parties, taking the form of funding, capacity building and instigating programmes and projects for the purpose of managing non-compliance.[29] In contrast, no supportive measures can be carried out under the law of armed conflict because it is a field in which the treaties lack treaty bodies

the Environment Against Damage: A Meaningless Obligation?' (2010) 92 *International Review of the Red Cross* 675, 680; M Orellana, 'Criminal Punishment for Environmental Damage: Individual and State Responsibility at a Crossroad' (2005) 17 *Georgetown International Environmental Law Review* 673, 683–84.

[29] Dupuy and Viñuales (n 20) 37–38.

and is more dependent on states for compliance.[30] The non-compliance mechanisms under environmental treaties, and their less state-focused approaches, are often neglected in the literature when looking at safeguarding the environment in relation to armed conflict.

In addition, environmental treaties contribute to the development of an institutional infrastructure on an international level. Apart from treaties bodies, such a structure consists of international organisations, non-governmental organisations and private actors, etc. These take part in decision- and policy-making, as well as collaborating to implement international environmental law to some extent.[31] As the international institutional structure is influential for the application of international environmental law, it also has to be examined in order to overview the protection offered under this legal field. Therefore, this book contributes to studying the processes under international environmental law, adopting new legal requirements as well as inventive methods to address global environmental problems, to provide an understanding of how these can operate together with the law of armed conflict, and in particular to advance the understanding of the operation of MEAs during armed conflicts.

[30] International criminal tribunals for individual criminal accountability are, in a way, institutions enforcing the law of armed conflict to some extent. Also, non-governmental organisations, such as Human Rights Watch and Amnesty International, are increasingly involved in monitoring the application of the law of armed conflict. See M Schmitt, 'Classification in Future Conflict' in E Wilmshurst (ed), *International Law and the Classification of Conflicts* (Oxford University Press, 2012) 476.

[31] Beyerlin and Marauhn (n 26) 244.

2

Wartime Environmental Damage

I. INTRODUCTION

THE ENVIRONMENT AND its resources have a complicated relationship with armed conflicts. Environmental issues can be traced through all phases of a conflict cycle: contributing to conflict outbreaks; fuelling and sustaining hostilities; being a direct as well as an indirect target during hostilities; and obstructing peacebuilding efforts.[1] In addition, the concerns of climate change are regarded as a 'threat-multiplier' that is likely to increase the vulnerability of societies already affected by, or at the risk of being affected by war.[2] This nexus between climate change and security has been under debate by the UN Security Council since 2007.[3] Thus, the need to protect the environment in the context of armed conflict is likely to be even more pressing in the future.

The overall purpose of this chapter is to show the particularities of the type of environmental damage that occurs in times of armed conflict and why it needs to be addressed. Section II presents the common types of environmental damage that occur during armed conflicts and section III discusses the larger implications of such damage, including its effect on preventing peace and recovery in war-torn societies.

II. CATEGORIES OF WARTIME ENVIRONMENTAL DAMAGE

The typical wartime environmental damage can be divided into four categories. The first relates to damage resulting from the direct and intentional targeting of

[1] A UN report highlighted the role of environmental problems in relation to international security concerns. See United Nations, 'A More Secure World: Our Shared Responsibility Report of the High-level Panel on Threats, Challenges and Change' (United Nations, 2004). See also O Das, *Environmental Protection, Security and Armed Conflict* (Edward Elgar Publishing, 2013) 66–67; UNEP, 'From Conflict to Peacebuilding: The Role of Natural Resources and the Environment' (UNEP, Switzerland, 2009) 8; UNEP, 'Lebanon Post-Conflict Assessment' (UNEP, Switzerland, 2007) 10.

[2] K Mach et al, 'Climate as a risk factor for armed conflict' *Nature* (2019), available at: www.nature.com/articles/s41586-019-1300-6.

[3] In March 2017, the Security Council highlighted the role of climate-related risks in regard to the conflict in the Lake Chad basin. See UN Security Council Resolution, UN Doc S/RES/2349 (31 March 2017) para 26. In July 2018, the Security Council discussed the climate-related security risks. See UN News, 'Climate change recognized as "threat multiplier", UN Security Council debates its impact on peace' (25 January 2019), available at: news.un.org/en/story/2019/01/1031322.

the environment. The second refers to unintentional, even if foreseeable, collateral environmental damage occurring as a side effect of attacks directed at other (military) targets; for instance, attacks aimed at weapons factories, oil refineries, infrastructure, etc, resulting in oil spills, leakage of toxic substances, and other forms of pollution. This type of damage is probably the most common form of wartime environmental damage. The third category covers damage caused by manipulating the forces of the environment as a weapon. This type of damage is unusual, and the only noted example of the use of these techniques in warfare is when the United States performed cloud seeding during the Vietnam War.[4] The fourth and final category refers to the indirect environmental damage caused by the collapse of domestic and regional institutions because of the armed conflicts. The lack of governance means that states are left unable to protect their environment which enables illegal exploitation of natural resources and wildlife, leakages of sewage and sanitation facilities, unsustainable refugee settlements, etc. This type of damage can in many cases be more severe than the environmental damage occurring as a direct consequence of warfare.

A. Directly Targeting the Environment

It is not uncommon for military operations to directly target the environment and its assets to achieve a military advantage. The employment of scorched earth policies is an example of such a military operation that may target farmlands for the purpose of denying the food supply to the enemy, forests to prevent the enemy places in which to hide, and dikes or dams to create flooding and prevent the transportation of soldiers.

The scorched earth policies have been frequently used in times of armed conflict, often resulting in massive environmental damage. During the Second World War, the German occupation forces destroyed the human settlements in northern Norway to escape Russian soldiers. All domestic animals were slaughtered; the buildings burned; the roads, bridges, and fishing boats ruined; all communications and utilities damaged; and the terrain and the harbours mined in order to hinder the advancement of the Russian forces.[5] Another use of the scorched earth policies occurred in 1953, when the United States bombed five dams in North Korea. These attacks were undertaken for the purpose of weakening the important rice production in the state, pressuring North Korea into signing a peace agreement.[6]

[4] JE Austin and CE Bruch, 'Introduction' in JE Austin and CE Bruch (eds), *The Environmental Consequences of War* (Cambridge University Press, 2000) 2.

[5] J Leaning, 'War and the Environment: Human Health Consequences of Environmental Damage of War' (1993) *Critical Condition: Human Health and the Environment* 123, 127, available at: mitpress.mit.edu/sites/default/files/titles/content/9780262531184_sch_0001.pdf.

[6] ibid.

One of the most notorious examples of employing scorched earth policies in modern warfare took place during the Vietnam War, when the United States directly attacked and destroyed vegetation as a response to the guerrilla warfare conducted by the North Vietnamese army and the Viet Cong guerrilla. The enemy were able to hide by blending into the surrounding vegetation, posing a particular challenge to the US military operations. Therefore, the United States developed a strategy with three aims: first, forest destruction to deny the enemy its ability to move freely and to seek cover; second, crop destruction to prevent food supplies to the enemy; and third, relocation of civilians to avert local support.[7]

Between 1961 and 1972, the United States sprayed approximately 70 million litres of herbicides and other chemical substances, notably Agent Orange, as part of its military operations to achieve these aims. As a result, allegedly, 43 per cent of the farmland and 44 per cent of the total forest area of South Vietnam were contaminated. An area covering approximately 1.7 million hectares and corresponding to one-tenth of the total land area of South Vietnam was affected.[8] The United States also employed napalm and bombs of high-explosive ammunition to damage large areas of forest and agricultural land.[9] In addition, so-called 'Rome Plows', which are heavy land-clearing tractors with large blades, were used to clear forests and crops.[10] All these military activities have had a severe impact on the Vietnamese environment, destroying entire biotic communities.[11] Overall, approximately 4.8 million persons have been exposed, or potentially exposed, to Agent Orange since the military operations. The exposure of Vietnamese civilians continued because of the persistence of dioxin in the environment.[12] The population has experienced birth defects, diseases and premature death that can be traced to the toxic substances released during the war.[13] The military actions caused disruption to the ecosystem and rendered arable land unusable, and the Vietnamese population still suffers from severe health disorders more than 40 years after the hostilities ended.[14]

[7] A Westing, *Pioneer on the Environmental Impact of War* (Springer, 2013) 40.

[8] ibid, 43.

[9] Approximately 2 per cent of Indochina was sprayed with herbicides, with most of the military operations taking in place in South Vietnam. Approximately 30 per cent of all the mangrove forest in South Vietnam was attacked and destroyed. A Westing, 'Ecological Consequences of the Second Indochina War: A Case Study' (1975) 4 *Ambio: A Journal of Human Environment* 216, 220–22.

[10] Companies with 30 tractors were able to clear 40 hectares of dense forest per day and 160 hectares of lighter jungle per day. Westing, *Pioneer on the Environmental Impact of War* (n 7) 47.

[11] ibid, 48.

[12] A Ngo et al, 'Association Between Agent Orange and Birth Defects: Systematic Review and Meta-analysis' (2006) 35 *International Journal of Epidemiology* 1220.

[13] Austin and Bruch (n 4) 2.

[14] See H Frumkin, 'Agent Orange and Cancer: An Overview for Clinicians' (2003) 53 *A Cancer Journal for Clinicians* 245; AD Ngo, R Taylor and C Roberts, 'Paternal Exposure to Agent Orange and Spina Bifida: A Meta-analysis' (2010) 25 *European Journal of Epidemiology* 37; M Allukian and P Atwood, 'Public Health and the Vietnam War' in BS Levy and VW Sidel (eds), *War and Public Health* (Oxford University Press, 1997).

From 1990–91, during its invasion of Kuwait, Iraq intentionally spilt between seven and nine million barrels of oil into the Persian Gulf[15] and set over 600 oil wells on fire.[16] Iraq also destroyed all oil refineries, oil gathering stations, water desalination plants, and other installations related to oil production in Kuwait.[17] This oil sabotage represents one of the worst environmental disasters in history,[18] and was labelled as 'environmental terrorism' by the international press.[19] Iraq claimed to have military motives for causing the oil spill, such as preventing amphibious landings in the Gulf.[20] However, the attacks appeared to be revenge for Kuwait's unwillingness to raise its oil prices. Therefore, Iraq wanted to destroy Kuwait's ability to produce and export oil, in order to control oil pricing and oil production.[21]

The oil leakage polluted the Gulf. Approximately 400 km of its coastline was affected – the coast of Saudi Arabia, in particular – with devastating impacts on marine life,[22] including adversely affecting the sea grass beds, coral reef communities, and the blue-green algae providing nutrients to fish.[23] The oil pollution from the wells formed oil lakes at the soil surface and polluted the water table.[24] The oil lakes were especially distressing for the migrating birds that mistook the oil for water.[25] The Kuwaiti oil fires created soot and other particles during the burning process of the crude oil, releasing dioxide, ozone, carbon monoxide, and nitrogen dioxide to unsafe emission levels.[26] The toxic smoke affected Turkey, Iran, and even eastern parts of India, creating black rainfall.[27] The black smoke from the burn remained in the region for several months, causing an increase in respiratory illnesses among the population in Kuwait, affecting the sick and elderly, in particular. Respiratory problems were also reported from neighbouring states; for instance, Bahrain. The smoke increased the risks of

[15] M Schmitt, 'Green War: An Assessment of the Environmental Law of International Armed Conflict' (1997) 22 *Yale Journal of International Law* 1, 18.

[16] Austin and Bruch (n 4) 2.

[17] G Plant, *Environmental Protection and the Law of War: A 'Fifth Geneva' Convention on the Protection of the Environment in Time of Armed Conflict* (Belhaven Press, 1992) 3.

[18] SAS Omar et al, 'The Gulf War Impact on the Terrestrial Environment of Kuwait: An Overview' in JE Austin and CE Bruch (eds), *The Environmental Consequences of War* (Cambridge University Press, 2000) 317.

[19] Steven Emerson coined Iraq's actions as 'environmental terrorism'. See S Emerson, 'When Earth Takes the Hit' (1991) 21 *International Wildlife* 38.

[20] Austin and Bruch (n 4) 2.

[21] JE Seacor, 'Environmental Terrorism: Lessons From the Oil Fires of Kuwait' (1994) 10 *American University Journal of International Law and Policy* 481, 484.

[22] Westing, *Pioneer on the Environmental Impact of War* (n 7) 63.

[23] FJ Yuzon, 'Deliberate Environmental Modification Through the Use of Chemical and Biological Weapons: "Greening" the International Laws of Armed Conflict to Establish an Environmentally Protective Regime' (1996) 11 *American University Journal of International Law and Policy* 793, 794–95.

[24] Omar et al (n 18) 329–330.

[25] ibid, 327.

[26] K Hulme, *War Torn Environment: Interpreting the Legal Threshold* (Nijhoff, 2004) 164–65.

[27] Austin and Bruch (n 4) 2.

cancer and mortality among people, as well as animals.[28] In addition, the black smoke obscured the sunlight and dropped the temperatures,[29] and the region experienced the coldest winter ever documented.[30]

Another, more recent, example of targeting vegetation, although on a lesser scale, is the ongoing civil war taking place in Syria. In a bid to deny rebels fighters cover, it is claimed that governmental forces have burned tens of thousands of hectares of forest in the north of Syria to the ground. Unfortunately, the fire also affected the Turkish forest because of strong winds. It is estimated that the damage to the ecosystem will take several decades to recover.[31] Also, in the northwest of Syria, thousands of hectares of crops and farmland were set on fire. Satellite images show the burning of fields, orchards and olive plantations. BBC News has reported that Syrian and Russian militaries have targeted farmland with missiles and shells containing flammable chemicals, to cause fires with the intention to destroy the crops and deny farmers their harvests.[32] Both rebel fighters and Syrian governmental forces have accused each other of turning food into a 'weapon of war'.[33]

Directly attacking the environment can also be a strategy forming part of ethnic cleansing or the crime of genocide. Damaging a specific environment that a group lives in or destroying the natural resources that a group depends on, means that the living conditions of that area can be radically changed, affecting a group's ability to survive. If such acts are committed with the intent to destroy a national, ethnic, racial, or religious group (in whole or in part), it can be regarded as ethnic cleansing or genocide.[34] It has been reported that these types of act have taken place in Iraq and Sudan, as well in several states particularly directed at indigenous peoples.[35] Indigenous peoples have historically

[28] Hulme (n 26) 165.

[29] Westing, *Pioneer on the Environmental Impact of War* (n 7) 60.

[30] E Hunay, 'Black Rain in Turkey: Possible Environmental Effects of the Gulf War' (1992) 26 *Environmental Science & Technology* 873.

[31] Al Jazeera English, 'Syria's forests pay a heavy price' (*YouTube*, 22 October 2012), available at: www.youtube.com/watch?v=mV6apaqmnPw. See also M Guzel, 'Syria Crisis: Turkey's Border Fires Were Deliberately Set by Syrian Forces, Say Turkish Officials' (*Huffington Post*, 7 April 2012), available at: www.huffingtonpost.com /2012/07/04/turkey-border-fires-syria-deliberate_n_1649091.html.

[32] BBC News, 'Syrian military "burning farmland in rebel-held north"' 29 May 2019, available at: www.bbc.com/news/world-middle-east-48444596.

[33] Al Jazeera English, 'UN: Syrian fighters burning vital farmland is "weapon of war"' 4 June 2019, available at: www.aljazeera.com/news/2019/06/syrian-fighters-burning-vital-farmland-weapon-war-190604175625835.html.

[34] See Article II(c) of the Convention on the Prevention and Punishment of the Crime of Genocide (adopted 9 December 1948, entered into force 12 January 1951) 78 UNTS 277 (Genocide Convention). See also ethnic cleansing as part of the crime against humanity in Article 7(1)(h) of the Rome Statute of the International Criminal Court (adopted 17 July 1998, entered into force 1 July 2002) 2187 UNTS 90 (1998 Rome Statute).

[35] One of the most infamous examples took place during the 1860s when the American army attempted to drive Native Americans off the plains and into reservations during the Plains Indian Wars. The situation got worse when gold was discovered in the Montana Territory and the American government wanted to get access to the ancestral lands of Plains Indigenous tribes. When the

suffered greatly when their environment has been under attack. This is because indigenous peoples have a special relationship to their ancestral land having a 'fundamental importance for their collective physical and cultural survival as peoples'.[36]

In the aftermath of the 1990–91 Gulf War, the Iraqi government initiated a campaign against the ethnic group of the Marsh Arabs. The Marsh Arabs, located in the Mesopotamian wetlands, have a long history of opposing the government. In June 1991, the government burned down villages, tightened the food supply, and attacked sacred sites of the Marsh Arabs. It also re-initiated an old plan to construct a water diversion project to dry the Mesopotamian wetlands in order to create arable land.[37] The project took place during 1991–97 and included building a system of dams, dikes and canals. The draining turned the wetlands into dry, salty lands. Many of the animals of the wetlands disappeared, including the grey wolf, Bashrah reed warbler, fishes, etc, as well as key staging areas for migrating waterfowl. In 2002, only 7 per cent of the wetlands remained.[38] The destruction of the Mesopotamian wetlands is one of the largest ecosystem losses in the Arab world adding to the water stress at a global level.

The loss of the wetlands has had serious consequences for the Marsh Arabs because their culture depends on the resources – the plants, animals and water – of the marshes. Therefore, the Iraqi government's actions to diminish the wetlands essentially changed the living conditions of the Marsh Arabs.[39] Most of them were displaced in camps and those who stayed in the marshes live in extreme poverty.[40] According to commentators, the destruction of the wetlands

negotiations with the tribes failed, the army decided to kill the millions of buffalo in order to remove the indigenous people from their lands. By killing the buffalo, the intent was to destroy and erase the indigenous people who relied on buffalo for food and to build tents with their skin. The campaign succeeded. By exterminating the buffalo, the tribes starved and ultimately were forced to move into the reservations. See *Indian Country Today*, 'Genocide by Other Means: US Army Slaughtered Buffalo in Plains Indian Wars' published 24 September 2017, available at: newsmaven.io/indiancountrytoday/archive/genocide-by-other-means-u-s-army-slaughtered-buffalo-in-plains-indian-wars-nEWiK2AZik-yWbnFLXOqfw/.

[36] Permanent Forum on Indigenous Issues, 'Who are indigenous peoples?', Fact Sheet, available at: www.un.org/esa/socdev/unpfii/documents/5session_factsheet1.pdf. See also *Advisory Opinion of the African Commission on Human and Peoples' Rights on the United Nations Declaration on the Rights of Indigenous Peoples*, Adopted by the African Commission on Human and Peoples' Rights at its 41st Ordinary Session, May 2007 in Accra, Ghana.

[37] The engineering plan originated from the 1950s. See T Weinstein, 'Prosecuting Attacks that Destroy the Environment: Environmental Crimes or Humanitarian Atrocities?' (2005) 17 *Georgetown International Environmental Law Review* 697, 715.

[38] UNEP, H Partow, 'The Mesopotamian Marshlands: Demise of an Ecosystem', Division of Early Warning and Assessment (UNEP, Kenya 2001).

[39] A Schwabach, 'Environmental Damage Resulting From the NATO Military Action Against Yugoslavia' (2000) 25 *Columbia Journal of Environmental Law* 117; UNEP, Partow, 'The Mesopotamian Marshlands' (n 38). See also Report of the United Nations Integrated Water Task Force for Iraq, 'Managing Change in the Marshlands: Iraq's Critical Challenge', UN White Paper (2011).

[40] Schwabach (n 39) 4. See also UNEP, Partow, 'The Mesopotamian Marshlands' (n 38); Report of the United Nations Integrated Water Task Force for Iraq, 'Managing Change in the Marshlands: Iraq's Critical Challenge', UN White Paper (2011).

was undertaken as part of a systematic effort to deliberately destroy the ethnic group of the Marsh Arabs.[41] Dellapenna states that, 'many of the canals and other engineering structures serve no legitimate agricultural, economic, or developmental purpose'.[42] He argues that, 'the only goal of the projects appeared to be to drain the marshes and thereby destroy the ability of the Marsh Arabs to continue to live in their homeland'.[43]

In Darfur, the Sudanese government, together with the rebel group of the Janjaweed, has attempted to drive black Africans away from their villages by abusing the vegetation and water supply. The water wells were directly targeted by bombs and poison or otherwise contaminated.[44] Trees were cut down to make the land infertile and food stores were burned. These acts are explained as being part of a military strategy to make it impossible to return to the villages and to drive the black Africans away from their land.[45] The acts that have taken place in Darfur have been regarded as crimes against humanity by a UN fact-finding mission.[46]

B. Collateral Environmental Damage

Most of the environmental damage in armed conflicts is collateral damage that occurs while attacking other objects, often of a military nature. The environmental damage that arises from such an attack is not intended, albeit it may be foreseeable and expected. Military operations aimed at cutting energy supplies are common targets resulting in large-scale collateral environmental damage and there are numerous examples.

During the 1980–88 Iran–Iraq war, several attacks were directed at major oil installations. The attack on the Iranian Nowruz offshore platform released two million barrels of oil into the Red Sea.[47] The attack had adverse impacts on the wildlife, including endangered species, and the smoke blocked the sunlight for four days.[48] Another oil incident took place during the 2006 Israeli–Lebanese

[41] Weinstein, (n 37) 715–17.

[42] J Dellapenna expressed this view at a Current Issues Briefing held at the United States Institute of Peace, 'Marshland Arabs of Iraq', 12 December 2002, available at: www.usip.org/publications/marshland-arabs-iraq.

[43] ibid.

[44] UNEP, 'Sudan Post-Conflict Environmental Assessment' (UNEP, Kenya, 2007) 92; Das (n 1) 82–83.

[45] UNEP, 'Sudan Post-Conflict Environmental Assessment' (n 44).

[46] Report of the International Commission of Inquiry on Darfur to the Secretary-General, UN Doc S/2005/60, 1 February 2005.

[47] UNEP, Partow, 'The Mesopotamian Marshlands' (n 38).

[48] J Wyatt, 'Law-making at the Intersection of International Environmental, Humanitarian and Criminal Law: The Issue of Damage to the Environment in International Armed Conflict' (2010) 92 *International Review of the Red Cross* 593 598. See also E Mann-Borgese, 'The Protection of the Marine Environment in the Case of War', The Future of the International Law of the Environment, Workshop (1984); Schmitt (n 15).

conflict. Israel bombed an oil storage facility in Jiyeh located on the Lebanese coast. It led to the release of at least 13,000 tonnes of oil into the Mediterranean Sea.[49] This affected 150 km of the 220 km Lebanese coast and reached into Syria, negatively affecting its beaches and rocky headlands.[50] In addition, five storage containers were burned in the attack, releasing a toxic cloud that drifted over southern Lebanon.[51]

Strikes at energy facilities, however, are not only a concern in international armed conflicts. As witnessed in the Colombian civil war, rebels exploded pipelines causing millions of barrels of oil to enter into rivers, contaminating drinking water, and killing fish and wildlife. In addition, warfare has caused forest fires and oil pollution with transboundary impacts on the environment of Venezuela.[52] Similar incidents have occurred in Turkey, involving Kurdish armed groups.[53]

During the 1999 bombing campaign in former Yugoslavia, the North Atlantic Treaty Organization (NATO) attacked the petrochemical complex in Pancevo and the industrial facilities of Novi Sad.[54] Consequently, there was a serious leakage of toxic chemicals from the facilities, polluting water, the atmosphere and land. According to a report of the UN Environment, formerly UN Environmental Programme (UNEP), metallic mercury entered the Danube river, threatening the water supply of the region's population of 10 million. The toxins also affected Romania and Bulgaria, located downstream of the Danube.[55] Furthermore, this targeting of infrastructure and sewage treatment facilities caused environmental damage all over former Yugoslavia, as well as its neighbouring states.[56]

The use of certain weapons and ammunition – for instance, depleted uranium ammunition, mines, napalm and cluster sub-munitions – leads to further collateral environmental wartime damage. Depleted uranium is a by-product of the enrichment process of uranium that is used for nuclear reactors and nuclear weapons. It contains radiological and chemical components that may cause problems for both human health and the environment.[57] During the 1991 Gulf War,

[49] UNEP, 'Lebanon Post-Conflict Assessment' (n 1) 10; LY Huang, 'Israel–Lebanese Conflict: A Case Study for Protection of the Environment in Times of Armed Conflict' (2006) 20 *Florida Journal of International Law* 103, 104.

[50] UNEP, Partow, 'The Mesopotamian Marshlands' (n 38).

[51] Huang, 'Israel–Lebanese Conflict' (n 49) 104.

[52] Austin and Bruch (n 4) 3–4.

[53] ibid.

[54] ibid.

[55] Although, even prior to the NATO attacks, this area of the Danube river had been seriously polluted by the release of toxic substances from the industrial facilities at Pancevo. See UNEP and UNCHS, 'The Kosovo Conflict, Consequences for the Environment and Human Settlements' (UNEP and Habitat, Nairobi, 1999) 37; Austin and Bruch (n 4) 4.

[56] Austin and Bruch (n 4) 4.

[57] See UNEP and United Nations Human Settlements Programme (UNCHS), 'The Kosovo Conflict, Consequences for the Environment and Human Settlements' (UNEP and Habitat, Nairobi, 1999) 62; UNEP, 'Lebanon Post-Conflict Assessment' (n 1) 148.

the United States and the United Kingdom used approximately 300 tonnes of depleted uranium ammunition.[58] It has been suggested that NATO used depleted uranium during the 1999 bombing campaign in the Balkans, but this has not been officially confirmed.[59] It was also used in Sarajevo in 1995 during the US peacekeeping mission.[60] However, the environmental consequences of the use of depleted uranium have never been scientifically established, and scientists are in disagreement regarding its effects.[61] Iraqi scientists have reported unusually high levels of radiation in air, water and soil samples because of the use of depleted uranium during the Gulf War in the 1990s.[62] As depleted uranium is chemically and radiologically toxic, the release of such substances into the environment could have impacts on the groundwater and the air because of the re-suspension of depleted uranium dust. Nevertheless, it depends on the concentration of the toxins, as well as the amount of ammunition used.[63]

Unexploded mines and cluster sub-munitions remain in nature and litter large-scale areas long after the armed conflict has ended. Anti-personnel, as well as anti-tank, mines are frequently used in a large number of international and non-international armed conflicts. There are thought to be approximately 100 million still active landmines across Europe, Africa, Asia and Latin America.[64] The former UN Secretary-General, Kofi Annan, labelled landmines as 'one of the most widespread, lethal and long-lasting forms of pollution we have yet encountered'.[65] They are mainly used to secure or deny land. In civil wars, mine fields are often unmarked, which means that civilians risk their lives to cut wood, to farm land, and to herd animals. When the mines and cluster munitions explode, they cause damage to humans, domestic animals and wildlife and they shatter soil systems and disrupt water flows.[66]

Cluster bombs have a dispenser that contains hundreds of smaller individual sub-munitions or bomblets. Thus, when cluster bombs explode they can cover large areas. There are many variations on the design and material of the cluster weapons, depending on their intended purpose.[67] In general, the sub-munitions have to land on hard surfaces to explode, which means that a large number will not detonate immediately. The use of cluster weapons in armed conflict leads to significant problems in cleaning up the environment at the end of hostilities;

[58] Austin and Bruch (n 4) 3.
[59] UNEP and UNCHS, 'The Kosovo Conflict' (n 57) 62–63.
[60] Hulme (n 26) 226.
[61] UNEP, 'Lebanon Post-Conflict Assessment' (n 1) 149.
[62] Hulme (n 26) 230–31.
[63] ibid, 231–32.
[64] J Leaning, 'Tracking the Four Horsemen: The Public Health to Approach the Impact of War and War-Induced Environmental Destruction in the Twentieth Century' in JE Austin and CE Bruch (eds), *The Environmental Consequences of War* (Cambridge University Press, 2000) 396–97.
[65] Report of the Secretary-General, 'Assistance in Mine Clearance', UN Doc A/49/357/Add.1, 20 September 1994.
[66] Leaning, 'Tracking the Four Horsemen' (n 64) 396–97.
[67] UNEP, 'Lebanon Post-Conflict Assessment' (n 1) 150.

in particular, because the bomblets cannot be deactivated, they have to explode. The presence of remnants of cluster bombs strictly limits or proscribes access to farmland for a long time period because clean-up teams prioritise urban areas.[68] Agriculture is affected because the unexploded cluster bombs mean that farmland cannot be accessed.[69] Furthermore, if they are left in the environment for a long time, the heavy metals – such as copper, lead, zinc, mercury and cadmium – can leak and contaminate the ground.[70]

The Israeli use of cluster bombs in the south of Lebanon left widespread farmland contaminated with remnant munitions. By the end of the armed conflict in November 2006, when an estimated 85 per cent of southern Lebanon was assessed, 813 cluster bomb strike locations had been identified. This covered an area of 32.7 km^2 with up to one million unexploded sub-munitions.[71] One of the four most important agricultural areas of Lebanon, which accounts for approximately 30 per cent of the State's agricultural production, is located in the affected area.[72]

In more recent conflicts, similar types of environmental damage from the use of certain weapons and ammunition have been reported. Although, the 2008 armed conflict between Russia and Georgia lasted less than a month, it caused extensive environmental damage through forest fires, oil spills and the remnants of unexploded fragments. Allegedly, incendiary bombs were dropped in Borjomi-Kharaguali National Park, resulting in a forest fire that reportedly damaged almost 10 km^2 of the forest.[73] In the armed conflict in Syria, governmental forces caused contamination as a by-product of the heavy metals used in munitions, toxic remainders from weaponry and attacks on an industrial complex and chemical facilities. For example, the so-called 'barrel bombs' contain hundreds of kilograms of explosive chemicals. In many cases, these bombs remain unexploded and may contaminate land, as well as groundwater, if they are not removed.[74]

C. The Environment as a Weapon

The forces of the environment may be employed as a weapon in warfare, although it is highly unusual. By manipulating the environment to create earthquakes,

[68] ibid.

[69] H Partow, 'Environmental Impact of Wars and Conflicts in "Future Arab Environmental Challenges"' (Arab Forum for Development Report, Lebanon, 2008) 167.

[70] Hulme (n 26) 251–54.

[71] UNEP, 'Lebanon Post-Conflict Assessment' (n 1) 154.

[72] ibid, 155.

[73] ILPI 2014, 'Protection of the Natural Environment in Armed Conflict: An Empirical Study', International Law and Policy Institute, Report 12/2014, 28–30.

[74] D Weir, 'The Civilian Health Risks from TNT in Syria's Barrel Bombs' (*Toxic Remnants of War Project Blog*, 27 March 2015), available at: www.toxicremnantsofwar.info/the-civilian-health-risks-from-tnt-in-syrias-barrel-bombs.

tsunamis, lightning, etc, the forces could be used for hostile purposes. The only known wartime example of the employment of environmental manipulation is the weather modification during the Vietnam War. The United States tried to prolong the monsoon season through cloud seeding. This means that chemical substances were placed into the air with the aim of altering the microphysical process inside the clouds. The purpose behind the cloud seeding was to increase the rainfall in order to soften the road surfaces, to make them muddy and impassable for the communication and transport of supplies to the enemy.[75]

The United States and New Zealand conducted secret tests during the Second World War that aimed to create a tsunami, although they never employed the technique during wartime. The so-called 'tsunami bomb' was designed to attack coastal cities by using underwater explosions to generate enormous tidal waves. The tests showed that the weapon was capable of inundating a small city and probably also able to cause substantial environmental damage.[76] To date, there are no known examples of larger environmental damage caused by these environmental manipulation techniques.

D. Knock-on Effects

Armed conflicts have knock-on effects that may cause in some cases even more environmental damage than the warfare. The knock-on effects are connected to the disruption of existing governmental structures and state functions followed by institutional vacuum and absence of governance.[77] There are typically three types of knock-on problems that affect the environment. First, the lack of upholding of environmental legislation can increase illegal exploitation of natural resources and wildlife poaching. Second, the collapsed infrastructure can result in failure to handle basic services such as sewage, sanitation and waste. Third, the large number of displaced persons that lack the means for their basic needs and are often forced to engage in unsustainable exploitation of natural resources and wildlife poaching for sustenance.

The first knock-on problem, relating to a shortage of means to uphold laws, leads to both belligerents and civilians being tempted to employ unsustainable exploitation of natural resources and other prohibited acts towards the environment. As the society cannot enforce the laws, the persons that are involved in the illegal activities do not risk any punishment.[78] The uncontrolled exploitation

[75] Westing, 'Ecological Consequences' (n 9) 221–22.

[76] J Pearlman, '"Tsunami bomb" tested off New Zealand coast' *The Telegraph* (1 January 2013), available at: www.telegraph.co.uk/news/worldnews/australiaandthepacific/newzealand/9774217/Tsunami-bomb-tested-off-New-Zealand-coast.html. See also TDJ Leech, 'The Final Report of the Project "Seal"', 18 December 1950, available at: www.wanttoknow.info/documents/project_seal.pdf.

[77] UNEP, 'From Conflict to Peacebuilding' (n 1) 17.

[78] Partow, 'Environmental Impact of Wars' (n 69) 167.

of natural resources has considerable environmental impacts. Mineral extraction causes damage by removing soil and rocks to access the minerals. Also, the use of chemicals in these processes pollutes the soil and water, in particular with mercury. In addition, overexploitation of forests for timber results in deforestation of large areas. In many cases, the activities take place in sensitive ecological areas.[79] The inability of the state to protect the environment poses a threat for both protected areas and endangered species. As mentioned in the first chapter, protected areas frequently suffer the adverse impacts of armed conflict,[80] because these areas are often rich in natural resources, isolated and remote from state authorities, and therefore unsustainable exploitation can take place without being stopped. For instance, environmentally destructive extraction activities have taken place in areas recognised as world heritage sites in the Democratic Republic of the Congo (DRC),[81] which will be further discussed in chapter eight.

Institutionally weak states, which may already struggle to uphold an effective legal system, may be further weakened by an outbreak of armed conflict – it creates a milieu that feeds the corruption of public officials, who can prioritise personal interests over the community. The result is that exploitation of natural resources is supported, or even directly carried out, by state officials.[82] Corrupt officials establish parallel systems of administration that mean the exploitation of natural resources and wildlife can continue without being addressed by the authorities, having severe environmental impacts. This has been noted in the armed conflicts taking place in Angola, Sierra Leone, Sudan, Liberia, the DRC, the Central African Republic, etc. The conflicts are characterised by the unsustainable exploitation of natural resources and wildlife poaching. In addition, species such as primates, reptiles, parrots, etc, are subjects for the bush meat trade and illegal export.[83]

The second typical knock-on problem relates to the incapacity of many states involved in armed conflicts to arrange for or maintain adequate facilities to handle waste, sewage, sanitation, and water, etc. War-torn societies often lack the means (and/or spend them on military activities instead) of investment in infrastructure for public services, which accelerates the problems.[84] The 2008–09 military operations conducted by Israeli forces had severe consequences on the already vulnerable environment in the Gaza Strip. Due to underinvestment in the infrastructure, combined with the collapse of governance mechanisms, the

[79] D Dam-de Jong, 'International Law and Resource Plunder: The Protection of Natural Resources During Armed Conflict' (2009) 19 *Yearbook of International Environmental Law* 27, 28.

[80] ILPI 2014, 'Protection of the Natural Environment' (n 73) 54.

[81] Dam-de Jong (n 79) 28.

[82] UNEP, 'From Conflict to Peacebuilding' (n 1) 17.

[83] UNEP, 'The Democratic Republic of the Congo Post-Conflict Environmental Assessment United Nations Environment Programme Synthesis for Policy Makers' (UNEP, Kenya, 2011) 25.

[84] Partow, 'Environmental Impact of Wars' (n 69) 17.

recurrent hostilities increased the burden on the already pressured and financially challenged institutions. Strikes damaging the sewage system, water wells and drinking water pipes caused additional stress on public services, such as access to clean water.[85] A UN report stated that 90 per cent of Gaza's groundwater was unfit to serve as drinking water.[86] Furthermore, attacks on fuel stations and tanks resulted in adverse environmental impacts, including the widespread destruction of agricultural areas, damage to smaller industrial enterprises, and an increase in pollution discharged into the Mediterranean and into the groundwater.[87] The environmental damage of the war in Gaza was clearly distinguishable by satellite image analysis, reports from other UN agencies, visual inspection of the age of the damage, and chemical analysis.[88] In the aftermath of the hostilities, the Palestinian institutional collapse resulted in a situation where there is no system in place to manage natural resources or to provide basic services to the population. In particular, the sewage system is extremely poor. In 2007, a sewage wall collapsed and flooded a village; in addition to its environmental contamination, it killed four Palestinians.[89]

The third type of knock-on problem is that large numbers of displaced persons resulting from hostilities put additional pressures on the environment. In many cases, there can be up to hundreds of thousands of persons arriving in certain areas within a short time period. They often settle in temporary, informal camps, which become permanent over the years. The camps, frequently located in areas already challenged by the fighting, struggle to manage food and fuel distribution, sewage and waste disposal, etc.[90] The local environment around the camps is reportedly damaged by deforestation, encroachment of vulnerable ecosystems, water pollution, air pollution, and the loss of endangered species.[91] In combination with the scarce enforcement powers of the authorities, overexploitation of natural resources is common in the nearby surroundings. This is because frequently the displaced persons' energy and housing needs cannot be provided for, and they are forced to search for alternative ways to sustain themselves. For instance, enormous environmental impacts of displaced persons have been witnessed in the areas surrounding camps located in Sudan. In a region with otherwise good forest cover, satellites can detect deforestation on a great scale around these camps, the result of collecting firewood in the dry climate.[92]

[85] UNEP, 'Environmental Assessment of the Gaza Strip Following the Escalation of Hostilities in December 2008–January 2009' (UNEP, Kenya, 2009) 6.

[86] United Nations Country Team, 'Gaza in 2020 A liveable place? A Report by the United Nations Country Team in the Occupied Palestinian Territory' (August 2012).

[87] UNEP, 'Environmental Assessment of the Gaza Strip' (n 85) 30.

[88] ibid, 27.

[89] UNEP, 'From Conflict to Peacebuilding' (n 1) 18.

[90] JE Austin and CE Bruch, 'Legal Mechanisms for Addressing Wartime Damage to Tropical Forests' (2003) 16 *Journal of Sustainable Forestry* 161, 166–67.

[91] Leaning, 'Tracking the Four Horsemen' (n 64) 399.

[92] UNEP, 'Sudan Post-Conflict Assessment' 105–06, available at: postconflict.unep.ch/publications/sudan/05_displacement.pdf.

In many cases, the humanitarian agencies are unable to provide for the basic needs of these displaced peoples. This was evident in the DRC, when the UN High Commissioner for Refugees (UNCHR) allowed the displaced persons fleeing the Rwandan genocide to cut firewood inside Virunga National Park, also listed as a world heritage site. At its peak, the site of Virunga National Park lost around 90 hectares of forest per day.[93] The cutting of the firewood imperilled the unique ecosystem and threatened the endangered mountain gorillas in the park.[94] These problems remain in eastern DRC, even after more than two decades. Informal camps have been established around, as well as inside, the world heritage sites, and the huge number of displaced persons, the presence of armed groups, the low production in agriculture, and the interrupted activities of conservationists have all led to an increase in wildlife poaching.[95]

Although these environmental problems are not directly caused by warfare, they arise in connection with armed conflict. War-torn states struggle to maintain effective environmental protection. Existing problems are exacerbated by the outbreak of war, because of the lack of functioning institutions in place. Foreign and higher educated national staff are often evacuated first during armed conflicts, often leading to a shortage of competent staff, operative facilities, intact premises and funds. Furthermore, in the aftermath of armed conflicts, most stakeholders involved in rehabilitation and restoration are focused on humanitarian assistance and democracy issues, while the environment is a low priority.[96] Consequently, much of the environmental protection work halts. The capability of a war-torn society to manage its natural resources in a sustainable manner is severely affected and may result in long-lasting negative environmental impacts. Furthermore, there may be no means available to restore a polluted area or destroyed ecosystem.[97]

III. WHY PROTECT THE ENVIRONMENT IN RELATION TO ARMED CONFLICT?

The environment should be protected from the destructive forces of armed conflict for three main reasons. First, the environmental effects may have devastating effects on human health. Second, the impacts are difficult to foresee because of how ecosystems are interconnected and lack of scientific knowledge,

[93] UNEP, 'The Democratic Republic of the Congo' (n 83) 26.

[94] ibid.

[95] JA McNeeley, 'War and Biodiversity: An Assessment of Impacts' in JE Austin and CE Bruch (eds), *The Environmental Consequences of War* (Cambridge University Press, 2000). See also UNEP, 'The Democratic Republic of the Congo' (n 83) 26–27.

[96] J Oglete, J Shambaugh and R Kormos, 'Parks in the Crossfire: Strategies for Effective Conservation in Areas of Armed Conflict' 14 War and Protected Areas, (2004) *International Journal for Protected Areas Managers* 3–4, available at: cmsdata.iucn.org/downloads/14_1.pdf.

[97] Special Rapporteur M Lehto, 'Second Report on the Protection of the Environment in Relation to Armed Conflicts', UN Doc A/CN.4/728, para 19.

which can make it impossible to repair. Third, environmental damage and lack of environmental regulations may obstruct building peace once the conflict is over. First, damage to the environment is different from other types of wartime damage because it affects all humans living in it. For instance, as witnessed after the Vietnam War, civilians continued to suffer because of the toxic substances released into the environment[98] resulting in birth defects, diseases and premature death among the local population.[99] While much of the other damage occurring during armed conflicts can be replaced and rebuilt – such as buildings, roads and infrastructure – the environment cannot. As technology develops, the means and methods of warfare become more advanced and new weapons with the ability to inflict graver environmental destruction than in previous wars become available.[100] In addition, weapons of mass destruction – namely nuclear, chemical and biological weapons – can be used to render states, continents, and even the entire planet uninhabitable for humans.[101] The call for protecting the environment at all times, particularly during armed conflicts, is important for the sake of human survival, because we depend on the existence of a healthy environment. Thus, environmental protection during war is as important as the protection of civilians.[102]

Second, the increased scientific knowledge of the global ecosystem has put a focus on the need to assess and legally prevent environmental damage in a holistic manner. The consequences of environmental damage are difficult to evaluate because they often create a chain of reaction among the interconnected ecological components. Therefore, it is not enough to protect one single ecosystem – the global ecosystem needs protection as a whole.[103] This also holds true in times of armed conflict; an isolated military attack on the environment may cause negative effects on a regional or even international scale. For instance, as explained by Hulme, setting oil wells on fire in Kuwait during the 1990–91 Gulf War created widespread air pollution, which, in addition to the local and regional pollution, had adverse impacts in India and China. Thus, environmental damage may have worldwide implications because neither the environment nor the environmental damage respect state borders.[104]

Environmental damage can remain long after the hostilities have ended and a peace agreement has been signed. Even if in some cases the environment is able to recover, it may take decades until full recuperation. Mines, cluster ammunition and other explosive remnants can be left for decades. Warfare can release substances that can disturb the ecological balance. For instance, the herbicides

[98] Ngo et al, 'Association Between Agent Orange and Birth Defects' (n 12) 1220.

[99] Oglete, Shambaugh and Kormos (n 96) 2.

[100] JA Cohan, 'Modes of Warfare and Evolving Standards of Environmental Protection Under the International Law of War' (2003) 15 *Florida Journal of International Law* 481, 532.

[101] Schwabach (n 39) 121.

[102] Hulme (n 26) 16.

[103] ibid, 13.

[104] ibid.

used in Vietnam introduced micro-organisms that have disrupted the biodiversity and vegetation.[105] Nevertheless, sometimes in rare cases the environment can profit from armed conflict. The Vietnam War was an ecological catastrophe, but interestingly the tiger population managed to increase at the time.[106] In the Nicaraguan civil war in the 1980s, the logging of timber, animal trafficking, and the vegetation clearance for agricultural purposes decreased. As a result, animal populations – for instance, white-tailed deer, peccaries, monkeys and crocodiles – recovered.[107] Additionally, fish stocks improved because of the fishermen's fear of the naval mines.[108] However, wildlife poaching and cutting forests for firewood increased, driven by the displaced population and the soldiers and the fact that the state's protected areas were mismanaged.[109] Another example is the Demilitarised Zone between South and North Korea, which has become a sanctuary for wildlife where species can recover because of the lack of development and hunting. This has led to the Demilitarised Zone becoming one of the most biologically diverse areas in the region.[110] Nonetheless, even though the environment might be able to profit from armed conflict in some instances, most wars have devastating environmental consequences.

Third, the environmental state can also be a factor affecting the recovery of post-conflict societies and the ability to create lasting peace. In war-torn societies, managing natural resources has been highlighted as an important aspect to meet the basic needs of the population, such as providing water, food, shelter and livelihoods, but also to reconstruct the financial system and to rebuild the governmental structure.[111] States that are unable to give their population the support they require can create additional environmental degradation and foster further conflicts. Consequently, it is not only the warfare in itself that challenges the environmental protection, but also the knock-on effects that can nurture further hostilities by creating instability in the affected areas.

In conflicts characterised by unsustainable exploitation, economic incentives can hamper peace building. Many armed groups, as well as governmental army members, benefit from the wars on a personal level due to corruption and therefore they may wilfully interfere with any peace efforts. States involved in environmentally linked conflicts are twice as likely to relapse into conflict within the first five years.[112] On a short-term basis, however, unsustainable natural resource exploitation can advance and boost the post-conflict economy. This was the case in Japan after the Second World War when investments were made in

[105] Yuzon (n 23) 795–96.
[106] McNeeley (n 95) 367.
[107] ibid, 368.
[108] Austin and Bruch (n 4) 5.
[109] McNeeley (n 95) 368.
[110] Austin and Bruch (n 4) 5.
[111] C Bruch et al, 'Post-conflict Peace Building and Natural Resources' (2009) 19 *Yearbook of International Environmental Law* 58, 67.
[112] UNEP, 'From Conflict to Peacebuilding' (n 1) 11.

coal mining, which fostered the Japanese economy and helped to stabilise peace, although at the same time had adverse environmental impacts.[113] Nevertheless, in many cases the environmental damage caused in relation to armed conflict impedes the outlook for peace and for societies to recover.[114]

To conclude, in war-torn societies, environmental degradation has the potential to endanger the health, livelihoods and security of the population, creating further degradation and nourishing future conflicts.[115] The relationship between armed conflict and the environment is an important aspect to address when trying to prevent conflicts, minimise their impact on societies, and achieve sustainable peace.[116] Therefore, reducing vulnerability to the environment during armed conflicts is important for the outlook of peace.[117] Managing natural resources has been highlighted as an important aspect to avoid a relapse to conflict; to meet the basic needs of the population by providing water, food, shelter and livelihoods; to reconstruct the financial system; and to build up governance.[118]

As the global environment is getting more vulnerable due to pollution, climate change, loss of biodiversity, etc, all kinds of activities, and the consequences of them, may become more significant than before. New scientific information, as well as the changing patterns on how armed conflicts are conducted, is a challenge for protecting the environment by legal means. One challenge, as phrased by Bodansky, is that 'environmental protection generally requires a long-term perspective, while warfare is usually dominated by short-term exigencies'.[119] Because of the changing circumstances with regard to environmental damage and armed conflict, Parson argues that, '[t]he scheme for protection of the environment during armed conflict must go beyond mere incidental protection; it must incorporate international environmental law'.[120]

[113] Bruch et al (n 111) 99.

[114] UNEP, 'From Conflict to Peacebuilding' (n 1) 19.

[115] Das (n 1) 122–23.

[116] For further reading, see UN, 'A More Secure World' (n 1); UNEP, 'From Conflict to Peacebuilding' (n 1).

[117] UNEP, 'From Conflict to Peacebuilding' (n 1) 19.

[118] Bruch et al (n 111) 67.

[119] D Bodansky, 'Effects of Military Activity on the Environment', Final Report, May 2003, 5 Executive summary, vi.

[120] RJ Parson, 'Fight to Save the Planet: US Armed Forces, Greenkeeping, and Enforcement of the Law Pertaining to Environmental Protection During Armed Conflict' (1997–98) 10 *Georgetown International Environmental Law Review* 441, 468–69.

3

Special Protection under the Law of Armed Conflict

I. INTRODUCTION

THIS CHAPTER SCRUTINISES the special protection of the environment that is provided under the law of armed conflict. This framework has traditionally emphasised the ability to conduct successful military operations with a minimum of civilian casualties, whereas environmental protection has been of low priority. Thus, wartime environmental protection has become a subject for critique from international organisations,[1] as well as legal scholars.[2] In this chapter, I argue that the environmentally specific rules in the law of armed conflict do not provide sufficient protection because they do not reflect the increased environmental awareness as incorporated in contemporary international environmental law. More specifically, I claim that the special environmental protection under the law of armed conflict has two limitations. First, the rules have a narrow scope of application given that they set a high threshold that excludes most of the environmental damage that results from conventional warfare. Second, the threshold is not only high, but it also contains unclear requirements, creating uncertainty about what type of damage is prohibited. I propose that the rules should be interpreted in an evolving manner that takes into account new scientific environmental knowledge, as well as novel legal

[1] UN Environment criticised rules under the law of armed conflict and suggested that the International Law Commission should address the issue. In 2013, the topic of Protection of the Environment in Relation to Armed Conflict was put on the agenda of the International Law Commission. For further reading on the background of the topic, see Annex E in the Report of the International Law Commission, 63rd Session (26 April–3 June and 4 July–12 August 2011) UN Doc A/66/10 *Yearbook of the International Law Commission*, 2011, Volume II, Part Two, 351–68.

[2] D Fleck, 'The Protection of the Environment in Armed Conflict: Legal Obligations in the Absence of Specific Rules' (2013) 82 *Nordic Journal of International Law* 7; K Bannelier-Christakis, 'International Law Commission and Protection of the Environment in Times of Armed Conflict: A Possibility for Adjudication?' (2013) 20 *Journal of International Cooperation Studies* 129, 132–33; C Droege and M-L Tougas, 'The Protection of the Natural Environment in Armed Conflict–Existing Rules and Need for Further Legal Protection' (2013) 82 *Nordic Journal of International Law* 21; S Vöneky, 'A New Shield for the Environment: Peacetime Treaties as Legal Restraints of Wartime Damage' (2000) 9 *Review of European, Comparative & International Environmental Law* 20, 32; M Bothe et al, 'International Law Protecting the Environment During Armed Conflict: Gaps and Opportunities' (2010) 92 *International Review of the Red Cross* 569.

requirements of international environmental law to remedy the limitations. In this way, the rules can be clarified in a manner that resembles the environmental protection provided under modern international law, and thereby lower the threshold.

This chapter is structured as follows. Sections II and III provide a background on the foundations of the law of armed conflict and how environmental protection has become a recognised concern within the framework. Section IV examines the ENMOD Convention (Convention on the Prohibition of Military or Any Other Hostile Use of Environmental Modification Techniques) that prohibits the manipulation of environmental forces for hostile use. Section V deals with the special environmental protection detailed in Articles 35(3) and 55 of Protocol I, and how these can be interpreted in an evolutionary manner. Finally, section VI concludes that the rules on direct environmental protection under the law of armed conflict remain vague, even if interpreted in the light of international environmental law. Nevertheless, applying such an interpretation may contribute to lowering the threshold in the rules.

II. THE FOUNDATIONS OF THE LAW OF ARMED CONFLICT

The inherent nature of armed conflict is to 'destroy life and property, and this will never change'.[3] Still, the law of armed conflict attempts to limit the harm of the hostilities. The law of armed conflict has a long history and originates from the concepts of chivalry and military necessity. It attempts to balance the needs of military demands and humanitarian concerns in relation to the direct consequences of warfare.[4] In short, the law of armed conflict covers rules of international law that regulate the treatment of 'protected persons' meaning individuals not taking part or no longer taking part in the hostilities; the practice of violence by prohibiting or limiting the use of certain means and methods of warfare; the governance of occupied areas; and the relation between belligerent and neutral states.[5]

As the rules of the law of armed conflict are human-centred, protecting the environment per se is not an objective.[6] Nevertheless, as part of humanitarian considerations, the environment has traditionally enjoyed – even if limited – protection because of its connection to civilians' security and sustenance and

[3] BK Schafer, 'The Relationship Between the International Laws of Armed Conflict and Environmental Protection: The Need to Reevaluate what Types of Conduct are Permissible During Hostilities' (1989) 19 *California Western International Law Journal* 287, 288.

[4] Y Dinstein, *The Conduct of Hostilities Under the Law of International Armed Conflict*, 3rd edn (Cambridge University Press, 2016) 8–9.

[5] C Greenwood, 'Historical Development and Legal Basis' in D Fleck (ed), *The Handbook of International Humanitarian Law* (Oxford University Press, 2008) 11.

[6] S Simonds, 'Conventional Warfare and Environmental Protection: A Proposal for International Legal Reform' (1992) 29 *Stanford Journal of International Law* 165, 168.

has to some extent evolved from there.[7] As an example, Article 55 in the Annex to the 1908 Fourth Hague Convention (Hague Regulations)[8] protects property during occupation in accordance with the rules of usufruct. The usufruct rules prohibit the destruction of civilian property by limiting the exploitation to the harvest of the 'fruits' of the crops only.[9] It allows the occupying state to use the property, but it may not permanently alter or destroy it.[10] For instance, property such as a forest may be logged but not in an arbitrary and unsustainable manner.[11] In 2018, the International Law Commission provisionally adopted an updated version of the usufruct rules by referring to an occupying power's obligations to ensure sustainable use and minimise environmental harm when administrating and using natural resources in an occupied territory.[12] Such an updated version of the rules shows how obligations under the law of armed conflict may evolve to incorporate environmental considerations. The draft principle received support in the debate of the Sixth Committee of the UN General Assembly.[13]

The environment also receives general protection through the prohibition of using the starvation of the civilian population as part of the warfare, by protecting drinking water installations, crops, foodstuff, etc.[14] The protection of the environment follows from the prohibition of wanton destruction for the sake of the civilian population's future ability to sustain itself in an area affected by armed conflict. However, explicit environmental protection did not exist until Protocol I was adopted in 1977.

III. ADOPTING SPECIAL ENVIRONMENTAL PROTECTION IN WARFARE

The environmental devastation occurring during the Vietnam War and the 1991 Gulf War has been particularly influential in the process towards adopting

[7] A Bouvier, 'Protection of the Natural Environment in Time of an Armed Conflict' (1991) 31 *International Review of the Red Cross* 438.

[8] Convention (IV) respecting the Laws and Customs of War on Land and its Annex: Regulations concerning the Laws and Customs of War on Land (adopted 18 October 1907, entered into force 26 January 1910) (Hague Regulations).

[9] K Hulme, *War Torn Environment: Interpreting the Legal Threshold* (Nijhoff, 2004) 4.

[10] E Talbot Jensen, 'The Intentional Law of Environmental Warfare: Active and Passive Damage During Armed Conflict' (2005) 38 *Vanderbildt Journal of Transnational Law* 145, 157.

[11] B Baker, 'Legal Protections for the Environment in Times of Armed Conflict' (1993) 33 *Virginia Journal of International Law* 351, 361.

[12] Draft Principle 21 [20] (as adopted at the first reading), International Law Commission, 'Protection of the Environment. Text and Titles of the Draft Principles Provisionally Adopted by the Drafting Committee on First Reading' (Protection of the Environment, First Reading) UN Doc A/CN.4/L.937 (2019). These principles have been numbered differently during the work of the International Law Commission. To avoid confusion, I will refer to the numbering of the draft principles as they appear on the first reading in 2019.

[13] See summary of the debate in Special Rapporteur M Lehto, Second Report on the Protection of the Environment in Relation to Armed Conflicts, UN Doc A/CN.4/728, para 8.

[14] See Article 54 of Protocol I and Article 14 of Protocol II.

the first wartime special environmental protection. In addition, the reports conducted by UN Environment on the environmental consequences arising from various armed conflicts have contributed to a growing awareness of the need to address the issue with legal means. Yet, resistance among states to modify the existing law to enhance wartime environmental protection persists.

Several instruments of the law of armed conflict are of relevance for environmental protection during armed conflicts.[15] However, only three instruments provide direct protection of the environment, namely the ENMOD Convention, Protocol I, and Protocol III on Incendiary Weapons (Incendiary Weapons Protocol) to the 1981 Convention on Certain Conventional Weapons.[16] Protocol I and the ENMOD Convention are the two most significant of these. Both instruments were negotiated in the 1970s and they are the first instruments under the law of armed conflict that specifically refer to the environment. Thus, they represent a new trend in the modern law of armed conflict to acknowledge the need for environmental protection in warfare. In addition, the Rome Statute of the International Criminal Court (1998 Rome Statute) contains a provision on environmental war crime.[17] However, the 1998 Rome Statute is an instrument of international criminal law concerning individual accountability for war crimes, which is omitted from this study.

Protocol I was the first instrument under the law of armed conflict that contained direct protection of the environment without reference to human harm. The Vietnam War was a turning point because of its large-scale environmental damage, in combination with the emerging environmental awareness of the 1970s followed by new international environmental legislation.[18] As an outcome, and due to the critical role that the environment played in the Vietnam War, states and international organisations, as well as scholars, expressed concern about the complex interrelationship between warfare and the environment. At the time, there was a rising advocacy to add environmental damage as a separate category of concern within the law of armed conflict.[19]

[15] These include the Fourth Hague Convention of 1907 and its Annex (Hague Regulations); the Fourth Geneva Convention of 1949, and its Protocols; the ENMOD Convention; Protocol III to the 1980 Conventional Weapons Convention restricting incendiary weapons; the Cultural Property Convention; the Biological Weapons Convention; and the Chemical Weapons Convention.

[16] Convention on Prohibitions or Restrictions on the Use of Certain Conventional Weapons Which May be Deemed to be Excessively Injurious or to Have Indiscriminate Effects (and Protocols) (as amended on 21 December 2001) (adopted 10 October 1980, entered into force 2 December 1983) 1342 UNTS 137 (Convention on Certain Conventional Weapons).

[17] Article 8(2)(b)(iv) of the 1998 Rome Statute: 'Intentionally launching an attack in the knowledge that such attack will cause incidental loss of life or injury to civilians or damage to civilian objects or widespread, long-term and severe damage to the natural environment which would be clearly excessive in relation to the concrete and direct overall military advantage anticipated'.

[18] For instance, in 1972, the Stockholm Declaration was adopted marking the birth of international environmental law. See JA Cohan, 'Modes of Warfare and Evolving Standards of Environmental Protection Under the International Law of War' (2003) 15 *Florida Journal of International Law* 481, 485.

[19] R Falk, 'Evaluating the Adequacy of Existing International Law Standards' in JE Austin and CE Bruch (eds), *The Environmental Consequences of War* (Cambridge University Press, 2000).

In 1972, at an academic conference held in Stockholm, a group of scholars encouraged the UN to organise a meeting to adopt an 'Ecocide' Convention. The purpose of the convention was to criminalise acts taken against the environment as a part of warfare.[20] The meeting never took place and the convention did not come into existence as a legally binding instrument.[21] Nonetheless, the need to protect the environment during armed conflicts had been introduced to the international agenda. Later, the notion of environmental protection in times of armed conflict was raised at the negotiations of the 1974–77 conference organised by the International Committee of the Red Cross (ICRC). Consequently, Articles 35(3) and 55, which specifically protected the environment, were adopted in Protocol I. Concurrently, the ENMOD Convention, regulating the use of environmental modification techniques, was negotiated and adopted under the leadership of the UN.[22] Protocol I and the ENMOD Convention introduced environmental protection as such to the law of armed conflict.

The 1991 Gulf War was the second historic event that influenced the legal debate on environmental protection during armed conflicts.[23] It caused enormous ecological harm because of the massive oil spill that occurred as a part of Iraq's deliberate warfare, as explained in chapter two. Consequently, states and legal scholars questioned the ability of the specific rules in the law of armed conflict to address wartime environmental damage. The criticism was partially related to events in the UN Security Council. The Security Council addressed the 1991 Gulf War events in Resolution 687 (1991),[24] in which Iraq was held liable for direct loss and damage, including environmental damage and the depletion of natural resources, inflicted during the invasion and occupation of Kuwait.[25] Iraq's liability for all damage was based on the breach of Article 2(4) of the UN Charter,[26] rather than the specific provisions in the law of armed conflict on environmental protection. However, Iraq was not a party to Protocol I or the ENMOD Convention. Even if Iraq had been a party to these instruments, legal scholars disagree whether these environmentally specific provisions would have applied due to their narrow scope of application.[27]

[20] ibid.

[21] M Schmitt, 'Green War: An Assessment of the Environmental Law of International Armed Conflict' (1997) 22 *Yale Journal of International Law* 1, 11–12.

[22] A Schwabach, 'Environmental Damage Resulting from the NATO Military Action Against Yugoslavia' (2000) 25 *Columbia Journal of Environmental Law* 117, 126.

[23] Report of the International Law Commission, 63rd Session (26 April–3 June and 4 July–12 August 2011) UN Doc A/66/10, 212. See also Schmitt, 'Green War' (n 21) 18.

[24] UN Security Council Resolution, UN Doc S/RES/687, 8 April 1991.

[25] A Compensation Claim Commission was established under the UN to review liability claims.

[26] Charter of the United Nations and Statute of the International Court of Justice (adopted 26 June 1945, adopted 24 October 1945) 1 UNTS XVI.

[27] S Vöneky, 'Peacetime Environmental Law as a Basis of State Responsibility for Environmental Damage Caused by War' in JE Austin and CE Bruch (eds), *The Environmental Consequences of War* (Cambridge University Press, 2000) 191; M Bothe, 'The Protection of the Environment in

The existing legal mechanisms that were in place at the time of the 1991 Gulf War to prohibit environmental damage during armed conflicts were arguably not able to deal with the serious environmental harm that was occurring.[28] Consequently, in 1991, a number of important expert meetings took place dealing with the issue.[29] These included the London Round Table Conference on a 'Fifth Geneva' Convention on the Protection of the Environment in Times of Armed Conflict; the Ottawa Conference of Experts on the Use of the Environment as a Tool of Conventional Warfare; and the Munich Consultation of Experts on the Law Concerning the Protection of the Environment in Times of Armed Conflict. The meetings did not lead to any new constraints on the law, but they raised the question of the adequacy of the contemporary environmental protection during armed conflicts. The Munich meeting proposed some specific recommendations that were submitted in a report to the UN Secretary-General.[30] It suggested the adoption of a 'Fifth Geneva Convention' to remedy the perceived deficiencies of the existing legal framework.[31] A symposium was held in 1995 to discuss the possibility of adopting such a convention. However, in the end, the pursuit of getting the convention adopted was abandoned because the discussants at the symposium concluded that it was neither necessary nor desirable and that it might do more harm than good.[32]

Parallel with the expert meetings, wartime environmental protection was debated in the UN General Assembly. Affected by the Iraqi warfare pollution, Jordan brought up the issue under the title 'Exploitation of the Environment as a Weapon in Times of Armed Conflict and the Taking of Practical Measures to Prevent Such Exploitation'.[33] The issue was assigned to the Sixth Committee of the UN General Assembly, which later changed the title into 'Protection of the Environment in Times of Armed Conflict'.[34] In the debate of the Sixth Committee, two positions were embraced among the states: the first considered

Times of Armed Conflict: Legal Rules, Uncertainty, Deficiencies and Possible Developments' (1991) 34 *German Yearbook of International Law* 54.

[28] Baker (n 11) 352.

[29] Falk's call for the need of establishing the crime of 'ecocide': Falk (n 19) 137–55. There was also a call for establishing a type of 'Fifth Geneva Convention' with the purpose to protect the environment during armed conflicts. For details, see G Plant, *Environmental Protection and the Law of War: A 'Fifth Geneva' Convention on the Protection of the Environment in Time of Armed Conflict* (Belhaven Press, 1992).

[30] See AO Adede, 'Protection of the Environment in Times of Armed Conflict: Reflections on the Existing and Future Treaty Law' (1994) 1 *Annual Survey of International & Comparative Law* 161, 169.

[31] RJ Parson, 'Fight to Save the Planet: US Armed Forces, Greenkeeping, and Enforcement of the Law Pertaining to Environmental Protection During Armed Conflict' (1997) 10 *Georgetown International Environmental Law Review* 441, 472–73.

[32] ibid, 476.

[33] Exploitation of the Environment as a Weapon in Times of Armed Conflict and the Taking of Practical Measures to Prevent Such Exploitation, UN Doc A/46/141, 8 July 1991.

[34] Summary Record of 18th meeting of the Sixth Committee of the General Assembly, held on 22 October 1991, UN Doc A/C.6/46/SR.18.

that the existing law was adequate to deal with environmental protection in warfare and rather emphasised improved acceptance and compliance of the law; and the second stressed the inadequacy of the existing legal framework and called for new rules and strengthened protection.[35] In 1992, the UN General Assembly adopted, without a vote, Resolution 47/37 on 'Protection of the Environment in Times of Armed Conflict'.[36] The resolution expressed deep concern about the environmental damage and the depletion of natural resources during conflicts. It also underscored that destruction of the environment that was not justified by military necessity, carried out wantonly, was clearly not in accordance with international law.[37]

In the resolution, the UN General Assembly gave the ICRC a mandate to continue to work on the issue. As a response, the ICRC organised expert meetings. These generated the drafting of a set of guidelines for military manuals on how to protect the environment during armed conflicts. In 1994, the ICRC guidelines were introduced to the UN General Assembly. At that time, the discussion on environmental protection during armed conflicts had cooled down. This was noted as the guidelines received an overall unreceptive response from states.[38] Without formally approving the guidelines, they were annexed to a UN General Assembly resolution, in which all states were invited to 'give due consideration to the possibility of incorporating them into their military manuals and other instructions addressed to their military personnel'.[39] Due to the lack of political support for any modification of the law of armed conflict from the states, the general debate on improving wartime environmental protection was removed from the international agenda, together with the unsuccessful reaction to the ICRC guidelines and the proposal for a new convention. However, interest in environmental protection and armed conflict has reappeared on the international agenda.

In 2011, during an international conference, the ICRC specifically acknowledged how environmental degradation caused during armed conflicts has added to the vulnerability of the victims of the armed conflict and how the natural environment plays a vital role in ensuring the survival of present and future generations. The ICRC concluded by stressing that the law protecting the environment during armed conflicts is not clear and not sufficiently developed. Furthermore, the ICRC expressed a wish to bring the law of armed conflict closer to international environmental law.[40] This represents a change in the

[35] Adede (n 30) 173–74.

[36] Protection of the Environment in Times of Armed Conflict, General Assembly, UN Doc A/RES/47/37, 25 November 1992.

[37] ibid, Preamble.

[38] Bothe et al (n 2) 573.

[39] General Assembly, UN Doc A/49/50, 15 February 1994. The Guidelines were published annexed to the report of the Secretary General, UN Doc A/49/323, 19 August 1994.

[40] At the 31st International Conference of the Red Cross and Red Crescent held in Geneva, Switzerland, 28 November–1 December 2011, the protection of the environment was raised as a

attitude of the organisation because the previous comments of its staff have opted for improvement of the implementation of the law of armed conflict rather than developing or modifying the law itself.[41] The ICRC is also updating its guidelines on environmental protection in relation to armed conflict, which has not yet been finalised.[42]

In 2013, the International Law Commission – encouraged by UN Environment[43] – decided to include the issue of 'the Protection of the Environment in Relation to Armed Conflict' on its programme of work. The aim of the topic is to clarify and develop rules protecting the environment in relation to armed conflict.[44] The first Special Rapporteur, Ambassador Marie Jacobsson, provided the Commission with three reports. Her successor, Ambassador Marja Lehto took over in 2017 and has since then provided two additional reports. In 2019, on the first reading a set of 28 draft principles were provisionally adopted by the International Law Commission.[45]

The renewed interest for wartime environmental protection during the 2010s is not connected to a particular event, as was the case in the 1970s and 1990s. It seems to be driven by an overarching environmental consciousness in the international society, coupled with the attention for the exposure and exploitation of the environment connected with conflicts, as well as the general development of international environmental law. As mentioned, UN Environment has conducted several post-conflict environmental assessment reports since 1999, which have highlighted the adverse impacts of armed conflict.[46] The reports are a reminder of the vulnerability of the environment during and after armed conflicts and the need of environmental protection in all situations. In addition, the character of environmental issues and the fact that these tend to permeate into other areas of international law – for instance international trade law, human rights law, refugee law, etc – mean that it is unsurprising that they also affect the law of armed conflict.

The exposé of the treatment of environmental protection in the law of armed conflict shows that historically there is a lack of political will to create clear and

concern to strengthening legal protection for victims of armed conflict. See Draft Resolution & Report of the 31st International Conference of the Red Cross and Red Crescent held in Geneva, Switzerland 28 November–1 December 2011, 31IC/11/5.1.1, 5, 16.

[41] Bouvier (n 7); J-M Henckaerts, 'International Legal Mechanisms for Determining Liability for Environmental Damage Under International Humanitarian Law' in JE Austin and CE Bruch (eds), *The Environmental Consequences of War* (Cambridge University Press, 2000).

[42] The updated ICRC environmental guidelines are expected to be published in 2020.

[43] See Recommendations in UNEP, 'Protecting the Environment During Armed Conflict: An Inventory and Analysis of International Law' (UNEP, Switzerland 2009).

[44] Report of the International Law Commission, 65th Session (6 May–7 June and 8 July–9 August 2013) UN Doc A/68/10, (2013) *Yearbook of the International Law Commission*, Volume II, Part Two, Chapter IX, paras 130–44.

[45] International Law Commission, 'Protection of the Environment, First Reading'.

[46] See UNEP's website for a list of publications on post-conflict environmental assessments: www.unep.org/disastersandconflicts/Publications/tabid/54718/Default.aspx.

robust legal rules – a large number of states wish to maintain as much leeway as possible when it comes to the battlefield. Environmental damage has been overlooked in wartime, and states do not wish to impose new rules to change that. Instead, a status quo approach to the rules in the law of armed conflict is frequently stressed. At the same time, there are other opinions. Initiatives by the ICRC, UN Environment, and the International Law Commission, for example, reflect considerable changes in the view of the environment and its role in armed conflicts.[47] In addition, states are starting to accept and to be aware of the fact that environmental damage is costly, also in terms of human lives. The suffering of environmental damage goes beyond the battlefield, having uncertain negative impacts in regions other than solely where the hostilities take place.[48] For that reason, environmental protection has become a renewed concern in times of armed conflict.[49]

The question of how to face these challenges without putting additional constraints on the military conduct generates an unsolvable equation, resulting in the creation of ambiguous and vague rules that leave much discretion to the law-applier. In particular, as I discuss further in section V, the existing ambiguity and vagueness of the environmental rules in Protocol I is probably a conscious choice of the negotiators for the purpose of reaching a compromise in the conflicting views on environmental protection during armed conflicts. Hence, the rules provide wide discretion for the law-applier, generating insecurity and unpredictability on how the rules apply.

IV. PROHIBITION ON ENVIRONMENTAL MODIFICATION TECHNIQUES: THE ENMOD CONVENTION

The ENMOD Convention prohibits the modification of environmental forces as a weapon. This Convention has a restricted scope of application as it only applies to intentional modification techniques and adds little to the environmental protection in wartime. The ENMOD Convention was prompted after the Vietnam War, during which the United States attempted to manipulate the environment through seed clouding.[50] The Convention was negotiated under a

[47] In addition, the Nordic Red Cross Societies made a joint pledge, Pledge P1290, presented at the 31st International Conference of the Red Cross and Red Crescent, Geneva, 28 November–1 December 2011.

[48] UNEP, 'Protecting the Environment'; UNEP, 'From Conflict to Peacebuilding: The Role of Natural Resources and the Environment' (UNEP, Switzerland, 2009).

[49] MD Deiderich, 'Law of War and Ecology – A Proposal for a Workable Approach to Protecting the Environment Through the Law of War' (1992) 136 *Military Law Review* 137, 158.

[50] Seed clouding is a technique to induce rainfall by adding silver-iodide or liquid nitrogen to clouds that makes the particles heavy as they freeze. The US employed this technique during the Vietnam War in an attempt to prolong the monsoon season and to flood strategic roads and make them unusable, thereby gaining military advantage. See ch 2.

UN conference,[51] as well as during bilateral discussions taking place between the United States and the Soviet Union.[52]

Article I(1) of the ENMOD Convention reads:

> Each State Party to this Convention undertakes not to engage in military or any other hostile use of environmental modification techniques having widespread, long-lasting or severe effects as the means of destruction, damage or injury to any other State Party.

The ENMOD Convention does not attempt to prohibit adverse environmental effects per se. Rather, it regulates environmental modification having certain adverse impacts on other states, which are most likely to consist of environmental damage.[53] Furthermore, the ENMOD Convention prohibits techniques having 'widespread, long-lasting or severe effects'. It is a similar formula to that which was used in Articles 35(3) and 55(1) of Protocol I. The ENMOD Convention has – unlike Protocol I – an attached Understandings section, which defines these terms. The definitions are submitted exclusively for the interpretation of the ENMOD Convention. The Understandings section defines the terms as follows:

a. 'Widespread': encompassing an area on the scale of several hundred square kilometres.
b. 'Long-lasting': lasting for a period of months, or approximately a season.
c. 'Severe': involving serious or significant disruption or harm to human life, natural and economic resources or other assets.

While the terms 'widespread' and 'long-lasting' are explained by quantifiable definitions, the explanation of 'severe' is not as clear and is open to various interpretations. As noted by Schmitt, the use of 'serious or significant' as a clarifying term of 'severe' tends to manifest a certain vagueness.[54]

Moreover, the legal value of the annexed Understandings section is not entirely clear. The ENMOD Convention has four attached Understandings that regard the interpretation of its articles.[55] The Understandings were included by the drafters or the 'Committee' in a report of the conference submitted to the

[51] The UN Conference of the Committee on Disarmament provided the negotiation forum.

[52] See UN General Assembly Resolution 3264 (XXIX) UN Doc A/RES/3264 (XXIX) (9 December 1974) on the Prohibition of Action to Influence the Environment and Climate for Military and Other Purposes Incompatible with the Maintenance of International Security, Human Well-Being and Health.

[53] W Verwey, 'Protection of the Environment in Times of Armed Conflict: In Search of a New Legal Perspective' (1995) 8 *Leiden Journal of International Law*, 7 17.

[54] M Schmitt, 'War and the Environment: Fault Lines in the Prescriptive Landscape' in JE Austin and CE Bruch (eds), *The Environmental Consequences of War* (Cambridge University Press, 2000) 106.

[55] EV Koppe, *The Use of Nuclear Weapons and the Protection of the Environment During International Armed Conflict* (Gildeprint, 2006) 108.

UN General Assembly. Hence, they are not a part of the official Convention text.[56] The Understandings attached to the ENMOD Convention are likely to be regarded as agreements relating to the treaty concluded between all the state parties at the conclusion of the Convention. As such, they form part of the context of the Convention and can be used as a primary means of interpretation in accordance with Article 31(2)(a) of the Vienna Convention on the Law of Treaties (VCLT).[57]

The Understandings could also be regarded as a part of the negotiation and drafting history. In such case, they would be used as a supplementary means of interpretation, according to Article 32 VCLT. Supplementary means of interpretation can only be applied if an interpretation using the primary means leaves the meaning of a treaty text ambiguous, obscure, absurd, or unreasonable; or if it can be used to confirm an interpretation established with the primary means. Consequently, regarded as a supplementary means of interpretation, the Understandings are of limited use in an interpretation process. However, as pointed out by Koppe, interpretative documents like the Understandings are more likely to be viewed as agreements between the parties.[58] Thus, I approach the Understandings as being part of the context, constituting a primary means of interpretation to establish the requirements in the terms used in the Convention, in particular regarding Article 1(I) of the Convention.

The requirements of 'widespread, long-lasting or severe effects' does not apply cumulatively because the provision contains the conjunction 'or'. Hence, it considerably lowers the threshold regarding the level of required damage. Once the requisite of any of the terms – 'widespread', 'long-lasting', or 'severe' – is met, the Convention applies and the prohibitions set out in the ENMOD Convention are absolute. In such a case, no reference to military necessity or the proportionality principle may override or justify a breach of its provisions.[59] However, the ENMOD Convention does not forbid a low-level manipulation of natural processes for hostile purposes. As noted by Dinstein, an environmental modification technique used with the intent to create fog over enemy areas may be harmless as such and therefore not reach the damage threshold.[60]

The modification techniques that the Convention covers are described in Article II as follows:

> [T]he term 'environmental modification techniques' refers to any technique for changing – through the deliberate manipulation of natural processes – the dynamics, composition or structure of the Earth, including its biota, lithosphere, hydrosphere and atmosphere, or outer space.

[56] Although, parts of the Understandings section were originally part of the treaty text. See ibid, 114.

[57] ibid, 114.

[58] ibid.

[59] Cohan (n 18) 518.

[60] Dinstein (n 4) 233.

The term 'biota' is intended to refer to flora and fauna, 'lithosphere' to the Earth's ground, 'hydrosphere' to water, and 'atmosphere' to air.[61] The explanatory Understandings section related to Article II of the ENMOD Convention provides examples of such modification techniques:

> [E]arthquakes, tsunamis; an upset in the ecological balance of the region; changes in weather patterns (clouds, precipitation, cyclones of various types, tornadic storms); changes in climate patterns; changes in ocean currents; changes in the state of the ozone layer; and changes in the state of the ionosphere.

The list is intended to be illustrative, but not exhaustive. Verwey suggests that the ENMOD Convention does not prohibit the abuse of the environment as a method in warfare. It does not apply when the environment itself constitutes a weapon, only when the weapon is the manipulated natural process. Such processes do not necessarily need to have adverse impacts on the environment.[62]

There have also been discussions on whether the introduction of chemical substances that interrupt ecosystems would fall within the scope of the ENMOD Convention. Cohan argues that the use of herbicides is prohibited under the Convention if causing 'widespread, long-lasting or severe effects'.[63] As witnessed during the Vietnam War, the use of Agent Orange caused ecological imbalance in the South Vietnamese regions. In 1984 and 1992, two review conferences were held for the state parties to discuss the application of the ENMOD Convention in accordance with Article VIII. At the conferences, different interpretations about the scope of the Convention were discussed. During the discussions, the parties concluded in a Final Declaration that herbicides used for the hostile purposes of upsetting the ecological balance are indeed covered by the ENMOD Convention.[64]

The Final Declaration should be regarded as a subsequent agreement in accordance with Article 31(3)(a) VCLT. Thus, a contemporary interpretation would probably come to the conclusion that employment of herbicides must be prohibited, in some cases, under the ENMOD Convention if their use has the effect of disrupting the ecological balance and fulfilling the threshold of 'widespread, long-lasting or severe'. In addition, the introduction of chemical substances to the environment – such as Agent Orange by the United States during the Vietnam War – as a part of military operations is also prohibited under the Geneva Protocol for the Prohibition of the Use in War of Asphyxiating,

[61] Koppe, *The Use of Nuclear Weapons* (n 55) 108.

[62] Verwey (n 53) 17.

[63] Cohan (n 18) 513.

[64] Article II. See Second Review Conference of the Parties to the ENMOD Convention, held in Geneva, 14–18 September 1992, Final Document, ENMOD/Conf.II/12, 22 September 1992, 11–12. See also M Orellana, 'Criminal Punishment for Environmental Damage: Individual and State Responsibility at a Crossroad' (2005) 17 *Georgetown International Environmental Law Review* 673, 683.

Poisonous and Other Gases, and of Bacteriological Methods of Warfare[65] (1925 Geneva Gas Protocol).

The examples of modification techniques, as included in the Understandings section, are rarely employed by military planners. Hence, the utility of the ENMOD Convention can therefore be questioned. The sophisticated environmental modification techniques that are listed in the Understandings section are largely remote from conventional warfare.[66] The Vietnam War, when the United States used cloud seeding in its warfare, stands out as a unique example. In total, only 76 states have ratified the ENMOD Convention, including militarily powerful states such as the United States, Russia (the Soviet Union at the time of ratification) and the United Kingdom.[67] The number of states is relatively low and can be explained by the fact that there are very few states with the capability to develop these types of weapons.[68] Therefore, the interest to prohibit such techniques may not be a prioritised issue for most states.

In Article III, it is however stated that the ENMOD Convention does not hinder the use of environmental techniques for peaceful purposes; but it may be difficult to draw a distinction between peaceful and hostile use. If, for example, a state seeks to alleviate a drought by cloud seeding and, consequently, produces a devastating flood that may serve military purposes as a side effect, it is not considered a violation of the Convention, even if it occurred in wartime. Nevertheless, the Convention may still be relevant as an instrument of future importance. Scientists might be able to develop techniques to control environmental forces for efficient military purposes – the ENMOD Convention may be able to prevent such a development.[69] However, it does not prohibit the research and experimentation of environmental modification, regardless of what the purpose may be, including hostile ones.

The application of the ENMOD Convention is also limited in another aspect – it only protects the environment within the territory of state parties to the Convention in accordance with Article I(1). Hence, the destruction, damage, or injury that affects the territory of the acting state, a state not a party to the ENMOD Convention, or an area outside the jurisdiction of all state parties will not fall within the scope of the Convention.[70] The ENMOD Convention does not contain an expressed scope of application to international armed conflict,

[65] Geneva Protocol for the Prohibition of the Use in War of Asphyxiating, Poisonous and Other Gases, and of Bacteriological Methods of Warfare (adopted 17 June 1925, entered into force 8 February 1928) 94 LNTS 65 (1925 Geneva Gas Protocol).

[66] Orellana (n 64) 683. See also Falk (n 19) 154.

[67] See the parties to the ENMOD Convention at the web page of UN Office for Disarmament Affairs: disarmament.un.org/treaties/t/enmod.

[68] Koppe, *The Use of Nuclear Weapons* (n 55) 106–07; S Freeland, *Addressing the Intentional Destruction of the Environment During Warfare Under the Rome Statute of the International Criminal Court* (Intersentia, 2015) 81.

[69] Cohan (n 18) 512–14.

[70] Verwey (n 53) 18.

but as it includes a transboundary element by requiring injury on other state parties' territory, it is more likely that it is mostly relevant in international armed conflicts.[71] Moreover, the ENMOD Convention obligates state parties to consult and cooperate to resolve an alleged violation. In addition, a state party accusing another state party for a breach of the Convention can lodge a claim at the UN Security Council – this mechanism has, however, not yet been used.[72]

To sum up, the application of the ENMOD Convention is subject to the following limitations. First, it only covers the very special cases of using environmental modification techniques as weapons during warfare.[73] It does not pertain to conventional acts of warfare that result in adverse effects on the environment or to acts where the environment is a target itself. Therefore, the Convention is not relevant to most cases of damage to the environment in armed conflicts.[74] Second, it only prohibits environmental modification techniques for hostile purposes. The techniques can be used if the purpose is peaceful, although it may cause harm for another state party. Third, it merely protects the environment within the territory of state parties to the Convention. Third states or territories outside state parties' jurisdiction are not protected from harmful effects under the Convention. The ENMOD Convention has more a symbolic value to hinder the development of manipulating the environment for hostile use, rather than providing substantial protection of the environment in relation to armed conflict. Thus, the ENMOD Convention, as a tool to protect the environment, could be disregarded in most armed conflicts.

V. ABSOLUTE ENVIRONMENTAL PROTECTION IN PROTOCOL I

In this section, I examine the two environmentally specific provisions in Protocol I: Article 35(3), which limits the means and methods of warfare that damage the environment; and Article 55, which contains an obligation to take care of the environment for the sake of the population's survival and forbids reprisals against the environment. I argue that these provisions set a high, as well as an unclear, threshold for application that makes them irrelevant in most cases of environmental harm occurring in relation to armed conflict. However, by applying an evolutionary interpretation approach to define 'environmental damage' and the standard of 'taking care' of the environment in the light of new

[71] CE Bruch, 'All's Not Fair in (Civil) War: Criminal Liability for Environmental Damage in Internal Armed Conflict' (2000) 25 *Vermont Law Review* 695, 703.

[72] JE Smith, *Weather Warfare: The Military's Plan to Draft Mother Nature* (Adventure Unlimited Press, Kempton, US, 2006) 126.

[73] Many commentators confirm such a view, see A Roberts, 'The Law of War and Environmental Damage' in JE Austin and CE Bruch (eds), *The Environmental Consequences of War* (Cambridge University Press, 2000) 59.

[74] ibid, 58–59.

scientific knowledge and requirements of international environmental customary law, I claim that the threshold can be lowered and – to some extent – clarified.

The following subsections scrutinise the content and application of Articles 35(3) and 55 of Protocol I. Subsection A provides a general description of the articles. Subsection B examines the threshold of 'widespread, long-term and severe' environmental damage and how it can be clarified by employing an evolutionary interpretation. Subsection C discusses the general obligation to take care of the environment, as stated in Article 55(1), and how it relates to other obligations in Protocol I. Finally, subsection D examines the foreseeability requirement in Article 35(3).

A. The Articles

Articles 35(3) and 55 of Protocol I provide direct protection of the environment in times of armed conflict. Article 35(3), placed in the chapter titled 'Methods and Means of Warfare' of Protocol I, states that:

> It is prohibited to employ methods or means of warfare which are intended, or may be expected, to cause widespread, long-term and severe damage to the natural environment.

Article 55 is situated in the chapter titled 'Civilian Objects' of Protocol I. It reads:

1. Care shall be taken in warfare to protect the natural environment against widespread, long-term and severe damage. This protection includes a prohibition of the use of methods or means of warfare which are intended or may be expected to cause such damage to the natural environment and thereby to prejudice the health or survival of the population.
2. Attacks against the natural environment by way of reprisals are prohibited.

At first glance, the two articles seem to replicate each other; however, there are some essential differences between them. The main difference is that Article 35(3) refers to the use of means and methods of warfare and lacks a reference to human harm. Article 55 instead contains a positive obligation to take care of the environment, as well as a specific prohibition on means and methods that mainly aims to ensure the health and survival of the population. In addition, Article 55 prohibits reprisals against the environment. A reprisal constitutes a legal act of retaliation that is undertaken for enforcing the rules of the law of armed conflict. Such an act would otherwise be unlawful. The prohibition against reprisals towards the environment demonstrates that environmental concerns are recognised under the law of armed conflict.[75]

[75] Schafer (n 3) 312–13.

The articles seem to be mainly intended for 'high-level policy decision-makers', as pointed out by Thomas.[76] They set an absolute prohibition for belligerents to cause environmental damage above the threshold of 'widespread, long-term and severe' damage, regardless of the military situation. This applies even if the environment constitutes a 'military objective';[77] if the military advantage outweighs the environmental damage;[78] or if the action is needed because of pressing military concerns.[79] Thus, the threshold represents a fixed upper limitation on permissible environmental harm in times of armed conflict.

The terms in the threshold are not defined in Protocol I and the provisions have not yet been subject to any court examination. However, Articles 35(3) and 55(1) of Protocol I have been analysed extensively in the legal doctrine.[80] Even so, it has proven to be a challenging interpretation exercise to establish the meaning of the terms in the articles and no consensus has yet been achieved about their content. The articles are generally described in the literature as being unable to set a precise threshold.[81] There seems, however, to be common agreement among scholars that the provisions set an exceptionally high threshold because they require cumulatively 'widespread, long-term *and* severe damage' (emphasis added).[82]

In its 2009 report, UN Environment similarly stated that Articles 35(3) and 55(1), 'do not effectively protect the environment during armed conflict due to the stringent and imprecise threshold required to demonstrate damage'.[83] The provisions are criticised, first, for the narrow scope of application because of the high threshold[84] and, second, for imposing vague constraints on environmentally harmful warfare, because the terms 'widespread', 'long-term' and 'severe' have not been clarified and the articles have never been put in to use.[85] The usefulness of the articles is questioned because they do not cover most of the environmental damage occurring in times of armed conflict. In the Final Report to the Prosecutor by the Committee Established to Review the NATO Bombing

[76] C Thomas, 'Advancing the Legal Protection of the Environment in Relation to Armed Conflict: Protocol I's Threshold of Impermissible Environmental Damage and Alternatives' (2013) 83 *Nordic Journal of International Law* 90; See also, M Bothe, KJ Partsch and W Solf, *New Rules for Victims of Armed Conflicts: Commentary on the Two 1977 Protocols Additional to the Geneva Conventions of 1949* (Nijhoff, 1982) 343.

[77] As defined in Article 52(2) of Protocol I.

[78] Such a balancing test is set out in the proportionality principle, as replicated in Article 51(5)(b) of Protocol I.

[79] See discussion in Simonds (n 6) 173.

[80] For further reading on the definitions of the requirements set out in Articles 35(3) and 55 of Protocol I, see Hulme, *War Torn Environment* (n 9) 88–100; Dinstein (n 4) 235–39; Thomas (n 76) 83–101; Schmitt, 'Green War' (n 21) 68–81; Parson (n 31) 452.

[81] Thomas (n 76) 84.

[82] See Hulme, *War Torn Environment* (n 9) 88–100; Dinstein (n 4) 237–39; Schmitt, 'Green War' (n 21) 68–81.

[83] UNEP, 'Protecting the Environment' (n 48) 4.

[84] Thomas (n 76) 110; Bothe et al (n 2).

[85] UNEP, 'Protecting the Environment' (n 48) 4.

Campaign (Review Committee Report for the ICTY Prosecutor), it was stated that the threshold of Articles 35 and 55 was set so high that the Committee could not determine prima facie if it had been reached during the bombing of the Pancevo complex.[86]

Nevertheless, the articles may have had an impact on warfare since 1977. For instance, the articles could apply to unconventional warfare, such as the substantial use of herbicides or chemical agents that have the potential to cause 'widespread, long-term and severe' environmental damage.[87] However, according to some scholars, Protocol I was not intended to apply to weapons of mass destruction, namely chemical, biological and nuclear weapons.[88] For instance, Marsh states that Protocol I is not at all applicable to nuclear weapons,[89] although there is nothing in the treaty text indicating the existence of such an exception. Thus, Protocol I is applicable to all kinds of warfare, except in those cases where state parties have made an explicit reservation regarding certain weapons.[90]

B. Interpreting the Threshold of 'Widespread, Long-term and Severe Damage'

In this subsection, I seek to establish the meaning of the terms used in the threshold in Articles 35(3) and 55(1) of Protocol I. I argue that the threshold must be assessed by using an evolutionary interpretation that takes into consideration the circumstances prevailing *at the time of interpretation*, rather than *at the time of the adoption* of Protocol I. Such an interpretation puts less emphasis on the negotiation and drafting history. It could also potentially lower the threshold in the articles because the interpretation process can be influenced by the contemporary requirements of customary international environmental law that may not have existed at the time of the adoption of Protocol I.

i. Justifying an Evolutionary Interpretation

An evolutionary interpretation functions on the premise that the meaning of certain expressions used in treaty provisions may have evolved over time. These are so-called 'dynamic generic expressions' that are intended by the parties of an instrument to be exposed to temporal variations and interpreted in its

[86] Final Report to the Prosecutor by the Committee Established to Review the NATO Bombing Campaign Against the Federal Republic of Yugoslavia, published 13 June 2000 on ICTY's web page, available at: www.icty.org/sid/10052.

[87] Thomas (n 76) 90.

[88] Simonds (n 6) 175.

[89] J Marsh, 'Lex Lata or Lex Ferenda? Rule 45 of the ICRC Study on Customary International Humanitarian Law' (2008) 198 *Military Law Review* 116, 138–39.

[90] The United States, the United Kingdom and France have made expressed reservations exempting them from Articles 35(3) and 55. See ICRC's web page on reservations: www.icrc.org/applic/ihl/ihl.nsf/States.xsp?xp_viewStates=XPages_NORMStatesParties&xp_treatySelected=47.

contemporary meaning (at the time of the interpretation).[91] As observed by Dam-de Jong, international courts frequently apply an evolutionary approach in their interpretation processes.[92] For instance, in the *Namibia* Advisory Opinion, the International Court of Justice stated that an international instrument has to be interpreted and applied with consideration of the rules of the whole legal system *at the time of the interpretation.*[93] For the same reason, the Court stated in the *Gabcikovo-Nagymaros Project* case that new rules have to be taken into account when states conduct activities, even if the activities started in the past when those new rules did not exist.[94] Such a view permits the result that even when the activities are regulated in a treaty concluded prior to the existence of the new rules, these may still be taken into consideration when applying the treaty.[95]

While interpreting the ordinary meaning, Linderfalk distinguishes between historical language – which is the meaning of the language used at the time when the treaty was concluded – and contemporary language – which is the meaning of the language at the time of the interpretation.[96] To determine whether historical or contemporary language should be used in the interpretation process and thus whether an evolutionary interpretation should be applied, Linderfalk makes a distinction between two categories of generic referring expressions that can be either static or dynamic. The distinction depends on what the parties intended with the choice of a certain expression in a provision. Linderfalk describes the differences as:

> [I]f it can be shown that the thing interpreted is a generic referring expression with a referent assumed to be alterable then the decisive factor for determining 'the ordinary meaning' of the expression shall be contemporary language. In all other cases, the decisive factor shall be historical.[97]

Consequently, it must be demonstrated that the parties of Protocol I intended that 'widespread, long-term and severe damage to the natural environment' should be regarded as a *dynamic* generic referring expression to be able to consider temporal variations in the interpretation process.

There seem to be indications that an evolutionary interpretation of treaty terms is generally preferred in relation to environmental matters under

[91] U Linderfalk, *On the Interpretation of Treaties* (Springer, 2007) 73 ff.

[92] DA Dam-de Jong, *International Law and Governance of Natural Resources in Conflict and Post-Conflict Situations* (EM Meijers Instituut, 2013) 30–31.

[93] *Legal Consequences for States of the Continued Presence of South Africa in Namibia (South West Africa) Notwithstanding Security Council Resolution 276 (1970)*, Advisory Opinion of 21 June 1971, ICJ Reports 1971, para 53.

[94] *Gabcikovo-Nagymaros Project (Hungary/Slovakia)*, Judgment of 25 September 1997, ICJ Reports 1997, para 80.

[95] Dam-de Jong (n 92) 31.

[96] Linderfalk (n 91) ff.

[97] ibid, 87.

international law.[98] For instance, in the case *Dispute Concerning Access to Information* of the OSPAR Arbitration (from the Convention for the Protection of the Marine Environment of the North-East Atlantic),[99] the Tribunal stated that it should avoid producing an outdated result that is inconsistent with current international law. It stated further that a tribunal should strive for a result that is in line with existing obligations, even when the international instrument in question was concluded in the past.[100] Similarly, the WTO Appellate Body in the *Shrimp/Turtle* case referred to contemporary law on environmental protection to interpret the term 'exhaustible natural resources' in the GATT 1947. The WTO Appellate Body concluded that such terms 'must be read by a treaty interpreter in the light of contemporary concerns of the international community of nations about the protection and conservation of the environment'.[101] In addition, it stated that, 'the generic term "natural resources" in article XX(g) is not "static" in its content or reference but is rather by definition, evolutionary'.[102]

In the *Gabcikovo-Nagymaros Project* case, the International Court of Justice was asked to interpret a treaty concluded between Hungary and Slovakia. The treaty included provisions regarding the preservation of the water quality, the environment and fisheries. Hungary decided to halt the project and based one of its arguments on the new requirements in international environmental law. Hungary argued that in relation to the water quality assessment, scientific discoveries had changed the view of how chemical substances in the water affect humans. Water that was accepted to have decent quality 20 or even 10 years ago may no longer be considered as decent quality. Thus, it was suggested by Hungary that scientific knowledge decides the definition of acceptable water quality, which may differ over time.

The Court did not accept the Hungarian conservation argument as a valid reason to terminate a treaty in accordance with the VCLT. Nevertheless, the Court stated that new rules within international environmental law are relevant for the implementation of the treaty with regard to conservation of the environment and its resources. The Court concluded that new environmental rules could be considered in the treaty application because the parties, namely Hungary and Slovakia, intended to have dynamic provisions that could adjust to new requirements with regard to the conservation of water quality, environment

[98] R Desgagné, 'The Prevention of Environmental Damage in Time of Armed Conflict: Proportionality and Precautionary Measures' (2000) 3 *Yearbook of International Humanitarian Law* 109, 113.

[99] Convention for the Protection of the Marine Environment of the North-East Atlantic (adopted 22 September 1992, entered into force 25 March 1998) 2354 UNTS 67 (OSPAR Convention).

[100] *Dispute Concerning Access to Information Under Article 9 of the OSPAR Convention, Ireland v United Kingdom*, Final Award (2003) XXIII RIAA 59, 2 July 2003, Permanent Court of Arbitration, para 103.

[101] *Shrimp/Turtle Case of 12 October*, WTO Appellate Body, 1998WT/DS58/AB/R, para 129.

[102] ibid, para 130.

and fisheries.[103] The Court ruled that safeguarding the environment can be estimated and treated differently depending on new rules and principles or new scientific knowledge, in accordance with the parties' intention.

The Court took an evolutionary approach to consider the law prevailing at the time of interpretation, by taking into account the context and using 'relevant rules of international law' as provided by Article 31(3)(c) VCLT.[104] For the same reason, in the *Rhine Iron* case, the Tribunal favoured an evolutionary interpretation of a treaty concluded in 1839 in relation to environmental concerns.[105] The Tribunal expressed that, based on Article 31(3)(c) VCLT, new rules of international environmental law could be taken into account when interpreting a generic term that is intended to follow the legal development.[106] In sum, there appears to be a tendency that courts and tribunals will apply an evolutionary interpretation when dealing with environmental concerns in international instruments, because they consider that the state parties have incorporated dynamic generic referring expressions.

Therefore, an intertemporal aspect needs to be taken into account to determine whether more recently developed environmental rules and principles can be used to interpret the older rules in the law of armed conflict. As expressed by Koppe in relation to the terms used in Protocol I:

> [E]nvironmental considerations tend to play an increasingly important role in other areas of international law, such as European law, international trade and investment law, the law of state responsibility, treaty law and even the law of individual criminal responsibility. It is therefore not unthinkable that all these developments will lead to a less restrictive interpretation of these terms.[107]

ii. Shedding New Light on the Threshold

The previous scholarly analysis of the articles has, in general, put most, if not all, emphasis on the negotiation and drafting history of Protocol I, as reproduced in the ICRC Commentary to the Protocols and the drafting records.[108] Such an approach is not consistent with the rules for treaty interpretation as formulated in Articles 31–33 VCLT. The interpretation of Articles 35(3) and 55(1) needs to put less weight on the circumstances at the conclusion of the treaty and seek to establish the common intention of the present state parties to Protocol I today.

[103] *Gabcikovo-Nagymaros Project (Hungary/Slovakia)*, Judgment of 25 September 1997, ICJ Reports 1997, para 112.

[104] Linderfalk (n 91) 185.

[105] *Award in the Arbitration Regarding the Iron Rhine ('Ijzeren Rijn') Railway Between the Kingdom of Belgium and the Kingdom of the Netherlands*, Decision of 24 May 2005.

[106] ibid, para 79.

[107] Koppe, *The Use of Nuclear Weapons* (n 55) 144–45.

[108] See, eg, Simonds (n 6) 173 ff.; Thomas (n 76) 88; Roberts, 'The Law of War' (n 73) 62; Schmitt, 'War and the Environment' (n 54) 105; Bouvier (n 7).

As mentioned above, few scholars have provided an interpretation that is faithful to the interpretation rules in the VCLT with regard to the phrase 'widespread, long-term and severe damage to the natural environment' by applying the primary means of interpretation. There are, of course, exceptions.[109] However, most commentators have based the interpretation mainly on the supplementary means, focusing on the negotiation and drafting history. The supplementary means of interpretation is permitted in case the result of an interpretation process, in conformity with the primary means, leaves the meaning of a treaty text ambiguous, obscure, absurd, or unreasonable; or if it is used to confirm a meaning established under an interpretation using the primary means. Consequently, the negotiation and drafting history is of limited use as a means of interpretation. This is neglected by most scholars who interpret the threshold in Articles 35(3) and 55(1) of Protocol I.

Bothe and Verwey have also criticised the use of the supplementary means of interpretation, such as drafting and negotiation history, when interpreting the articles.[110] Bothe notes that at the time when the negotiations took place, the participants in the 1974–77 ICRC Conference had limited experience and expertise in relation to environmental damage in general and wartime environmental damage in particular.[111] He stresses that interpreting the threshold in Articles 35(3) and 55(1) of Protocol I according to their negotiation history heavily restricts the application. Instead, he suggests that an interpretation conducted in an evolving manner could provide new answers as to whether the environmental effect of an attack is 'widespread, long-term and severe'.[112]

Koppe also supports the view that the terms may change over time and that this change may even be a desirable development.[113] Similarly, Verwey highlights that the terms were not clarified in the preparatory work, and, even if they were, it cannot provide any authoritative answers on the type of environmental damage intended.[114] Using the primary means of interpretation can therefore shed some new light on how to interpret the 'widespread, long-term and severe' environmental damage because they may provide for using an evolutionary interpretation.

iii. 'Natural Environment' versus 'Environment'

Articles 35(3) and 55(1) of Protocol I include the qualifying word of '*natural* environment' to distinguish from the 'human-made environment' in the provisions.[115]

[109] See, for instance, Hulme, *War Torn Environment* (n 9).
[110] See Verwey (n 53) 10; Bothe, 'The Protection of the Environment' (n 27) 56.
[111] Bothe, 'The Protection of the Environment' (n 27) 56.
[112] M Bothe, 'The Ethics, Principles and Objectives of Protection of the Environment in Times of Armed Conflict' in R Rayfuse (ed), *War and the Environment: New Approaches to Protecting the Environment in Relation to Armed Conflict* (Brill Nijhoff, 2014) 103.
[113] Koppe, *The Use of Nuclear Weapons* (n 55) 144.
[114] Verwey (n 53) 10.
[115] Lehto, Second Report (n 13) para 194.

Thus, this would favour a restricted definition of the environment. The International Court of Justice in the *Kasikili/Sedudu Island* case[116] stated that the ordinary meaning can be determined by using the language of international law as a means of interpretation, like treaties, which express the language of international law. By making such a remark, the Court implied that the language of international law is a technical variation of the language as used by international lawyers.[117] For that reason, a review of treaties dealing with the environment is appropriate to establish what is generally meant by the notion of the 'environment' in international law and, thus, also in the provisions of Protocol I.

The term 'environment' lacks, however, a universal definition in international law.[118] Although various definitions have been suggested, many international environmental law instruments make general references to the dependence of humans on the environment.[119] For instance, the 1972 Declaration of the Conference on the Human Environment (Stockholm Declaration) broadly refers to both aspects of 'the natural and the man-made' environment and how these are crucial for humans' 'well-being and enjoyment of basic human rights'.[120] Thus, much of the focus lies in the interaction between humans and the natural world. The Council of Europe's Convention on Civil Liability for Environmental Damage broadly defines the environment to include abiotic and biotic natural resources, property forming part of the cultural heritage, and the characteristic aspects of the landscape.[121] The International Law Commission adopted a similar broad definition of the environment in its work on transboundary harm arising out of hazardous activities, although it did not include any reference to cultural heritage.[122]

Further support for a broad definition of the environment is also found in the expanding reach that environmental issues are gaining. For instance, in an advisory opinion of the Inter-American Court of Human Rights, the interdependence between humans and the environment was established in relation by stating that environmental harm affects human rights.[123] The overall trend in

[116] *Kasikili/Sedudu Island (Botswana/Namibia)*, Judgment of 13 December 1999, ICJ Reports 1999, 1045.

[117] See Linderfalk's reasoning in relation to the case in Linderfalk (n 91) 67–69.

[118] P Birnie, A Boyle and C Redgwell, *International Law & the Environment* (Oxford University Press, 2009) 4.

[119] ibid.

[120] Principle 1, Declaration of the United Nations Conference on the Human Environment, Stockholm, 16 June 1972, 11 I.M 1416 (1972) (Stockholm Declaration).

[121] Articles 1(2) and 2 Convention on Civil Liability for Environmental Damage.

[122] The definition reads: 'The "environment" includes natural resources, both abiotic and biotic, such as air, water soil, fauna and flora and the interaction between the same factors, and the characteristic aspects of the landscape'. See Report of the International Law Commission, 58th Session (1 May–9 June and 3 July–11 August 2006) UN Doc A/61/10, (2006) *Yearbook of the International Law Commission*, Volume II, Part Two, para 66.

[123] Inter-American Court of Human Rights, Advisory Opinion No OC 23-17, *Medio Ambiente y Derechos Humanos*, 15 November 2017, Series A, No 23.

international law is to interpret references to the environment in treaties in an extensive manner without separating humans and nature.[124] Consequently, the conventional language may presumably support a broad definition of the environment seeing it as a complex system, in which components of the natural environment interact with each other and with humans making a clear division difficult to uphold.

The Commentary to Protocol I states that the 'natural environment' in Protocol I should be understood as 'in the widest sense to cover the biological environment in which a population is living'.[125] Defined as a 'biological environment' indicates that something that is human-made can be omitted; for instance, cultural heritage. Simultaneously, the Commentary refers to an environment that is inhabited by a population. The presence of a population will most likely have some sort of impact on the environment and change its character from being purely natural to at least partly human-made. Thus, the notion of 'natural environment' cannot be intended to refer to a nature untouched by humans while at the same time referring to an environment in which humans live. It must include both human-made as well as uninhabited nature. Furthermore, Simonds argues that the Commentary to the Protocol supports 'an expansive view' on how to define the environment by embracing the expression 'in the widest sense'.[126] She bases this view on the fact that the parties to Protocol I intended to refer to a broad definition of the environment because several restricted definitions of the environment were rejected during the drafting process.[127]

In relation to the ICRC's 2005 Customary Law Study, Hulme points out that the authors make no distinction between man-made and natural parts of the environment in the customary rules applicable to the environment.[128] In the Study, the environment is referred to, interchangeably, both as the 'natural environment' and 'environment' in the rules dealing with environmental protection.[129] This supports the notion that the language of international law does not separate between the natural and the human-made environment. In addition, in the debate of the Sixth Committee of the UN General Assembly in 2018, some states expressed that the term 'natural environment' included in several of the draft principles provisionally adopted by the International Law Commission applicable during armed conflicts may be overly restrictive.[130] Also, Special Rapporteur Lehto argues in her Second Report that the term 'natural

[124] Lehto, Second Report (n 13) para 196.

[125] Y Sandoz, C Swinarski and B Zimmerman (eds), *Commentary on the Additional Protocols of 8 June 1977* (ICRC, Geneva, 1987) 662.

[126] Simonds (n 6) 173.

[127] ibid.

[128] K Hulme, 'Natural Environment' in E Wilmshurst and S Breau (eds), *Perspectives on the ICRC Study on Customary International Humanitarian Law* (Cambridge University Press, 2007) 208.

[129] See Rules 43–44 in J-M Henckaerts and L Doswald-Beck (eds), *Customary International Humanitarian Law Study*, Volume I: Rules (Cambridge University Press, 2005).

[130] See the summary of the debate in Lehto, Second Report (n 13) para 5.

environment' should be replaced with 'environment'. She supports this argument by referring to recent research that views the environment as a complex interactive system in which humans and the natural environment interact with each other to an extent that these cannot be separated.[131] The general trend of international law taken together with the Commentary to Protocol I, indicates that the parties of Protocol I aimed at communicating a broad definition of the environment that may include human-made formations.[132]

iv. 'Widespread, Long-term and Severe'

As there is no universal definition of the 'environment', it follows that there cannot be any universal definition of 'environmental damage' either. In fact, most international environmental treaties do not define 'damage' or the more commonly used term 'pollution'. Instead, these focus on the state parties' duty to prevent environmental damage, which is an obligation to minimise the risk of causing harm. When environmental damage, or pollution, is defined, international treaties described it as deleterious or adverse effects on the environment, including harm to living resources or ecosystems and/or human health.[133]

Since the adoption of Protocol I in 1977, states have adopted new international legal standards for how to protect the environment in accordance with increased scientific knowledge.[134] As 'environmental damage' appears to be a term that could constitute a generic expression of a dynamic character when it appears in treaties, it may change the view of such damage and the responses to it. The explanation is rooted in the fact that what may be considered as 'environmental damage' at one point in history may be altered over time due to increased scientific knowledge and/or new rules developed to address new risk factors. In other words, the accepted levels of harm that may be done to the environment will most likely change over time and new types of measures to care for the environment may be required by new rules of international law.

As environmental damage tends to be treated as a dynamic generic expression, it is likely that the state parties to Protocol I intended that 'widespread, long-term and severe' environmental damage should be determined with the use

[131] ibid, paras 196–97.

[132] As pointed out by Henckaerts and Constantin, almost 95 per cent of what exists on the planet would fall under the definition of environment. See J-M Henckaerts and D Constantin, 'Protection of the Environment' in A Clapham and P Gaeta (eds), *The Oxford Handbook of International Law in Armed Conflict* (Oxford University Press, 2014) 471.

[133] See, for instance, Article 1(4), United Nations Convention on the Law of the Sea (adopted 10 December 1982, entered into force 16 November 1994) 1833 UNTS 3 (UNCLOS); Article 1, Convention on Long-Range Transboundary Air Pollution (adopted 13 November 1979, entered into force 16 March, 1983) 1302 UNTS 217 (LRTAP); Article 1(1), Framework Convention on Climate Change (adopted 9 May 1992, entered into force 21 March 1994) 1771 UNTS 107 (Climate Change Convention).

[134] Bothe, 'The Ethics, Principles and Objectives' (n 112) 103.

of the conventional language of international law applicable at the time of interpretation, and not with the language applicable at the time of the conclusion of Protocol I in 1977. Thus, the ordinary meaning of environmental damage must have evolved in the light of the development of international environmental law, given that this branch of law was only in its infancy at the time of the adoption of Protocol I. It may also have been affected by increasing scientific knowledge on the effects of warfare on the environment; for instance, the reports generated by UN Environment have augmented the knowledge on how conflicts affect the environment. Thus, the notion of environmental damage is likely to have changed over the years. However, because the level of damage still has to fulfil the requirements of 'widespread, long-term and severe', an evolutionary interpretation may have limited impact.

Within international environmental law, 'significant' or 'serious' damage to the environment is often the legal yardstick for state responsibility, at least when referring to transboundary damage.[135] Consequently, as Protocol I uses the terms 'widespread, long-term and severe' to qualify the environmental damage, the intention of the parties must be to set a standard different from the one of international environmental law (existing at the time). Hulme underscores that 'serious damage' is a lower standard than 'severe' alone, and it is considerably lower than the three cumulative requirements in the threshold in Articles 35(3) and 55(1) of Protocol I.[136] International environmental treaties may not be able to assist in establishing the meaning of 'widespread, long-term and severe' environmental damage because these do not use the terms at all.

The inclusion of 'widespread, long-term and severe' is obviously deliberately used to refer to something that goes beyond 'significant damage' – the 'normal' damage standard in international environmental law. Effects on future generations may be incorporated into the meaning of 'long-term' damage, because the principle of intergenerational equity has gained recognition within international environmental law.[137] Bothe states that it may be necessary to take into account ecological values in determining what is intended by 'severe'.[138] To conclude, the environmental damage referred to in Protocol I must be lowered in accordance with existing international law, even if the content cannot be fully established and will still go beyond the damage level established in international environmental law.

[135] The threshold of prohibited damage set in the *Trail Smelter* case is damage of 'serious consequence'. See *Trail Smelter Case (United States/Canada)*, Award of 11 March 1941. The treaties and practice have referred to 'significant damage' which has lowered the threshold. See Principle 2 of the International Law Commission Draft Articles on Prevention of Transboundary Harm From Hazardous Activities, Report of the International Law Commission, adopted at the 65rd Session (2001) *Yearbook of the International Law Commission*, Volume II, Part Two.

[136] Hulme, 'Natural Environment' (n 128) 229.

[137] Bothe, 'The Ethics, Principles and Objectives' (n 112) 103.

[138] ibid.

v. Using the ENMOD Convention as a Means of Interpretation

The ENMOD Convention could serve as a means of interpretation to assist in establishing the meaning of 'widespread, long-term and severe' environmental damage in Articles 35(3) and 55(1) of Protocol I. The language of the ENMOD Convention can be a source of information to determine the ordinary meaning of the terms 'widespread, long-term and severe' in Protocol I because these are also used in the ENMOD Convention and are defined in an Understandings section attached to the Convention. Most scholars have rejected this option, however, mainly based on reasons relating to the negotiation history of the two instruments. The negotiating states were united in the fact that the threshold included in Protocol I is higher than the threshold of the ENMOD Convention.[139] Unlike Protocol I, the ENMOD Convention does not require that the terms are cumulatively fulfilled. As put by Thomas, with regard to the ENMOD Convention, 'its interpretative guidance specifically disclaims equivalence with Protocol I'.[140] Protocol I is not only considered to set a higher threshold altogether, but it is also considered higher for each of the individual requirements as well. For instance, according to the drafting records, in Protocol I 'long-term' is suggested in the Commentary to cover a period of decades, while in the Understandings section to the ENMOD Convention, 'long-lasting' refers to a season.

I argue that the provisions in the ENMOD Convention can be used as a source of information to establish the 'ordinary meaning' of the articles in Protocol I in accordance with Article 31(1) VCLT. As mentioned earlier, the negotiation and drafting records are supplementary means of interpretation, while the ordinary meaning of the treaty text is at the heart of the interpretation process. In addition, the ordinary meaning may be subject to temporal variations in the language in accordance with the parties' intentions. In this case the 'widespread, long-lasting or severe effects' in the ENMOD Convention – as defined in the Understandings section – represent the contemporary language of international law. Therefore, it can serve to advance the interpretation of 'widespread, long-term and severe damage' written in Protocol I.

As the Understandings section provide the definitions of the terms of the provisions in the ENMOD Convention (based on a contextual interpretation as discussed in section IV), the same definitions could be a possible source of information to shed some light on how to define the terms in Articles 35(3) and 55(1) of Protocol I. Such an interpretation attempts to apply a uniform interpretation of terms used in other provisions of international law by applying the language of international law.

In relation to the Committee Report to the Prosecutor of the ICTY, Marauhn argues that the Committee could have interpreted the terms used in

[139] Thomas (n 76) 89–90.
[140] ibid.

the ENMOD Convention to establish the meaning of 'long-term' as a period of several months.[141] He bases this suggestion on, 'the recent tendencies'.[142] However, one has to acknowledge that the term 'long-lasting' is used in the ENMOD Convention, whereas the term 'long-term' is used in Protocol I. The difference is subtle, but perhaps the choice was a conscious one to separate the two terms – with the intention that 'long-term' covers a lengthier time period than 'long-lasting'.[143] Nevertheless, at least in relation to 'widespread' and 'severe', the Understandings section to the ENMOD Convention could provide a plausible interpretation of the terms.

To conclude, it is likely that the parties to Protocol I have intended that the expression 'damage to the natural environment' could be subject to new scientific knowledge and evolving legal requirements that may alter the view of what such damage consists of. Thus, the terms in the threshold in Articles 35(3) and 55(1) of Protocol I may be interpreted in an evolutionary manner that takes into account temporal variations in the language. Nevertheless, the terms remain unclear, even when applying an evolutionary interpretation. However, it can be established that the threshold of the environmental damage must be lower than what has been noted in the negotiation and drafting records of Protocol I and that the identical terms used in the provision in the ENMOD Convention could be used a source of information to establish the meaning of 'widespread' and 'severe'.

vi. Two Standards of Widespread, Long-term and Severe Damage

The internal relationship between Articles 35(3) and 55(1) of Protocol I is contradictory because they use the identical terms 'widespread, long-term and severe damage' slightly differently. Contrary to Article 35(3), Article 55(1) defines 'widespread, long-term and severe damage' as including a reference to the human population. This has the implication that the articles set an ambiguous legal standard in regard to whether the requirement of 'widespread, long-term and severe' damage must include human harm to reach the damage threshold.

a. Interpretation Departing from the 'Context'

As the terms are utilised repeatedly in both articles, the same type of damage should be intended in both in order to uphold a consistent meaning of the terms. This is in line with a systemic interpretation. Such an interpretation departs from the treaty context and requires that all treaty provisions must be viewed

[141] T Marauhn, 'Environmental Damage in Times of Armed Conflict – Not "Really" a Matter of Criminal Responsibility?' (2000) 82 *International Review of the Red Cross* 1029, para 3.
[142] ibid.
[143] Koppe, *The Use of Nuclear Weapons* (n 55) 138.

as part of a larger context or system, as provided in Article 31(2) VCLT.[144] The context includes the rest of the treaty text (the other provisions), including the Preamble and Annex. A systemic interpretation assumes all treaty rules to have a legal meaning and to be logically compatible within the treaty system as a whole.[145] Thus, identical terms must be assumed to have a uniform meaning within the same treaty.[146] This presumption is disturbed by the fact that Article 55(1) contains a second sentence that inserts an additional element referring to harm to the population with regard to what constitutes 'widespread, long-term and severe' environmental damage. At the same time, according to the Commentary to Protocol I, the prohibition in Article 35(3) applies irrespective of whether the population is affected or not.[147]

While analysing the articles, the first sentence in Article 55(1) prescribes a general obligation to take care of the environment against 'widespread, long-term and severe' damage. The second sentence reads as follows:

> This protection includes a prohibition of the use of methods or means of warfare which are intended or may be expected to cause such damage to the natural environment and thereby to prejudice the health or survival of the population.

The human reference in Article 55(1) could be seen as a clarification of the 'widespread, long-term and severe' environmental damage, providing a further limitation to the general applicability by inserting the reference of harm to the population.[148] By adding this reference, the second sentence introduces a new element of the requirement when compared with Article 35(3).[149] Such an addition may be regarded as a contradiction between the two articles, because it goes beyond what is stated in Article 35(3), even though it refers to the same threshold of damage. This reading would not give 'widespread, long-term and severe' damage a uniform meaning. However, Schmitt supports such an interpretation. He states that in cases where the population is not affected, Article 55(1) does not apply, regardless of the amount of damage to the environment.[150] However, Article 35(3) setting the same threshold would not require any human harm to apply. Consequently, such a reading would give the identical terms in Articles 35(3) and 55(1) different meanings, which would amount to contradiction within the treaty.

An alternative interpretation suggests that the insertion of the word 'includes' in the second sentence in Article 55(1) implies that the human reference is only an example of the damage referred to in the first sentence that contains a general obligation to take care. This view would not regard the reference

144 Linderfalk (n 91) 105.
145 ibid.
146 ibid, 107.
147 Sandoz, Swinarski and Zimmerman (n 125) 420.
148 Verwey (n 53) 13.
149 Dinstein (n 4) 236.
150 Schmitt, 'War and the Environment' (n 54) 93.

to human as a qualifier or clarifier of the definition of the damage threshold. As formulated by Hulme, 'the care obligation does not refer to environmental protection only on those occasions when people might be harmed'.[151] Thus, the use of 'includes' indicates that the article intends to prohibit more than what is explicitly mentioned.[152] Such an interpretation regards the second sentence in Article 55(1), not as an additional condition, but as a 'paramount category' of harm incorporated within the boundaries of a larger restriction.[153] It does not assume that 'widespread, long-term and severe damage' requires harm to the population, but suggests that human harm might be a consequence of such damage. This reading avoids any logical contradiction between Articles 35(3) and 55(1) of Protocol I, and it enables the phrase 'widespread, long-term and severe damage' to have the same meaning throughout the treaty, in accordance with a systemic interpretation that sees the provisions as parts of a coherent system in the context of Protocol I.

b. Interpretation Departing from the 'Object and Purpose'

As provided in Article 31(1) VCLT, the object and purpose can be used as a means to clarify the intended meaning in a treaty text.[154] In the literature, one of the main dissimilarities between Articles 35(3) and 55(1) is often described as their raison d'être of providing protection based on the reason of protecting the environment. Article 35(3) has been suggested to protect the environment per se, while Article 55(1) focuses on preventing adverse effects on humans because of environmental damage.[155] The distinction is established on the population reference in the second sentence of Article 55(1), which may suggest that Article 55(1) has a different object and purpose from Article 35(3).

Seeking to establish the provisions' meaning interpreted against the object and purpose of the treaty as a whole, the object and purpose of a treaty is the intended or desired effect of the application of the treaty. The principal purpose behind the instruments of the law of armed conflict is to safeguard human life and ameliorate human suffering, but at the same time enable military operations to be carried out.[156] Thus, Protocol I aims to balance humanitarianism with military necessity. Consequently, it can be said – as pointed out by Koppe – that Protocol I has the purpose of protecting humans.[157] Despite this, the population

[151] K Hulme, 'Taking Care to Protect the Environment Against Damage: A Meaningless Obligation?' (2010) 92 *International Review of the Red Cross* 675, 677.
[152] Verwey (n 53) 13.
[153] Dinstein (n 4) 236.
[154] Linderfalk (n 91) 203.
[155] Simonds (n 6) 172.
[156] FJ Yuzon, 'Deliberate Environmental Modification Through the Use of Chemical and Biological Weapons: "Greening" the International Laws of Armed Conflict to Establish an Environmentally Protective Regime' (1996) 11 *American University Journal of International Law and Policy* 793, 813.
[157] See Koppe, *The Use of Nuclear Weapons* (n 55) 96–97.

reference in Article 55(1) should be regarded as a paramount restriction and not as an additional qualification according to a systemic interpretation that aims for a coherent uniform reading of the provisions in Protocol I. At the same time, the reference specifies that the protection for the environment in the article applies for the sake of humans.[158] Such a reading is in line with the overall object and purpose of Protocol I. However, it implies that Article 55(1) has an additional requirement of human harm incorporated in the damage. As mentioned earlier, such an interpretation would create an inconsistent meaning of the phrase 'widespread, long-term and severe damage to the natural environment' that is contrary to a systemic interpretation.

Furthermore, the object and purpose of Article 35(3) is to protect the environment itself 'irrespective of its context and relationship' with the human population.[159] In fact, the adoption of Article 35(3) is based on the new threats that environmental degradation poses. This reading can be drawn from the Commentary to Protocol I stating that, '[w]ar is still a threat but it no longer has a monopoly' as a threat.[160] Chemical components of certain war remnants can have permanent harmful effects on humans, animals, vegetation, water, land and the ecosystem as a whole.[161] These aspects are recognised in the Commentary, which highlights the serious and constant danger a degraded environment implies. Environmental damage may be of serious nature even though it does not jeopardise the health of the population. In addition, Article 35(3) is not limited to the environment of the enemy, but recognises the global character of the environment and the transnational adverse effects on it.[162] Schmitt states that, '[A]rticle 35(3) is the sole provision that operates in isolation of anthropocentric values'.[163] It is not a provision that has been adopted to minimise human harm, but to protect the environment in itself. Its object and purpose do not seem to be linked with the principal objective of Protocol I.[164] However, a treaty may have several objects and purposes.[165]

The illogicality of the two articles within the same instrument prohibiting the same type of damage, but responsive to different aims, is explained by the dynamics of the negotiations and drafting of Protocol I.[166] The division of the articles was mainly a result of two camps having conflicting views.

[158] See further discussion, EV Koppe, 'The Principle of Ambiguity and the Prohibition against Excessive Collateral Damage to the Environment During Armed Conflict' in R Rayfuse (ed), *War and the Environment: New Approaches to Protecting the Environment in Relation to Armed Conflict* (Brill Nijhoff, 2014).

[159] ibid, 66.

[160] Sandoz, Swinarski and Zimmerman (n 125) 410–11.

[161] ibid, 411.

[162] ibid.

[163] Schmitt, 'War and the Environment' (n 54) 128.

[164] Koppe, 'The Principle of Ambiguity' (n 158) 66.

[165] Linderfalk (n 91) 111–12.

[166] Schmitt, 'War and the Environment' (n 54) 128.

One camp advocated a provision protecting the environment for its importance for humans, while the other camp wanted protection for the environment as such. As a demand from several delegations during the ICRC Conference (between 1974 and 1977), an informal working group called the Group Biotope was established within Conference Committee III to consider proposals submitted for environmental protection.

Some members of Group Biotope suggested adopting articles that inclined towards treating the environment, from an instrumental perspective, based on its value for humans, which merits protection because of the harm to the population that can be caused by environmental damage. As a result of these efforts, Article 55 was adopted. Some other members of the group urged for the adoption of a standard protecting the environment for its inherent value, unqualified by the human factors. This led to the adoption of Article 35(3).[167]

The inclusion of the two articles in Protocol I can be seen as a compromise of two factions of conflicting views on the environment and the reasons for its protection. As a result, the two articles are not fully and logically compatible, and two conflicting interpretations are possible. One alternative is to see that the environmental damage intended in both articles must include a reference to human health, which would follow the line of the principal object and purpose of Protocol I. The other alternative is that Article 55 of Protocol I adds such reference as an example in conformity with the context of Protocol I, to provide the phrase 'widespread, long-term and severe' damage with a uniform meaning throughout the treaty. In such a case, Article 35(3) is indeed noteworthy since it lacks references to human protection and therefore does not need to balance such values against safeguarding the environment. This means that Article 35(3) must have an object and purpose of its own – to protect the environment per se. Consequently, an act that causes the required degree of 'widespread, long-term and severe damage' is prohibited, even if such action would prevent human suffering or save lives.

To sum up, an interpretation using the object and purpose, as well as the context, as a means of interpretation leaves the meaning of Articles 35(3) and 55(1) of Protocol I with ambiguous results. Due to that fact that different interpretations are possible, Articles 35(3) and 55(1) provide unclear and unsatisfactory protection of the environment. However, because a treaty may have several objects and purposes, I suggest an interpretation that provides Article 55(1) with a two-fold object and purpose – to both protect the environment as well as the population from environmental damage. Such a reading provides 'widespread, long-term and severe damage' with a consistent meaning with regard to both the context as well as with the object and purpose. As discussed above, the added reference to humans should be seen as an example of what 'widespread, long-term and severe damage' can consist of, because both the

[167] Schmitt, 'Green War' (n 21) 70. See also Koppe, *The Use of Nuclear Weapons* (n 55) 121–22.

articles have the object and purpose to protect the environment. Nevertheless, Article 55(1) would emphasise protecting the environment in order to spare the population as well – thereby having two objects and purposes.

vii. No Use of the Drafting and Negotiation History at All?

As stated earlier, Article 32 VCLT invites the interpreter to use the supplementary means in cases when, in accordance with the primary means, an interpretation process, '(a) leaves the meaning ambiguous or obscure; or (b) leads to a result which is manifestly absurd or unreasonable'. The supplementary means may also be used to confirm a meaning established with the primary interpretation means. The interpretation of the terms in Articles 35(3) and 55(1) of Protocol I using the primary means can be clarified to a certain extent, at least in relation to 'widespread' and 'severe'. However, the interpretation using the primary means has not been able to fully clarify the requirements of the threshold. Therefore, the supplementary means can be utilised to provide some further clarity.

Protocol I was negotiated and drafted at the ICRC Conference that took place between 1974 and 1977. The conference's discussion concerning the environment was very much influenced by the environmental damage that was caused in the Vietnam War, when the United States caused extensive environmental damage as a part of its warfare. Thus, it seems like the intention of drafting Articles 35(3) and 55(1) was to prohibit a similar scenario in future wars. From the official records, 'severe' was discussed in relation to the environmental adverse impact on humans. The term 'widespread' was not subject to any lengthy discussions.[168] There were some discussions that the requirement of 'long-term' should be defined as a time period measuring up to several decades. This definition was not however an official position, rather it was a view expressed by some participants at the conference.[169] No additional clarification or description on the other terms was included.[170] Hence, the supplementary means establishes a yardstick for 'long-term' as several decades, while the other terms remain undefined.

As the view of the environment and environmental damage has developed since 1977 when Protocol I was adopted, it is problematic that the view that just a few delegates expressed at the negotiation should be authoritative for determining the meaning of one out of the three requirements of the threshold. This is especially concerning because their views set a very restricted scope of application in terms of the lasting effects of environmental damage. In fact, the time aspect of several decades might not even have been fulfilled in the case of the Vietnam War, the war that initiated the adoption of the articles. Nature has

[168] Sandoz, Swinarski and Zimmerman (n 125).
[169] ibid.
[170] Parson (n 31) 451.

recovered in many areas of Vietnam concerned. However, depending on how environmental damage and its consequences are assessed, the adverse effects on the public health of the Vietnamese population – as a direct result of the wartime environmental damage – remain. These effects have already had negative impacts on the next generation born after the war and may continue to affect future generations.[171]

To conclude, the supplementary means do not add much to the interpretation of the terms in the threshold of Protocol I. The changing view of what constitutes environmental damage and its impacts on human health would be completely neglected if the negotiation history was seen as a decisive act in the interpretation process. Thus, at the time, the most plausible interpretation of the terms in Protocol I are the definitions found in the ENMOD Convention, because it is the only instrument using similar language that can assist as a source of information to determine the ordinary meaning.

C. The Obligation of Care for the Environment

The present subsection focuses on the obligation of care in Article 55(1) of Protocol I. First, it deals with its internal liaison with Article 35(3). Second, it examines the relationship between the obligation of care and the obligation to minimise civilian damage (also referred to as the principle of precaution), as formulated in Article 57(1) of Protocol I. I argue that the duty to care for the environment described in Article 55(1) sets a due diligence standard that applies beyond the means and methods of warfare, in contrast to Article 35(3). It also applies, unlike Article 57(1), when the environment or parts of it constitute a military objective in accordance with Article 52(2) of Protocol I.

i. Two of the Same Kind: The Internal Relation between Articles 35(3) and 55(1)

As Articles 35(3) and 55(1) of Protocol I are both prohibiting 'widespread, long-term and severe' environmental damage, they appear to encompass identical legal obligations. However, although the articles have overlapping scope, they stress different aspects of environmental protection.[172] Taking a closer look at the text in the articles, the first sentence in Article 55(1) contains a duty to take care to protect the environment in warfare. Hulme views the obligation of care as being an underlying concept that acknowledges the particular value of the environment to humankind and recognises that it functions as a reminder that environmental protection has to be ensured during armed conflicts.[173]

[171] Bothe et al (n 2) 576.
[172] Hulme, 'Taking Care to Protect' (n 151) 676.
[173] ibid, 677.

The 'care obligation' encourages a greater protection since it rises above the minimum standard described in the second sentence of Article 55(1), indicating a positive obligation to actively take measures in favour of the environment.[174] As suggested by Hulme, it could require measures to protect the environment from pollution resulting from the use of means and methods of warfare, including attacks on certain facilities and limiting the use of depleted uranium or cluster bombs (which have polluting effects).[175] In addition, Article 55(1) states that the 'protection *includes* a prohibition of the use of methods or means of warfare', which suggests that the obligation of care goes beyond the means and methods of warfare. Such a reading differentiates from Article 35(3), which only applies to damage occurring because of the means and methods of warfare.

Nevertheless, some commentators are of the opinion that both articles require that the environmental damage has to be a result of the means and methods of warfare.[176] Such an understanding would take away some of the significance and the benefit of the inclusion of Article 55(1) of Protocol I. According to Fitzmaurice, provisions in a treaty need to be interpreted to provide them with 'the fullest weight and effect' that is in conformity with a reading of the wording used, together with other parts of the treaty, in a manner that a reason and a meaning can be given to every part of the provision.[177] Such a view is in line with the principle of effectiveness, departing from a systemic interpretation, which builds from the understanding that all provisions in a treaty must have a legal meaning in the treaty system.

Any redundancy must be avoided in an interpretation process, meaning that a treaty should be interpreted in a manner in which no part of it seems superfluous.[178] Therefore, in the case of two plausible interpretations of a treaty text, the option that allows all norms to have a meaning without contradicting each other should prevail. Following this logic, to circumvent any repetition between the provisions within Protocol I, the obligation of care must be given a meaning that goes beyond what is required under Article 35(3). Thus, the obligation of care must contain other obligations that limit the use of the means and methods of warfare. This indicates that other sources causing damage may be covered; for instance, damage deriving from military base camps, moving troops, transport, etc.[179] It could also include, as suggested by Hulme, the restriction of the 'environmentally destructive exploitation of conflict resources, as well as, to address the contribution of warfare to climate change and its potential impacts'.[180]

[174] Schmitt, 'Green War' (n 21) 73.

[175] Hulme, 'Taking Care to Protect' (n 151).

[176] See, for instance, Bannelier-Christakis (n 2) 135.

[177] G Fitzmaurice, 'The Law and Procedure of the International Court of Justice 1951–1954: Treaty Interpretation and Other Treaty Points' (1957) 33 *British Yearbook of International Law* 203, 211. See also Linderfalk (n 91) 110.

[178] Linderfalk (n 91) 109–10.

[179] Hulme makes a similar argument in Hulme, 'Taking Care to Protect' (n 151).

[180] ibid, 690.

According to Hulme, 'the obligation to "take care" requires States to, at least, contemplate what environmental damage might be caused by their military operations and just how serious a level of harm is foreseeable'.[181] This observation is closely related, viewing 'taking care' as applying 'due diligence' to avoid injury.[182] Such an understanding suggests that Article 55 contains elements of positive obligations of prevention.[183] The protection could involve the reduction of collateral environmental effects to avoid the threshold of 'widespread, long-term and severe damage'.[184]

One could argue that commanders are required by the care obligation to take more precautions when dealing with sensitive environmental areas or components, such as areas rich in biodiversity and environments containing endangered species. These areas are likely to be injured more easily and rapidly if exposed to harm. Hulme states that, '[i]n theory therefore, in regard to such fragile or important environmental components, the standard of care (for fulfilment of the care obligation) would require greater cautionary measures'.[185] Such a view must be based on an evolutionary interpretation, defining taking care of the environment to include requirements formulated under international environmental law.

The rules in the law of armed conflict do not distinguish between different environmental components, only between civilian objects and military targets. Nevertheless, under international environmental law, a duty of due diligence has developed. The duty requires a state to undertake active measures 'to control or restrain likely harmful activities that it can reasonably be expected to take' to avoid transboundary harm.[186] In relation to Article 55(1), Hulme argues that the obligation includes a standard of the measures undertaken by a reasonable commander to avoid widespread, long-term and severe environmental damage.[187]

The provision does not specify what the duty of care requires in any practical terms, however. Similarly, the due diligence standard under international environmental law does not further specify its requirements, rather these need to be determined on a case-by-case basis. Thomas argues that:

> If states take this obligation seriously, they will have to undertake some sort of environmental impact assessment when there is a danger of exceeding the threshold, a process likely to have protective value even if the action's consequences are ultimately deemed to lie beneath the threshold.[188]

[181] ibid, 689.
[182] ibid, 679.
[183] HH Almond, 'Weapons, War and the Environment' (1990) 3 *Georgetown International Environmental Law Review* 117, 165.
[184] Hulme, 'Taking Care to Protect' (n 151) 681.
[185] ibid.
[186] U Beyerlin and T Marauhn, *International Environmental Law* (Hart Publishing, 2011) 42.
[187] Hulme, 'Taking Care to Protect' (n 151) 680.
[188] Thomas (n 76) 96.

Hulme suggests that such measures could include avoiding locating military camps in important environmental areas, such as national parks, or attacking facilities containing large concentrations of toxins, both for the purpose of avoiding 'widespread, long-term and severe' damage to the environment. This interpretation of the obligation of care in Article 55(1) is partly informed by international environmental law that requires a higher protection of certain areas and operates from some degree of uncertainty regarding environmental damage.

Hulme divides the 'care obligation' into three types of conduct required for the attacking party. First, to undertake environmental assessments that examine intelligence data and estimate the potential environmental damage of a particular military operation, including a review of the environmental impacts of the proposed weapons, as well as threats to certain kinds of environment. Second, to adjust their military operations to circumvent any potential environmental damage identified. Third, and finally, calling off planned operations because of the potential environmental damage.[189] This could be achieved by using less artillery, by using other types of weapons, by changing tactics, and by altering the military objective of the military operation.[190]

As suggested by Hulme, the defending party would have a corresponding obligation of care. It has to reduce environmental risks, particularly with regard to its 'rare, endangered, biodiverse, and fragile environments'.[191] The obligation could consist of removing military objectives from the surrounding areas of its national parks or other significant environmental areas. It could also include measures to close down certain high risk or vulnerable toxic facilities.[192] These actions could materialise the obligation of 'taking care to protect the environment against damage' in Article 55(1).

Some margin of appreciation is allowed because the standard is not fixed.[193] This flexibility could however impinge on the effectiveness of the article and be interpreted as to lower the standard for environmental protection. At the same time, discretion permits the law-applier to interpret the obligations in the light of the due diligence standard and the principle of prevention, as formulated under international environmental law. An interpretation informed by international environmental law could include more far-reaching measures to prevent environmental damage. During the NATO bombing campaign in Kosovo in 1999, attempts were made by the former Yugoslavia to remove or make safe dangerous substances in order to reduce any potential damage in case of an attack.[194] However, these precautions may not necessarily be acts resulting from

[189] Hulme, 'Taking Care to Protect' (n 151) 681–82.
[190] ibid.
[191] ibid.
[192] ibid.
[193] Sandoz, Swinarski and Zimmerman (n 125) 663.
[194] Hulme, 'Taking Care to Protect' (n 151) 681–82. See also UNEP analysis on Kosovo Conflict, 1999, 5.

the obligations formulated by Article 55(1) of Protocol I, but rather to minimise the damage in general. It still indicates the possibility of taking care of the environment during armed conflicts.

Furthermore, as noted by Hulme, to take care of the environment in Article 55(1) appears to be an obligation of conduct rather than of result.[195] While an obligation of conduct encourages a certain action *towards* a specific objective, an obligation of result has a clear defined objective that should *be achieved*, sometimes within a fixed time limit.[196] In addition, because the obligation to take care only refers to damage intended or expected to cause widespread, long-term, and severe damage, its use is significantly restricted – in particular because the threshold is cumulative. This limits the reach of the obligation of care considerably. For instance, potential environmental damage that is irreversible and fulfilling the requirements of long-term and severe would not require that a party take care, if the damage is not widespread at the same time.[197] To conclude, even though there is a general obligation to take care of the environment, it still only applies in relation to exceptional cases of damage fulfilling the damage threshold.

ii. Relation between the 'Constant Care Obligation' (Civilian Objects) and the 'Care Obligation' (Environment)

There are scholars suggesting that Article 55 only applies to the environment as far as it is a civilian object because the provision is situated in the chapter titled 'Civilian Objects'.[198] Such an interpretation would render Article 55 meaningless because Article 57(1) of Protocol I already entails a duty to take 'constant care' with regard to civilian objects, but without the limiting threshold of 'widespread, long-term and severe' damage. Article 57(1) codifies the general principle of precaution, which requires the belligerents to adopt positive measures to spare civilians and civilian objects.[199] It would cover the same scope (and more) if Article 55 only applied to civilian parts of the environment. Thus, a systemic interpretation of Article 55(1) of Protocol I, in a manner that ensures its legal meaning in relation to the other treaty provisions, would obligate parties to take care to protect the environment, even if it constitutes a military objective.

The 'Civilian Objects' chapter contains provisions providing special protection for certain civilian objects. For instance, Article 53 provides protection 'of cultural objects and of places of worship'; Article 54 protects 'objects indispensable to the survival of the civilian population'; and Article 56 protects

[195] Sandoz, Swinarski and Zimmerman (n 125) 679.
[196] Beyerlin and Marauhn (n 186) 37–38.
[197] ibid, 682.
[198] Verwey (n 53) 13.
[199] Hulme, 'Taking Care to Protect' (n 151) 687.

'works and installations containing dangerous forces'. These objects ought to be immune from attacks. If the objects turn into military objects, the provisions explicitly regulate under which circumstances the special protection would cease. In relation to 'objects indispensable to the survival of the civilian population' and the 'works and installations containing dangerous forces', Articles 54(3) and 56(2) state that these objects lose their immunity if they are used for military purposes and become military targets. Such an exception is not however included in regard to Article 55.

Putting Article 55 in the 'Civilian Objects' chapter does not mean that the environment is not protected if it becomes a military target. Rather, it indicates that it should be viewed as a prima facie civilian object.[200] A similar view was adopted in the Review Committee Report for the ICTY Prosecutor.[201] In addition, in her Second Report to the International Law Commission, Special Rapporteur Jacobsson suggests, in a draft principle, that the environment is civilian in its nature.[202] Furthermore, Article 55 does not only protect the *civilian* population; according to the report of Committee III that reproduces the negotiations of Protocol I, the omission of 'civilian' is intentional. It emphasises the fact that environmental damage may continue for a long time and affect the whole population, with no distinction between civilian populations and combatants.[203]

Nevertheless, there are some overlaps between Articles 55(1) and 57(1) of Protocol I because they are likely to require similar types of measures. The obligations of precaution are developed in the remainder of Article 57, as well as in Article 58 of Protocol I. For instance, Article 57(2)(c) of Protocol I requires advance warning to the opposing party and permits that party to change the location of military objectives to spare civilians or civilian objects. In this sense, Hulme suggests that it can also be employed to spare environmentally sensitive areas or to take some protective measures to move samples of endangered species, just as states can do with cultural property.[204] However, the environment is a part of the surroundings in warfare and as such can never be completely spared from the hostilities.[205] Article 57 of Protocol I is further discussed in relation to the indirect protection of the environment in chapter five.

To sum up, although the duty of care in Article 55(1) is not entirely clear with regard to its content, two conclusions can be established. First, it must go beyond restricting means and methods to not replicate Article 35(3). Second, it applies

[200] ibid, 677–78.
[201] Final Report to the Prosecutor, para 15.
[202] See Second Report on the Protection of the Environment in Relation to Armed Conflicts, UN Doc A/CN.4/685, 28 May 2015, Draft principle 1 in para 151. It states: 'The natural environment is civilian in nature and may not be the object of an attack, unless and until portions of it become a military objective. It shall be respected and protected, consistent with applicable international law and, in particular, international humanitarian law'.
[203] Sandoz, Swinarski and Zimmerman (n 125) 663.
[204] Hulme, 'Taking Care to Protect' (n 151) 687.
[205] ibid.

even if the environment turns into a military objective. Articles 55(1) and 57(1) have overlapping scope, yet they have different legal meanings. Article 57(1) requires parties to take constant care exclusively with regard to civilian objects, which also applies to the environment to the extent that it does not constitute a military objective. Article 55(1) applies, and requires care to be taken, even in cases where the environment has become a military objective.

D. Level of Foreseeability

Article 35(3) of Protocol I poses some additional challenges because it requires that the 'widespread, long-term and severe' environmental damage of an attack must be 'intended, or may be expected'. The inclusion of the word 'expected' is meant to ensure that the provisions cover foreseeable damage as well, even in cases when the damage is not deliberate. The damage must be 'objectively foreseeable' based on the information at the time the attack is launched.[206] The Commentary to Protocol I states that the provision refers both to geophysical weapons, which are exclusively intended to affect the environment or parts of it, and conventional warfare that is unintentionally harming the environment.[207] In relation to Article 55(1), the foreseeability is only relevant to the second sentence regarding means and methods because the obligation of care has wider scope, as discussed in the previous subsection (subsection C).

Koppe states that:

> Requiring that the environmental damage is reasonably foreseeable means that those who deploy these means or methods of warfare must know beforehand to a certain extent that they may have detrimental effects on the environment. This implies that if they cannot reasonably know that they may have adverse environmental impact and such damage is accidental, no violation of either Article can be established.[208]

This 'foreseeability' test may take into account both the actor's and the observer's perception, and thereby broaden the environmental protection.[209] Some scholars argue that it creates an ambiguous standard regarding what a commander 'should have known' and imposing imprecise and unfeasible requirements.[210] However, Schmitt points out that this concern may be an overstatement. He argues that 'lack of actual knowledge is a mitigating factor, not a defence based on the absence of an element of the offense'.[211] In addition, assessing and predicting environmental damage is complex because the numerous interactive and natural

[206] Simonds (n 6) 173; Bruch (n 71) 704.
[207] Sandoz, Swinarski and Zimmerman (n 125) 418.
[208] Koppe, *The Use of Nuclear Weapons* (n 55) 126.
[209] Orellana (n 64) 682.
[210] A Roberts, 'Environmental Destruction in the 1991 Gulf War' (1992) 32 *International Review of the Red Cross* 538.
[211] Schmitt, 'Green War' (n 21) 72.

processes are not fully comprehensible. This means that adverse environmental impacts may not be recognisable at the time of launching an attack. As raised by Verwey: 'Only quite recently, science has become able to demonstrate that even apparently restricted, relatively short-term and seemingly insignificant forms of environmental impact may subsequently turn out to have triggered serious or significant ecological disruption'.[212] Thus, environmental damage may not be visible or objectively verifiable as perceptible harm.

When Protocol I was adopted, France and the United Kingdom stated that the risk of environmental damage that reaches the threshold of 'widespread, long-term and severe' has to be assessed objectively based on the information at the time.[213] The declaratory statements may have been intended by these states to avoid the situation that the lack of scientific knowledge about the environment, which was not accessible at the time for the attack, should not be a burden to the commanders. Thus, there seems to be an intention of the state parties to circumvent the situation that unknown environmental impacts are included with regard to what a commander should have known at the time of an attack.

As opposed to international environmental law, the law of armed conflict operates based on what is known at the time of the decision to launch an attack. Articles 35(3) and 55(1) suggest that the same standard of what a reasonable commander should have known applies, even though the articles concern environmental damage. As pointed out by Koppe, the articles do embody a 'precautionary element' by including the phrase 'may be expected', but do not include obligations that are as far-reaching as the requirements under the precautionary approach in international environmental law.[214] Thus, the foreseeability of expected damage in Articles 35(3) and 55(1) of Protocol I appears to cover only the damage that can be estimated based on the information known at the time of the attack, and it does not require a state to take into account scientific uncertainty with regard to environmental damage.

VI. CONCLUSIONS

The special environmental protection provided under the ENMOD Convention, as well as in Articles 35(3) and 55 of Protocol I, is of limited use. As I have disclosed in this chapter, it has two constraints in particular. First, the rules have a narrow scope of application because they set a high threshold that excludes most environmental damage resulting from conventional warfare. Second, the threshold sets unclear requirements, which creates uncertainty with regard to what type of damage they address.

[212] Verwey (n 53) 12.
[213] Henckaerts and Doswald-Beck (n 129) 152.
[214] Koppe, *The Use of Nuclear Weapons* (n 55) 126.

The ambiguous language in the rules of the law of armed conflict can be used in a manner that excuses grave wartime environmental damage.[215] In addition – and a key issue – there has not been any political will from states to revise the high threshold in Protocol I or the ENMOD Convention.[216] The unwillingness of states to limit the level of environmental damage can partly be explained by the abstractness of the notion of the environment and the uncertainty on how its regulation may constrain their warfare.[217]

Concerning the first constraint, both the ENMOD Convention and Protocol I have a restricted scope. The ENMOD Convention only regulates environmental modification techniques and the provisions in Protocol I are not likely to apply to any type of conventional warfare because it rarely creates such extensive damage as required by the threshold of 'widespread, long-term and severe'. Thus, the rules on direct environmental protection only apply in extreme cases of environmental damage. According to Schmitt, the articles 'must be applied in an extraordinary circumscribed manner'.[218] The analysis in the literature is consistent on this point.

The second constraint regards the vagueness in the protection. Fleck describes the environmental protection 'as far-reaching absence of specific rules' that results in constant challenges to apply them in situations they were not intended for.[219] In relation to the vague content, Schmitt argues that the law of armed conflict does not provide satisfactory notice of what level of environmental destruction is prohibited.[220] He formulates it as follows, '[t]he textual law reveals in insufficient environmental specificity, an indispensable requirement for predictability'.[221] There is no consensus among scholars on what the special environmental rules in the law of armed conflict prohibit.

Even if the rules in Protocol I interpreted in an evolutionary manner, can – to some extent – lower the damage threshold, the content of the provisions remains unclear, mainly because the requirements in the threshold are cumulative.[222] The articles may have been intentionally drafted with an ambiguous and vague wording, meaning that the intended communicative meaning of the provisions cannot be fully established through the means of interpretation. Conclusively, the content of the articles is unclear, contradictory and unable to set a standard, but such a standard would be higher than the 'normal' collateral damage resulting from conventional warfare. Thus, the result is similar to an interpretation based solely on the preparatory work, but with the difference that the statements made during the negotiations can be largely dismissed.

[215] Yuzon (n 156) 825.
[216] Thomas (n 76) 85. See also Falk (n 19).
[217] Almond (n 183) 130.
[218] Schmitt, 'War and the Environment' (n 54) 109.
[219] Fleck (n 2) 7.
[220] Schmitt, 'War and the Environment' (n 54) 113.
[221] ibid.
[222] Desgagné (n 98) 113.

As the vague content in the provisions renders them unsettled, it allows the possibility to interpret them in the light of other areas of international law. For instance, the rules in international environmental law can inform the application of the special environmental protection under the law of armed conflict. This is similar to how international human rights law can be used to complement unclear requirements or provisions under the law of armed conflict.[223] For instance, just as human rights law has been applied to determine the content/ meaning of a fair trial as provided in Common Article 3 of the Geneva Conventions, international environmental law can inform the requirements of determining the level of environmental damage required for the application of Articles 35(3) and 55(1) of Protocol I. Such an approach can contribute to harmonise the law of armed conflict with the international environmental legal field.

As the development is moving towards applying other fields of law concurrently with the law of armed conflict in times of armed conflict, this view would sit well with contemporary international legal scholarship. The intended ambiguous meaning of Articles 35(3) and 55(1) may be given clarity by using international environmental law. The threshold of environmental damage could be informed by looking at how different parts of the environment are affected by warfare. This may be a way to incorporate the complexity of nature and provide it with long-term protection. As suggested by Hulme, the positive measures that may be required under the obligation to take care of the environment in Article 55(1) could be established by looking at the legal requirement of the principle of prevention or due diligence within international environmental law.

When the possibilities to interpret the treaty provisions are exhausted, the meaning of the provisions is left to the law-applier to decide. In this case, it will rely on the military commanders and decision-makers to apply Articles 35(3) and 55(1) of Protocol I. In practice, military commanders are inclined to have a tendency to prioritise military concerns at the cost of environmental protection. Nevertheless, the ambiguous and unclear content does not include a complete discretion for the law-appliers to apply the provisions in accordance with his or her preferences.

To conclude, the main problem with the excessively restraining and vague definition of the level of impermissible environmental damage during wartime is the potential use of it to justify, rather than restrict, environmental destruction when harm is unmistakably below the threshold. Nevertheless, the ENMOD Convention and Articles 35(3) and 55 remain the most explicit and articulated treaty provisions regulating environmental warfare and damage during armed conflicts.[224] The direct protection represents an important development

[223] Human rights do however remain specifically applicable under certain conditions during armed conflicts, directly based on Protocol I. See Article 72 of Protocol I and the Preamble to Protocol II.
[224] Thomas (n 76) 91.

that acknowledges the unique character of the environment and its need to be protected in times of armed conflict. Thus, the provisions strengthen the idea that environmental protection is a consideration to be taken into account when applying the rules of the law of armed conflict.[225] However, customary environmental law seems to be of limited assistance in the interpretation process. For this reason, environmental treaties may offer further clarification because they are more specific.

[225] Desgagné (n 98) 113.

4

Special Environmental Protection under Customary International Law

I. INTRODUCTION

THIS CHAPTER EXAMINES the content and status of customary international law that provides direct environmental protection during armed conflicts. The examination serves three purposes. First, all states are not parties to the ENMOD Convention and/or Protocol I. Currently, Protocol I has 174 state parties, while the ENMOD Convention has 76 state parties.[1] In addition, several militarily powerful states have not ratified Protocol I.[2] While treaty law is binding for the state parties that have ratified or accessed a specific treaty, customary international law applies to all states (with the exception of persistent objectors). However, if the rules on direct environmental protection in the ENMOD Convention and/or Protocol I can be regarded as having customary law status, all states would be bound to follow them.

Second, since the treaty-based special environmental protection was adopted, the International Committee of the Red Cross (ICRC) has published the 2005 Customary Law Study containing three rules on special environmental protection, and the International Law Commission has provisionally adopted 28 draft principles on the topic 'Protection of the Environment in Relation to Armed Conflict', of which at least eight draft principles specifically apply during armed conflicts. These two studies of the law serve as indicators on the status of the law on environmental protection in relation to armed conflict. I will examine whether the studies have considered new developments in the law that provide more progressive environmental protection compared with the protection in Protocol I and the ENMOD Convention.

Third, customary law is relevant to establish special environmental protection in non-international armed conflicts, given that no treaty provides rules on direct environmental protection during these types of armed conflict.

[1] See International Committee of the Red Cross web page for state parties. For Protocol I see: www.icrc.org/applic/ihl/ihl.nsf/States.xsp?xp_viewStates=XPages_NORMStatesParties&xp_treatySelected=470. For ENMOD Convention see: www.icrc.org/applic/ihl/ihl.nsf/ States.xsp?xp_viewStates=XPages_NORMStatesParties&xp_treatySelected=460.

[2] eg, the United States, Israel, Pakistan, India, Iran and Turkey.

For instance, Protocol II has no corresponding environmental provisions to those included in Protocol I. The ENMOD Convention contains a transnational element requiring damage to another state party, which makes it mainly relevant in international armed conflicts. Therefore, it is essential to establish whether direct environmental protection is reflected in customary law and applicable in non-international armed conflicts. In addition, although treaty-making is an important tool to develop international law to respond to new problems, such as environmental concerns, the development of customary law is of equal importance to respond to such problems.

I divide the examination into two parts. First, I analyse customary international law with regard to international armed conflicts. Second, I investigate the application of these rules to non-international armed conflicts.

II. ICRC CUSTOMARY LAW STUDY AND THE DRAFT PRINCIPLES OF THE INTERNATIONAL LAW COMMISSION

In this section, I use the ICRC 2005 Customary Law Study as a point of reference to assess the development of customary rules relating to direct environmental protection during armed conflicts. I also look at the International Law Commission's draft principles on 'Protection of the Environment in Relation to Armed Conflict'.

Rules 43–45 in the 2005 Customary Law Study protect the environment during armed conflicts. Rules 44 and 45 are partly revised versions of Articles 35(3) and 55(1) of Protocol I and the ENMOD Convention. Draft Principles 13(2) and 16 provisionally adopted by the International Law Commission at first reading also reflect these rules.[3] Rule 43 and the last two sentences of Rule 44 as well as Draft Principles 13(2), 14 and 15 reflect the general rules of protection under the law of armed conflict. These include the principle of distinction, the rule on military necessity, the principle of proportionality, and the principle of precaution. Even though the rules in the 2005 Customary Law Study as well as the draft principles explicitly refer to the environment, they are based on the general rules providing indirect environmental protection. Therefore, these aspects of the rules are discussed in chapter five. However, to draw a strict dividing line between the special and general environmental protection with regard to these rules and draft principles is difficult because they mix both sets of rules. Thus, some of the aspects are discussed in this chapter as well as the next (chapter five).

When Articles 35(3) and 55 of Protocol I were adopted in 1977, they were considered to be a progressive development of the law.[4] For instance,

[3] International Law Commission, 'Protection of the Environment. Text and Titles of the Draft Principles Provisionally Adopted by the Drafting Committee on First Reading' (Protection of the Environment, First Reading) UN Doc A/CN.4/L.937 (2019).

[4] S Simonds, 'Conventional Warfare and Environmental Protection; A Proposal for International Legal Reform' (1992) 29 *Stanford Journal of International Law* 165, 177.

the United States was and continues to be a persistent objector to the rules.[5] The main concern for the United States is that the articles are too broadly formulated.[6] Nevertheless, the United States stated in relation to the 1991 Gulf War that its practice did not apply any means or methods of warfare causing 'widespread, long-term and severe' environmental damage. In addition, the United States, as reported, abstained from certain attacks because of environmental concerns during the 1991 Gulf War.[7]

Even though the environmental provisions represented a progressive legal development in 1977, much has changed since then – in particular, regarding regulation of environmental matters. However, in 1991, faced with the aftermath of the 1991 Gulf War, the customary status of Articles 35(3) and 55 of Protocol I remained uncertain. Some states including Germany and Iran – according to the Commentary to the ICRC's study – declared that the damage caused by Iraq indeed violated Articles 35(3) and 55 of Protocol I.[8] At the same time, the UN Security Council did not address the liability of Iraq based on violating the rules in the law of armed conflict, but on those in the UN Charter.[9] As Iraq was not a party to Protocol I, it may have been considered controversial to directly declare its actions as being breaches against customary law as reflected in Articles 35(3) and 55(1) of Protocol I. In addition, there was disagreement among states and scholars as to whether the oil spill caused by Iraq reached the threshold in the articles. Nevertheless, given that several states expressed criticism for the large-scale damage to the environment and condemned it as an act of 'ecocide', it may indicate the existence of a customary law obligation of taking general care of the environment during armed conflicts.

Between 1991 and 2005, the attitude towards the articles seems to have changed among states, perhaps triggered by the events during the Gulf War and the following debates on wartime environmental protection. The change is noted in the 2005 Customary Law Study. The Study is an important and influential document because of the prominent role of the ICRC in relation to the law of armed conflict and the thorough work behind the Study.[10] Taking a decade to

[5] RJ Parson, 'Fight to Save the Planet: US Armed Forces, Greenkeeping, and Enforcement of the Law Pertaining to Environmental Protection During Armed Conflict' (1997) 10 *Georgetown International Environmental Law Review* 441, 452.

[6] C Thomas, 'Advancing the Legal Protection of the Environment in Relation to Armed Conflict: Protocol I's Threshold of Impermissible Environmental Damage and Alternatives' (2013) 82 *Nordic Journal of International Law* 83, 89.

[7] J-M Henckaerts and L Doswald-Beck (eds), *Customary International Humanitarian Law Study*, Volume I Rules (Cambridge University Press, 2005) 148.

[8] ibid, 153.

[9] JE Austin and CE Bruch, 'Existing and Emerging Wartime Standards, Introduction' in JE Austin and CE Bruch (eds), *The Environmental Consequences of War* (Cambridge University Press, 2000) 40.

[10] I Scobbie, 'The Approach to Customary International Law in the Study' in E Wilmshurst and S Breau (eds), *Perspectives on the ICRC Study on Customary International Humanitarian Law* (Cambridge University Press, 2007) 17.

complete, it consists of three volumes that contain 161 rules with commentaries and supporting materials counting over 5,000 pages.[11] Many scholars would probably agree that the 2005 Customary Law Study is 'a quasi-official codificatory text in a broad sense, inasmuch as it is an attempt to discern "unwritten rules" and reduce them to an authoritative written form'.[12] Bothe regards the Study to be 'based on a realistic, well considered, cautious yet not unnecessarily timid methodological approach to the proof of customary law'.[13]

The 2005 Customary Law Study has, however, been criticised on a number of points, including its methodology. Notably, the criticism has been directed at the Study's progressive approach which cannot be perceived as a pure codification of existing customary law. It is rather to be regarded as a statement on what the law ought to be. Marsh states that the Study 'represents the ICRC's idealistic notion of what States should consider customary international humanitarian law'.[14] The state practice and *opinio juris* supporting the rules in the Study are, in parts, not fully evaluated to demonstrate the existence of a certain customary rule.[15] In particular, Rules 43–45, related to direct environmental protection, have been the subject of criticism because they may go beyond *lex lata*.[16] Nevertheless, the 2005 Customary Law Study is a considerable contribution to the development of the law of armed conflict, although the Study must be assessed with some caution regarding the rules' legal status. It cannot be considered as having the same authority as treaty law.[17] It is merely a starting point of reviewing state practice and *opinio juris*, rather than a photograph of the reality, as it is claimed to be in the Study.[18] To the extent that the Study and the work of the International Law Commission overlap, it can be seen as representing customary international law.[19]

[11] D Bethlehem, 'The Methodological Framework of the Study' in E Wilmshurst and S Breau (eds), *Perspectives on the ICRC Study on Customary International Humanitarian Law* (Cambridge University Press, 2007) 3.

[12] Scobbie (n 10) 17.

[13] M Bothe, 'Customary International Humanitarian Law: Some Reflections on the ICRC Study' (2005) 8 *Yearbook of International Humanitarian Law* 143, 163.

[14] Marsh criticises Rule 45 in the Study for being a *lex ferenda* rule. See J Marsh, 'Lex Lata or Lex Ferenda? Rule 45 of the ICRC Study on Customary International Humanitarian Law' (2008) 198 *Military Law Review* 116, 117–18.

[15] Scobbie (n 10) 17; S Freeland, *Addressing the Intentional Destruction of the Environment During Warfare Under the Rome Statute of the International Criminal Court* (Intersentia, 2015); Bethlehem (n 11) 9–11.

[16] Freeland (n 15) 175; K Hulme, 'Taking Care to Protect the Environment Against Damage: A Meaningless Obligation?' (2010) 92 *International Review of the Red Cross* 675, 676; Bothe (n 13); Parson (n 5). Also, for a further discussion on the concept of *lex ferenda*, see H Thirlway, 'Reflections on *lex ferenda*' (2001) 32 *Netherlands Yearbook of International Law* 3.

[17] Bethlehem (n 11) 13–14.

[18] In the 'Foreword', Sandoz claims that, '[t]he study is still a photograph of reality, taken with great concern for absolute honesty, that is, without trying to make the law say what one wishes it would say'. Henckaerts and Doswald-Beck, *Customary International Humanitarian Law Study*, Volume I: Rules (n 7) xiv.

[19] In regard to the study, a cautious approach was adopted by the first Special Rapporteur on Protection of the Environment in Relation to Armed Conflict with regard to her work for the

Since 2011, the International Law Commission has dealt with the topic of 'Protection of the Environment in Relation to Armed Conflict'.[20] The 28 provisionally adopted draft principles codify and develop the law in this field. The Commission has, as suggested by the first Special Rapporteur Jacobsson, adopted a temporal approach addressing the topic from the various phases of an armed conflict – before, during and after. The following subsections will mainly focus on the draft principles applicable during and – to some extent – also after armed conflict (post-conflict). As the work of the International Law Commission is still in progress, the study will only cover the work of the Commission up until 2019, when the last set of draft principles were provisionally adopted at the first reading of the topic in 2019.

A. Prohibition of 'Widespread, Long-term and Severe Damage'

The first sentence of Rule 45 of the Study states: 'The use of methods or means of warfare that are intended, or may be expected, to cause widespread, long-term and severe damage to the natural environment is prohibited'. The sentence reproduces Articles 35(3) and 55(1) of Protocol I and it recognises the same high threshold by requiring 'widespread, long-term and severe damage'. It sets an absolute prohibition, just like Articles 35(3) and 55(1) – if the threshold is reached, exceptions cannot be justified based on military necessity.[21] The International Law Commission adopted provisionally Draft Principle 13(2) also restating the first sentence of Article 55(1). It reads: 'Care shall be taken to protect the natural environment against widespread, long-term and severe damage'. The formulation used by the International Law Commission does not specifically refer to means and methods. Instead, the term 'care shall be taken' should be interpreted as a general duty for parties to an armed conflict to be attentive of how military activities can impact the environment.[22] Neither Rule 45 nor Draft Principle 13(2) have incorporated the reference to the population as stated in Article 55(1).

The Commentary to the 2005 Customary Law Study explicitly refers to both articles in Protocol I. The ICRC states in its Commentary to the Study that:

> Practice, as far as methods of warfare and use of conventional weapons are concerned, shows a widespread, representative and virtually uniform acceptance of

International Law Commission. Special Rapporteur M Jacobsson, Second Report on the Protection of the Environment in Relation to Armed Conflicts, UN Doc A/CN.4/685, 28 May 2015, para 7.

[20] In 2013, the topic was included in its programme of work.

[21] Henckaerts and Doswald-Beck, *Customary International Humanitarian Law*, Volume I: Rules (n 7) 157.

[22] Report of the International Law Commission on the Work of its 68th Session (2016) Chapter X 'Protection of the environment in relation to armed conflicts' Commentaries to the draft principles provisionally adopted by the Commission, 329, para 6.

the customary nature of the rule found in article 35(3) and 55(1) of the Additional Protocol I.[23]

To support the rule, the Study refers to: military manuals of both state parties and non-state parties to Protocol I; state submissions to the International Court of Justice regarding the Advisory Opinion on the *Legality of Use of Nuclear Weapons* (*Nuclear Weapons* Advisory Opinion); policy statements of Israel and the United States (both are non-state parties to Protocol I); the condemnation of the environmental destruction during the 1991 Gulf War; the ICRC Guidelines on the Protection of the Environment in Times of Armed Conflict; the environmental war crime included in the 1998 Rome Statute; and the offence of ecocide in the national legislation of state parties and non-state parties to Protocol I.

In total, according to the Commentary of the Study, the study mentions 18 military manuals that represent evidence of state practice and *opinio juris* supporting the customary status of the rule. The manuals are from Argentina, Australia, Belgium, Benin, Canada, Colombia, France, Germany, Italy, Kenya, Netherlands, New Zealand, Russia, Spain, Sweden, Switzerland, Togo and Yugoslavia.[24] As noted by Hulme, of the quoted military manuals only Kenya is not a state party to Protocol I. Training manuals of the United Kingdom and United States are also referred to in the Commentary to the Study, although these are not binding documents.[25] In addition, Koppe notes that the number of manuals that the ICRC has referred to is too limited to confirm a general state practice that supports the view that Articles 35(3) and 55(1) of Protocol I represent customary law.[26] In addition, the United States has expressly stated that it does not recognise Articles 35(3) and 55(1) of Protocol I as customary law.[27] In relation to this, the ICRC stated that it is not sufficient that a state that is not considered 'specially affected' can block the development of customary law. Furthermore, the 2005 Customary Law Study refers to the numerous state submissions to the International Court of Justice in relation to the 1996 *Nuclear Weapons* Advisory Opinion that suggest that Articles 35(3) and 55 represented customary law.[28]

[23] Henckaerts and Doswald-Beck, *Customary International Humanitarian Law*, Volume I: Rules (n 7) 154.

[24] See ibid, 152, fn 52.

[25] K Hulme, 'Natural Environment' in E Wilmshurst and S Breau (eds), *Perspectives on the ICRC Study on Customary International Humanitarian Law* (Cambridge University Press, 2007) 230.

[26] EV Koppe, *The Use of Nuclear Weapons and the Protection of the Environment During International Armed Conflict* (Gildeprint, 2006) 183.

[27] Written statement submitted by the United States to the International Court of Justice in the *Nuclear Weapons* Advisory Opinion. Letter dated 20 June 1995 from the Acting Legal Adviser to the Department of State, together with Written Statement of the Government of the United States of America, available at: www.icj-cij.org/docket/files/95/8700.pdf.

[28] The ICRC refers to the oral pleading and written statements in the *Nuclear Weapons* Advisory Opinion of Australia, Ecuador, New Zealand, Sweden and Zimbabwe, and the written statements of Rwanda and Ukraine in the *Nuclear Weapons* Advisory Opinion (WHO). See Henckaerts and Doswald-Beck, *Customary International Humanitarian Law*, Volume I: Rules (n 7) 152, fn 56.

The ICRC also draws attention to the Review Committee Report to the Prosecutor of the ICTY that investigated the 1999 NATO bombing campaign, in which the articles were regarded as emerging customary law. In its report, the Review Committee for the ICTY Prosecutor stated that: 'Article 55 may, nevertheless, reflect current customary law'.[29] Also, the ICRC points out that a Report on the Practice of Israel, which is not party to Protocol I, affirms that the Israeli defence forces do not use or tolerate the use of methods or means of warfare which are intended, or may be expected, to cause 'widespread, long-term and severe' damage to the environment.[30]

The International Union for Conservation of Nature and Natural Resources (IUCN) Draft International Covenant on Environment and Development has included a provision that prohibits the employment or threat to employ 'methods or means of warfare which are intended or may be expected to cause widespread, long-term, or severe harm to the environment'.[31] According to the IUCN Commentary, the provision reflects the 'threshold of permissible harm that departs from existing precedents'.[32] The Draft International Covenant on Environment and Development is the outcome of an ongoing collaboration among eminent environmental lawyers, practitioners and diplomats and it aims to provide a blueprint for an international framework agreement consolidating and developing existing legal principles related to environment and development.[33]

In addition, the 1998 Rome Statute, although being an instrument of international criminal law, defines an environmental war crime as prohibiting wilfully launching an attack that will cause 'widespread, long-term and severe' environmental damage that is not in proportion to the military advantage anticipated.[34] The crime does not fully correspond to the articles in Protocol I because it introduces a proportionality assessment as an additional restriction with regard to how the environmental damage relates to the military advantage. Nevertheless, as noted by several scholars, the inclusion of the environmental war crime in the 1998 Rome Statute is not a consequence of binding treaty law obligations,

[29] Final Report to the Prosecutor by the Committee Established to Review the NATO Bombing Campaign Against the Federal Republic of Yugoslavia, 13 June 2000 on ICTY's web page, para 15. See: www.icty.org/sid/10052.

[30] Henckaerts and Doswald-Beck, *Customary International Humanitarian Law*, Volume I: Rules (n 7) 152–53.

[31] Article 40(1)(c) of the IUCN Draft International Covenant on Environment and Development (IUCN Draft Covenant), IUCN, 'Draft International Covenant on Environment and Development – Implementing Sustainability', 5th edn, IUCN Environmental Policy and Law Paper No 31 Rev 4 (IUCN, Gland).

[32] ibid, 121.

[33] ibid.

[34] Article 8(2)(b)(iv) of the 1998 Rome Statute states: 'Intentionally launching an attack in the knowledge that such attack will cause incidental loss of life or injury to civilians or damage to civilian objects or widespread long-term and severe damage to the natural environment which would be clearly excessive in relation to the concrete and direct overall military advantage anticipated'.

but the result of a customary rule applicable to individuals to not cause such damage to the environment in wartime.[35]

The environmental war crime as incorporated in the 1998 Rome Statute has its roots in an underlying customary rule. Although, as pointed out by Bothe, the restrictive formulation of the crime – as well as referring to states' national criminal codes that incorporate the environmental crime in the Commentary to the Study – does not provide any evidence that the customary rule underlying the war crime is as equally restricted in regard to the added proportionality requirement. As explained by Bothe, a rule of criminal law is a secondary rule and it is not required that it has the same scope as the underlying prohibition being the primary rule, which, in this case, was established under the law of armed conflict. Thus, the secondary rule can have a more narrow scope than the primary rule, but not a broader.[36] Consequently, the incorporation of the environmental war crime in the 1998 Rome Statute, as well in several states' national legislation, could indicate that states have a similar customary law obligation to not harm the environment during armed conflicts, but that obligation could be wider than the restricted version of the environmental war crime.

The United States, the United Kingdom and France are persistent objectors with regard to a customary rule corresponding to the environmental rules in Protocol I applying to nuclear weapons. In fact, most NATO Member States have stated that Protocol I is not applicable to nuclear weapons.[37] According to the Commentary to the Study – as opposed to the case with the United States as a persistent objector to the rule in general – these three states are considered to be 'specially affected' because they possess nuclear weapons. Consequently, the Commentary states that these states are able to block the development of the environmental rule applying to nuclear weapons as customary law and they are not bound by such a rule in relation to its application to nuclear weapons.[38] The Commentary is confusing at this point, but its position is that states having expressly rejected the application of the environmental rules in Protocol I to nuclear weapons are not bound by a corresponding customary rule, but that rule applies as customary law to other states. Thus, the specially affected objecting states have not been able to prevent the development of a customary law applicable to nuclear weapons in general, contrary to the conclusion of the International Court of Justice in the *Nuclear Weapons* Advisory Opinion.[39] Freeland points out that the qualifications related to the persistent objector claims of the United States to the rule in general, and by the United States, France and the United Kingdom to the application of the rule in relation to

[35] Hulme, 'Natural Environment' (n 25) 206. See also Freeland (n 15).

[36] Bothe (n 13) 168.

[37] Henckaerts and Doswald-Beck, *Customary International Humanitarian Law,* Volume I: Rules (n 7) 151.

[38] ibid, 154–55.

[39] Compare *Legality of the Threat or Use of Nuclear Weapons*, Advisory Opinion of 8 July 1996, ICJ Reports 1996, para 73.

nuclear weapons, raise some doubts as to whether there is adequate state practice to establish a customary rule. He states that this is especially dubious when relating to the use of nuclear weapons because the objectors are all powerful nuclear powers.[40]

Several scholars tend to treat the environmentally specific provisions of Protocol I as having customary law status and agree with many of the conclusions of the 2005 Customary Law Study with regard to the first sentence in Rule 45.[41] Yet, some commentators remain sceptical about the customary status of Rule 45. For instance, Hulme states that it cannot be established that states 'generally' consider Articles 35(3) and 55(1) of Protocol I as customary law.[42] Schmitt highlights the fact that many militarily powerful states have not ratified Protocol I precisely because the specific environmental provisions are not part of customary law.[43] Koppe notes that because of the limited number of states that clearly support a customary rule based on Articles 35(3) and 55(1), in combination with the militarily powerful states that are expressly against such a rule, it cannot be justified to conclude that such a customary rule exists.[44] Bothe, on the other hand, is of the opinion that the rule is not going far enough with regard to environmental protection. This is because of the criticisms of the restrictive interpretation of the requirements in the threshold of the articles in Protocol I and because of the increased attention for environmental protection in recent conflicts; therefore he argues that customary law might have developed to go beyond the treaty-based law.[45]

The majority of state parties have ratified Protocol I without making any significant reservations to the environmental provisions.[46] Articles 35(3) and 55 of Protocol I appear to be respected. There have not been any violations of them, but the high and imprecise threshold for application may explain this.[47] Thus, it is unclear what the customary status of Articles 35(3) and 55(1) of Protocol I is. The state practice quoted in the 2005 Customary Law Study is not extensive and many commentators are doubtful about the rule as stated in the Study. Consequently, Rule 45 may not reflect customary international law, although, this view may have altered since the adoption of Protocol I and since the 2005 Customary Law Study was published.

[40] Freeland (n 15) 168–69.

[41] First sentence reads: 'The use of methods or means of warfare that are intended, or may be expected, to cause widespread, long-term and severe damage to the natural environment is prohibited'. For scholars confirming this, see Parson (n 5) 452.

[42] Hulme, 'Natural Environment' (n 25) 232.

[43] M Schmitt, 'War and the Environment: Fault Lines in the Prescriptive Landscape' in JE Austin and CE Bruch (eds), *The Environmental Consequences of War* (Cambridge University Press, 2000) 93.

[44] Koppe (n 26) 189.

[45] Bothe (n 13) 168.

[46] See Henckaerts and Doswald-Beck, *Customary International Humanitarian Law*, Volume I: Rules (n 7) 154.

[47] Hulme, 'Natural Environment' (n 25) 232.

To conclude, Rule 45 may not be considered an exact reflection of customary law. Nevertheless, a rule establishing that it is prohibited to cause 'widespread, long-term and severe' damage during international armed conflicts appears to exist as a threshold of the maximum of permissible environmental damage in wartime. Such understanding is supported by the adopted Draft Principle 13(2) provisionally adopted by the International Law Commission and the IUCN Draft Covenant. Nevertheless, the precise scope of the rule remains unclear, in particular in regard to the cumulative criteria of widespread, long-term and severe, which despite its vague content, has firm support from the ICRC, the International Law Commission, scholars and states.

B. Environment as a Weapon

The second part of Rule 45 in the 2005 Customary Law Study reads, 'Destruction of the natural environment may not be used as a weapon'. It is not the modification of environmental forces that is prohibited as a means of warfare in Rule 45, but the destruction of the environment as such for hostile purposes. Unfortunately, the Study is not specific on what the prohibition actually covers, but it appears to extend beyond the prohibition of environmental modification techniques as established under the ENMOD Convention. The International Law Commission has provisionally adopted Draft Principle 19, which replicates to a large extent the prohibition in Article 1(1) of the ENMOD Convention.[48] It also reflects the prohibition in the 1996 ICRC Guidelines.[49] Thus, the draft principle refers only to environmental modification techniques for hostile use and does not, like Rule 45, go beyond that scope.

The use of the environment as a weapon was highlighted after the Iraqi oil burning and deliberate destruction of the environment. According to the Commentary to the Study, state practice supports the prohibition of deliberate attacks on the environment as a weapon.[50] As the ENMOD Convention was intended to address environmental modification techniques, it does not deal with the 'use of destruction of the natural environment as weapon' or any other types of acts labelled as 'environmental terrorism'. The reference to using the environment and its resources 'as a weapon of terrorism' was used by Kuwait to describe the acts undertaken by Iraq during the 1991 Gulf War in a letter to the UN Secretary-General, which the Commentary refers to.[51]

[48] International Law Commission, Protection of the Environment, First Reading (n 3).

[49] See Guideline 12 in Report of the Secretary General, UN Doc A/49/323, 19 August 1994; see Annex for the Guidelines for Military Manuals and Instructions on the Protection of the Environment in Times of Armed Conflict.

[50] Henckaerts and Doswald-Beck, *Customary International Humanitarian Law*, Volume I: Rules (n 7) 155–56.

[51] ibid, 156. See also Kuwait's 1991 Letter to the UN Secretary-General.

Furthermore, the ICRC states in the Commentary, 'that it is unclear whether the provisions of ENMOD [Convention] have developed into customary rules of international law'.[52] Other commentators have noted the same conclusion – there is not sufficient state practice or *opinio juris* supporting the prohibition to employ environmental modification techniques.[53] There are however only a small number of states that would have the ability and/or the wish to develop such techniques to modify environmental forces. Therefore, the vast majority of states would have little interest in the provisions in the ENMOD Convention. However, it must be in the interests of all states to prevent other states from manipulating environmental forces for hostile purposes and upsetting the ecological balance, weather patterns, etc.

Nevertheless, the prohibition on destroying the environment as a weapon could be a customary rule, irrespective of the customary status of the rules in the ENMOD Convention and Protocol I.[54] The Commentary to the Study states that, 'significant practice exists prohibiting a deliberate attack on the environment as a method of warfare'.[55] The Commentary refers to the strong reactions of states condemning the environmental destruction during the Gulf War – these reactions may signify a customary rule against the wilful destruction of the environment as a part of warfare.[56] In some cases, such acts would, however, be prohibited by the principle of distinction and the prohibition of wanton damage to the extent that they are directed against civilian objects.[57] The IUCN Draft also includes a prohibition on using 'the destruction or modification of the environment as a means of warfare or any other hostile activity'.[58] Moreover, the ICRC Commentary refers to the legislation of several states that criminalises 'ecocide' as a state practice.[59] Thus, there seems to be some support to conclude

[52] Henckaerts and Doswald-Beck, *Customary International Humanitarian Law,* Volume I: Rules (n 7) 151.

[53] Koppe (n 26) 177.

[54] Henckaerts and Doswald-Beck, *Customary International Humanitarian Law*, Volume I: Rules (n 7) 155–56.

[55] ibid, 155.

[56] Iraq and Kuwait stated in separate letters to the Secretary-General that natural resources should not be used as a weapon as they were by Iraq and Kuwait. A declaration was adopted in 1991 by the Ministers of the Environment of the Organisation for Economic Co-operation and Development that condemned Iraq's burning of oil fields and discharging of oil into the Gulf as a violation of international law and urged Iraq to cease resorting to environmental destruction as a weapon. In addition, in the Sixth Committee, statements were made by Sweden and Canada that the environment should not be used as a weapon or be the object for direct attacks during warfare. See Henckaerts and Doswald-Beck, *Customary International Humanitarian Law*, Volume I: Rules (n 7) 156.

[57] Hulme, 'Natural Environment' (n 25) 234.

[58] Article 40(1)(d) of the IUCN Draft Covenant (n 31).

[59] The Study lists the legislation of Armenia, Belarus, Kazakhstan, Kyrgyzstan, Moldova, Russia, Tajikistan, Ukraine and Vietnam. A definition of the notion of 'ecocide', as formulated in the penal codes of the countries of the former Soviet Union, is included in a footnote to the Study: 'mass destruction of the flora and fauna and poisoning of the atmosphere or water resources, as well as other acts capable of causing an ecological catastrophe'. Vietnam's Penal Code refers to 'ecocide' as

that the destruction of the environment as a weapon may constitute a customary rule, at least as far as it regards environmental modification techniques.

C. Care for the Environment

Rule 44 in the 2005 Customary Law Study concerns the obligation to care for the environment. It mainly replicates Article 55(1) of Protocol I, but also aspects of the principle of precaution as formulated in Article 57 of Protocol I. The first sentence of Rule 44 states: 'Methods and means of warfare must be employed with due regard to the protection and preservation of the natural environment'.

The Commentary to the 2005 Customary Law Study states that safeguarding the environment per se, and not only in as far as it is regarded as a civilian object, is shown by state practice. The rule confirms a general obligation of respecting the environment and it requires taking measures and precautions in warfare to spare it.[60] Thus, Rule 44 goes beyond the care obligation incorporated in Article 55(1), as well as Article 57 of Protocol I. This is evident for two reasons. First, it does not include any threshold level for taking care, as in Article 55(1). Second, it separates the environment from other civilian objects, as opposed to Article 57. As mentioned above, the International Law Commission provisionally adopted a more restricted version of the care obligation by keeping the requirement of 'widespread, long-term and severe' environmental damage in Draft Article 13(2) suggesting that the customary law obligation to care for the environment during armed conflicts is not as far-reaching as suggested by the ICRC Study.

Rule 44 acknowledges that due regard must be employed for the specific purpose of protecting and preserving the environment during warfare; therefore it may include obligations to take precautions that are influenced by the general development of international environmental law. This is based on the fact that the 2005 Customary Law Study refers to international environmental treaties – such as the Biodiversity Convention (Article 3) and the African Convention on the Conservation of Nature and Natural Resources (Article XV) – and non-binding environmental instruments – such the Stockholm Declaration (Principle 21), the World Charter for Nature (Principles 5 and 20), and the Rio Declaration (Principle 24).[61]

In addition, the ICRC states in the Commentary to the Study:

> The extensive development of international law to protect the environment over the last few decades has been motivated by a recognition of the dangerous degradation

'destroying the natural environment'. See Henckaerts and Doswald-Beck, *Customary International Humanitarian Law*, Volume I: Rules (n 7) 155, fn 77.

[60] Hulme, 'Natural Environment' (n 25) 206.

[61] J-M Henckaerts and L Doswald-Beck, *Customary International Humanitarian Law*, Volume II: Practice (Cambridge University Press, 2012) Rule 44A.

> of the natural environment caused by mankind. This development has been such that a state's interest in the protection of its natural environment has now been recognised by the International Court of Justice in the *Gabcıkovo-Nagymaros Project case* as an 'essential interest' that could justify that state invoking the doctrine of 'necessity' to renege from other international obligations.[62]

The reference is somewhat confusing because the quote of the *Gabcıkovo-Nagymaros Project* case refers to the rules on state responsibility and more specifically to the circumstances precluding wrongfulness by invoking a state of necessity. These rules do not contain any material standard on precaution towards the environment.[63] The inclusion of the reference may be intended to indicate a general development of taking environmental considerations into various areas of international law – in this case, state responsibility – to show its growing influence.

The use of the term 'due regard' differs from 'care', as incorporated in Article 55(1). It may be a conscious choice in order to distance Rule 44 from Article 55(1) of Protocol I and to indicate an independent rule of 'due regard' for the environment. The main difference is the exclusion of the damage threshold. Rule 44 therefore suggests, as correctly argued by Koppe, 'that a customary duty of care for the environment during international armed conflict has developed since the early 1970s'.[64] The concern for the environment in relation to armed conflict has indeed been affirmed in other contexts as well. For instance, Principle 5 in the non-binding instrument, the 1982 World Charter for Nature, states that the environment shall be safeguarded from the damage caused by warfare or other hostile activities.[65] Likewise, the non-binding Article 40(1)(b) of the IUCN Draft Covenant suggests parties to an armed conflict are under the obligation to 'take all reasonable measures to protect the environment against avoidable harm'. Also, the non-binding, but aimed at codifying customary law, 1994 San Remo Manual on International Law Applicable to Armed Conflicts at Sea (San Remo Manual) includes a reference to employ due regard for the environment in warfare at sea.[66] Consequently, there seems to be a customary rule to take care of the environment during armed conflicts.

The core of the obligation in Rule 44 and Article 55(1) appears to be similar, with the major difference being that Rule 44 has omitted the

[62] ibid, 147.

[63] See, in particular, Draft Article 25 of the International Law Commission's Draft Articles on Responsibility of States for Internationally Wrongful Acts, Report of the International Law Commission, adopted at the 65th Session (2001), *Yearbook of the International Law Commission*, Volume II, Part Two.

[64] Koppe (n 26) 199.

[65] The World Charter was annexed to a resolution adopted by the UN General Assembly and it was drafted by a Group of Experts established by the Secretary-General. See World Charter for Nature, UN Doc A/Res/37/7, adopted 28 October 1982.

[66] L Doswald-Beck, *1994 San Remo Manual on International Law Applicable to Armed Conflicts at Sea, Prepared by International Lawyers and Naval Experts at the International Institute for Humanitarian Law* (Cambridge University Press, 1995).

damage threshold.[67] Hulme points out that the omission of the threshold is the 'real value' of the rule – states have to employ due regard no matter the level of the potential environmental damage.[68] Thus, Rule 44 recognises the general need to protect and respect the environment without requiring a certain level of harm, which seems to have become a growing trend within warfare. However, this rule was not confirmed by the International Law Commission that kept the damage threshold, which may question the customary law status of Rule 44.

Although the terms 'due regard' and 'care' have a comparable meaning, they set separate standards. As noted by Hulme, the 'due regard' formula contains an element of balancing interests against each other, and it seems to slightly lower the protection in terms of the required positive obligations of parties.[69] Hulme is of the view that the requirement of employing due regard does not involve taking measures to protect the environment to the same extent as the 'care' obligation in Article 55(1) of Protocol I. Thus, the 'due regard' formula seems to provide a lower level of protection because it contains fewer incentives to take action and a requirement to balance different interests against each other. Hulme argues that there is no reason to depart from the wording used in the Protocol, in particular since the word 'care' is more likely to be understood by the ordinary soldier than 'due regard'.[70]

The 'due regard' formula is used in several provisions in the UN Law of the Sea Convention (UNCLOS). The employment of due regard requires states to refrain from certain acts in order to not interfere with the rights of other states when those states are exercising their freedoms on the high seas. The due regard formula was adopted in relation to environmental protection in the rules on naval warfare in the San Remo Manual.[71] As pointed out by Hulme, Rule 44 of the 2005 Customary Law Study imposes a similar obligation to conduct a 'balancing exercise' with regard to military necessity and the interest of environmental protection during warfare.[72] This is reasonable, given that Rule 44 does not require a level of harm for its application, to ensure a balance between military interests and other interests in an armed conflict context, such as humanitarian interests, against the interest of protecting the environment.

[67] See Hulme, 'Natural Environment' (n 25) 218; Hulme, 'Taking Care to Protect' (n 16) 686.

[68] Hulme, 'Taking Care to Protect' (n 16) 686.

[69] ibid.

[70] Hulme, 'Natural Environment' (n 25) 218.

[71] See Rule 44 in Part III on Basic Rules and Targets Discrimination, Section I in the *San Remo Manual on Naval Warfare*. Rule 44, relating to the environment, states that, '[m]ethods and means of warfare should be employed with due regard for the natural environment taking into account the relevant rules of international law. Damage to or destruction of the natural environment not justified by military necessity and carried out wantonly is prohibited'. See Doswald-Beck (n 66).

[72] Hulme, 'Taking Care to Protect' (n 16) 686.

In addition, Rule 44 requires due regard in relation to protection as well as *preservation* of the environment during armed conflicts. The term 'preservation' also originates from UNCLOS, applying to marine environmental protection, and it was used in the San Remo Manual on Naval Warfare.[73] Hulme interprets the term 'preservation' as representing a 'heightened standard of conservation' of the environment. She notes that the phrase 'preservation measures' is generally associated with safeguarding endangered species and fragile ecosystems and in the context of ensuring sustainable use and for keeping the ecosystems as intact as possible.[74] While 'protection' relates more to a specific threat.[75]

The inclusion of preservation into the customary rules protecting the environment during armed conflicts further indicates a rapprochement towards the international environmental legal field. Hulme supports such a view and that Rule 44 signifies a recognition of the importance of the environment to humankind.[76] In fact, the environmental rules in the 2005 Customary Law Study have moved the law of armed conflict closer to international environmental law as many of the terms as well as references are originating from this corpus of law.[77]

The type of environmental protection embodied in the care/due regard obligation seems to be practised in armed conflict, at least to some extent. Most states have incorporated environmental procedures in their rules of engagement and voluntarily engage in cleaning-up operations after hostilities.[78] Several states have stopped using depleted uranium and lead ammunition or at least exchanged it for the less polluting option of tungsten; the United States has adopted carbon-cutting measures on its military bases; and German scientists claim to have developed nitrogen-based 'environmentally friendly' bombs.[79] In general, states seek to avoid the adoption of new environmental regulations within the law of armed conflict that restrict warfare. At the same time, state practice shows that there is an awareness and interest for environmental protection in times of armed conflict. Thus, the regulations in the law of armed conflict represent the minimum level of environmental protection that states have officially accepted.

[73] Article 192 UNCLOS.

[74] Hulme, 'Natural Environment' (n 25) 220.

[75] V Frank, *The European Community and the Marine Environmental Protection in the International Law of the Sea: Implementing Global Obligations on a Regional Level* (Nijhoff, 2007) 19.

[76] Hulme, 'Taking Care to Protect' (n 16) 691.

[77] Hulme, 'Natural Environment' (n 25) 237.

[78] *The Guardian*, 'What's the environmental impact of modern war?' (6 November 2014), available at: www.theguardian.com/environment/2014/nov/06/whats-the-environmental-impact-of-modern-war.

[79] M Rutherford, 'German Scientists Developing Green Bombs. New Environmental Friendly, Nitrogen-based Explosives Could Deliver More of a Bang While Being Safer to Handle Than Traditional Charges, German Scientists Say' (*Cnet*, 5 June 2008), available at: www.cnet.com/news/german-scientists-developing-green-bombs.

States' environmental policies in relation to military operations, however, are often more ambitious than reflected in the law.[80] For instance, the United States has an advanced environmental programme for its military operations. Its army carries out detailed studies on the environmental impacts with regard to their operations overseas, verifying to what extent their military forces can comply with local environmental laws.[81] This shows that a general 'care' or 'due regard' standard towards the environment is reflected in the practice of the United States. In addition, NATO has developed environmental guidelines for its military engagements, both in peacetime and wartime. The Joint NATO Doctrine Document provides guidelines to take environmental protection into account while planning and executing military operations, including targeting. NATO commanders have to take into account the military mission objectives and threat level, and balance these with environmental considerations.[82]

Many states seem to have been influenced by the rising awareness of the degradation of the environment during warfare. Consequently, there is evidence showing that warfare is becoming 'greener', which is not reflected in the treaty law.[83] However, this greener practice does not appear to be undertaken in the belief that it is legally required, which means that it may lack an *opinio juris*, thus obstructing it from being regarded as part of customary law.

To sum up, the obligation to employ methods and means of warfare with due regard to environmental protection seems to be a rule of customary law. However, Hulme questions whether the first sentence of Rule 44 has sufficient support in general state practice to reflect customary law. She is particularly sceptical whether this rule represents customary law because it has omitted the threshold and replaced the care standard with due regard requiring a balancing exercise.[84] Nonetheless, she has expressed (prior to the ICRC publishing the Study) that care for the environment is a customary law obligation, affirming that 'all states when making military decisions must now recognise the basic customary obligation to have regard to protection of the environment'.[85] It is most likely that a customary rule containing an obligation for states to pay attention to the environment during warfare exists, albeit that the content of such an obligation is uncertain.

[80] Hulme, 'Taking Care to Protect' (n 16) 689.

[81] J Burger, 'Environmental Aspects of Non-International Conflicts: The Experience in Former Yugoslavia' in R Grunawalt, J King and R McClain (eds), *Protection of the Environment During Armed Conflict* (1996) 69 *International Law Studies* 336.

[82] Joint NATO Doctrine for Environmental Protection During NATO-led Military Activities (STANAG 7141/AJEPP-4). See, in particular, chapter 2.2 regarding environmental planning guidelines for military activities and chapter 3.1 regarding environmental risk management in military activities planning, 3–1. See also NATO Military Principles and Policies for Environmental Protection (MC 469/1), which is the NATO environmental policy document as drafted by the Military Committee, available at: nso.nato.int. The author is grateful for the help provided by Jeroen Rottink, Chairman EP WG.

[83] Hulme, 'Taking Care to Protect' (n 16) 689.

[84] ibid, 686–87.

[85] K Hulme, *War Torn Environment: Interpreting the Legal Threshold* (Nijhoff, 2004) 108.

D. Reprisals

The International Law Commission provisionally adopted a draft principle prohibiting reprisals directed against the natural environment. The draft principle replicates Article 55(2) of Protocol I.[86] A belligerent reprisal is according to the ICRC Customary Law Study 'an action that would otherwise be unlawful but that in exceptional cases is considered lawful under international law when used as an enforcement measure in reaction to unlawful acts of an adversary'.[87] The term 'reprisals' or 'belligerent reprisals' is mainly used in the context of international armed conflict, while the term 'countermeasures' is used outside such a context.[88] Reprisals are permitted, but heavily restricted during armed conflicts. According to Protocol I, reprisals are expressly prohibited against protected persons and protected objects,[89] civilian population or civilians,[90] civilian objects,[91] cultural property or places of worship,[92] objects indispensable to the survival of the civilian population,[93] the natural environment,[94] and works or installations containing dangerous forces.[95]

Clearly, reprisals taken against the environment are prohibited under treaty-based law. However, whether the prohibition represents customary international law generated a lively debate in the International Law Commission. The deviating opinions regarded whether the prohibition of reprisals against the environment could be considered to have customary legal status, and if so, whether such a customary law rule would apply in international as well as non-international armed conflicts.[96] Furthermore, concerns were also expressed by some members due to the fact that the draft principle was literally a replicate of Article 55(2). As Protocol I does not have universal ratification, the adoption of an identical provision as representing customary law could therefore be misunderstood as an attempt to create a binding rule on non-state parties, in particular as Article 55(2) of Protocol I had been subject to reservations and declarations by some state parties.[97] In the Commentary to the Draft Principle the position of Article 55(2) is summarised accordingly:

> [T]he prohibition of attacks against the natural environment by way of reprisals is a binding rule for the 174 State parties to Additional Protocol I. The extent to which

[86] Draft Principle 16, UN Doc A/CN.4/L.937.
[87] ICRC Study, Commentary to Rule 145, 513.
[88] Jacobsson, Second Report (n 19) 43, available at: legal.un.org/docs/?symbol=A/CN.4/685.
[89] Article 20 Protocol I.
[90] Article 51(6) Protocol I.
[91] Article 52(1) Protocol I.
[92] Article 53(c) Protocol I.
[93] Article 54(4) Protocol I.
[94] Article 55(2) Protocol I.
[95] Article 56(4) Protocol I. The prohibition remains even in cases where they constitute military objectives.
[96] Report of the International Law Commission, 68th Session (2 May–10 June and 4 July–12 August) (2016) *Yearbook of the International Law Commission* Volume II, Part Two, 336.
[97] ibid, 337.

> States have made declarations or reservations that are relevant to its application must be evaluated on a case by case basis, since only a few States have made an explicit reference to paragraph 2 of article 55.[98]

The inclusion of a draft principle on the prohibition of reprisals against the environment was regarded as being particularly pertinent and needed in the light of the overall aim of the draft principles to enhance environmental protection in relation to armed conflict. Thus, the inclusion of the draft principle should be seen 'as promoting the progressive development of international law' in accordance with the Commission's mandate.[99]

E. Protected Zones

The International Law Commission has provisionally adopted two draft articles that deal with the designation of major important environmental and cultural areas as protected zones. Draft Principle 4 stipulates that states should designate such areas by entering 'agreements or otherwise', which could also be done in peacetime, while Draft Principle 17 states that designated areas subject to such agreements shall be protected against attacks, as long as the areas do not contain a military objective.[100] The concept of area-based protection is an established practice in both international environmental (eg, protected areas) and law of armed conflict (eg, demilitarised zones). Article 40(3) in the non-binding IUCN Draft Covenant also includes an area-based protection mechanism for the protection of natural and cultural sites, 'in particular for sites designated for protection under applicable national laws and international treaties'. Furthermore, the ICRC suggested a similar approach at the thirty-first Conference in 2011. In the conference report, it was suggested that:

> To avoid the consequences of hostilities, certain fragile environments or areas of major ecological importance, such as groundwater aquifers, national parks and habitats of endangered species, should be off-limits to any form of military activity. Such areas should therefore be delineated and designated as demilitarized zones before an armed conflict occurs, or at the latest when the fighting breaks out.[101]

At the time of the negotiations of Protocol I, a special protection to 'publicly recognized nature reserves' had already been proposed.[102] The proposal was

[98] ibid, 338.

[99] ibid.

[100] The Draft Principles were first provisionally adopted in 2015 at International Law Commission's 67th meeting and later adopted on the first reading together with 26 other draft principles in 2019. See International Law Commission, Protection of the Environment, First Reading (n 3).

[101] Draft resolution and Report of the 31st International Conference of the Red Cross and Red Crescent held in Geneva, Switzerland, 28 November–1 December 2011, 31IC/11/5.1.1.

[102] Y Sandoz, C Swinarski and B Zimmerman (eds), *Commentary on the Additional Protocols of 8 June 1977* (ICRC, Geneva, 1987) 664.

never adopted but the idea of sparing areas of ecological importance in armed conflict has remained alive. It has roots not only in the law of armed conflict debate, but also within international environmental law. The World Heritage Convention refers to the 'outbreak of an armed conflict' as a reason to enhance the protection of world heritage sites (natural, cultural or mixed), which clearly indicates that these sites should also remain protected in times of armed conflict.[103] This provision was indeed essential for the inclusion of the Special Rapporteur's proposed draft principle on designation of major ecological and cultural areas[104] as well as for the inclusion of the area-based protection of natural and cultural sites in the IUCN Draft Covenant.[105]

While the ICRC's proposal at the thirty-first Conference referred to the possibility of establishing demilitarised zones for protecting specific natural areas, the International Law Commission choose the term 'protected zones' thereby departing from the Special Rapporteur's original proposal which was in line with the ICRC's.[106] According to the Commentaries to Draft Principle 4, the intention of choosing another term was to stress the different meanings of the two types of zone.[107] Demilitarised zones are established by the parties to an armed conflict by entering into agreement stating that the parties are prohibited from extending their military operations to that zone if such an extension is contrary to the terms of their agreement.[108] Protected zones are established in accordance with the Commission's Draft Principle 4 emphasising the environmental and cultural importance of these areas.[109]

Draft Principle 17 provides protection only for the areas that have been designated by an express agreement, which may have been concluded in peacetime or during armed conflicts. According to the Commentary to the Draft Principle, 'the reference to the term "agreement" should be understood in its broadest sense as including mutual as well as unilateral declarations accepted by the other party, treaties and other types of agreements, as well as agreements with non-State actors'.[110]

An area of major environmental and cultural importance designated by agreement as a protected zone shall be protected against any attack, as long as it does not contain a military objective. Thus, if a party to an armed conflict has military objectives within the area, or uses the area to carry out any military activities during an armed conflict, the area may lose its protection. This formula replicates the provision on demilitarised zones in Article 60 of

[103] Article 11(4) World Heritage Convention. See ch 8 for how such protection could be materialised.
[104] Jacobsson, Second Report (n 19) para 227.
[105] IUCN, 'Draft International Covenant' (n 31) 122.
[106] See Jacobsson, Second Report (n 19) para 229.
[107] Report of the International Law Commission, 68th Session (n 96) 323.
[108] Article 60 Protocol I.
[109] Report of the International Law Commission, 68th Session (n 96) 323.
[110] ibid, 339.

Protocol I, which states that if a party to an armed conflict uses a protected area for specified military purposes, the protected status shall be revoked.[111]

The inclusion of the two draft principles may not in practice add any protection to the environment as such. The protection depends on the fact that the parties to the armed conflict must have entered agreements to spare areas of major ecological and cultural importance. Such agreements would be equally binding even without the Commission's draft principles. Yet, the inclusion may be seen as a reminder to warring parties on the possibility of sparing environmentally and culturally important areas in warfare and respecting areas protected under international law in general also in times of armed conflict.

III. SPECIAL ENVIRONMENTAL PROTECTION IN NON-INTERNATIONAL ARMED CONFLICTS

This section examines whether any of the customary rules providing direct environmental protection also apply in non-international armed conflicts. Treaty rules applicable to non-international armed conflicts are scarce in general, and they are non-existent with regard to special environmental protection. States have been reluctant to adopt rules regulating internal armed conflicts because they historically have regarded these as national concerns. Hence, most of the law of armed conflict instruments have been created for applying to international armed conflicts. The limited number of treaties applying to non-international armed conflicts include Common Article 3 to the Geneva Conventions and Protocol II. In addition, more recently adopted treaties apply to all situations of armed conflict alike. For instance, the 1972 Biological Weapons Convention,[112] the 1993 Chemical Weapons Convention,[113] the 1997 Ottawa Convention[114] and the 2001 Amendment, which extends the Convention on Conventional Weapons and its protocols to non-international armed conflicts.

The differences regarding the applicable rules of the law of armed conflict between international and non-international armed conflict have diminished through the expansion of customary international law.[115] The Appeals Chamber in the *Tadić* case stated: 'What is inhumane, and consequently proscribed, in

[111] See ibid, 339–40.

[112] Convention on the Prohibition of the Development, Production and Stockpiling of Bacteriological (Biological) and Toxin Weapons and on Their Destruction (adopted 10 April 1972, entered into force 26 March 1975) 1015 UNTS 163 (Biological Weapons Convention).

[113] Convention on the Prohibition of the Development, Production, Stockpiling and Use of Chemical Weapons and on Their Destruction (adopted 13 January 1993, entered into force 29 April 1997) UNTS 45 (Chemical Weapons Convention).

[114] Convention on the Prohibition of the Use, Stockpiling, Production and Transfer of Anti-Personnel Mines and on Their Destruction (adopted 18 September 1997, entered into force 1 March 1999) 2056 UNTS 211 (Ottawa Convention).

[115] D Akande, 'Classification of Armed Conflicts: Relevant Legal Concepts' in E Wilmshurst (ed), *International Law and the Classification of Conflicts* (Oxford University Press, 2012) 35.

international wars cannot but be inhumane and inadmissible in civil strife'.[116] There is an increasing consensus on the fact that what is not tolerated in international armed conflicts should not be tolerated in non-international conflicts either.[117] In contemporary conflicts, regardless of international or non-international character, civilians are the main victims. Thus, there is no reason why the level of protection should be different in situations of non-international armed conflicts. For comparable reasons, a similar level of environmental protection should apply in both types of conflict.[118] For instance, the ICRC stated at a conference in 2011 that 'the law needs to be strengthened with a view to establishing territorial protection applicable to areas of major ecological importance in international and non-international armed conflicts'.[119]

In its 2005 Customary Law Study, the ICRC acknowledged that most rules applying to international armed conflicts also apply to non-international armed conflicts. One of the main reasons that the ICRC initiated the Study was to address the fact that most treaty laws did not regulate non-international armed conflicts, which represent the majority of the current armed conflicts.[120] Nevertheless, important differences persist between the two types of conflict, such as combatant privileges that are only relevant in international armed conflicts.[121]

The 2005 Customary Law Study suggests that some of its environmentally specific rules are applicable in non-international armed conflicts. Therefore, this section addresses the application of Rule 45, followed by Rule 44, to non-international armed conflicts. Furthermore, at the first reading concluded in 2019 of the topic 'Protection of the Environment in Relation to Armed Conflict', the International Law Commission did not differentiate between international and non-international conflict in regard to the application of the set of draft principles provisionally adopted.[122] It is still not certain whether this non-separation will be kept in at the second reading, given that some states have expressed criticisms towards the approach adopted by the Commission.[123]

[116] *Prosecutor v Tadić*, IT-94-1-AR72, Decisions on Defence Motion for Interlocutory Appeal on Jurisdiction (Appeals Chamber) 2 October 1995 (Tadić Jurisdiction) para 119.

[117] C Bruch, 'All's Not Fair in (Civil) War: Criminal Liability for Environmental Damage in Internal Armed Conflict' (2000) 25 *Vermont Law Review* 695, 738.

[118] ibid.

[119] Draft resolution and Report of the 31st International Conference (n 101).

[120] J-M Henckaerts and Doswald-Beck, 'Introduction' in *Customary International Humanitarian Law*, Volume I: Rules (Cambridge University Press, 2005) xxxiv.

[121] Akande (n 115) 36–37.

[122] Regarding the *ratione materiae* of the draft principles provisionally adopted by the International Law Commission, reference is made to the term 'protection of the environment' as it relates to the term 'armed conflicts'. No distinction is made between international armed conflicts and non-international armed conflicts. See Report of the International Law Commission, 68th Session (n 96) 322.

[123] For instance, China, Republic of Korea and Viet Nam. See the discussion in S-E Pantazopoulos, 'Protection of the Environment during Armed Conflicts: An Appraisal of the ILC's Work' (2016) 43 *Questions of International Law* 7, 9–10.

Yet, the approach chosen by the International Law Commission is indeed an attempt to expand the application of the law to enhance the environmental protection in both types of armed conflict.

A. ENMOD Convention and Protocol I

In its Study, the ICRC concluded that it is not entirely established if Rule 45 applies to non-international armed conflicts. As mentioned, the first part of the rule – incorporating Article 35(3) and Article 55(1) of Protocol I – prohibits the means and methods of warfare causing 'widespread, long-term and severe' damage to the environment. The second part of the rule prohibits the destruction of the environment as a weapon. At the adoption of the protocols in 1977, a proposal to include a corresponding Article 35(3) in Protocol II was rejected at the conference. It is stated in the Commentary to the 2005 Customary Law Study that the grounds for the rejection were not clear, but it may have been to simplify the negotiations in order to ensure that Protocol II was adopted.[124] This is also showing that including special environmental rules was not a priority for the delegates at the conference for non-international conflicts. Perhaps it is because the major environmental devastation at the time had only occurred in international armed conflicts.

It is noted in the Commentary to the Study, however, that Rule 45 has been included in other instruments applicable to non-international armed conflicts. The Study refers to two examples, namely a Memorandum of Understanding on the Application of International Humanitarian Law between Croatia and the Socialist Federal Republic of Yugoslavia, and an Agreement on the Application of International Humanitarian Law Between the Parties to the Conflict in Bosnia and Herzegovina.[125] Furthermore, the Commentary supports the customary status of the rule on practice in the form of several military manuals that have included a prohibition on 'widespread, long-term and severe' environmental damage in non-international armed conflicts.[126]

The 2005 Customary Law Study also asserts that a large number of states have criminalised 'ecocide' or intentional 'widespread, long-term and severe' environmental damage, without distinguishing between international and non-international armed conflicts.[127] At present, there seems to be sparse state

[124] See Henckaerts and Doswald-Beck, *Customary International Humanitarian Law*, Volume I: Rules (n 7) 156.

[125] See Henckaerts and Doswald-Beck, *Customary International Humanitarian Law*, Volume I: Rules (n 7) 157 fn 86.

[126] The Study makes references to military manuals of Australia, Benin, Colombia, Germany, Italy, Kenya, South Korea, Togo and Yugoslavia. See Henckaerts and Doswald-Beck, *Customary International Humanitarian Law*, Volume I: Rules (n 7) 157, fn 87.

[127] See Henckaerts and Doswald-Beck, *Customary International Humanitarian Law*, Volume I: Rules (n 7) 157. The 2005 Customary Law Study refers to the legislation of Armenia, Azerbaijan,

practice and *opinio juris* showing that the environmentally specific rules in the law of armed conflict apply to non-international conflict as customary law. However, the Commentary states that:

> [E]ven if this rule is not yet customary, present trends towards further protection of the environment and towards establishing rules applicable in non-international armed conflicts mean that it is likely to become customary in due course. This is particularly true as major damage to the environment rarely respects international frontiers, and also because the causing of such damage may violate other rules that apply equally in international and non-international armed conflicts, for example the prohibition of indiscriminate attacks.[128]

It is expressed in the 2005 Customary Law Study, that the rule is not a customary rule applicable to non-international armed conflicts, which seems to be the correct conclusion at the time.[129] Practice after the publication of the 2005 Customary Law Study has not shown any significant change in relation to the customary status of Rule 45 and its applicability in non-international armed conflicts. The 2006 Manual on the Law of Non-International Armed Conflict (the IIHL Manual), a non-binding document with the intention to replicate customary law, only provides the environment with an indirect protection as a civilian object. Furthermore, the IIHL Manual has only one rule on regarding environmental protection. It reads: 'damage to the natural environment during military operations must not be excessive in relation to the military advantage anticipated from those operations'. Furthermore, the Manual states explicitly that Articles 35(3) and 55 are not part of customary law in either international or non-international armed conflicts.[130] Thus, Rule 45 cannot be confirmed as applying to non-international armed conflicta as a customary law in 2019: there is not sufficient state practice or *opinio juris* demonstrating such status. In addition, there are still ongoing debates whether the rule has customary law status in international armed conflicts (see chapter three). Nevertheless, the IIHL Manual states that 'the natural environment is a civilian object' and, as such, parts of the environment are therefore protected under all the rules regarding protection of civilian objects. The IIHL Manual also takes note that the ENMOD Convention bans environmental modification as a method of warfare if doing so results in widespread, long-lasting or severe effects on the environment.

Belarus, Bosnia and Herzegovina, Colombia, Croatia, Kazakhstan, Kyrgyzstan, Moldova, Slovenia, Spain, Tajikistan, Ukraine and Yugoslavia.

[128] Henckaerts and Doswald-Beck, *Customary International Humanitarian Law*, Volume I: Rules (n 7) 157.

[129] ibid. Similar conclusions are made by Hulme: see Hulme, 'Natural Environment' (n 25) 233.

[130] International Institute of Humanitarian Law, The Manual on the Law of Non-International Armed Conflict With Commentary, issued by Drafting Committee consisting of M Schmitt, C Garraway and Y Dinstein, *San Remo 2006* (the IIHL Manual). See para 4.2.4 on the environmental protection in general, and in the related Commentary in para 4.2.4.1. The IIHL Manual, prepared on behalf of the International Institute of Humanitarian Law, is an attempt to draft an 'authoritative restatement of the law' governing these types of conflict.

Thus, the IIHL Manual supports that the ENMOD Convention applies in non-international armed conflicts. This is also the conclusion of the International Law Commission while adopting Draft Principle 19 prohibiting environmental modification techniques. Nevertheless, the ENMOD Convention as well as Draft Principle 19 incorporate a transnational element meaning that another state must have been the subject of the technique.

B. Care for the Environment

Rule 44 in the 2005 Customary Law Study, stating that methods and means of warfare shall be employed with due regard to the environment, possibly applies in non-international armed conflicts. The Commentary states that: 'It can be argued that the obligation to pay due regard to the environment also applies in non-international armed conflicts if there are effects in another State'. The study supports this view by referring to the recognition of the International Court of Justice in the *Gabcíkovo-Nagymaros Project* case. In this case, environmental concerns were regarded as an 'essential interest' and it was found that states have an obligation to 'ensure that activities within their jurisdiction and control respect the environment of other States as part of customary law'.[131] This would suggest that it would only apply if there were an injury to another state, which would then probably concern the rules of state responsibility, rather than the law of armed conflict, as discussed in chapter three.

The ICRC claims that there is to some extent state practice suggesting that Rule 44 is applicable in non-international armed conflicts. This claim is supported in the Commentary by references to military manuals, official statements, and state submissions to the International Court of Justice regarding the *Nuclear Weapons* Advisory Opinion and that environmental protection is for the interest of all states.[132] Hulme raises doubts whether the practice referred to in the 2005 Customary Law Study supports the applicability of a due regard obligation in non-international armed conflicts. The statements submitted to the International Court of Justice regarding the *Nuclear Weapons* Advisory Opinion do not refer to non-international armed conflicts. Rather these are general statements emphasising that environmental protection for the benefit of all states, as noted by Hulme.[133] Nevertheless, a rule to take general care or due regard for the environment may still apply in non-international armed conflicts as customary law. There seem to be certain indications to view the environment as an object that should be regarded with some degree of care, also during non-international armed conflicts. Indications of such an obligation would be more

[131] Henckaerts and Doswald-Beck, *Customary International Humanitarian Law*, Volume I: Rules (n 7) 148–49.

[132] ibid, 149.

[133] Hulme, 'Natural Environment' (n 25) 220–21.

likely to have its roots in international environmental law, given that it is a legal field providing obligations for states to protect the environment within their territory. As minimum, an obligation to take care against widespread, long-term and severe damage applies in non-international armed conflicts in accordance with International Law Commission's Draft Principle 13(2).

To conclude, the applicability of the Rules 43 and 44 in non-international armed conflicts is not entirely established. However, there is a growing tendency to prohibit the same things that are considered inhumane in international armed conflicts in non-international armed conflicts. If the view of the environment has changed under international warfare, a similar development should then be mirrored in non-international armed conflicts, as suggested by the draft principles provisionally adopted by the International Law Commission.

IV. CONCLUSIONS

The ENMOD Convention and Protocol I have influenced the development of customary law. Environmental awareness is growing within the military sector, which potentially pushes state practice in a more environmentally friendly direction.[134] According to the 2005 Customary Law Study and the International Law Commission, the special environmental protection in customary law of armed conflict is broader in scope than the treaty-based protection. In addition, compared with the treaty-based protection of the environment under the law of armed conflict, the customary rules incorporate references to international environmental law to enhance the protection further.

The emerging set of rules in customary international law has attempted to extend the application of provisions regulating international armed conflict to apply to non-international armed conflicts. The 2005 Customary Law Study takes the position that its environmentally specific rules may also apply in non-international armed conflicts.[135] However, little state practice is provided to support this position. The International Law Commission does not separate the two types of conflict indicating that the draft principles apply alike, which has received varied reactions among states. Consequently, there is no consensus as to whether any of the rules on direct environmental protection in the ENMOD Convention or Protocol I apply in non-international armed conflicts. Nevertheless, such a weakness may not be of pressing concern because in these internal conflicts the environment remains protected by the rules of general protection under the law of armed conflict. The general protection rules probably offer a broader protection than the special environmental protection, as discussed in the next chapter (chapter five).

[134] A Westing, *Pioneer on the Environmental Impact of War* (Springer, 2013) 131.

[135] See Rules 43–45; Henckaerts and Doswald-Beck, *Customary International Humanitarian Law, Volume I: Rules* (n 7) 143–58.

5

General Protection under the Law of Armed Conflict

I. INTRODUCTION

THIS CHAPTER ANALYSES the indirect protection of the environment under the law of armed conflict. It examines the rules of the general protection of the environment as a civilian object and the protection provided under other rules of importance, including protection for cultural property, work installations containing dangerous forces, objects indispensable for civilians, and relevant weapons conventions. Even though the law of armed conflict contains rules specifically directed at environmental protection, it is often argued that a broader environmental protection is offered under the general rules.[1] I support this position, given that the general rules have a more generous scope of application compared with the rules in the ENMOD Convention and Protocol I. The general rules of protection have customary law status and apply alike to international and non-international armed conflicts.[2] Thus, there is no need to distinguish between the two categories in this chapter. At the same time, however, the indirect protection is also subject to a number of limitations.

This chapter has the following structure. Section II studies how the environment is defined as a civilian object. Section III examines the environmental protection offered under the principle of distinction and the prohibition on wanton damage. Section IV analyses the subjective element in attacking the environment. Section V scrutinises the exercise of balancing environmental

[1] C Droege and M-L Tougas, 'The Protection of the Natural Environment in Armed Conflict – Existing Rules and Need for Further Legal Protection' (2013) 82 *Nordic Journal of International Law* 21; D Fleck, 'The Protection of the Environment in Armed Conflict: Legal Obligations in the Absence of Specific Rules' (2013) 82 *Nordic Journal of International Law* 7; M Bothe et al, 'International Law Protecting the Environment During Armed Conflict: Gaps and Opportunities' (2010) 92 *International Review of the Red Cross* 569; K Hulme, 'Taking Care to Protect the Environment Against Damage: A Meaningless Obligation?' (2010) 92 *International Review of the Red Cross* 675, 678.

[2] See also Rules 7–10 in the Customary Law Study: J-M Henckaerts and L Doswald-Beck, *Customary International Humanitarian Law Study*, Volume I: Rules (Cambridge University Press, 2005) 25–35.

collateral damage and military advantage. Section VI addresses the environmental protection offered under the principle of precaution and its relation to the precautionary approach, as formulated under international environmental law. In section VII, I study the protection under the Martens Clause (also referred to as the principle of humanity), and discuss how scientific knowledge has altered the view on the environment and thereby may have modified its protection in warfare. Sections VIII and IX explore the importance of other rules and conventions of the law of armed conflict to provide environmental protection. The last section, section X, provides some concluding remarks on the limitations of the general rules to safeguard the environment.

II. APPLYING THE GENERAL RULES OF PROTECTION TO THE ENVIRONMENT

In this section, I argue that the environment is prima facie a civilian object (unless it is specifically used for military purposes in a concrete situation) and, therefore, the general rules should apply. I also claim that the environmentally specific provisions in Protocol I are not intended to apply *lex specialis*, but rather they complement the general rules of protection to the environment.

A. Environment as a Civilian Object

Parts of the environment can be regarded as civilian objects, as long as they do not contribute to the war efforts and thereby constitute military objectives. Consequently, in such a case, the principles of distinction, proportionality and precaution – as well as the rule of military necessity – provide a general protection of the environment.[3] The general rules have customary law status,[4] but they are also codified in Protocol I. In addition, Rule 43 in the 2005 Customary Law Study has formulated the general rules of protection to explicitly apply to the environment. It reads:

> The general principles on the conduct of hostilities apply to the natural environment:
>
> No part of the natural environment may be attacked, unless it is a military objective.
>
> Destruction of any part of the natural environment is prohibited, unless required by imperative military necessity.
>
> Launching an attack against a military objective which may be excessive in relation to the concrete and direct military advantage anticipated is prohibited.

[3] See Henckaerts and Doswald-Beck, *Customary International Humanitarian Law*, Volume I: Rules (n 2); Droege and Tougas (n 1) 24.

[4] See also Rules 7–10 in the Customary Law Study. Henckaerts and Doswald-Beck, *Customary International Humanitarian Law*, Volume I: Rules (n 2) 25–35.

Rule 43A restates the principle of distinction and confirms the general requirement to distinguish between military objectives and civilian objects.[5] Draft Principle 13(3) provisionally adopted by the International Law Commission contains an identical provision.[6] Rule 43B refers to the rule of military necessity and to the prohibition of wanton destruction of civilian objects. Rule 43C corresponds to the principle of proportionality.[7] The International Law Commission has also provisionally adopted Draft Principles 14 and 15 referring to general rules specifically applicable to the environment.[8] The principle of precaution is included in Rule 44 in the Study and its two last sentences read as follows:

> In the conduct of military operations, all feasible precautions must be taken to avoid, and in any event to minimise, incidental damage to the environment. Lack of scientific certainty as to the effects on the environment of certain military operations does not absolve a party to the conflict from taking such precautions.

The principle of distinction is a cornerstone of the law of armed conflict. It was formulated in the 1868 St Petersburg Declaration, stating that only military objectives are lawful to attack in armed conflict. Thus, it excludes civilians and civilian objects as legitimate targets. The modern version of the principle of distinction is codified in Article 48 of Protocol I. It compels the parties to an armed conflict to always distinguish between civilians and fighters, as well as civilian objects and military objectives. Article 52(1) of Protocol I provides a general protection for civilian objects, meaning all objects that are not a 'military objective'.[9] Article 52(2) of Protocol I defines a military objective as one 'whose total or partial destruction, capture or neutralization, in the circumstances ruling at the time offers a definite military advantage'. Thus, lawful attacks must be expected to attain a certain military advantage as a direct result, based on the available information at the time of the attack. Therefore, the environment, or a part of it, can become a military objective if attacking it would offer a military advantage. For instance, a river used for military transport and communication could become a military target, or a forest providing cover to soldiers.

Historically, the protection under the principle of distinction was limited to 'civilian property' of the enemy, as provided for in Article 23(g) of the Hague Regulations. Tangible parts of the environment that have some sort of economic value would most likely fall under the definition of 'property', such as forests, fields, rivers, farmland, animals, crops and water supplies; while

[5] ibid 143–44.

[6] International Law Commission, 'Protection of the Environment. Text and Titles of the Draft Principles Provisionally Adopted by the Drafting Committee on First Reading' (Protection of the Environment, First Reading) UN Doc A/CN.4/L.937 (2019).

[7] Henckaerts and Doswald-Beck, *Customary International Humanitarian Law*, Volume I: Rules (n 2) 146.

[8] International Law Commission, Protection of the Environment, First Reading (n 6).

[9] Article 52(1) of Protocol I and Rules 7, 10 and 43(a) in Henckaerts and Doswald-Beck, *Customary International Humanitarian Law*, Volume I: Rules (n 2).

other environmental components of a more abstract character – atmosphere, ecosystems, ozone layer, or biodiversity – may over-extend the notion of property.[10] However, Article 52 of Protocol I introduced the notion of the 'civilian object', instead of referring to civilian property. Rule 7 in the 2005 Customary Law Study, which codifies the principle of distinction, refers to civilian objects.[11] Thus, the modern law of armed conflict tends to use the term 'civilian object' in relation to the principle of distinction.

The term 'civilian object' is likely to have a more generous scope of application with regard to the environment. From an environmental perspective, the notion of an object is probably able to cover more abstract components of the environment, which would otherwise be excluded from the more restricted notion of property. However, the reference to the environment as a whole, as being an object, may be somewhat misleading. As pointed out in the 2015 plenary debate in the International Law Commission in relation to the topic of 'Protection of the Environment in Relation to Armed Conflict', parts of the environment may be considered as civilian objects. However, some of the members questioned referring to the entire natural environment as an 'object', mainly because it was viewed as confusing terminology.[12] In accordance with the ordinary meaning of the term 'object', it would be used to describe tangible things that can be seen or touched; thus, it omits abstract (environmental) components.[13] It could be more correct to refer to the environment as being *civilian in nature*, as suggested by Special Rapporteur Jacobsson in her Second Report to the International Law Commission.[14]

Nevertheless, the environment and its abstract components have been referred to as 'civilian objects', for example by the International Court of Justice.[15] As expressed by Fleck:

> In all military operations it is essential today to recognise the legal status of the natural environment as a civilian object; as a heritage of mankind that should not be damaged, misused or targeted as a military objective.[16]

[10] R Desgagné, 'The Prevention of Environmental Damage in Time of Armed Conflict: Proportionality and Precautionary Measures' (2000) 3 *Yearbook of International Humanitarian Law* 109, 115.

[11] Henckaerts and Doswald-Beck, *Customary International Humanitarian Law*, Volume I: Rules (n 2) 25.

[12] Report of the International Law Commission, 67th Session (4 May–5 June and 6 July–7 August 2015) (2015) *Yearbook of the International Law Commission*, Volume II, Part Two, Chapter IX, para 154.

[13] Droege and Tougas (n 1) 25–26.

[14] See Draft Principle 1 in the Annex in Special Rapporteur M Jacobsson, Second Report on the Protection of the Environment in Relation to Armed Conflicts, UN Doc A/CN.4/685, 28 May 2015. See also Droege and Tougas (n 1).

[15] *Legality of the Threat or Use of Nuclear Weapons*, Advisory Opinion of 8 July 1996, ICJ Reports 1996, paras 23 and 33; Also, by the Review Committee in the Final Report to the Prosecutor by the Committee Established to Review the NATO Bombing Campaign Against the Federal Republic of Yugoslavia (Final Report to the Prosecutor) published 13 June 2000 on the ICTY's web page at: www.icty.org/sid/10052.

[16] Fleck (n 1).

The San Remo Manual states that the environment is a civilian object.[17] The 2005 Customary Law Study does not expressly refer to the environment as a civilian object, but the rules in the Study offer the corresponding civilian protection to the whole environment without differentiating between its concrete and abstract components. The Study mentions 'parts' of the environment. As highlighted by Hulme, the use of the word 'part' is a new term appearing in the law of armed conflict. The reason the term is used could be to indicate that the environment can be broken down into smaller entities that do not necessarily have to be seen as one unit.[18] Thus, the general protection under the law of armed conflict applies to the environment as a whole, and, when it is appropriate, to its parts.[19]

B. Applying the General Rules to the Environment

In accordance with the *lex specialis* rule, the most explicit treaty provisions should apply at the cost of the more general ones in case two provisions apply, inconsistently, to same subject matter.[20] Protocol I entails special environmental rules, as well as the general rules of protection. If taking the *lex specialis* rule seriously, then Articles 35(3) and 55 should prevail over the general principles codified in Protocol I in relation to environmental matters. Donner and von Heinegg claim that the environmental provisions in Articles 35(3) and 55 were incorporated with the purpose of sidestepping the general protection rules.[21] Verwey points out that no decisive evidence has been presented that can completely exclude such a reading because there are no authoritative interpretations of the articles to this date.[22] If interpreted in this manner, the special environmental protection in Articles 35(3) and 55 of Protocol I would exclude the general protection and thereby lower considerably the level of environmental protection under Protocol I.[23] This is because, unlike Articles 35(3) and 55, the principle of distinction in Article 48 of Protocol I protects the environment from attacks, even if the damage is of low scale.

[17] L Doswald-Beck, *1994 San Remo Manual on International Law Applicable to Armed Conflicts at Sea, Prepared by International Lawyers and Naval Experts at the International Institute for Humanitarian Law* (Cambridge University Press, 1995).

[18] K Hulme, 'Natural Environment' in E Wilmshurst and S Breau (eds), *Perspectives on the ICRC Study on Customary International Humanitarian Law* (Cambridge University Press, 2007) 210.

[19] Droege and Tougas (n 1) 26.

[20] C Thomas, 'Advancing the Legal Protection of the Environment in Relation to Armed Conflict: Protocol I's Threshold of Impermissible Environmental Damage and Alternatives' (2013) 82 *Nordic Journal of International Law* 83, 117.

[21] WH von Heinegg and M Donner, 'New Developments in the Protection of the Natural Environment in Naval Armed Conflicts' (1994) 37 *German Yearbook of International Law* 281, 289. See also Droege and Tougas (n 1) 26.

[22] W Verwey, 'Protection of the Environment in Times of Armed Conflict: In Search of a New Legal Perspective' (1995) 8 *Leiden Journal of International Law* 7, 11; Bothe et al (n 1).

[23] EV Koppe, *The Use of Nuclear Weapons and the Protection of the Environment During International Armed Conflict* (Gildeprint, 2006) 221.

On the contrary, Droege and Tougas claim that the environmentally specific rules have a different purpose from sidestepping the general rules, which is to set an absolute limitation on environmental damage.[24] Similarly, Bothe states that the special environmental protection rules in Protocol I are not intended to lower, but rather to complement, the general protection in the law of armed conflict.[25] In addition, in the *Nuclear Weapons* Advisory Opinion, the International Court of Justice stated that environmental considerations must be taken into account in the assessment of what is considered as necessary and proportionate when pursuing legitimate military objectives.[26] Such an assessment is exclusively made in relation to civilians and civilian objects. This indicates that the Court does not regard Articles 35(3) and 55 of Protocol I as preventing the general rules from applying for the purpose of protecting the environment.

The Review Committee Report for the ICTY Prosecutor further shows that the special protection in Articles 35(3) and 55 would not prevent the general rules of protection provided in the Protocol or in customary law applying to environmental damage.[27] The report concluded that the damage during the NATO bombings did not reach the thresholds of Articles 35(3) and 55(1) of Protocol I, and continued to address the damage based on the general principles of law of armed conflict.[28] In addition, Rule 43 in the 2005 Customary Law Study seems to solve the issue by explicitly stating in its chapeau that, 'The general principles on the conduct of hostilities apply to the natural environment'. Also, the International Law Commission has provisionally adopted Draft Principles 13, 14 and 15 that confirm that the rules of general protection apply to the environment.[29] In sum, there are strong indications that the general protection rules apply to the environment as a civilian object, regardless of the existence of Articles 35(3) and 55 of Protocol I.

III. TURNING THE ENVIRONMENT INTO A MILITARY TARGET

This section examines how the environment and its parts can turn into military objectives, as defined in Article 52(2) of Protocol I.[30] The possibility for the environment to be considered as a military objective is the first limitation of protection provided under the general rules.

[24] Droege and Tougas (n 1) 27. This view has support from other scholars, such as Hulme, 'Natural Environment' (n 18) 204.

[25] M Bothe, 'The Protection of the Environment in Times of Armed Conflict: Legal Rules, Uncertainty, Deficiencies and Possible Developments' (1991) 34 *German Yearbook of International Law* 54.

[26] *Legality of the Threat or Use of Nuclear Weapons* (n 15) para 30.

[27] Final Report to the Prosecutor (n 15).

[28] ibid.

[29] International Law Commission, Protection of the Environment, First Reading (n 6).

[30] Bothe et al (n 1) 576.

According to Article 52(2) of Protocol I, the causal link between the military advantage and the attack must be clearly established. This means that an attack must be directed towards the war fighting capabilities of the enemy to give such a 'direct military advantage'. Using such reasoning, attacks on the natural resources contributing to financing the war would not have the required causal link and would therefore not be considered legal under the provisions of the law of armed conflict.[31] Because of the required causal link, Droege and Tougas state that the environment cannot *easily* turn into a military target. They argue that it would be difficult to see how environmental components such as the air, the ozone layer, or underground water resources could make an effective military contribution and offer a military advantage if subjected to an attack.[32] However, although it is correct that these environmental components would not in most cases be a primary target for an attack, they would still be at risk as collateral damage when other parts of the environment turn into military objectives and are under attack. For instance, if a forest used as a hiding place for the enemy is set on fire, such an attack would most likely also cause air pollution from the smoke, the destruction of the forest may have adverse effects on the ozone layer, and pollutants mobilised from the fire may enter and pollute the underground water. Thus, environmental components – such as the air, ozone layer, soil, and underground resources – cannot be separated from the parts of the environment that constitute military objectives.

Environmental damage is complex and no part of the environment can be attacked in isolation; environmental components are interconnected in ecosystems that are connected to other ecosystems, damage to one part of the environment will affect other parts as well. In addition, loss of biodiversity and environmental degradation can have unforeseeable damage, for instance in combination with climate change. Furthermore, the boundaries of the parts of the environment that are considered as military targets are difficult to appreciate. Thus, even if it is only a certain part of the environment that represents a military target, an attack on that part can still have adverse indirect impacts on other parts. It might not be possible to fully distinguish where the line of the civilian part of the environment is to be drawn.

Moreover, regardless of which part of the environment is considered, it may turn into a military target if it is contributing to military operations and the contribution can be prevented by attacking it. For instance, if enemy troops enter a forest to seek cover, parts of the forest become a military objective. This would be the case even if it concerns a protected national park or an area inhabiting endangered species.[33] Consequently, even if the environment is civilian in its nature, parts of it can become a military target when an attack on it offers a

[31] Droege and Tougas (n 1) 28–29.

[32] ibid, 28.

[33] Bothe et al make a similar conclusion suggesting that sensitive areas need to be immune against attacks. See Bothe et al (n 1) 577.

military advantage.[34] However, the inclusion of Draft Principle 13(1) adopted by the International Law Commission, serves as a reminder that warring parties are still under the obligation to respect and protect the environment.

IV. UNDERSTANDING THE ATTACKER

The environment and its parts can be lawfully attacked under certain conditions, even when remaining civilian. As restated in Rule 43B in the 2005 Customary Law Study, the environment is protected from destruction as a civilian object, unless it is required by imperative military necessity. The rule of military necessity has its origins in Article 23(g) of the Hague Regulations, which prohibits wanton destruction of civilian property.[35] It bans acts that are excessively destructive or harmful to secure a military advantage. Thus, there must be a sufficient link between the destruction of the object and the needs of the military operations.[36]

The 2005 Customary Law Study reproduces the original Article 23(g) in Rule 50 that expressly applies to 'civilian property', while Rule 43B has reformulated the article to expressly apply to the 'environment'. Rule 43B suggests an approach that views the environment as a category of a need for special protection. At the same time, certain parts of the environment may still be regarded as property – for instance, cattle, crops, trees, etc – and fall under the application of Rule 50 as well.[37]

Moreover, it may be difficult to determine when parts of the environment are destroyed with reference to military necessity. This is because it requires an understanding of the attacker's subjective intention and knowledge of the military advantage anticipated as an outcome of the operation. As Schmitt points out with regard to the 1991 Gulf War, if Iraq set the oil wells on fire with the intention to create smoke and aggravate the sight of the Iraqi targets for the coalition's aircraft (the enemy), then such actions may have been lawful based on military necessity. The defence of military necessity depends on the context and could apply to any objects that are not inherently military in nature, such as the environment.[38] Thus, it is difficult to determine when the environment has lawfully been attacked with reference to pressing military concerns. Even though there are boundaries on how far such speculations can be taken, the rule

[34] M Schmitt, 'War and the Environment: Fault Lines in the Prescriptive Landscape' in JE Austin and CE Bruch, (eds), *The Environmental Consequences of War* (Cambridge University Press, 2000) 112–13.

[35] Article 23(g) of the Hague Regulations: 'Destruction or seizure of the enemy's property unless imperatively demanded by the necessities of war'.

[36] Hulme, 'Natural Environment' (n 18) 213.

[37] ibid.

[38] Schmitt, 'War and the Environment' (n 34) 112–13.

of military necessity contains an uncertainty with regard to the environment and its contribution and use in military operations.[39]

V. PROPORTIONALITY TEST

This section examines how environmental considerations could be balanced against military advantage when applying the principle of proportionality. The proportionality principle, as codified in Article 51(5)(b) of Protocol I, protects civilians and civilian objects from the excessive collateral damage of an attack directed at a lawful military target.[40] It permits collateral damage, including damage to the environment, as long as it is not excessive compared with the direct military advantage anticipated. I will assess the level of environmental considerations that can be expected by a reasonable decision maker (law-applier), usually a military commander, in accordance with the principle before launching a lawful military attack.

The standard prescribed by the principle is 'excessive' in comparison to the military advantage. Such a standard is not fixed. In other words, the protection is not absolute, but subject to a balancing test.[41] A direct military advantage is a result that weakens the enemy's military power. In contrast, an indirect military advantage, such as weakening the civilian population's fighting spirit, cannot be considered in the balancing test under the proportionality principle. Furthermore, the lawfulness of an attack is based on the information known at the time of the attack, irrespective of the actual consequences.[42] What a commander had reason to believe regarding the consequences of an attack, based on the known information, determines whether the requirements under the proportionality principle were fulfilled.

When applying the proportionality principle to the environment, I will address three issues. First, the problem of introducing environmental considerations into the test of balancing humanitarian needs and military necessity. Second, the specific problem with foreseeability in relation to complex environmental damage, as discussed earlier. It may not be possible to establish certain environmental consequences prior to an attack. Third, the discretionary power that the proportionality principle provides to the law-applier. This means that, to a certain extent, the principle can be applied in accordance with the law-applier's personal preferences rather than legal requirements.

[39] ibid, 112.

[40] The principle of proportionality is also included in the 2005 Customary Law Study in Rule 14, and applies both in international and non-international armed conflicts. See Henckaerts and Doswald-Beck, *Customary International Humanitarian Law*, Volume I: Rules (n 2) 46–50.

[41] Bothe et al (n 1) 577.

[42] M Schmitt, 'Green War: An Assessment of the Environmental Law of International Armed Conflict' (1997) 22 *Yale Journal of International Law* 1, 55.

First, it has been established that environmental concerns should be taken into account in the application of the proportionality principle. For instance, the International Law Commission adopted a draft principle confirming that environmental considerations should play a role when assessing proportionality and necessity in relation to military targets.[43] The draft principle was based mainly on a statement made by the International Court of Justice in the *Nuclear Weapons* Advisory Opinion.[44] The introduction of environmental considerations in the proportionality test complicates the balancing act by adding another interest to the calculation.[45] The environment is, however, a valid and recognised object protected under the law of armed conflict. In addition, it is mainly protected for the sake of the population and public health. Thus, an operation should be thoroughly planned and executed to avoid damage that is excessive to the environment and human health compared with the military advantage.[46]

Nonetheless, environmental concerns may be awkward to balance against human life or human suffering,[47] in particular, given that there appears to be little guidance on how it should be conducted within the framework of the law of armed conflict. As mentioned in section II, the proportionality principle is codified specifically in relation to the environment in Rule 43C in the 2005 Customary Law Study. This rule is formulated in a manner that views environmental damage occurring in isolation from other war-related damage. In reality, most environmental destruction would take place together with other collateral damage. Neither the Study nor its Commentary provide any answer on how to deal with the environmental damage in relation to the death of civilians or other type of collateral damage.[48] As noted by the Review Committee for the ICTY Prosecutor, the proportionality principle is difficult to apply because it involves comparing different quantities and interests.[49] The proportionality test also depends on the context and its contemporary setting, since interests change over time along with the development of prevailing societal values.[50]

Second, while dealing with a highly complex issue such as environment damage, it might be challenging for a military commander deciding on an attack to determine the foreseeable environmental effects. The proportionality principle provides that the expected damage is assessed based on the known risk at the

[43] Draft principle 15 [II-3, 11], International Law Commission, Protection of the Environment First Reading (n 6).

[44] *Legality of the Threat or Use of Nuclear Weapons* (n 15) para 30.

[45] Schmitt, 'Green War' (n 42) 55.

[46] The key to environmental risk management is balancing environmental protection with mission objectives. Joint NATO Doctrine for Environmental Protection During NATO-led Military Activities (STANAG 7141/AJEPP-4).

[47] Schmitt, 'Green War' (n 42) 59.

[48] Hulme, 'Natural Environment' (n 18) 216.

[49] Final Report to the Prosecutor (n 15) para 48.

[50] Schmitt, 'Green War' (n 42) 57.

time when the attack is planned or launched. This means that at a tactical level, a commander needs to take into account the information that is *reasonably* available to a person in such position.[51] In the case of an attack on an oil refinery or other facility that releases toxic substances, data on the surroundings is required to be able to determine the environmental consequences. For instance, knowledge about a nearby aquifer or protected area can lead to the conclusion that the attack could result in poisoning an underground aquifer that provides ground water for the local population or could threaten endangered species and/or sensitive ecosystems.

The question is, however, what level of knowledge of the surrounding environment, as well as of the environmental impacts of various toxins, is it reasonable for a commander to have prior to an attack in order to comply with the proportionality principle? Scientific discoveries on how the environment is affected by different acts are constantly made, which makes the notion of environmental damage subject to an evolutionary interpretation, as discussed in chapter three. For instance, environmental consciousness has increased over the last 50 years, and is related to the increased knowledge of the environment and how it is globally interconnected. Acts that were tolerated as collateral environmental damage decades or just several years ago may be seen as unacceptable nowadays.[52] Also, the fact that the absolute non-derogable human right to life is increasingly recognised as being interconnected with a healthy environment is adding to this view.[53] Therefore, the demand of the level of information, as well as the environmental risks, that a reasonable commander should obtain prior to an attack are difficult to establish.[54]

In addition, as unforeseeable risks and scientific insecurity are intertwined with environmental problems, serious and irreversible environmental damage may not be evident at first sight; it might not be revealed until years after an incident has occurred. The question is what a commander should have known in these cases. The reasonable level of knowledge may become higher alongside the increasing scientific knowledge of the environment. However, according to the standard provided under the law of armed conflict, a commander is probably

[51] Droege and Tougas (n 1) 34–35.

[52] Desgagné (n 10) 116.

[53] See, for instance, Special Rapporteur M Lehto, First Report on the Protection of the Environment in Relation to Armed Conflicts, UN Doc A/CN.4/720, 30 April 2018, paras 4 and 50; Special Rapporteur M Lehto, Second Report on the Protection of the Environment in Relation to Armed Conflicts, UN Doc A/CN.4/728, 27 March 2019, para 195. See also how the relationship between human rights and environmental protection is affirmed in the Inter-American Court of Human Rights, Advisory Opinion No OC 23-17, *Medio Ambiente y Derechos Humanos* [The environment and human rights], 15 November 2017, Series A, No 23. Furthermore, see the established link between biodiversity and human health in World Health Organization, 'Our Planet, Our Health, Our Future: Human Health and the Rio Conventions: Biological Diversity, Climate Change and Desertification' Discussion Paper (2012) 2, available at: www.who.int/globalchange/publications/reports/health_rioconventions.pdf.

[54] Bothe et al (n 1) 578.

not required to obtain special knowledge of the local environment or of the scientific risks of the intended action. This follows from a reading of the law of armed conflict that operates based on the known information. The proportionality rule is formulated in a manner where a commander is not obligated to take into account unforeseeable damage or assess scientific uncertainty in a balancing test. In fact, the uncertainty of the effects on the environment during military operations could instead be turned into a defence to justify the action with regard to proportionality.[55] The Commentaries to Draft Principle 14 suggest, however, that 'environmental considerations cannot remain static over time. They should develop as human understanding of the environment develops'.[56]

Third, the proportionality principle is a balancing test that leaves a wide discretionary power to the law-applier to weigh different interests against each other. According to the comments made in the Review Committee Report for the ICTY Prosecutor, as long as a substantial military advantage can be shown, attacks causing grave environmental harm are lawful.[57] On the other hand, the Review Committee Report for the ICTY Prosecutor investigated environmental damage that corresponded to a standard for the purposes of the prosecution of war crimes of individuals, rather than establishing a standard for state responsibility. The Report partly studied the standard as incorporated in Article 8(b)(iv) of the 1998 Rome Statute for environmental war crimes. This crime includes a threshold of 'widespread, long-term and severe' damage in combination with such damage that is 'clearly excessive' in relation to the military advantage, which raises the required damage level even higher.[58] As the proportionality principle allows a large measure of discretion for the law-applier, usually the military commanders or the military forces, an important military advantage will typically outweigh serious collateral damage to the environment.[59] Thus, as Hulme points out, the proportionality principle when applied to the environment prohibits very little.[60]

The Review Committee Report for the ICTY Prosecutor notes that, 'the notion of "excessive" environmental destruction is imprecise and the actual environmental impact, both present and long term, of the NATO bombing campaign is at present unknown and difficult to measure'.[61] Hence, as the proportionality principle opens up a certain amount of discretion for the law-applier, it will most likely be used in a manner that puts the needs of the military operations before the environmental concerns. The standard used to establish

[55] Schmitt, 'War and the Environment' (n 34) 112–13.

[56] Report of the International Law Commission, 68th Session (2 May–10 June and 4 July–12 August) (2016) *Yearbook of the International Law Commission*, Volume II, Part Two, 336.

[57] Final Report to the Prosecutor (n 15) para 22.

[58] ibid.

[59] Hulme, 'Natural Environment' (n 18) 215–16.

[60] ibid, 216.

[61] Final Report to the Prosecutor (n 15) para 23.

this balancing exercise is that of the 'reasonable commander', although such a standard will be of a flexible kind.[62]

The Review Committee for the ICTY Prosecutor comments that the principle may be applied differently depending on the decision-maker. A human rights lawyer and a qualified military commander may not assign the same relative value to military advantage and harm to civilians. In addition, military commanders with different doctrinal backgrounds and experience or different national military historical records may not always come to the same conclusions in similar cases.[63] This means that such a test will be subject to a certain level of unpredictability and inconsistency, because of the context-based decisions of whoever compares the interests at stake. The standard and requirement of the application of the principle may vary depending on the resources of the performer.

This is further complicated by the fact that the view of the environment may also differ, for instance, between different societies and cultures. Much of the application of the principles will depend on the discretion of the decision-maker; this is a further incentive to leave less room for such discretion. Therefore, the proportionality principle needs to be strengthened to narrow the gap for biased decision-making, as it probably cannot be completely closed. The balancing test could be made tighter by permitting legal requirements in international environmental law to inform the application of the principle and by allowing the legal requirements to influence the assessment.

According to Droege and Tougas, there is a trend to include more distant environmental damage in the proportionality assessment during warfare.[64] An example could be that if an electricity network is targeted, risks that may be considered in the assessment could involve disruptions of sewage or waste management that would harm the quality of the water and soil as a result of the attack. The close causality between such an attack and the resultant harm would justify such a damage calculation.[65] The Joint NATO Doctrine for Environmental Protection During NATO-Led Military Activities illustrated the tendencies to consider distant environmental damage. As the Joint NATO Doctrine stipulates, commanders must know how NATO-led activities affect the environment, and environmental planning must be performed.[66] The Joint NATO Doctrine does not provide more tangible guidance on how this will be achieved. It only states that environmental risks are to be balanced against mission objectives.

In practice, certain precautions are undertaken to prevent accidents within the military. For instance, in NATO's 1993 Operation Deny Flight to enforce

[62] ibid.

[63] ibid.

[64] Droege and Tougas (n 1).

[65] Joint NATO Doctrine for Environmental Protection During NATO-led Military Activities (n 46).

[66] ibid. See also Droege and Tougas (n 1) 30.

a UN no-fly zone over Bosnia and Herzegovina, as well in the joint operation Provide Promise of the United States in former Yugoslavia in 1992, precautions were taken to transport arms and munitions that were considered hazardous. Accidents had to be prevented and installations where the materials were stored had to be kept safe. All these were factors were considered in the planning of operations as precautionary measures to control the handling of pollutants.[67] In addition, the UN has an extensive claims programme and has regularly paid claims for damages caused during its operations caused by negligence or improper acts by the UN.[68] These range from typical motor vehicle accidents to damage that includes environmental damage, for instance to farmland.

To sum up, there are three issues with regard to environmental matters when applying the proportionality principle. First, an important military advantage may legally outweigh serious collateral damage to the environment because environmental considerations have not been properly accommodated in the proportionality assessment.[69] The environment may be considered less important in times of war in comparison to military necessity and humanitarian distress. Second, only the foreseeable damage based on the information that can be reasonably available for a commander at the time of the attack is relevant when deciding on launching a lawful attack. To ensure adequate protection of the environment, it is probably necessary to introduce unforeseeable risks into the proportionality test.[70] The problem is to determine when unforeseeable risks are 'excessive' in the sense required by the proportionality principle, in particular, since the extent of the damage cannot always be fully established. Third, the environment is dependent on how it is valued by the law-applier to some extent. The proportionality principle is a flexible and context-based principle. Thus, it is unable to provide stable environmental protection.

VI. CALCULATING THE UNKNOWN: THE PRINCIPLE OF PRECAUTION VERSUS THE PRECAUTIONARY APPROACH

Closely related to the proportionality principle is the principle of precaution. It obligates belligerents prior to an attack to take 'constant care' and adopt precautionary measures to avoid or minimise the adverse effects on civilians and civilian objects to the furthest extent possible. The principle functions in a context-based scenario by requiring measures of precaution in line with 'everything feasible', 'all feasible precautions', 'unless circumstances do not permit', 'may be expected' and 'becomes apparent'. This means that the standard must

[67] J Burger, 'Environmental Aspects of Non-International Conflicts: The Experience in Former Yugoslavia' in R Grunawalt, J King and R McClain (eds), *Protection of the Environment During Armed Conflict* (1996) 69 *International Law Studies* 333, 342.

[68] ibid.

[69] Hulme, 'Natural Environment' (n 18) 215–16.

[70] Bothe et al (n 1) 578.

be applied in a manner establishing what a reasonable commander in a similar position would do in his capacity in similar situations, like in the case of the proportionality principle. The information available to those planning or conducting an attack determines if an action or a result can be considered as feasible or reasonably expected. The level of precaution can vary and belligerents have different legal burdens of precaution given by the information, equipment and ability that they have at a certain time and place.[71]

The principle of precaution is codified in Articles 57 and 58 of Protocol I. Article 57 contains the obligations of the attacker concerning the verification of the exact nature of an object exposed to an attack to ensure it is a military objective, and to undertake feasible measures to minimise and avoid civilian casualties. Article 58 relates to the precautions required by the attacked party to minimise the civilian loss of an attack, including removing civilians from the vicinity of military installations and avoiding placing such installations in populated areas.

Rule 44 in the 2005 Customary Law Study is based, to some extent, on Articles 57 and 58. It requires of parties of armed conflicts that 'all feasible precautions must be taken to avoid, and in any event to minimise, incidental damage to the environment'.[72] Rule 44 also requires parties of armed conflicts to take 'due regard' of the environment, which is mainly based on the duty to take care of the environment in Article 55(1) of Protocol I, as discussed in chapter four. In addition, the last sentence of the rules states that, 'Lack of scientific certainty as to the effects on the environment of certain military operations does not absolve a party to the conflict from taking such precautions'. This formulation is based on the 'precautionary principle' or the 'precautionary approach' in international environmental law.[73] Rule 44 in the 2005 Customary Law Study states that lack of scientific certainty of military operations cannot excuse parties for not taking proper precautionary measures to prevent undue damage with regard to the environment.[74]

To avoid confusion, I use the term 'precautionary approach' when referring to the obligation to take precaution, as formulated in international environmental law, and 'principle of precaution' when referring to the principle, as articulated under the law of armed conflict. The International Committee of the Red Cross (ICRC) refers to Principle 15 in the Rio Declaration in the Commentary to the Study to provide a basis for including Rule 44 referring to 'lack of scientific

[71] Y Sandoz, C Swinarski and B Zimmerman (eds), *Commentary on the Additional Protocols of 8 June 1977* (ICRC, Geneva, 1987).

[72] Rule 44. Henckaerts and Doswald-Beck, *Customary International Humanitarian Law*, Volume I: Rules (n 2). See also Droege and Tougas (n 1) 34.

[73] The precautionary principle is often referred to as the precautionary approach in international environmental law, indicating a less restricted use of it. See P Birnie, A Boyle and C Redgwell, *International Law & the Environment* (Oxford University Press, 2009) 155.

[74] Henckaerts and Doswald-Beck, *Customary International Humanitarian Law*, Volume I: Rules (n 2) 150.

certainty'. The choice of codifying the precautionary approach in the Study could be seen as a way to acknowledge the particular nature of the environment and environmental damage. It addresses the uncertainty of how the environment is affected by warfare and the difficulty of repairing environmental damage. The precautionary approach in international environmental law is rooted in the fact that environmental risks are often vague and difficult to prove scientifically.[75] The approach is therefore created to address this complexity and to prevent potential environmental destruction.[76] It encompasses the obligation that when facing risks that are scientifically uncertain, this uncertainty cannot be used as a reason to proceed with the activity involving such potential risks. As a result, the precautionary approach lowers the burden of establishing a causal link between an action (an attack) and environmental damage.[77]

Precautionary measures undertaken in accordance with Article 57 of Protocol I (principle of precaution) are based on *foreseeable* risks given the information at the time of planning or conducting an attack. In comparison, precautionary measures according to the precautionary approach are based on the risks that may be *unforeseeable* at the time of the attack. According to the principle of precaution, under the law of armed conflict, the known information appears to be the determining factor on which precautionary measures should be undertaken. Such an interpretation excludes that precautions are carried out based on scientific uncertainty.[78] In a conflict scenario, scientific certainty of the environmental effects prior to an attack would be rare because conflict scenarios are often characterised by fast decision-making and insufficient knowledge on the other party's territory and capacity. Furthermore, it is unclear how a commander could know what precautions to take if there is no scientific certainty as to the effects on the environment.[79]

The inclusion of the precautionary approach in Rule 44 of the 2005 Customary Law Study is controversial as it sets a different standard from the principle of precaution in the law of armed conflict rules. The ICRC's inclusion of this formulation in Rule 44 may be regarded as an attempt to move the law of armed conflict closer to international environmental law. Thus, the protection of the environment provided under the law of armed conflict could be improved by allowing an assessment that considers the unknown risks in relation to military conduct. Such an assessment reflects the approach of international environmental law on how to safeguard the environment.

The ICRC states in its Commentary that: 'The precautionary [approach] in environmental law has been gaining increasing recognition. There is, furthermore, practice to the effect that this environmental law principle applies to

[75] See Birnie, Boyle and Redgwell (n 73) 155.
[76] Hulme, 'Natural Environment' (n 18) 225.
[77] Bothe et al (n 1) 578.
[78] ibid.
[79] Hulme, 'Natural Environment' (n 18) 222.

armed conflict'.[80] However, the statement is supported by scarce practice in the Commentary. This includes: (1) environmental law treaties and non-binding declarations; (2) state comments submitted to the International Court of Justice in relation to the 1995 *Nuclear Test* case and the 1996 *Nuclear Weapons* Advisory Opinion; and (3) a statement in relation to ICRC's own report on the protection of the environment in times of armed conflict presented in 1993 to the UN General Assembly. Little of this practice can establish that the use of the precautionary approach during armed conflicts is a part of customary law.

Regarding the first type of practice, the Commentary states that the precautionary approach, as formulated in international environmental law, has gained recognition in international law. In this regard, it refers to both environmental treaties and non-binding environmental declarations as evidence.[81] Hulme is critical that these instruments are able to demonstrate that the precautionary approach has attained customary law status in international law, because its status is controversial in environmental law.[82] On the other hand, other commentators are of the view that the precautionary approach, as formulated in the Rio Declaration has received sufficient support to be recognised as a customary law principle.[83] Because of the lack of consensus on this matter, it is unclear whether the precautionary approach can be considered as customary law based on the environmental instruments as referred to in the Commentary. Thus, these instruments are unable to demonstrate the customary law status of the precautionary approach during armed conflicts.

The second type of practice that the Commentary refers to is the *Nuclear Tests* case because of the central role of the precautionary approach in the case, as New Zealand based it arguments on it. However, France, the respondent state, challenged the status of the precautionary approach as having customary law status.[84] The Court never confirmed the status. Nevertheless, the Commentary refers to this case to support the argument that the precautionary approach does have customary law status.[85] However, in his dissenting opinion, Judge Weeramantry did advocate that the precautionary approach has growing support to become a part of the international law of the environment.[86] The Commentary

[80] Henckaerts and Doswald-Beck, *Customary International Humanitarian Law*, Volume I: Rules (n 2) 150.

[81] ibid.

[82] Hulme, 'Natural Environment' (n 18) 225–28.

[83] P Sands et al, *Principles of International Environmental Law*, 4th edn (Cambridge University Press, 2018) 239–40.

[84] *Request for an Examination of the Situation in Accordance with Paragraph 63 of the Court's Judgment of 20 December 1974 in the Nuclear Tests (New Zealand v France) Case*, Order of 22 September 1995, ICJ Reports 1995, 288.

[85] Henckaerts and Doswald-Beck, *Customary International Humanitarian Law*, Volume I: Rules (n 2) 150.

[86] *Request for an Examination of the Situation in Accordance with Paragraph 63 of the Court's Judgment of 20 December 1974 in the Nuclear Tests (New Zealand v France) Case*, Order of 22 September 1995, ICJ Reports 1995, Dissenting Opinion of Judge Weeramantry, C, 342. See Hulme, 'Natural Environment' (n 18) 223–24.

also refers to the *Nuclear Weapons* Advisory Opinion, in which the Court states that the basic environmental principles it has recognised also apply to the actual use of nuclear weapons in armed conflicts.[87] However, the Court did not affirm the status of the precautionary approach. Thus, the reference to the case does not support that the precautionary approach has customary law status.

The third type of practice that the 2005 Customary Law Study supported the rule with was the 1993 Report of the ICRC itself, in which it was suggested that the precautionary approach was, at the time, an emerging principle of international law.[88] The 1993 report was submitted to the General Assembly, in which, during the discussions, no state contested the assertion to refer to the precautionary approach as an emerging principle of international law.[89] As noted by Hulme, it is difficult to attach any significant weight to the absence of contesting a report, in particular given that the report did not propose any binding rules, which may also be the reason why states did not contest it.[90]

Moreover, no references are made to military manuals of states to support the environmental precautionary approach as being part of the customary law of armed conflict. Overall, the practice supporting the reference to the precautionary approach in the Study is rather limited. Therefore, to declare a principle of environmental law to be applicable as customary law during armed conflicts without convincing practice must be regarded with some scepticism.[91] In addition, the International Law Commission did not adopt any draft principle with a similar content, at least not up until the first reading (2019), which indicates further the absence of customary law status. Similarly, Article 40 of the International Union for Conservation of Nature and Natural Resources (IUCN) Draft Covenant does not include any reference to the precautionary approach either.

Bothe agrees that state practice supporting the rule is 'somewhat scarce'. However, the Study recognises – correctly according to Bothe – that the general development of the precautionary approach in environmental law cannot be ignored within the law of armed conflict. He argues that the inclusion of the precautionary approach in the rules of the Study is based on legal reasoning, rather than state practice. Such legal reasoning is based on the structure of international law as one system – because of its fragmented nature, international law needs to include the requirements of different areas of international law to give them meaning.[92] Bothe describes it as:

> The development of customary law which has been described can be explained as a recognition of, and, adherence to common values … respect for the interest of future

[87] Henckaerts and Doswald-Beck, *Customary International Humanitarian Law*, Volume I: Rules (n 2) 150. See also *Legality of the Threat or Use of Nuclear Weapons* (n 15) para 32.

[88] J-M Henckaerts and L Doswald-Beck (eds), *Customary International Humanitarian Law Study*, Volume II: Practice (Cambridge University Press, 2012) 876.

[89] ibid, 150.

[90] Hulme, 'Natural Environment' (n 18) 223–24.

[91] Hulme, 'Taking Care to Protect' (n 1) 686.

[92] M Bothe, 'Customary International Humanitarian Law: Some Reflections on the ICRC Study' (2005) 8 *Yearbook of International Humanitarian Law* 143, 167.

> generations through an enhanced protection of the environment in times of armed conflict – is a part of the recognition and realization of common values. They are documented in the 2005 Customary Law Study and the study strengthens them.[93]

Consequently, the inclusion of the precautionary approach into the 2005 Customary Law Study is an important step forward. It shows that the law of armed conflict can be interpreted in the light of international environmental law, and that the legal requirements of this legal field can influence the application of the rules of the law of armed conflict. It also shows that there are tendencies within the law of armed conflict that acknowledge the special character of the environment and how environmental damage could be assessed. Thus, the uncertainty of environmental impacts and the growing scientific knowledge of these are demonstrated to play a potential role in the application of the law of armed conflict in relation to the environment. Even if the reference to the precautionary approach may not reflect it as the precautionary approach is incorporated in international environmental law, it indicates the general notion of precaution in warfare towards the environment.[94] It could be an obligation for states to carry out assessments of potential outcomes and effects of military operation on the environment and undertake feasible precautionary measures based on the result in order to protect common values protected by other international law, such as the interests of future generations.[95] This view is also supported by the inclusion of Article 40(1)(b) in the IUCN Draft Covenant that requires states to 'take all reasonable measures to protect the environment against avoidable harm in areas of armed conflict'. Although this provision is based on Principle 5 in the World Charter for Nature requiring nature to be 'secured against the degradation caused by warfare or other hostile activities' and that 'military activities damaging to nature are to be avoided' according to the IUCN Draft Covenant Commentary rather than the precautionary approach.[96]

VII. 'GREENING' THE MARTENS CLAUSE

This section looks at how the Martens Clause can be used to incorporate rules of other fields of international law into the law of armed conflict to enhance environmental protection.

The Martens Clause, also referred to as the humanity principle, is generally considered to have customary law status. The Martens Clause was first incorporated in the Preamble to the 1907 Hague Convention IV[97] and named

[93] ibid, 178.
[94] Hulme, 'Natural Environment' (n 18).
[95] ibid, 227–28.
[96] IUCN, 'Draft International Covenant on Environment and Development – Implementing Sustainability' 5th edn, IUCN Environmental Policy and Law Paper No 31 Rev 4 (IUCN, Gland) 121.
[97] It reads: 'Until a more complete code of the laws of war has been issued, the High Contracting Parties deem it expedient to declare that, in cases not included in the Regulations adopted by them,

after its creator, Professor Friedrich von Martens, the Russian delegate at The Hague Peace Conferences. The purpose of including the Clause was to ensure that even if there were no expressed rules prohibiting a certain conduct, it could still be prohibited with the reference to standards of 'humanity' and 'public conscience'.[98] Thus, the Martens Clause broadens the range of applicable rules governing warfare beyond those that are expressly laid out in the treaties. The Martens Clause has been incorporated into many instruments since then.[99] In Protocol I, an updated version reads: 'Civilians and combatants remain under the protection and authority of the principles of international law derived from established custom, from the principles of humanity and from the dictates of public conscience'.[100]

The legal implications of the Martens Clause are, however, complex and unsettled.[101] The Commentary to the Protocols states that the Clause has a dynamic element enabling interpretations by taking new developments and technology into account.[102] In the *Nuclear Weapons* Advisory Opinion, the International Court of Justice recognised that the Clause provides the basis for an evolutionary interpretation of existing rules.[103] In essence, the Clause is intended to fill potential gaps in the existing law of armed conflict, by stipulating that states should respect a minimum standard of 'humanity' and 'public conscience'.[104] Implicitly, this principle refers to both military necessity and proportionality calculations, but it prohibits, in particular, acts that

the inhabitants and the belligerents remain under the protection and the rule of the principles of the law of nations, as they result from the usages established among civilized peoples, from the laws of humanity, and the dictates of the public conscience'.

[98] C Greenwood, 'Historical Developments and Legal Basis' in D Fleck (ed), *The Handbook of International Humanitarian Law* (Oxford University Press, 2008), 34.

[99] Article 63 Geneva Convention I; Article 62 Geneva Convention II; Article 142 Geneva Convention III; Article 158 Geneva Convention IV; Preamble, para 4 of Protocol II; and Preamble, para 5 Convention on Certain Conventional Weapons.

[100] Article 1(2) Protocol I.

[101] Cassese has even referred to it as a 'legal myth' of the international community, because of its multiplicity of often conflicting interpretations and frequent use by national and international courts, as well as states, and many invocations by organisations and individuals. See A Cassese, 'The Martens Clause: Half a Loaf or Simply Pie in the Sky?' (2000) 11 *European Journal of International Law* 187.

[102] Sandoz, Swinarski and Zimmerman (n 71) 39.

[103] With regard to the applicability of the Martens Clause to nuclear weapons, the International Court of Justice referred to the Clause as being 'proved to be an effective means of addressing the rapid evolution of military technology'. See *Legality of the Threat or Use of Nuclear Weapons* (n 15) para 78. Dam-de Jong and Desgagné describe the Court's use of the Clause as a way to justify an evolutionary interpretation of the law of armed conflict principles of distinction and necessity in the light of new technologies. See DA Dam-de Jong, *International Law and Governance of Natural Resources in Conflict and Post-Conflict Situations* (EM Meijers Instituut, 2013) 244; Desgagné (n 10) 114.

[104] UNEP, 'Protecting the Environment During Armed Conflict: An Inventory and Analysis of International Law' (UNEP, Switzerland, 2009) 12.

'civilised people' are not supposed to undertake, like acts that cause unnecessary suffering.[105] Consequently, the Martens Clause limits the selection of methods, weaponry and targets by prohibiting acts that are inhumane or otherwise not accepted by the general opinion of actors in the international arena.

The Clause has been of use in ensuring human protection in cases where a legal void in the law of armed conflict conventions has been claimed.[106] Meron notes that the Martens Clause is reinforcing a tendency to base customary law on *opinio juris*, rather than actual practice on the battlefield. He states that:

> It serves as a powerful vehicle for governments and especially [non-governmental organisations] to push the law ever more to reflect human rights concerns. Where there already is some legal basis for adopting a more humanitarian position, the Martens clause enables decision makers to take the extra step forward.[107]

Meron also claims that the principles of humanity and dictates of public conscience are restraining factors on the freedom of states to do what is not explicitly prohibited according to the treaty-based law and customary law of the law of armed conflict.[108] However, Meron adds that the Clause has limits and that it alone cannot prohibit certain weapons or methods of warfare based on references to principles of humanity and dictates of public conscience. Thus, it is unclear how the Clause operates in practical terms.

It has been suggested that the Martens Clause cannot be a rule prohibiting potential means and methods of warfare because it would be too imprecise to use the standard of 'the public conscience'.[109] However, a large number of the rules in the law of armed conflict are vague and imprecise, such as the proportionality principle in Article 51(5)(b) of Protocol I that uses the standard of 'military advantage'. Nevertheless, the proportionality principle is still influential in regulating warfare and its application as such has never been in dispute. Thus, an imprecise standard in itself cannot be a valid argument for discarding the Martens Clause. Just like the proportionality principle, the Martens Clause is a principle and not a precise rule. Principles have a more dynamic character compared with norms formulated as rules. Even though principles may be abstract and vague, which makes it difficult to agree on specific and concrete

[105] Schmitt, 'Green War' (n 42) 61.

[106] Cassese describes that the Martens Clause was interpreted in this manner by a US Military Tribunal sitting at Nuremberg in the *Krupp* case, Washington: Government Printing Office (1950) 1341. However, Cassese argues that the Tribunal misquoted the Clause and actually never applied it in the case to introduce new sources as these were already applicable in the case. See Cassese (n 101) 204. Dam-de Jong interprets the same case to use the Clause directly to advance the given protection to private property for the sake of the civilians. See Dam-de Jong (n 104) 244.

[107] T Meron, 'The Martens Clause, Principles of Humanity, and Dictates of Public Conscience' (2000) 94 *American Journal of International Law* 78, 88.

[108] ibid.

[109] Greenwood (n 98) 34.

entitlements or obligations derived from them,[110] the abstractness and vagueness of the principles is not a reason to not apply them. As a principle, the Martens Clause can provide a flexible standard, opting for certain considerations to be balanced against each other. Hence, the Martens Clause is as equally applicable as the proportionality principle or the principle of precaution under the law of armed conflict.

The Martens Clause was used by the International Court of Justice in the *Nicaragua* case to validate the applicability of customary law along with treaty law. In this case, the Court referred to the version of the Martens Clause that is incorporated in Article 158 of Geneva Convention IV to conclude that customary law principles of the law of armed conflict still apply, even though the treaties that incorporate the same principles are not applicable.[111] This understanding of the Clause seems to be of less significance today because the majority of the norms of the law of armed conflict are now recognised to have customary law status.[112]

According to some scholars, however, the Martens Clause merely implies that in the absence of treaty rules, customary law applies because it is only a reminder of the application of customary international law.[113] Such a reading would mean that the Martens Clause would not have any significant value within the modern law of armed conflict. However, there is little support for such an interpretation because it seems to be incompatible with the ordinary meaning, as the Clause is expressed in Article 1(2) of Protocol I (and also in the previous versions of the Clause). The absence of treaty rules is not expressly required for application of the Clause. In contrast, the Clause must go beyond the established legal framework of the law of armed conflict, because it refers to 'principles of international law derived from established custom, principles of humanity and from the dictates of public conscience', as formulated in Article 1(2) of Protocol I. It is not clearly established what is intended by this phrase, but it is clear that the Clause entails more than only confirming the applicability of customary law alongside treaty law of the law of armed conflict.

Scobbie claims that the Martens Clause has a 'dynamic function', which gives the law of armed conflict an 'inherent malleability' that could opt for a complementary application of other areas of law – at least human rights law – to the law of armed conflict.[114] Greenwood expresses the view that the Martens Clause could be applied to assess which factors are expected to guide states in determining what types of conduct should be prohibited. The Clause could be of

[110] See the general discussion in Verwey (n 22) 22–23.

[111] See *Military and Paramilitary Activities in and against Nicaragua (Nicaragua v United States of America)* Merits, Judgment of 27 June 1986, ICJ Reports 1986, para 218. See also that Dam-de Jong has a similar conclusion, Dam-de Jong (n 104) 244–45.

[112] Dam-de Jong (n 104) 244–45.

[113] Greenwood (n 98) 34.

[114] I Scobbie, 'Principle or Pragmatics? The Relationship between Human Rights Law and the Law of Armed Conflict' (2009) 14 *Journal of Conflict & Security Law* 449.

relevance when adopting rules of prohibition on a particular weapon or means of warfare.[115] This means that the Martens Clause could push for prohibitions within warfare that have their basis in other rules or principles of international law. The point of the Clause seems to be to provide protection of such principles and dictates, even when the new regulation is not in place.

Furthermore, environmental concerns in general could be regarded as part of the 'dictates of public conscience' of today.[116] The state of the environment has a high impact on the population and its health, and in the past years the threat of climate change has permeated into most areas, such as security, trade, aid and development. Moreover, Cohan argues that environmentally harmful acts – such as poisoning water supplies, dispersing chemical or biological agents to infect a human population or contaminate its crops or livestock, or destroying a population's food source either directly or by blockade – are banned in warfare because of humanity reasons.[117] Additionally, even though the Martens Clause primarily aims at safeguarding respect for humanity, protection of the environment per se could be taken into account as well. The dictates of public conscience could presumably be interpreted as containing an obligation of avoiding environmental damage during military engagements. Such a view is supported by the International Law Commission as a 'green Martens Clause' and has been provisionally adopted at the first reading, which states: 'In cases not covered by international agreements, the environment remains under the protection and authority of the principles of international law derived from established custom, from principles of humanity and from the dictates of public conscience'.[118] This is not the first attempt at 'greening' the Clause; in 2000, the World Conservation Congress called on its Member States to endorse a policy of a green Martens Clause to apply in peacetime as well as in wartime.[119] In addition, the IUCN Draft Covenant included a Martens Clause specifically calling to protect the environment for present as well as future generations.[120]

The green Marten Clause refers to a general contemporary environmental awareness among actors in the international arena and also expressed by

[115] Greenwood (n 98) 34–35.

[116] Desgagné (n 10) 114.

[117] JA Cohan, 'Modes of Warfare and Evolving Standards of Environmental Protection Under the International Law of War' (2003) 15 *Florida Journal of International Law* 481, 495–96.

[118] Draft Principle 12, International Law Commission, Protection of the Environment, First Reading (n 6).

[119] World Conservation Congress Resolution 2.97 entitled 'A Martens Clause for environmental protection' (Amman, 4–11 October 2000).

[120] Article 40(2) of the IUCN Draft Covenant reads: 'The Parties shall cooperate to further develop and implement rules and measures to protect the environment during armed conflicts; until a more complete code of environmental protection has been adopted, in cases not covered by international agreements and regulations, the biosphere and all its constituent elements and processes remain under the protection and authority of the principle of international law derived from established custom, from dictates of the public conscience, and from the principles and fundamental values of humanity acting as steward for present and future generations'.

international environmental law. Such a view would mean that the Martens Clause could be a trigger to inject an evolutionary interpretation of the rules of the law of armed conflict that includes shifting and emerging standards from international environmental law. As the overall perception of the environment within the law of armed conflict lacks firm guidance on how to protect vulnerable environmental areas, aquifers, endangered species, etc, the use of the Martens Clause has the potential to clarify such a protection. Consequently, the application of the Martens Clause can remedy some of the uncertainty and vagueness of its environmental protection by interpreting the rules in the law of armed conflict in accordance with rules and principles as developed within international environmental law.

As mentioned earlier, the emphasis within the law of armed conflict is on military necessity and the direct military advantage, as determined based on the known and foreseeable risks under the principles of proportionality and precaution. Thus, the environmental protection is restricted. However, the Martens Clause may offer a way to interpret these principles in the light of other principles of international law, including those of international environmental law. The interpretation of the law of armed conflict in the light of international environmental law is frequently acknowledged and encouraged. For example, as explained by Verwey, it was stated at the 1991 Ottawa Conference that, 'the application and development of law of armed conflict have to take account of the evolution of environmental concerns generally'.[121]

In this regard, the International Law Commission and ICRC have pushed the law of armed conflict towards international environmental law, since they advocate that the environment needs to be treated differently from other civilian objects. In particular, in Rule 44 in the 2005 Customary Law Study, precaution towards the environment is not solely based on its protection as a civilian object, but also on the particular needs of the environment. The introduction of the requirement of taking precautions to spare the environment in military engagements, despite the lack of scientific certainty, is a major step to incorporating a view of the environment that is much closer to the one within international environmental law. It can be seen as an effort to try to establish a common view of the environment and how it should be cared for under international law. At the same time, it can bridge the fields of the law of armed conflict and international environmental law. However, as mentioned earlier, doubts must be raised as to whether Rule 44 on its own can be considered customary law. Nevertheless, the attempt to include a reference to an environmental principle may be a step towards demonstrating, or at least opting for, an evolutionary interpretation of the law of armed conflict rules.

Moreover, the international environmental law's precautionary approach is closely related to another principle of international environmental law,

[121] Verwey (n 22) 22–23.

namely the principle of prevention.[122] In contrast to the precautionary approach, the principle of prevention is clearly recognised as having customary law status.[123] In relation to the *Pulp Mills* case, the International Court of Justice acknowledged that a state must take specific measures to prevent harm to neighbouring states.[124] The primary distinction between the principle of prevention and the precautionary approach is based on the degree of proof required before establishing an obligation to undertake measures to prevent environmental harm. The principle of prevention focuses on measures based on the knowledge or the ability to foresee environmental harm, while the precautionary approach demands action even without scientific certainty on any harm.[125] If the environmental effects of a particular activity are known, then the measures taken to avoid them are *preventative*; if the effects are unknown, then the same measures would be labelled as *precautionary*.

One could elaborate that the principle of precaution, as formulated under the law of armed conflict, could be reinterpreted by using the standards of 'public conscience', which take into account the principle of prevention as formulated within international environmental law, rather than the precautionary approach because its customary law status is debated. Such an interpretation could imply that the principle of precaution (under the law of armed conflict) imposes obligations on belligerents to undertake certain preventative measures to minimise environmental damage. However, these suggestions have been discussed, to a certain extent, in relation to the principle of precaution, and have also been proposed by other scholars.[126] In concrete terms these may include:

- Gathering information on the environmental surroundings to map out rivers, underground aquifers, sensitive environmental areas, and endangered species that may be threatened by the military activities.
- Seeking information about the quantity, toxicity, and the possibility to avoid leakages, etc, if attacking a target containing toxic substances.

[122] K Hulme, *War Torn Environment: Interpreting the Legal Threshold* (Nijhoff, 2004) 52.

[123] For instance, the International Law Commission incorporated it into Draft Article 3. See Draft Articles on Prevention of Transboundary Harm from Hazardous Activities, Report of the International Law Commission, adopted at the 65th Session (2001) *Yearbook of the International Law Commission*, Volume II, Part Two. It has also been endorsed in the 1972 Stockholm Declaration and the 1982 World Charter. It is included in many international treaties, for instance in Article 194(1) UNCLOS; Article 2 LRTAP Convention; Article 2 Climate Change Convention; and Articles 8(h) and 14(1)(d) Biodiversity Convention.

[124] *Pulp Mills on the River Uruguay (Argentina v Uruguay)*, Judgment of 20 April 2010, ICJ Reports 2010, para 101. See also, Bothe et al (n 1).

[125] Several instruments refer to them as two distinct principles, but in practice it is not so straightforward. This is because the separation of the two concepts is difficult to maintain in operation of the principles. There are references to the precautionary principle in the sense of a preventive and precautionary approach. See A Trouwborst, *Evolution and Status of the Precautionary Principle in International Law* (Kluwer Law International, 2002).

[126] Droege and Tougas (n 1) 34–35. Hulme suggests that an environmental impact assessment can be performed prior to an attack. The examples given are based on her idea on how such an impact assessment could be carried out. See Hulme, *War Torn Environment* (n 122) 82–83.

- Gathering the necessary information about the environmental conditions surrounding specific military operations.
- Determining between choices of military targets that will cause the least danger to the environment.
- Considering the adverse environmental effects of the weaponry arsenal and using available weaponry that reduces the risk of environmental damage.
- Changing the timing of attack if this can contribute to reducing harm to the environment; giving warnings before the attack, if time permits, to allow for measures to safeguard the environment.
- Performing an environmental impact assessment during the planning phase of an attack.

The law of armed conflict's principle of precaution could also impose obligations for the attacked party to take preventative measures. These could involve not making environmentally sensitive areas or areas with endangered species into military objectives or not installing military facilities in such areas.[127] The suggestions would work better with the law of armed conflict because they are based on the same standard of known risks, rather than on elements of scientific uncertainty.

In international environmental law, however, the obligations attached to the principle of prevention are referring to transboundary harms. Therefore, it may be difficult to claim that the principle of precaution, as stated in the law of armed conflict, can be fully translated into the context of a non-international armed conflict with the requirements transferred from the principle of prevention (international environmental law). Furthermore, it may be claimed that the main objective of the Martens Clause is to ensure protection of humans and protect them from unnecessary suffering. Thus, it may follow that the legal requirements for environmental protection can only be introduced when they have a human focus. However, the Martens Clause refers to principles of international law, as well as dictates of public conscience, which, in accordance with its ordinary meaning, must be able to go beyond human suffering. This view is also supported by the provisional adoption of a green Martens Clause by the International Law Commission. In addition, the meaning of human protection may have been altered over time, in accordance with the dictates of public conscience, to include broader aspects such as protecting future generations or providing a healthy environment for the sake of humankind in accordance with the IUCN Draft Covenant.[128]

[127] See Hulme, *War Torn Environment* (n 122) 82–83.

[128] See also Dam-de Jong for a similar conclusion with regard to protecting natural resources. Dam-de Jong (n 104) 248.

VIII. OTHER RULES OF IMPORTANCE

Besides the special environmental rules and the general rules of protection, the environment is indirectly protected under other rules of the law of armed conflict. These include the protection of objects for the civilians' survival, the protection of installations containing dangerous forces, the prohibition of pillage and the protection of cultural property. They provide some additional environmental protection, although it is of limited use because they have the specific aim of protecting other objects and values other than the environment.

A. Objects Indispensable to the Civilian Population

To secure civilians' survival during armed conflicts, certain objects required for their basic needs receive special protection under Article 54 of Protocol I and Article 14 of Protocol II. These provisions forbid the use of starvation of civilians as a method of warfare. The prohibition to attack, destroy, remove, or render these objects useless applies during international as well as non-international armed conflicts. The prohibition also has customary law status.[129] Article 54 of Protocol I is more detailed than Article 14 of Protocol II, but both articles provide a non-exhaustive list of 'objects indispensable to the survival of the civilian population'. The articles list the following objects: 'food-stuffs, agricultural areas for the production of food-stuffs, crops, livestock, drinking water installations and supplies and irrigation works'. As most of these objects are all dependent on a fertile and healthy environment, the articles indirectly protect the environment as well. In a way, they materialise the notion of a human's dependence on the environment. For instance, the provisions prohibit practices like targeting water supply systems and crops. Such practice does occur, as in the armed conflicts in Sierra Leone,[130] Sudan[131] and Syria.[132] However, the articles protect only the objects that are indispensable to civilians. Thus, other objects or assets of the environment that are not essential for the survival of civilians fall outside the scope of these provisions.[133]

[129] Rule 54. See Henckaerts and Doswald-Beck, *Customary International Humanitarian Law*, Volume I: Rules (n 2) 189.

[130] Dam-de Jong (n 104) 233. See also UNEP, 'Sierra Leone, Environment, Conflict and Peacebuilding Assessment, Technical Report' (UNEP, Switzerland, 2010) 45.

[131] UNEP, 'Sudan Post-Conflict Environmental Assessment' (UNEP, Kenya, 2007) 92.

[132] Al Jazeera English, 'UN: Syrian fighters burning vital farmland is "weapon of war"' 4 June 2019, available at: www.aljazeera.com/news/2019/06/syrian-fighters-burning-vital-farmland-weapon-war-190604175625835.html.

[133] FJ Yuzon, 'Deliberate Environmental Modification Through the Use of Chemical and Biological Weapons: "Greening" the International Laws of Armed Conflict to Establish an Environmentally Protective Regime' (1996) 11 *American University Journal of International Law and Policy* 793, 817.

Article 54 of Protocol I expressly prohibits operations aimed at indispensable objects 'for the specific purpose of denying them for their sustenance value to the civilian population or to the adverse party, whatever the motive, whether in order to starve out civilians, to cause them to move away, or for any other motive'. Consequently, the provision is only applicable in those cases where a belligerent's goal is to deny these objects to the civilian population. Protocol II lacks this clarification, but, according to the Commentary to the Protocols, it applies in a similar manner.[134]

Both articles are subject to a number of limitations. They do not apply when these objects are used exclusively by the armed forces; are not used as sustenance and destruction and will not therefore deprive the civilian population of food or water; or if they are required in the defence of, and executed on, one's own territory.[135] For instance, if an underground water supply, providing drinking water, is targeted and intentionally contaminated, the provision would not apply if there is another source of drinking water, because the survival or health of the population would not be at stake. In such a case, the underground water would not be an object that is indispensable to the population.

Another example, given by Schmitt, is that if fields are set on fire to hinder an advancing enemy, Article 54 of Protocol I (and also Article 14 of Protocol II) would not apply despite the consequences for the civilian population, since the act has a clear military purpose. If the action created excessive suffering of civilians, the principle of proportionality and the prohibition of starvation in Article 54(1) of Protocol I and Article 14 of Protocol II could still prohibit such action.[136] As long as the intent of the attacker is not to deny civilians these objects, the articles do not apply. Thus, the element of intent clearly limits the reach of the articles' application. In addition, Article 54 does not ban scorched earth operations undertaken on a state's own territory to deny nourishment for the enemy.[137]

Furthermore, an evolutionary interpretation of the articles could extend the list of objects to include, for instance, clean air and soil. However, any assertion that a healthy and clean environment in general is indispensable to the population's survival is probably insufficient as a reference, because it lacks specificity and would not be conforming to the ordinary meaning of the articles.

[134] Sandoz, Swinarski and Zimmerman (n 71) 1457.

[135] Schmitt, 'Green War' (n 42) 77.

[136] Schmitt, 'War and the Environment' (n 34) 125.

[137] In a case in one of the 'Nuremberg Follow-up Trials' conducted by US Military Tribunals after the Second World War, General Rendulic was accused of adopting a scorched earth operation during the German retreat from Norway. According to General Rendulic, he had committed the acts in the belief that the Soviet troops were chasing him, and to prevent their advancement. It turned out that they were not. Nevertheless, General Rendulic was not held guilty for the scorched earth operation. This trial took place prior to the protocols being adopted. See Schmitt, 'War and the Environment' (n 34) 99. See also S Freeland, *Addressing the Intentional Destruction of the Environment During Warfare Under the Rome Statute of the International Criminal Court* (Intersentia, 2015) 62–63.

Besides, such an interpretation is also not supported by the drafting history of Protocol I.[138] Nevertheless, as argued by Dam-de Jong, natural resources generating income for the civilian population could be included in the definition. She bases this on a broad interpretation of Article 54(2) of Protocol I and Article 14 of Protocol II in the light of the human rights law instruments; for instance, the International Covenant on Economic, Social and Cultural Rights.[139] Article 1(2) of this instrument extends protection for the population to include all objects providing means of subsistence – like natural resources providing basic incomes – and the parties to an armed conflict would be prohibited from denying the population access to these resources.[140] The articles may be able to provide added environmental protection, but in a limited form.

B. Installations Containing Dangerous Forces

Article 56 of Protocol I and Article 15 of Protocol II (applicable in international and non-international armed conflicts, respectively) protect certain works and installations. These are 'dams, dykes, and nuclear electrical power generating stations', which contain dangerous forces. A release of these forces could result in severe losses among the civilian population. Although the purpose of the articles is to protect civilians, they provide indirect environmental protection as releasing dangerous forces would have devastating effects on the environment. The protection applies even if the installations are valid military objectives. While the provision in Protocol I is lengthy, the corresponding provision in Protocol II is shorter and less detailed.

Article 56 of Protocol I also prohibits attacks on any surrounding military objectives that might result in the release of dangerous forces. Article 15 of Protocol II 'covers attacks on military objectives in the direct vicinity of works or installations which might very well have the incidental effect of releasing dangerous forces and seriously injuring the civilian population'.[141] Article 56 of Protocol I contains a number of exceptions to the prohibition. If a dam or a dyke is used for purposes *other than its normal function* in regular, significant and direct support of military operations, and an attack is the only feasible way to terminate such support, the installation loses its special protection.[142] Nuclear electricity generating stations similarly lose their protection if used in regular, significant and direct support of military operations and where an

[138] B Baker, 'Legal Protections for the Environment in Times of Armed Conflict' (1993) 33 *Virginia Journal of International Law* 351, 371.

[139] International Covenant on Economic, Social and Cultural Rights (adopted 16 December 1966, entered into force 3 January 1976) 993 UNTS 3.

[140] Dam-de Jong (n 104) 236.

[141] Sandoz, Swinarski and Zimmerman (n 71) 1463.

[142] Article 56(2)(a) Protocol I (1977).

attack is the only feasible way to terminate such support, even if it maintains its normal function.[143] Furthermore, unless the release of the forces of the dangerous installations leads to severe losses among the civilian population, the installation will not receive any special protection. Article 15 of Protocol I has not expressed any exceptions. It states the rule, 'more categorically'.[144]

Given that the provisions are phrased to refer to specific installations, using the inclusion of 'namely' is a clear indication that the list is exhaustive and not illustrative. It has been suggested expanding the definition of 'works or installations containing dangerous forces' to include oil tankers, refineries, or facilities for the manufacture or storage of poisonous chemicals. Such an interpretation has not been accepted by states.[145] Consequently, other installations than those expressly mentioned are not likely to be protected under these provisions.

C. Pillage

Pillage in wartime is prohibited under all circumstances and is included in the Hague Regulations,[146] Geneva Convention IV,[147] as well in Protocol II.[148] The ICRC Study has confirmed its customary law status in Rule 52, which applies in international and non-international armed conflicts. It covers both public and private property as well as both organised pillage and isolated acts of indiscipline. It is also included in the Rome Statute and constitutes a war crime in both international and non-international armed conflicts.[149]

The prohibition of pillage was not drafted with the intention of preventing illegal exploitation of natural resources.[150] Nevertheless, the International Court of Justice in its *Armed Activities on the Territory of the Congo* case (*Armed Activities* case) held Uganda internationally responsible 'for acts of looting, plundering and exploitation of the DRC's natural resources' committed by members of the Ugandan army in the context of occupation.[151] Furthermore, a draft principle was provisionally adopted by the International Law Commission in 2019, which explicitly addresses the prohibition of pillage of natural resources.[152]

[143] Article 56(2)(b) Protocol I (1977).

[144] Sandoz, Swinarski and Zimmerman (n 71) 1462.

[145] A Schwabach, 'Environmental Damage Resulting from the NATO Military Action Against Yugoslavia' (2000) 25 *Columbia Journal of Environmental Law* 117, 128.

[146] Articles 28 and 47 Hague Regulations.

[147] Article 33 Geneva Convention IV.

[148] Article 4(2)(g) Protocol II.

[149] Articles 8(2)(b)(xvi) and 8(2)(e)(v) Rome Statute.

[150] L van den Herik and D Dam-de Jong, 'Revitalizing the Antique War Crime of Pillage: The Potential and Pitfalls of Using International Criminal Law to Address Illegal Resource Exploitation during Armed Conflict' (2011) 22 *Criminal Law Forum* 237.

[151] *Armed Activities on the Territory of the Congo (Democratic Republic of the Congo v Uganda)*, Judgment of 19 December 2005, ICJ Reports 2005, para 250.

[152] Draft Principle 18, International Law Commission, Protection of the Environment, First Reading (n 6).

In her Second Report, Special Rapporteur Lehto explains how the widespread illegal exploitation of natural resources taking place in the context of armed conflict results in environmental degradation, thereby confirming the link between exploitation of natural resources, armed conflicts and environmental degradation, which motivates the adoption of the draft principle. In particular, she addressed the illegal exploitation of natural resources taking place in the protracted conflicts in Angola, Côte d'Ivoire, the DRC, Liberia and Sierra Leone, which has caused substantial ecological destruction.[153] She also referred to the reports of the Expert Panels appointed by the UN Security Council, stating that 'highly organized and systematic exploitation activities at levels never before seen' are taking place in national parks in the DRC, including 'poaching for ivory, game meat and rare species, logging, and mining for coltan, gold and diamonds'.[154] Special Rapporteur Lehto also points out how '[t]he overexploitation of the forests of Liberia has been said to threaten "the long-term viability of the forest and the forest industry, as well as the lives, livelihoods and culture of Liberians who depend on the forest"'. She takes note of how deforestation threatens biodiversity, which 'contributes to the loss of ecosystem functions, including extreme weather mitigation, and accelerates climate change by weakening the forest carbon sink'.[155] Thus, the prohibition of illegal exploitation of natural resources has the potential to enhance environmental protection in an armed conflict context.[156]

By adopting a draft principle that specifically prohibits pillage of natural resources, the International Law Commission has given the ancient war crime of pillage a green coating.

D. Cultural Property

The 1954 Hague Convention, together with its two protocols adopted in 1954 and 1999, protect cultural property in relation to armed conflict.[157] The term 'cultural property' covers 'movable or immovable property of great importance to the cultural heritage of every people'.[158] The rules protect certain places, institutions and objects of cultural importance. The protection of cultural property

[153] Lehto, Second Report (n 53) para 17.

[154] ibid, para 18.

[155] ibid.

[156] For instance, Article 4 and the Preamble of the Lusaka Protocol of the International Conference on the Great Lakes Region explicitly prohibits the illegal exploitation of natural resources for, inter alia, environmental protection. Protocol against the Illegal Exploitation of Natural Resources of the International Conference on the Great Lakes Region (Lusaka Protocol) (Nairobi, 30 November 2006), available at: ungreatlakes.unmissions.org/sites/default/files/icglr_protocol_against_the_illegal_exploitation_of_natural_resourcess.pdf.

[157] C Forrest, 'The Doctrine of Military Necessity and the Protection of Cultural Property During Armed Conflicts' (2007) 37 *California Western International Law Journal* 177, 200.

[158] Article 1 1954 Hague Convention.

may offer indirect protection of the environment, particularly in the case where cultural property is protected through an 'area-based mechanism'.

The 1954 Hague Convention was the first instrument that specifically dealt with this matter and it was adopted under the auspices of UNESCO as a response to the extensive damage of cultural property that occurred during the Second World War.[159] The First Protocol was adopted at the same time and it regulates the export of cultural property during armed conflicts. The 1999 Second Protocol is formulated as being a complementary instrument to the 1954 Hague Convention, but, in fact, it has reinvented the protection scheme under the Convention.[160]

More specifically, the cultural property regime provides two kinds of protection. First, a general protection prohibits attacks on cultural property, unless required by military necessity. Second, certain property receives special or enhanced protection requiring a higher degree of military necessity.[161] Prior to an armed conflict, state parties are under an obligation to establish inventories of cultural property items that should receive protection in case of an armed conflict. State parties are also required to prepare in peacetime by taking other measures, as they find appropriate, for the purpose of protecting their cultural heritage from any anticipated adverse impacts of armed conflicts.[162] According to Article 4 of the 1954 Hague Convention, parties are under the obligation to not destroy property regardless of who it belongs to, if it has been identified as cultural property in accordance with the Convention. However, the protection can only be granted as long as the cultural property is not used for military purposes.[163] In addition, the obligations under the 1954 Hague Convention can be subject to a waiver if required by military necessity.[164] Articles 7 and 8 of the 1999 Second Protocol specify measures of precaution that the parties have to undertake to minimise damage to cultural property.

According to Article 18 of the 1954 Hague Convention, the Convention applies to international armed conflicts. Article 19 of the 1954 Hague Convention states that participants in non-international armed conflicts are 'bound to apply, as a minimum, the provisions of the present convention, which relate to respect for cultural property'. It also encourages parties to the

[159] Freeland (n 137) 73.

[160] L Lixinski, 'Environment and War: Lessons from International Cultural Heritage Law' in R Rayfuse (ed), *War and the Environment: New Approaches to Protecting the Environment in Relation to Armed Conflict* (Brill Nijhoff, 2014) 162–63.

[161] ibid, 168–69.

[162] Articles 3 and 7 Hague 1954 Convention and Article 5 1999 Second Protocol. For a general discussion on the various duties in the different phases of war, see Lixinski (n 160) 164.

[163] Article 8 1954 Hague Convention.

[164] Article 4(2) 1954 Hague Convention. Article 6(b) in the 1999 Second Protocol clarifies that a waiver can be invoked on the basis of imperative military necessity only 'to use cultural property for purposes which are likely to expose it to destruction or damage when and for as long as no choice is possible between such use of the cultural property and another feasible method for obtaining a similar military advantage'.

conflicts to enter special agreements to bring the Convention into force. Thus, the Convention is not explicitly applicable to non-international armed conflicts. However, the 1999 Second Protocol has extended the application of the 1954 Hague Convention to these conflicts.[165] Moreover, Article 53 of Protocol I and Article 16 of Protocol II (to the 1949 Geneva Conventions), applicable to international and non-international armed conflicts, protect 'historic monuments, works of art or places of worship which constitute the cultural or spiritual heritage of peoples' from attacks, to be used to support military operations, and to direct reprisals towards these objects. The articles do not provide for a waiver in the case of imperative military necessity. In addition, Rules 38–40 in the 2005 Customary Law Study deal with protection of cultural property in both international and non-international armed conflicts.[166] Thus, the rules on protection of cultural property apply as customary law as well. In sum, the environment is protected under the cultural property regime to the extent that the instruments provide an area-based protection mechanism. Thus, it may provide protection for natural areas that have cultural, religious, or historical significance. For instance, it could be triggered to protect the environment in a sacred land or archaeological site. Otherwise, the environmental protection is rather limited under these rules.

Suggestions of ways to include protection for natural heritage under the cultural property regime have been discussed, in particular, after the adoption of the World Heritage Convention in 1972. This Convention protects cultural and natural heritage on an equal footing and it has highlighted the environment's significance for humankind similar to cultural heritage. At the time when the 1954 Hague Convention was adopted, 'cultural property' reflected the understanding of 'cultural heritage'.[167] However, 'cultural property' is a more restricted term compared with 'cultural heritage'. The use of the term 'property' has in fact been described as one of the Convention's deficiencies.[168] Its restrictive terminology of 'cultural property' limits the environmental protection offered under the regime. An update to the terminology used in the regime was discussed during the negotiations of the 1999 Second Protocol to include protection of 'natural heritage' under the Second Protocol. The suggestion was rejected because the protection of the natural heritage appeared to be too distant from that of cultural property. According to the negotiators, such an inclusion would have required a new instrument and not only an update of the

[165] Article 22, 1999, Second Protocol to the 1954 Hague Convention. For a more detailed discussion on the protection of cultural property in non-international armed conflicts, see C Bruch, 'All's Not Fair in (Civil) War: Criminal Liability for Environmental Damage in Internal Armed Conflict' (2000) 25 *Vermont Law Review* 695, 712.

[166] See Henckaerts and Doswald-Beck, *Customary International Humanitarian Law*, Volume I: Rules (n 2) 127–38.

[167] Lixinski (n 160) 163.

[168] ibid.

existing regime, contrary to the purpose of the adoption of the 1999 Second Protocol.[169]

An attempt to bring natural and cultural protection in times of armed conflict closer to each other has been made by the International Law Commission by provisionally adopting two draft principles on designated areas of major environmental and cultural importance as protected zones, as discussed in chapter four.[170] The underlying reason for including a reference to both environmental and cultural areas of major importance alike is linked to the difficulty to clearly distinguish between these areas. The Commentaries to the Draft Principles state that: 'The reference to the term "cultural" is intended to infer the existence of a close linkage to the environment'.[171] It builds on the acknowledgment of the close link between the natural environment, cultural objects and characteristics in the landscape included in environmental protection instruments. For instance, the 1993 Convention on Civil Liability for Damage Resulting from Activities Dangerous to the Environment (adopted under the Council of Europe) is provided as an example in the Commentaries to the Draft Principles.[172]

The Commentaries also refers to the intricate relationship between environment and cultural heritage in relation to indigenous peoples' rights to their environment as a cultural and natural resource. Cultural sites of major importance include 'ancestral lands of indigenous peoples, who depend on the environment for their sustenance and livelihood'.[173] Furthermore, international law has acknowledged the need to preserve indigenous culture and knowledge which often connects with environmental protection.[174] Many sites protected under the World Heritage Convention are so-called mixed sites meaning that they are both cultural and natural world heritage. There are tendencies to recognise sacred sites for indigenous peoples with this dual status, which has historically been granted protection mainly as natural world heritage.[175]

[169] ibid.

[170] Draft Principles 4 [I-(x), 5] and 17 [II-5, 13], International Law Commission, Protection of the Environment, First Reading (n 6).

[171] Report of the International Law Commission, 68th Session (n 56) 323 ff.

[172] Article 2(10) defines the term 'environment' for the purpose of the Convention to include: 'natural resources both abiotic and biotic, such as air, water, soil, fauna and flora and the interaction between the same factors; property which forms part of cultural heritage; and characteristic aspects of the landscape'.

[173] Report of the International Law Commission, 68th Session (n 56) 326. See also Special Rapporteur M Jacobsson, Third Report on the Protection of the Environment in Relation to Armed Conflicts, UN Doc A/CN.4/700, 3 June 2016, paras 121–29.

[174] The Convention on Biological Diversity and the United Nations Declaration on the Rights of Indigenous Peoples, although not a binding instrument, refers to the right to manage, access and protect religious and cultural sites. See UN General Assembly, United Nations Declaration on the Rights of Indigenous Peoples, resolution adopted by the General Assembly, 2 October 2007, UN Doc A/RES/61/295.

[175] For instance, Chiribiquete National Park, inscribed in 2018, is the largest protected area in Colombia located in the Amazon. The indigenous communities, which are not directly present on

Also, Article 40(2) of the IUCN Draft Covenant includes references to cultural sites. It states that: 'Parties shall take the necessary measures to protect natural and cultural sites and objects of special interest'. To sum up, protecting the environment as such and sites of cultural and natural importance appears to correspond or overlap on many occasions.[176]

IX. PROTECTION UNDER THE WEAPONS CONVENTIONS

The purpose of adopting conventions regulating the use of certain weapons is seldom to protect the environment, but for other reasons connected to unnecessary suffering or protecting civilians from weapons unable to distinguish between military targets and civilians. However, certain weapons are particularly harmful to the environment. Therefore, prohibitions or restrictions on the use of such weapons have, for obvious reasons, positive effects for environmental protection. Several of the weapon conventions apply in both international and non-international armed conflicts. In addition, Article 36 of Protocol I requires states to ensure that new weapons and means and methods of warfare do not violate existing rules of international law.[177]

This section will provide an overview of the most important weapons conventions from an environmental perspective, and their contribution to safeguarding the environment during armed conflicts.

A. Poison, Biological and Chemical Weapons

Chemical weapons operate by using toxins, described as 'inanimate poisonous substances produced by living organisms', while biological weapons use 'living organisms that infect their victims, causing incapacitation and often death: some spread to other living entities, even those not initially attacked'.[178] Chemical and biological agents are often invisible and have enduring and toxic

the site, consider Chiribiquete as a sacred place that cannot be visited and that should be preserved unaltered. The Pimachiowin Aki ('The Land That Gives Life') in Canada, inscribed in 2018, is a landscape of rivers, lakes, wetlands and boreal forest. It forms part of the ancestral home of the Anishinaabeg, an indigenous people living from fishing, hunting and gathering. While Yellowstone National Park in the United States, inscribed 1978, considered as sacred land by native Americans, is only regarded as a natural world heritage site.

[176] For further reading, see A Dienelt, '"After War is Before the War" – The Environment, Preventative Measures Under International Humanitarian Law, and their Post-Conflict Impact' in C Stahn, J Iverson and JE Easterday (eds), *Environmental Protection and Transitions from Conflict to Peace* (Oxford University Press, 2017) 430–31.

[177] Report of the International Law Commission, 68th Session (n 56) 30.

[178] B Kellman, 'The Chemical Weapons Convention: A Verification and Enforcement Model for Determining Legal Responsibility for Environmental Harm Caused by War' in JE Austin and CE Bruch (eds), *The Environmental Consequences of War* (Cambridge University Press, 2000) 579.

effects. Because of the ability of these weapons to contaminate environmental components and destroy ecosystems, they can cause grave environmental harm if used in warfare.[179] Thus, prohibiting the use of such weapons also serves to safeguard the environment; in particular, because it is often easier for the army to defend themselves against these weapons through equipment or vaccination, but for civilians – as well as the exposed environment – these agents have severe and long-lasting effects.[180]

When the 1868 St Petersburg Declaration and the 1907 Hague Conventions were adopted, one of the most terrifying weapons existing was poison gas. Its use was prohibited by Article 23(a) and (e) of the Hague Regulations, which forbid poison or poisoned weapons, as well as arms causing unnecessary suffering. Despite the prohibition, poison gas, in particular mustard gas, was used on a great scale during the First World War, in violation of the Hague Regulations. As a consequence, the 1925 Geneva Gas Protocol was adopted, which prohibited chemical and bacteriological warfare.[181] More specifically, it banned the use of 'asphyxiating, poisonous, or other gases, and all analogous liquids, materials, and devices', and declared the ban as a universally accepted part of international law in its preamble. The Protocol also prohibited the use of biological and chemical weapons, whether they are directed at humans or plants.[182] In terms of environmental protection, the prohibitions are of significance, albeit its application directly to this end has been debated.

The 1925 Geneva Gas Protocol has proven to be effective in relation to poison gas. However, in the prevention of the use of other types of poison, the treaty has been less successful.[183] The application of the Protocol in relation to environmental matters has also involved some controversies. In 1969, after reports from the Vietnam War on the United States use of chemical agents such as herbicides, the UN General Assembly passed a resolution declaring that the 1925 Geneva Gas Protocol prohibits the use of chemical and biological agents of warfare with certain effects on the environment.[184] The resolution states that the 1925 Geneva Gas Protocol prohibits the use of:

> (a)any chemical agents of warfare – chemical substances, whether gaseous, liquid or solid – which might be employed because of their direct toxic effects on man, animals or plants; (b) any biological agents of warfare – living organisms, whatever their nature, or infective material derived from them – which are intended to cause disease

[179] ibid, 580.

[180] ibid.

[181] A Roberts, 'The Law of War and Environmental Damage' in JE Austin and CE Bruch (eds), *The Environmental Consequences of War* (Cambridge University Press, 2000) 53.

[182] Yuzon (n 133) 831.

[183] Schwabach (n 145) 124.

[184] UN General Assembly Resolution 2603 (XXIV) Question of Chemical and Bacteriological (Biological) Weapons (adopted 16 December 1969), available at: documents-dds-ny.un.org/doc/RESOLUTION/GEN/NR0/257/37/IMG/NR025737.pdf?OpenElement.

> and death in man, animals or plants, and which depend for their effects on their ability to multiply in the person, animal or plant attacked.[185]

The UN General Assembly Resolution is not a binding document, but it indicates a common position of states on how the 1925 Geneva Gas Protocol should be interpreted and applied. Nevertheless, it is still controversial whether the 1925 Geneva Gas Protocol covers all these chemical substances, mainly because the United States did not accept the broad scope of application.[186]

Due to the controversies, it remains uncertain whether the 1925 Geneva Gas Protocol prohibits the use of herbicides.[187] At least, under the precondition that states can ensure that the effects of the herbicide used are not lethal or injurious to the health of combatants or civilians, it cannot completely dismiss the legality of such usage.[188] Therefore, to address the deficiencies of the 1925 Geneva Gas Protocol, all acts related to chemical warfare have been prohibited in the Chemical Weapons Convention. The Chemical Weapons Convention was adopted in 1993 and it has 191 state parties.[189] The prohibition of the use of herbicides was addressed in the Preamble. The definition of 'toxic chemicals' in the Convention reads, 'any chemical which through its chemical action on life processes can cause death, temporary incapacitation or permanent harm to humans or animals'.[190] The prohibition of the chemicals implicitly protects the environment from harm.[191] The chemical agents are persistent and capable of moving up the food chain and concentrating in the tissues of the host organism. They can have carcinogenic, teratogenic and mutagenic effects on the life forms that they come into contact with.[192] Thus, chemical warfare has serious environmental impacts when it comes to the use of herbicides.[193]

The 1972 Biological Weapons Convention has restricted all types of acts related to these types of weapons. Biological weapons have never been employed in warfare.[194] However, they have been tested away from the battlefield. In 1942, the British tested an agent causing anthrax at Gruinard Island. Since the test, the island remains uninhabitable, primarily because the micro-organism that was introduced has become a permanent part of the ecosystem. Hence, these types of weapons have the potential to cause major

[185] ibid.
[186] Cohan (n 117) 498.
[187] Yuzon (n 133) 834.
[188] ibid.
[189] See the parties on the UN Treaty Collection's web page: treaties.un.org/pages/ViewDetails.aspx?src=TREATY&mtdsg_no=XXVI-3&chapter=26&lang=en.
[190] Article II Chemical Weapons Convention.
[191] Yuzon (n 133) 837.
[192] BK Schafer, 'The Relationship Between the International Laws of Armed Conflict and Environmental Protection: The Need to Reevaluate what Types of Conduct are Permissible During Hostilities' (1989) 19 *California Western International Law Journal* 287, 302.
[193] ibid.
[194] Yuzon (n 133) 833.

environmental damage,[195] and, consequently, the prohibition on biological weapons protects the environment.

Both the Biological Weapons Convention and the Chemical Weapons Convention apply in international as well as non-intentional armed conflicts. This is because being disarmament agreements, and not pure law of armed conflict instruments, they prohibit state parties from engaging in any activity related to handling these types of weapons, under any circumstances.[196]

B. Incendiary Weapons

It is not only weapons of mass destruction, like chemical and biological weapons, that can have grave environmental impacts, but also conventional weapons. The 1981 UN Convention on Certain Conventional Weapons prohibits or restricts the use of certain conventional weapons in the attached protocols to protect civilian life.[197] The Preamble to the Convention restates Article 35(3) of Protocol I (of the 1949 Geneva Conventions). The Preamble does not create any obligations, but it can be used for interpretation purposes because it reflects the motives of the state parties and the rationale for the Convention.[198] Protocols II and III to the Convention on Certain Conventional Weapons are of environmental interest. Protocol III (Incendiary Weapons Protocol) prohibits the indiscriminate use of incendiary weapons, while Protocol II covers mines, booby traps and similar devices. This section focuses on the former and the next section on the latter.

The definition of 'incendiary weapons' in the Incendiary Weapons Protocol is restricted to

> any weapon or ammunition which is primarily designed to set fire to objects or to cause burn injury to persons through the action of flame, heat, or a combination thereof, produced by a chemical reaction of substance delivered on the target.[199]

The scope is narrow because the provisions do not restrict the use of incendiary weapons that have primary effects other than to cause fire or flames. Incendiary weapons could have a devastating environmental impact as they could potentially create forest fires. The Incendiary Weapons Protocol contains a specific provision protecting the environment in Article 2(4). It reads:

> It is prohibited to make forests or other kinds of plant cover the object of attack by incendiary weapons except when such natural elements are used to cover, conceal or camouflage combatants or other military objectives, or are themselves military objectives.

[195] Schafer (n 192) 303–04.
[196] Article I(1) Chemical Weapons Convention; and Article I Biological Weapons Convention.
[197] Yuzon (n 133) 823.
[198] Koppe (n 23) 151–52.
[199] Article 1 Protocol II to Convention on Certain Conventional Weapons.

The provision is, however, restricted in its application. First, it relates to merely a small part of the environment – forests or other types of plant cover. Second, the Incendiary Weapons Protocol enables a proportionality assessment, because it does not prohibit collateral damage. Third, the protection ceases when the enemy is using the forest for cover or if they constitute military objectives.[200] It does not provide for absolute protection because it enables exceptions if required by military necessity. Therefore, the protection provided in the article is rather meaningless, since the cases when plant cover is most likely to be attacked are excluded from the protection.[201]

As observed by Koppe, the practical importance of the provision is undermined. He questions why a military commander would use incendiary weapons against a forest if there were no military advantage to obtain.[202] In addition, the wanton destruction of civilian objects is already prohibited by the rules of general protection under the law of armed conflict. Hence, the prohibition merely restates the importance of protecting parts of the environment during warfare, and adds little from a substantive point of view.

C. Remnants, Mines and Cluster Ammunition Weapons

Mines and cluster ammunition can cause harm to humans, animals and land. Landmines and explosive remnants from cluster bombs, etc, widely scattered over land demonstrate the long-lasting effects of conventional warfare on the environment. They also render land areas impossible to use, unless proper clearance is carried out. For instance, in states such as Mozambique, Cambodia and Angola, landmines remain in the surroundings with adverse impacts on civilians, as well as wildlife. These continue to take their toll long after they no longer serve a military purpose.[203] Lebanon has suffered from environmental damage following the Israeli war in 2006. Large numbers of cluster bombs lie unexploded throughout much of southern Lebanon.[204] There can be some positive benefits on the environment from the use of landmines, however. If properly marked and fenced off, such area-denial tactics can permit the restoration of damaged and overexploited environments by keeping the population away.[205] The Demilitarised Zone between North and South Korea is an example of this.

The indiscriminate use of anti-personnel landmines is prohibited under the 1997 Ottawa Convention, and restricted under Protocol II to the Convention

[200] Schmitt, 'Green War' (n 42) 89–90.

[201] Y Dinstein, *The Conduct of Hostilities Under the Law of International Armed Conflict*, 3rd edn (Cambridge University Press, 2016) 241.

[202] Koppe (n 23) 153.

[203] Bruch (n 165) 710.

[204] UNEP, 'Lebanon Post-Conflict Assessment' (UNEP, Switzerland, 2007) 154–56.

[205] Hulme, 'Natural Environment' (n 18) 222.

on Certain Conventional Weapons. Cluster ammunition is prohibited under the 2008 Convention on Cluster Munitions.[206]

While the 1997 Ottawa Convention prohibits the use of anti-personnel landmines altogether, Protocol II of the Convention on Certain Conventional Weapons only restricts their use. Protocol II provides environmental protection in two ways. First, it provides indirect environmental protection by providing a proportionality standard to balance damage to civilian objects against direct military advantage. Second, it forbids the indiscriminate use of landmines, requires mine locations to be recorded, and permits the remote delivery of only self-neutralising mines.[207] The Protocol has had little practical effect because it does not prohibit the use of anti-personnel mines as such and it does not deal with the production or transfer of them at all. On the other hand, the 1997 Ottawa Convention contains a total ban of the use of anti-personnel mines and it applies in both international and non-international conflicts. It is also a disarmament treaty, which prohibits any action related to anti-personnel mines including developing, producing, stockpiling, or transferring them.[208] Similarly, the Convention on Cluster Munitions prohibits any action related to cluster ammunition, and applies both to international and non-international armed conflicts.

Protocol V on Explosive Remnants of War to the Convention on Certain Conventional Weapons covers unexploded ordnance and abandoned ordnance, other than landmines, that remain after an armed conflict is over. They include artillery shells, grenades, mortars, rocket and air-dropped bombs as well as cluster bombs. Protocol V on Explosive Remnants of War[209] entered into force in 2006. It states that participants in an armed conflict bear responsibility for all explosive remnants of war in territory under their control. This means that such a participant to an armed conflict has to mark, remove and destroy explosive remnants after the cessation of hostilities. It should also record and retain information on the use of explosive remnants and make it available to the party in control of the affected areas.[210]

The International Law Commission provisionally adopted two draft principles dealing with remnants of war. Draft Principle 27 deals with remnants more generally, while Draft Principle 28 only deals with remnants that have been placed or dumped at sea.[211] The draft principles cover toxic and hazardous remnants, going beyond the term 'explosive remnants'. The draft principles

[206] Convention on Cluster Munitions (adopted 30 May 2008, entered into force 1 August 2010) 2688 UNTS 39.

[207] Schmitt, 'Green War' (n 42) 89–90.

[208] Article 1 Ottawa Convention.

[209] Protocol on Explosive Remnants of War (Protocol V) (entered into force 23 November 2003).

[210] Articles 3 and 4 Protocol V.

[211] International Law Commission, Protection of the Environment, First Reading (n 6).

also cover all remnants of war that cause danger or risk causing danger to the environment.[212]

X. CONCLUSIONS

In this chapter, I have examined the indirect wartime environmental protection under the general rules of the law of armed conflict. The protection provided by these rules applies both to international and non-international armed conflicts. It provides a broader environmental protection compared with direct environmental protection because it does not require a certain threshold for its application. The constraints within the law of armed conflict fall short of reflecting increasing environmental awareness, as expressed within international environmental law. As concluded by the International Court of Justice in the *Gabcíkovo-Nagymaros Project* case, 'the awareness of the vulnerability of the environment and the recognition that environmental risks have to be assessed on a continuous basis have become much stronger'.[213] I have highlighted three constraints of the protection. First, these rules cannot regulate which parts of the environment can become military objectives, meaning that these rules do not acknowledge the specific nature of the environment. Once parts of the environment constitute military objectives, these rules do not apply at all. Second, the general rules leave room for a wide discretion to the law-applier when balancing environmental damage against the other interests of the military operations. This often leads to favouring military interests at the expense of environmental considerations. Third, the general rules fail to address the special characteristics of the environment, in particular, when assessing environmental damage due to the uncertainty of its effects. I will go over the main points of these constraints and propose how they may be remedied.

The first constraint relates to the fact that any part of the environment can become a military target under the law of armed conflict, no matter how it may be protected under other international (environmental) rules. As long as the parts of the environment fulfil the requirements under Article 52 of Protocol I, they can become legitimate military targets. Thus, there are no obligations under the law of armed conflict requiring any consideration for more sensitive parts of the environment, even though the damage may have particularly harmful impacts.

The second constraint relates to the lack of legal guidance on how to apply the proportionality principle and the principle of precaution in relation to

[212] Report of the International Law Commission, 70th Session (30 April–1 June and 2 July–10 August 2018), (2018) *Yearbook of the International Law Commission*, Volume II, Part Two.

[213] *Gabcikovo-Nagymaros Project (Hungary/Slovakia)*, Judgment of 25 September 1997, ICJ Reports 1997, para 112.

environmental protection. It creates a large margin of appreciation for the law-applier that may then make decisions based on his or her preferences. Additional legal clarifications are therefore desirable and could be found within international environmental law. The unclear obligations under the law of armed conflict could therefore be interpreted in the light of international environmental law, clarifying how to appreciate and prevent environmental damage.

The third constraint is related to the two other because it regards the difficulties of assessing the exact effects of environmental damage. For instance, an attack on a wetland that would result in the loss of a certain animal species may cause an imbalance in the ecosystem that could have uncertain impacts. For instance, the adverse effects on the general biodiversity may have serious implications for public health. However, such effects will not be foreseeable at the time of the attack and may only be evident later Any possible damage to the environment may therefore be difficult to see at the time of the decision for the attack. The law of armed conflict fails to recognise the particular aspects of the environment and the implications of the damage that can be created in warfare.

An examination of the law of armed conflict rules demonstrates that the protection of the environment is vague, heavily restricted, and not reflecting the increasing awareness of environmental concerns. Although the law of armed conflict is developed to permit exceptions from peacetime rules, the vagueness of the rules relating to environmental protection could be clarified and informed by international environmental law. Bothe highlights that international environmental law is a growing international legal field which has considerably transformed in character.[214] As the consequences of environmental damage are difficult to assess and foresee, international environmental law contains the principle of prevention and the precautionary approach. These are developed to address the particularity of dealing with uncertain aspects that are inherent in environmental issues.

The Martens Clause opts for the possibility of allowing other principles of international law to influence the application of the law of armed conflict in order to better reflect the 'dictates of the public conscience'. Thus, it opens a door to the principles of international environmental law. For instance, the application of the principles of proportionality and precaution of the law of armed conflict could be informed by the environmental principles of prevention and the precautionary approach.

[214] Bothe, 'The Protection of the Environment' (n 25) 57.

6

International Environmental Treaties: A Missed Opportunity

I. INTRODUCTION

THIS CHAPTER EXPLAINS why the operation of MEAs (multilateral environmental agreements) in relation to armed conflict has not been fully investigated in the legal doctrine, while the next chapter (chapter seven) addresses how MEAs may enhance wartime environmental protection. The scholarly literature has primarily focused on the law of armed conflict – and to some extent customary international environmental law – to deal with environmental damage during armed conflicts. However, the examination of environmental treaties – for example, MEAs – during armed conflicts remains an underexplored area.

Overlooking the application of MEAs in relation to armed conflict could be a missed opportunity, especially because MEAs have three advantages. First, they have the potential to complement the rules of the law of armed conflict because they are specialised in dealing with the environment and the particularities involved in addressing environmental problems. Given that the rules within the law of armed conflict that are applicable to environmental protection are vague and not fully adapted to deal with environmental issues (as discussed in chapters three, four and five), environmental treaties offer the possibility to complement these rules. Second, environmental treaties form part of peacetime law and their application is not triggered by the outbreak of an armed conflict, as opposed to the law of armed conflict that is applicable depending on whether an armed conflict exists in a legal sense.[1] Environmental treaties, on the other hand, provide consistent protection of the environment, regardless of the existence or the classification of an armed conflict. Third, being a relatively young field of international law, international environmental law has its own specific strategies and mechanisms to address environmental problems of a global scale.[2] These strategies and mechanisms represent new possibilities to

[1] S Vöneky, 'Peacetime Environmental Law as a Basis of State Responsibility for Environmental Damage Caused by War' in JE Austin and CE Bruch (eds), *The Environmental Consequences of War* (Cambridge University Press, 2000) 192.

[2] ibid, 224.

also address environmental damage in times of armed conflict. Consequently, to better reflect the ability of international law to deal with wartime environmental protection, the law of armed conflict and international environmental treaties should be applied together. In general, when state parties negotiate and ratfy MEAs, there is intention to restrict warfare.

This chapter is structured as follows. Section II gives an overview of the emerging field of international environmental law. Section III summarises the explanations of why there is a lack of research on the application of MEAs during armed conflicts. These explanations will be thoroughly explored in sections IV, V and VI. In section IV, I discuss the applicability of environmental treaties during armed conflicts. Section V examines the application of the law of armed conflict as the *lex specialis* during armed conflicts, when facing a normative conflict with peacetime law. Section VI investigates the particular characteristics of environmental treaties and the perception of these among scholars specialised in the law of armed conflict. The last section, section VII, provides my conclusions that emphasise why the operation of MEAs should be carefully examined during armed conflicts.

II. INTERNATIONAL ENVIRONMENTAL LAW AT A GLANCE

Modern international environmental law has developed sophisticated legal techniques to conserve and protect the environment.[3] It brings new challenges of how to legally respond to environmental damage by offering innovative ways, often affecting other areas of law and involving actors other than states.[4] The emergence of this area of law represents a bigger transformation of the international legal system – both in regard to normative and institutional development.

Traditional international law is considered to be focused on the coexistence of states, as incorporated in the field of diplomatic law, sovereign immunity, treaty law and the law of armed conflict, etc. Apart from transboundary environmental damage, international environmental law is on the other hand mainly concerned with international cooperation between states to achieve the common interest of safeguarding the environment.[5] Given that many of the complex environmental problems are global and do not respect state borders (climate change, biodiversity loss, or depletion of the ozone layer, etc), actions undertaken to address these issues by one state alone may not have any

[3] P-M Dupuy and JE Viñuales, *International Environmental Law*, 2nd edn (Cambridge University Press, 2018) 3.

[4] See, for instance, A Boyle, 'Relationship between International Environmental Law and Other Branches of Law International Law' in D Bodansky, J Brunnée and E Hey (eds), *Oxford Handbook of International Environmental Law* (Oxford University Press, 2007).

[5] D Bodansky, *The Art and Craft of International Environmental Law* (Harvard University Press, 2010) 18.

substantial impact.[6] Instead, these problems frequently require collective and far-reaching measures – for example, cutting carbon emissions or preserving particular ecosystems and/or species. State cooperation is crucial for such measures to have effect and the focus of common concerns is a main feature in international environmental law.[7]

Three different phases can be distinguished in the growth of international environmental law. The first phase, taking place around 1920 to 1970, is described as a 'conservationist stage' that mainly focused on the protection and preservation of wildlife, as well as on the rational use of natural resources. During this phase, the types of environmental problems addressed were often limited to direct and concrete threats of pollution or loss of species.[8] For instance, the 1946 Whaling Convention is a typical environmental treaty signed during this phase for the conservation of the whale population,[9] because whales were endangered due to extensive hunting at that time.

The second phase is associated with the Stockholm Conference in 1972 and the adoption of the Stockholm Declaration that represented the 'birth' of modern international environmental law. The Stockholm Conference was highly influenced by the *1941 Trail Smelter* case concerning state responsibility for transboundary environmental damage.[10] Based on the principles of international law, the tribunal in this case reached the conclusion that no state has the right to allow its territory to be used in a manner that has adverse environmental effects on another state. The tribunal's conclusion has become a cornerstone of international environmental law.[11] In comparison with the first phase, the second phase is more concerned with the prevention of pollution, dealing with the risks of environmental damage caused by accidents. For instance, the issue of oil spills and marine pollution were highly topical after the accident with the oil tanker the Torrey Canyon in 1967.[12] Many of the instruments adopted during this phase address threats such as oil spills, as well as accidents involving nuclear weapons and nuclear energy. The focus of the second stage can be summarised as to respond to concrete but not imminent environmental threats. In addition, UN Environment is created during this phase entrusted to promote

[6] B Desai, *Multilateral Environmental Agreements: Legal Status of the Secretariats* (Cambridge University Press, 2010) 63–64.

[7] See also D Bodansky, J Brunnée and E Hey, 'International Environmental Law: Mapping the Field' in D Bodansky, J Brunnée and E Hey (eds), *Oxford Handbook of International Environmental Law* (Oxford University Press, 2007) 1–25.

[8] Bodansky (n 5) 21–24.

[9] Article V of the International Convention for the Regulation of Whaling (1946 Whaling Convention) (adopted 2 December 1946, entered into force 10 November 1948) 161 UNTS 72.

[10] The case involved the United States, which raised complaints of sulphur dioxide emissions released by a smelter located in Canada. The United States reported that the emissions were damaging crops and lands. *Trail Smelter Case (United States/Canada)*, Award of 11 March 1941.

[11] See Dupuy and Viñuales (n 3) 5.

[12] Bodansky (n 5) 26–28.

international cooperation in environmental matters, also including initiatives of legislative character.[13]

The third phase in the growth of international environmental law addresses environmental problems that are more complex, including climate change and biodiversity loss. These problems may require solutions of an integrated character, with regard to economic and social aspects. This phrase is marked by the Earth Summit Meetings, resulting in the adoption of the Rio Declaration in 1992, the Johannesburg Declaration on Sustainable Development in 2002, and the Rio+20 Document in 2012.[14] Consequently, the third phase focuses on sustainable development, attempting to achieve a balance between development and environmental protection.[15] For instance, it has dealt with the North–South dimension, as embodied in the commitments, ensuring that the developed states should carry a greater responsibility than the developing states. Such commitments emphasise capacity building and transfer in technology from developed states to developing states. During this stage, the ecosystem approach was introduced, which ensures an integrated management strategy of land, water and living resources to promote conservation and sustainable use.[16] In addition, the third phase is characterised by the need to take action against environmental risks, even if these have not yet been scientifically established.[17]

Contemporary international environmental law comprises elements of all three phases.[18] It introduces legal concepts and principles, such as the rights of future generations, the principle of prevention, the precautionary approach, common but differentiated responsibility, sustainable development, and the ecosystem approach. These concepts and principles suggest that the environment needs holistic long-term protection from the known risks, as well as the unknown risks.[19] International environmental law has become a multifaceted area of law, with an increased number of actors, treaties and initiatives at different levels.[20] In fact, it develops constantly by adopting new instruments to respond to new environmental challenges, in which novel scientific discoveries play a central role. Given that the instruments have been adopted at different times with different focuses, they form a patchwork of environmental obligations that lack overall coordination and can be perplexing to navigate around.

[13] Bodansky (n 5); Dupuy and Viñuales (n 3) 11.

[14] Dupuy and Viñuales (n 3) 3; Bodansky (n 5) 21.

[15] PH Sand, 'The Evolution of International Environmental Law' in D Bodansky, J Brunnée and E Hey (eds), *Oxford Handbook of International Environmental Law* (Oxford University Press, 2007) 39; Dupuy and Viñuales (n 3) 3.

[16] See the website of the Biodiversity Convention: www.cbd.int/ecosystem.

[17] Bodansky (n 5) 30–32; S Andresen and JB Skjaerteth, 'Science and Technology: From Agenda Setting to Implementation' in D Bodansky, J Brunnée and E Hey (eds), *Oxford Handbook of International Environmental Law* (Oxford University Press, 2007) 183.

[18] Bodansky (n 5) 21–24.

[19] P Birnie, A Boyle and C Redgwell, *International Law & the Environment* (Oxford University Press, 2009) 7–8, 119.

[20] Bodansky (n 5) 35.

MEAs provide most of the substantive content of international environmental law.[21] They set limitations on activities affecting the environment by balancing different interests, for instance the needs of present and future generations, economic growth, and the maintenance of the ecosystems and their equilibrium. MEAs are usually constructed to protect a certain component or part of the environment – such as biodiversity, the climate, wetlands, the ozone layer, etc – even though more general (non-binding) instruments exist – such as the Rio Declaration and the Stockholm Declaration. The environmental instruments arrange for collective measures to be undertaken by the state parties, but also in collaboration with other actors. As formulated by Ulfstein, MEAs 'represents a new form of international cooperation'.[22] The treaties can be described as institutionalising international cooperation.

The environmental treaties are, in general, preventative and/or precautionary orientated.[23] They set out general objectives to achieve and provide guidance on how to achieve them.[24] Although they have a limited number of prescriptive rules, MEAs are still able to influence changes in behaviour of the state. One way could be through the treaty bodies established under many environmental treaties. The treaty bodies adopt binding decisions, non-binding recommendations, provide guidance on how to apply the treaty, but also initiate projects, programmes, and provide capacity building and technology transfer to enhance compliance with the treaty obligations among its state parties.[25] The instruments of the law of armed conflict lack such treaty bodies. Therefore, the application of environmental treaties could complement environmental protection under the law of armed conflict, not only in a normative manner but also on an institutional level through the treaty bodies.

Moreover, the rules of international environmental law challenge the classical view of enforcing and reacting to breaches of international law.[26] To avoid state responsibility in relation to environmental damage, state behaviour is assessed based on its response to certain risks.[27] This is because international environmental law mainly aims at preventing harm, not only protecting the environment from actual harm. Due diligence, the principle of prevention, and the precautionary approach set a standard for a reasonable level of responding to environmental risks.[28] A state may be responsible for present or future, actual

[21] Birnie, Boyle and Redgwell (n 19) 9.

[22] G Ulfstein, 'Treaty Bodies' in D Bodansky, J Brunnée and E Hey (eds), *Oxford Handbook of International Environmental Law* (Oxford University Press, 2007) 878.

[23] A Bouvier, 'Protection of the Natural Environment in Time of an Armed Conflict' (1991) 31 *International Review of the Red Cross* 438, 438–39.

[24] L Boisson de Chazournes, 'Features and Trends in International Environmental Law' in Y Kerbrat and S Maljean-Dubois (eds), *The Transformation of International Environmental Law* (Hart Publishing and Editions A Pedone, 2011) 10.

[25] Ulfstein (n 22).

[26] Bodansky, Brunnée and Hey (n 7) 9.

[27] Boisson de Chazournes (n 24) 14.

[28] ibid, 13–15.

or potential, or even probable environmental damage. Much focus is on preventing and minimising environmental damage, even if the exact consequences of certain damage cannot be established. Consequently, even anticipated environmental damage requires certain behaviours to prevent it from occurring, based on the notion of risk. A state has to show that it has employed due diligence and provided the necessary precautionary and preventative measures, according to a required standard determined on the activity, in order to not be held internationally responsible for environmental damage. Such risk anticipation is grounded on the fact that environmental damage may be irreversible, in particular with regard to issues such as climate change or biodiversity loss. As highlighted by Maljean-Dubois, once a species is extinct it will be extinct forever, with no possible way of restoring it.[29] This is a view in contrast with environmental protection as formulated under the law of armed conflict, which mainly addresses the immediate and foreseeable environmental damage without including a long-term perspective of the possible unknown and irreparable consequences.

III. EXPLAINING THE MISSED OPPORTUNITY

Despite the shortcomings of the vague rules within the law of armed conflict, scholars seldom examine MEAs to address environmental damage during armed conflicts. I have identified three reasons explaining why. First, given that the applicability of environmental treaties during armed conflicts has been a disputable and unsolved issue under international law for a long time, it has made legal scholars focus on the instruments of the law of armed conflict instead. Second, even if MEAs apply during armed conflicts, the law of armed conflict applies as the *lex specialis* in case a normative conflict arises between the rules, which may undermine the impact of peacetime law, such as international environmental law. Third, most scholars focus on customary international environmental law to address the environment in relation to armed conflict and they rarely apply the environmental treaties. Scholars often dismiss MEAs because, in many cases, they constitute framework conventions that have vaguely formulated provisions and therefore their contribution during an armed conflict is questioned.[30] As a consequence of these explanations, little research has been

[29] S Maljean-Dubois, 'The Making of International Law Challenging Environmental Protection' in Y Kerbrat and S Maljean-Dubois (eds), *The Transformation of International Environmental Law* (Hart Publishing and Editions A Pedone, 2011) 26.

[30] Roberts raises the applicability of MEAs but without discussing them further. See A Roberts, 'The Law of War and Environmental Damage' in JE Austin and CE Bruch (eds), *The Environmental Consequences of War* (Cambridge University Press, 2000) 83; T Weinstein, 'Prosecuting Attacks that Destroy the Environment: Environmental Crimes or Humanitarian Atrocities?' (2005) 17 *Georgetown International Environmental Law Review* 697.

adopted a resolution on the Protection of the environment in areas affected by armed conflict.[53] These instruments express a political and a moral position for states to respect and protect the environment during armed conflicts. Consequently, they provide an indication that the peacetime law protecting the environment might have some normative impact in relation to armed conflict. However, these non-binding instruments are unable to establish a uniform legal position that settles the matter.

In the following subsections, I examine how this issue has been dealt with in practice, and thereafter, I address the work of the International Law Commission on the Effects of Armed Conflicts on Treaties.

A. State Practice in Relation to the Applicability of Environmental Treaties

The Gulf Wars, in the 1990s, spurred the criticism of the law of armed conflict, which gave rise to a debate in the Sixth Committee of the UN General Assembly on the possibility to protect the environment during armed conflicts through peacetime law. At the time, there was no common position among the states on the applicability of (peacetime) environmental law during armed conflicts. Some states contested such an idea, while other states expressed a more positive attitude towards it.[54]

The 1994 Guidelines, compiled by the International Committee of the Red Cross (ICRC), endorsed the continued applicability of international environmental treaties during armed conflicts, but only as far as they are consistent with the applicable law of armed conflict. However, the Guidelines were not formally approved by the UN General Assembly, which confirmed the divided positions on the issue.[55] In 1996, the International Court of Justice delivered its *Nuclear Weapons* Advisory Opinion, in which the Court stated that the question was not whether environmental treaties apply during armed conflicts, but whether the obligations arising from these 'were intended to be obligations of total restraint during military conflict'.[56] The approach chosen by the International Court of Justice, vaguely and ambiguously formulated, focuses on the applicability of the material obligations stemming from environmental treaties and not on the applicability of them as such. In that way, the Court managed to avoid determining the effects of armed conflicts on environmental treaties.

[53] UN Environment Assembly of the UN Environment Programme, adopted Nairobi 23–27 May 2016, UN Doc UNEP/EA.2/Res.15.

[54] See the summary of the debate in the UN General Assembly in Vöneky, 'Peacetime Environmental Law' (n 1) 196.

[55] Report of the Secretary General, UN Doc A/49/323, 19 August 1994. See also Vöneky, 'A New Shield' (n 31) 22.

[56] *Legality of the Threat or Use of Nuclear Weapons* (n 43) para 30.

In relation to the *Nuclear Weapons* Advisory Opinion, differing views on the issue were conveyed by states.[57] Among those that contested the applicability of environmental treaties were the United Kingdom, the United States and France.[58] In the Commentary to the 2005 Customary Law Study, in regard to the rules on environmental protection during armed conflicts, the ICRC states that: 'There appears to be insufficient uniformity of opinion on whether environmental law treaties continue to be applicable during armed conflict when no reference is made to this in the treaty concerned'.[59]

Some practice supports the continued applicability of MEAs. During the Iran–Iraq War in the 1980s, the two states continued to cooperate through the Regional Organization for the Protection of the Marine Environment to implement the 1978 Kuwait Regional Convention for Co-operation on the Protection of the Marine Environment from Pollution,[60] as noted by Vöneky.[61] Similarly, NATO forces abided by the environmental obligations set out in the UN Convention on Law of the Sea(UNCLOS)[62] during the Kosovo bombing campaign in 1999.

According to Article 192 of UNCLOS, states have an obligation to protect and preserve the marine environment. Article 194 of UNCLOS provides that states shall also take measures to prevent, control and reduce pollution of the marine environment, including the control of the release of pollutants from vessels, dumping wastes, the prevention of accidents, and the prevention of pollution from installations. However, Article 236 states that provisions related to environmental protection do not apply to 'any warship, navel auxiliary, other vessels or aircraft owned or operated by a State and used, for the time being, only on government non-commercial service'. Still, state parties need to ensure that they act in a manner consistent with the rules 'so far as reasonable and practicable'.

NATO forces did observe the obligations described above during Operation Sharp Guard, when monitoring and enforcing compliance with the sanctions adopted by the UN Security Council.[63] The maritime forces prevented all unauthorised shipping from entering the territorial waters of the Federal Republic

[57] Vöneky, 'Peacetime Environmental Law' (n 1) 196.

[58] See the debate summarised by Loets: A Loets, 'An Old Debate Revisited: Applicability of Environmental Treaties in Times of International Armed Conflict Pursuant to the International Law Commission's "Draft Articles on the Effects of Armed Conflict on Treaties"' (2012) 21 *Review of European, Comparative & International Environmental Law* 127, 130; Vöneky, 'Peacetime Environmental Law' (n 1) 195.

[59] J-M Henckaerts and L Doswald-Beck (eds), *Customary International Humanitarian Law Study*, Volume I: Rules (Cambridge University Press, 2005) 151.

[60] Kuwait Regional Convention for Co-operation on the Protection of the Marine Environment From Pollution (adopted 24 April 1978, entered into force 1 July 1979) 1140 UNTS 133.

[61] Vöneky, 'Peacetime Environmental Law' (n 1) 195.

[62] United Nations Convention on the Law of the Sea (adopted 10 December 1982, entered into force 16 November 1994) 1833 UNTS 3 (UNCLOS).

[63] See the UN Security Council Resolution, UN Doc S/RES/713, 25 September 1991. See also UN Security Council Resolution, UN Doc S/RES/757, 30 May 1992; UN Security Council Resolution,

of Yugoslavia and all arms from entering the former Yugoslavia.[64] On the other hand, however, NATO forces also conducted many environmentally harmful attacks, including those at the Pancevo Complex, which were probably contrary to the Biodiversity Convention, the Basel Convention on Transboundary Movement of Hazardous Wastes and Their Disposal,[65] as well as the Danube River Protection Convention.[66] For instance, the toxic and chemical release from the Pancevo attack caused substantial damage to the wetlands of the Danube Delta. These wetlands are protected under the Ramsar Convention that requires the 'wise use' of the wetlands. It is highly questionable that releasing toxins would constitute a 'wise use' of the wetlands, and therefore such an attack must have been a violation of the Ramsar Convention.[67]

Moreover, the 1979 Convention on Conservation of Migratory Species of Wild Animals[68] has encouraged developing transboundary cooperation among the DRC, Rwanda, and Uganda to preserve gorillas during armed conflicts. These states have adopted an agreement on conservation of gorillas and their habitat applicable in Central Africa – the Gorilla Agreement[69] to provide for robust cooperative mechanisms to address conservation challenges. Also, in 2015, the DRC, Rwanda and Uganda entered a treaty regarding transboundary collaboration of the Greater Virunga to conserve wildlife and promote the development of tourism.[70] One of the main objectives of the treaty is to promote and support safety and security within the Greater Virunga Landscape.[71] For instance, park rangers working in the conflict areas have conducted joint patrolling.[72] In addition, as will be discussed thoroughly in chapter eight, the World Heritage Convention[73] has been operational in the armed conflicts taking place in the DRC to protect the environment.

UN Doc S/RES/787, 16 November 1992; UN Security Council Resolution, UN Doc S/RES/820, 17 April 1993; UN Security Council Resolution, UN Doc S/RES/943, 23 September 1994.

[64] See Implementation Force Final Factsheet, 2 October 1996, available on NATO's website: www.nato.int/ifor/general/ shrp-grd.htm.

[65] Convention on Transboundary Movement of Hazardous Wastes and Their Disposal (adopted 22 March 1989, entered into force 5 May 1992) 1673 UNTS 126 (Basel Convention).

[66] Convention on Co-operation for the Protection and Sustainable Use of the Danube River (adopted 29 June 1994, entered into force 22 October 1998) (Danube River Protection Convention).

[67] Hulme, *War Torn Environment* (n 34) 194.

[68] Convention on the Conservation of Migratory Species of Wild Animals (adopted 23 June 1979, entered into force 8 October 1981) 1651 UNTS 333.

[69] Agreement on the Conservation of Gorillas and Their Habitats (Gorilla Agreement) (adopted 26 October 2007, entered into force 1 June 2008) 2545 UNTS 55.

[70] For further reading, see E Hsiao, 'Protecting Places For Nature, People, and Peace: A Critical Socio-Legal Review of Transboundary Conservation Areas' (PhD Thesis, University of British Colombia, 2018).

[71] Article 6(7) 2015 Greater Virunga Transboundary Collaboration Treaty on Wildlife Conservation and Tourism Development.

[72] A Crawford and J Bernstein, *MEAs, Conservation and Conflict: A Case Study of Virunga National Park, DRC* (International Institute for Sustainable Development, Winnipeg, 2008).

[73] Convention Concerning the Protection of the World Cultural and Natural Heritage (adopted 23 November 1972, entered into force 15 December 1979) 1037 UNTS 151 (World Heritage Convention).

B. The Issue under the International Law Commission

In 2011, the International Law Commission completed its work on the topic of the Effects of Armed Conflicts on Treaties by adopting 18 draft articles at the second reading. These draft articles have shed some light on how to deal with the applicability of MEAs in times of armed conflict. Draft Article 3 states that an outbreak of an armed conflict does not *ipso facto* terminate or suspend the operation of treaties.[74] The article affirms the contemporary view within international law that recognises the applicability of treaties of other legal areas besides the law of armed conflict during both international and non-international armed conflicts. The Commission expresses in Draft Article 3 that the termination of treaties is restricted to those that are 'political' and 'incompatible with the existence of hostilities' and those whose maintenance is 'incompatible with national policy' during armed conflicts. With regard to other treaties, the presumption is continued operation in times of armed conflict. The International Law Commission seeks to establish a general principle of legal stability and continuity to support solid treaty relations, as described in the Commentary to the Draft Articles.[75] However, treaties may be suspended because of other factors related to their nature or the characteristics of the conflict as I will explain below.[76]

The International Law Commission's draft articles set up a three-staged assessment of a treaty's ability to remain in operation during armed conflicts. It includes: first, determination of whether the treaty expressly regulates the issue; second, applying the rules on treaty interpretation to determine the continued applicability; and third, overall assessment of the continued applicability based on factors related to (a) the nature of the treaty and (b) the characteristics of the armed conflict. According to Draft Article 4, the first stage of the assessment is to establish whether a treaty provides for continued applicability in case of an outbreak of hostilities. The position originates from Article 30(2) of the VCLT, which states that if a treaty contains a derogation clause, it applies in order to meet the intention of the parties. Thus, the starting point for examining the applicability of environmental treaties in armed conflict is to look at the provisions in the specific treaty in question. If it is expressly regulated under the treaty, those regulations apply because the will of the parties constitutes the decisive element in an interpretation process. However, MEAs seldom contain any provisions on how the outbreak of an armed conflict affects their operation. There are, however, a few exceptions. Article XIX in the 1954 Oil Pollution Convention[77] expresses a possibility

[74] Draft Articles on the Effects of Armed Conflicts on Treaties, with Commentaries (n 42); see Draft Article 3.

[75] ibid; see Draft Article 3, para 1.

[76] ibid; see Draft Article 3, para 2.

[77] International Convention for the Prevention of Pollution of the Sea by Oil, 1954, as amended in 1962 and 1969 (adopted 12 May 1954, entered into force 26 July 1958) 973 UNTS 3 (OILPOL).

of suspension in case of war.[78] The 1997 UN Convention in International Watercourses includes a provision related to armed conflicts, stating that international watercourses and related installations shall be protected in accordance with the principles and rules of international law applicable during armed conflicts.[79] The provision could be interpreted as that the rules specially designed for armed conflict have priority over the provisions in the Convention, but that the treaty remains applicable to the extent it conforms to the law of armed conflict. Article 3 in the Ramsar Convention provides for the possibility to restrict or delete boundaries of wetlands in case of national interests of urgency, which could include a situation of an armed conflict. This means that boundaries of the wetlands may be amended due to the hostilities, if it is necessary for national security. However, if such an amendment results in loss of wetland resources, it must be compensated for by creating additional natural reserves.[80] The Convention does not specifically state anything in regard to its application during armed conflicts.

The World Heritage Convention provides indirectly for continued operation during armed conflicts. In fact, the protection of a world heritage site may be strengthened in case of an outbreak of an armed conflict. Pursuant to Article 11(4), the World Heritage Convention lists 'World Heritage Sites in Danger' (Danger List) in case a world heritage site's integrity is threatened by certain events that mean the site requires enhanced protection, such as in the 'outbreak of an armed conflict'.[81] In addition, the revised version of the African Convention on the Conservation of Nature and Natural Resources[82] arranges explicitly for state parties to take measures during armed conflicts and stipulates continued applicability during armed conflicts. Article XV of the Convention reads:

> Military and Hostile Activities:
>
> 1. The Parties shall:
>
>   (a) take every practical measure, during periods of armed conflict, to protect the environment against harm;

[78] Article XIX reads: '(1). In case of war or other hostilities, a Contracting Government which considers that it is affected whether as a belligerent or as a neutral, may suspend the operation of the whole or any part of the present Convention in respect of all or any of its territories. The suspending Government shall immediately give notice of any such suspension to the Bureau'.

[79] Article 29 Convention on the Law of the Non-Navigational Uses of International Watercourses (adopted 21 May 1997, entered into force 17 August 2014) (Convention on International Watercourses).

[80] Article 4(2) Convention on Wetlands of International Importance Especially as Waterfowl Habitat (adopted 2 February 1971, entered into force 21 December 1975) 996 UNTS 245 (Ramsar Convention).

[81] Other serious and specific dangers listed in Article 11(4) of the World Heritage Convention include, 'threat of disappearance caused by accelerated deterioration; large-scale public or private projects or rapid urban or tourist development projects; destruction caused by changes in the use or ownership of the land; major alterations due to unknown causes; abandonment for any reason whatsoever; calamities and cataclysms; serious fires, earthquakes, landslides; volcanic eruptions; changes in water level, floods and tidal waves'.

[82] African Convention on the Conservation of Nature and Natural Resources (adopted 15 September 1968, entered into force 6 June 1969) (revised version 11 July 2003).

(b) refrain from employing or threatening to employ methods or means of combat which are intended or may be expected to cause widespread, long-term, or severe harm to the environment and ensure that such means and methods of warfare are not developed, produced, tested or transferred;
(c) refrain from using the destruction or modification of the environment as a means of combat or reprisal;
(d) undertake to restore and rehabilitate areas damaged in the course of armed conflicts.

2. The Parties shall cooperate to establish and further develop and implement rules and measures to protect the environment during armed conflict.

The parties to the Convention on the Conservation of Migratory Species of Wild Animals entered the Gorilla Agreement, as mentioned in the previous subsection (subsection IV.A). The Preamble of the Agreement states that it is concerned with protecting gorillas, also during armed conflicts. Its treaty body has adopted action plans for each individual subspecies. The key objectives of the action plans include the monitoring of gorilla populations and threats, the strengthening of law enforcement and anti-poaching measures, the building of international collaboration between states, and the development of national strategies for gorilla conservation.

Thus, there are examples of MEAs that explicitly or implicitly provide for continued operation during armed conflicts. However, most environmental treaties – as in fact most treaties – do not expressly regulate for an outbreak of hostilities.[83] Vöneky argues that the loosely formulated language used in MEAs could be considered as constituting inherent derogation clauses. It would mean that a state party could derogate from certain obligations because of reasons connected to the armed conflict.[84] Nevertheless, the fact that MEAs formulate obligations creating some flexibility in the parties' application of them is not the same as being derogation clauses. For instance, if an MEA states that a state party shall adopt measures that are 'appropriate' to protect the environment, the standard of what is 'appropriate' during an armed conflict may not be the same as what is 'appropriate' in peacetime. However, such an assessment is based on the circumstances that a state party faces in peace or in war, and not on the possibility to derogate from the treaty. If a state party acts in accordance with what is considered appropriate, it is applying the treaty fully, even though the 'appropriate action' as well as its capacity to protect the environment may be altered during an armed conflict compared with peacetime.

Given that most MEAs do not expressly regulate the situation of an armed conflict, the applicability assessment's second stage would apply in such cases as proposed by the International Law Commission. Pursuant to Draft Article 5, the second stage consists of applying international rules on treaty interpretation

[83] A Pronto, 'The Effect of War on Law – What Happens to their Treaties when States go to War?' (2013) 2 *Cambridge Journal of International and Comparative Law* 227, 229.
[84] Vöneky, 'A New Shield' (n 31) 30.

to determine if a treaty is 'susceptible to termination, withdrawal or suspension in the event of an armed conflict'. The broader reference of 'international rules on treaty interpretation' in the Draft Article corresponds to Articles 31 and 32 VCLT, but keeps in mind that not all states are parties to the VCLT.[85] Thus, the second stage requires an examination in accordance with the treaty's ordinary meaning, object and purpose and subsequent practice, as well as the preparatory work and circumstances of its conclusion, to establish whether the treaty continues to apply. Hence, Draft Articles 4 and 5 focus on the factors relating to the treaty to pursue indications on whether it continues to operate during armed conflicts.[86]

The approach of the International Law Commission, as expressed in the draft articles, differs in two aspects from the one adopted by the International Court of Justice with regard to the *Nuclear Weapons* Advisory Opinion. First, the Court focused its attention on whether certain obligations within a treaty could apply, rather than the applicability of the treaty as such. Second, the Court could be understood that it meant that treaty obligations only apply if they were *intended* to constrain military behaviour during armed conflicts.[87] Hulme interprets the Court's statement to mean that the peacetime obligations that protect the environment are suspended during armed conflicts, unless they are adopted with the intention to apply in such situations. She states that: 'Seemingly, if such obligations were not so intended they would be suspended as between the belligerent States for the duration of the conflict'.[88] According to this interpretation of the *Nuclear Weapons* Advisory Opinion, the Court must have implied – given that most environmental treaties were adopted with the intention to regulate peacetime activities and not to restrain warfare – that the provisions of these treaties are not applicable during armed conflicts.

In contrast to the Court's view (as interpreted by Hulme), the International Law Commission has adopted a more progressive approach that provides for the possibility for MEAs' continued operation during armed conflicts. The Commission deliberately omitted an express reference to the intentions of the parties regarding the treaty's status in relation to warfare as a determining factor of its applicability. The reason is the rarity of the drafters discussing the possibility for a treaty to remain in operation in times of armed conflict.[89] In fact, multilateral treaties, often anchored in international organisations, have been negotiated and ratified for 'transnational, regional and even global interests' including environmental protection, free trade, disarmament and protection of human rights. Given this background, as pointed out by Arnold Pronto, '[i]t is

[85] Draft Articles on the Effects of Armed Conflicts on Treaties, with Commentaries (n 42); see Draft Article 5, para 2.

[86] ibid; see Draft Article 5, paras 1–2.

[87] *Legality of the Threat or Use of Nuclear Weapons* (n 43) para 30.

[88] Hulme, *War Torn Environment* (n 34) 141.

[89] Draft Articles on the Effects of Armed Conflicts on Treaties, with Commentaries (n 42); see Draft Article 5, para 3.

increasingly difficult to conceive of States opting-out from such a web of legal norms simply as a consequence of their involvement in an armed conflict'.[90] However, the intention of the parties is the decisive element in any interpretation process. To establish the ordinary meaning is in fact an exercise to determine the will of the parties. Consequently, it is contradictory of the International Law Commission to state in its Commentaries to the Draft Principles that a reference to the intentions of the parties is omitted. Yet, it seems like the International Law Commission is trying to avoid giving weight to the statement made by the Court in the *Nuclear Weapons* Advisory Opinion, in order to favour a more progressive approach. Instead, the Commission's position should rather be regarded as staying loyal to the interpretation process as expressed in the VCLT, given that it puts emphasis on the primary means of interpretation rather than on the supplementary, which would include the intentions of the negotiators as expressed in the preparatory work. As explained by Pronto: 'The emphasis is placed less on a subjective approach (implied in assertions of the intention of the parties) and more on the objective *meaning* of the treaty'.[91]

The third, and last, stage of the assessment suggested by the International Law Commission is formulated in Draft Articles 6 and 7. Draft Article 6 provides for an overall assessment based on factors related to (a) the nature of the treaty and (b) the characteristics of the armed conflict.[92] The first set of factors in (a) refers, in particular, to the treaty's subject matter, object and purpose, content, and the number of state parties (the draft articles apply to multilateral and bilateral treaties alike).[93] There is some overlap in relation to Draft Article 5, but Draft Article 6 is intended to offer a broader perspective by including factors that go beyond the rules of interpretation.[94]

Given that the subject matter and number of state parties are mentioned as factors that may affect the applicability of a treaty, it could include considerations as to what kind of interests the treaty protects or how derogations from it would affect other state parties. For instance, if it is an interest shared by all state parties protected under the treaty in question and a suspension would have negative effects on the third states, it could justify continued applicability during armed conflicts. As many of the environmental treaties protect a common concern owed to all the state parties, it concerns rights and obligations owed to the group (*erga omnes partes*), meaning that the group decides the matter. Sometimes the concern is even shared by the whole international community in order to mitigate global environmental problems.[95] MEAs often require that

[90] Pronto (n 83) 231.

[91] ibid, 236.

[92] Draft Articles on the Effects of Armed Conflicts on Treaties, with Commentaries (n 42); see Draft Article 6, para 2.

[93] ibid; see Draft Article 3, para 3.

[94] ibid; see Draft Article 6, para 3.

[95] J Brunnée, 'Common Areas, Common Heritage, and Common Concern' in D Bodansky, J Brunnée and E Hey (eds), *Oxford Handbook of International Environmental Law* (Oxford University Press, 2007) 553–55.

all state parties cooperate for the measures to be effective and it is not up to a particular state party to decide unilaterally. Therefore, to allow derogation from the obligations in times of armed conflict would undermine the operation of these treaties, as they do not work in a reciprocal way.[96] It would also affect third states that are not involved in the armed conflict.

According to Bannelier-Christakis, it would be technically impossible to allow for derogation because the obligations contained in MEAs are 'indivisible', meaning that the rights and obligations are interdependent.[97] She explains it that as the treaty provisions are owed to all state parties, so it is impossible to break them into bilateral relations based on reciprocity.[98] Removing some of the provisions from the rest of the treaty could threaten the operation of the entire treaty. Bannelier-Christakis provides an example of the 2011 Libyan conflict, in which it would be difficult to visualise how MEAs

> such as [the Convention of International Trade in Endangered Species[99] (CITES)] or the [Montreal Protocol on Substances that Deplete the Ozone Layer][100] on the protection of the ozone layer can be inapplicable in relation between belligerents while being at the same time applicable in all other type of relations between these states and third states.[101]

Within these types of treaties, fulfilling obligations does not lead to any advantage for any particular state because they serve a common concern of all the parties. They often include an intertemporal perspective going beyond the benefit of the community of today, to also refer to future generations. For instance, protecting world heritage must be seen as such an obligation that is not owed to a particular state but to all state parties and to be preserved for humankind in the future. In general, environmental treaties have to remain in operation for all state parties to be effective, even in times of armed conflict, because they often function on the cooperation of the state parties to protect a common concern. If this is a correct reading of the Commission's third stage of the assessment, environmental treaties should continue to operate during armed conflicts. Vöneky proposed a similar approach that MEAs should

[96] N Matz and R Wolfrum, *Conflicts in International Environmental Law* (Springer, 2003) 132–33.

[97] A similar discussion was raised in the International Law Commission in relation to the Reservation to Treaties, with regard to human rights treaties. It was claimed that these treaties have interdependent rights and obligations, meaning that the reservation to these treaties poses particular problems because its interdependence and the raison d'etre of the treaty may be threatened by a reservation relating to one of its elements. Therefore, such reservations would be invalid. See Reservation to Treaties (Continued), Report of the International Law Commission, 63rd Session (26 April–3 June and 4 July–12 August 2011) (2011) *Yearbook of the International Law Commission*, Volume II, Part Two: Guideline 3.1.5.6, 383.

[98] Bannelier-Christakis (n 33) 141.

[99] Convention on International Trade in Endangered Species (adopted 3 March 1973, entered into force 1 July 1975) 993 UNTS 243 (CITES).

[100] Montreal Protocol on Substances that Deplete the Ozone Layer (adopted 16 September 1987, entered into force 1 January 1989) 1522 UNTS 3 (Montreal Protocol).

[101] Bannelier-Christakis (n 33) 140–41.

remain in operation during armed conflicts based on the shared interest that they protect.[102]

In addition, a similar discussion has been raised by Verwey with regard to the application of the law of neutrality. He argues that this corpus of law provides that peacetime treaties entered between belligerent and neutral states continue to apply, while belligerents have the possibility, in case it is required by the 'necessities of war', to suspend the operation of multilateral treaties between them. However, according to Verwey, such a suspension would not be permissible if it negatively affects the rights of the neutral states under these treaties. Such negative impacts must be visible or evident.[103] As stated by Verwey, suspension of MEAs between the belligerents may negatively affect the rights of the other state parties being neutral third states. However, with regard to MEAs, it may be difficult to demonstrate the negative harm on the rights owed to the third states.[104] Nevertheless, the fact that most MEAs protect a common concern shared by all its state parties, with rights and obligations that are interdependent, indicates that the factors relating to the nature of the treaty, as provided in Draft Article 6, calls for the continued operation of MEAs during armed conflicts.

The other set of factors in Draft Article 6 regarding the characteristics of the armed conflict refers to, 'its territorial extent, its scale and intensity, its duration, and in the case of non-international armed conflict, also degree of outside involvement'.[105] For instance, whether the armed conflict takes place on land or at sea could be a factor. With regard to non-international armed conflicts, the inclusion of the element of 'degree of outside involvement' is intended to secure the treaty's stability because a higher degree of outside involvement increases the risk of affecting states' treaty relations.[106] The factors, in particular the scale of destruction and the intensity of the hostilities, are likely to affect the operation of an environmental treaty because they affect the ability of the state to act in accordance with the treaty obligations.

To provide further guidance, Draft Article 7 comprises an indicative list based on the treaty's subject matter. The list details the types of treaties that continue to operate, in whole or in part, during armed conflicts.[107] These are:

a. Treaties on the law of armed conflict
b. Status treaties

[102] Vöneky, 'A New Shield' (n 31) 27; Vöneky, 'Peacetime Environmental Law' (n 10) 211.

[103] Verwey refers to Convention (V) respecting the Rights and Duties of Neutral Powers and Persons in Case of War on Land (concluded 18 October 1907, entered into force 26 January 1910) and Convention (XIII) concerning the Rights and Duties of Neutral Powers in Naval War (concluded 18 October 1907, entered into force 26 January 1910). See W Verwey, 'Protection of the Environment in Times of Armed Conflict: In Search of a New Legal Perspective' (1995) 8 *Leiden Journal of International Law* 7, 26–28.

[104] Verwey (n 103) 26–28.

[105] Draft Articles on the Effects of Armed Conflicts on Treaties, with Commentaries (n 42); see Draft Article 6(b).

[106] ibid; see Draft Article 6, para 4.

[107] ibid; see Annex, para 2.

c. Multilateral law-making treaties
d. Treaties on international justice
e. Treaties on friendship, commerce and navigation
f. International human rights treaties
g. Treaties relating to the international protection of the environment
h. Treaties relating to international watercourses
i. Treaties relating to aquifers
j. Treaties which are constituent instruments of international organisations
k. Treaties relating to international peaceful dispute settlements
l. Treaties relating to diplomatic and consular relations.[108]

International environmental treaties are specified in (g) and may therefore, allegedly, continue to operate during armed conflicts. Bannelier-Christakis argues that the rationale of the International Law Commission to incorporate environmental treaties in the indicative list rests on their indivisible nature with 'the inability to "break" these multilateral agreements into a multitude of bilateral relations dominated by reciprocity'.[109] The incentive of why environmental treaties should remain in operation during armed conflicts is the fact that they contain interdependent obligations owed to all the state parties, as discussed above. Derogation because of an armed conflict would indeed complicate their operation and ability to fulfil treaty objectives.

According to Loets, however, the position of the Commission to include environmental treaties as the group of treaties with presumed wartime continuation does not reflect a consensual opinion of states or scholars. He describes the legal foundation of the inclusion as 'shaky'.[110] In that respect, the Commission's indicative list may be regarded as a progressive step towards applicability of MEAs during armed conflicts. Loets correctly points out that the indicative list provides a 'quasi-presumption' of continued operation of environmental treaties. As the remaining draft articles provide factors that are decisive to determine continued operation, the presumption can be broken based on these. The structure of the draft articles appears, therefore, to contradict them, thereby weakening the presumption. Thus, given that other factors are also relevant, an environmental treaty may not apply during an armed conflict after completing the three-stage assessment in accordance with the draft articles.[111]

In addition, as a concluding remark, Draft Article 18 conserves, 'the possibility of termination or withdrawal of a treaty, or of suspension thereof, arising from the application of other rules of international law'. The existence of an armed conflict does not preclude the operation of other grounds for termination, withdrawal, or suspension, as also provided under the VCLT.[112]

[108] ibid.
[109] Bannelier-Christakis (n 33) 140.
[110] Loets (n 58) 133.
[111] ibid, 132.
[112] Draft Articles on the Effects of Armed Conflicts on Treaties, with Commentaries (n 42); see Draft Article 18, paras 1–2.

In sum, the International Law Commission offers certain guidance in the draft articles on how different types of treaties could be affected by armed conflicts. Nevertheless, there are unresolved issues regarding the assessment of the applicability of environmental treaties during armed conflicts. No fixed general rule can be formulated based on the draft articles. However, Bannelier-Christakis underlines that the work of the International Law Commission has progressively moved the position forward towards a common understanding on the applicability of MEAs during armed conflicts that they are presumed to continue to operate. She stresses, however, that the progress made is not sufficient and that the work of the Commission is somewhat conceptionally vague.[113]

The general conclusion of the Commission solves the previous debate on whether environmental treaties *can* apply during armed conflicts, as there are scholars that have previously argued against such a possibility.[114] Nevertheless, many questions remain in regard to the applicability of environmental treaties in armed conflicts. For instance, do MEAs apply in relation to an armed conflict even in the parts of a territory that are no longer under control of the state party? How do the environmental treaties operate in times of armed conflict? How do they relate to obligations stemming from the law of armed conflict? The draft articles do not touch on these issues.

Overall, the benefit of the draft articles can be questioned. The draft articles appear to merely reproduce the existing treaty law, as provided under the VCLT. As international law is dispositive, the state parties to a treaty ultimately regulate the question on applicability of a treaty during armed conflicts. Instead, the importance of the work of the International Law Commission with regard to this topic is the establishment of the presumption that environmental treaties are not *ipso facto* terminated or suspended because of the outbreak of an armed conflict, as stated in Draft Article 3.

To conclude, environmental treaties can apply during an armed conflict, although it is unclear how the operation will be conducted. Thus, the focus appears to have shifted because the present problem is not whether the peacetime environmental treaties can apply or not, but whether they can provide any added environmental protection during armed conflicts.

V. THE *LEX SPECIALIS* RULE DURING ARMED CONFLICTS

The International Law Commission's draft articles on Effects of Armed Conflict on Treaties stipulate the possibility for environmental treaties to continue to

[113] Bannelier-Christakis (n 33) 140.

[114] See R Falk, 'The Environmental Law of War: An Introduction' in G Plant (ed), *Environmental Protection and the Law of War: A 'Fifth Geneva' Convention on the Protection of the Environment in Time of Armed Conflict* (Belhaven Press, 1992) 78; L Low and D Hodgkinson, 'Compensation for Wartime Environmental Damage: Challenges to International Law After the Gulf War' (1994) 35 *Virginia Journal of International Law* 405.

operate during armed conflicts. However, the draft articles do not ensure that MEAs remain 'effective' in such situations, meaning that they can enhance the environmental protection.[115] They may be subject to constraints if they are not compatible with the rules of the law of armed conflict being the *lex specialis* in times of armed conflict. The International Law Commission does not comment on the interrelation between the applicable treaties during armed conflicts.

The present section deals with the application of the *lex specialis* rule during armed conflicts, its establishment as the prevailing conflict solution technique, and how the law that applies as the '*lex specialis* law' relates to other applicable rules.

A. The Application of the *Lex Specialis* Rule

The *lex specialis derogat generali* (the *lex specialis* rule) prescribes that specific laws take precedence over general laws in cases where these are incompatible. As the law of armed conflict is the specialised legal regime regulating warfare, it is considered as the *lex specialis* law in times of war, in relation to peacetime law. The *lex specialis* rule applies to solve situations of normative conflicts.[116] A normative conflict occurs when two rules deal with the same subject matter and are applicable in the same context and time frame, with some amount of inconsistency between them, and both rules are prevented from being applied concurrently.[117]

In the literature, the views on the *lex specialis* rule vary and give rise to some confusion regarding the terminology, as well as the application, of the rule.[118] Milanovic has identified three different takes on the *lex specialis* rule: first, as a rule of total displacement of an entire legal area; second, as a rule of partial displacement or as a normative conflict solutions technique; or third, as an interpretative tool to avoid normative conflicts.[119] I will address and clarify these three takes on the rule in the sub-subsections below.

i. *The* Lex Specialis *Rule as Totally Displacing Entire Areas of Law*

The first take on the *lex specialis* rule is closely related to the debate on whether peacetime law can be fully displaced during armed conflicts. It is based on the

[115] Loets (n 58) 135.

[116] I have chosen to refer to 'normative tensions' rather than 'normative conflict' in this book, as I will explain in the next chapter (ch 7). However, in the present chapter I mainly use the term 'normative conflicts' while discussing the application of the *lex specialis* rule.

[117] A Lindroos, 'Addressing Norm Conflicts in a Fragmented Legal System: The Doctrine of *Lex Specialis*' (2005) 74 *Nordic Journal of International Law* 27, 39.

[118] P Eden and M Happold, 'Symposium: The Relationship between International Humanitarian Law and International Human Rights Law' (2010) 14 *Journal of Conflict & Security Law* 2.

[119] M Milanovic, 'The Lost Origins of *Lex Specialis*: Rethinking the Relationship Between Human Rights and International Humanitarian Law' in JD Ohlin (ed), *Theoretical Boundaries of Armed Conflict and Human Rights* (Cambridge University Press, 2016).

historical division between the law of peace and the law of war (law of armed conflict).[120] As discussed above, this view holds that all treaty relations between the parties to an armed conflict are suspended and that their relation would be solely regulated under the law of armed conflict.[121] This view of the *lex specialis* rule would mean that the obligations of any other field would not apply during war. Instead, all issues that arise would be addressed under the law of armed conflict, consisting of law of neutrality, law of occupation, and international humanitarian law. Thus, according to this view, matters related to environmental protection would exclusively be dealt with under the law of armed conflict, setting a certain wartime standard of the permitted environmental damage during an armed conflict.

This take on the application of the *lex specialis* rule lacks support in the modern practice, as well as in the legal doctrine. For instance, the International Law Commission has confirmed that peacetime treaties can remain in operation in situations of armed conflict, as discussed above. Similarly, the practice of the International Court of Justice confirms the applicability of peacetime law in times of armed conflict.[122] The Court refers mainly to human rights law, which – in contrast to international environmental law – explicitly continues to apply during armed conflicts.[123] However, the analysis on how MEA obligations might apply together with the law of armed conflict is similar to the conclusion drawn in relation to human rights law.[124]

More in detail, in the *Nuclear Weapons* Advisory Opinion, the International Court of Justice examined the application of different areas of international law, including the law of armed conflict, human rights law, international environmental law, and the prohibition of the use of force, in respect to the use of nuclear weapons. The Court only made some general observations regarding the relation between international environmental law and the law of armed conflict. Instead, it devoted more attention to clarify the relation between human rights law and the law of armed conflict. More specifically, the Court had to decide what constitutes an 'arbitrary deprivation of life' under Article 6 of the International Covenant on Civil and Political Rights (ICCPR).[125] The Court decided that the standard of killing should be determined in accordance with the law of armed conflict during armed conflicts.[126]

[120] ibid.

[121] G Plant, *Environmental Protection and the Law of War: A 'Fifth Geneva' Convention on the Protection of the Environment in Time of Armed Conflict* (Belhaven Press, 1992) 14.

[122] See *Legality of the Threat or Use of Nuclear Weapons* (n 43) 226; *Legal Consequences of the Construction of a Wall in the Occupied Palestinian Territory* (n 43) 136; *Armed Activities on the Territory of the Congo (Democratic Republic of the Congo v Uganda)*, Judgment of 19 December 2005, ICJ Reports 2005, 168.

[123] Article 72 Protocol I; and Preamble Protocol II.

[124] See K Hulme, 'Armed Conflict and Biodiversity' in M Bowman, P Davies and E Goodwin (eds), *Research Handbook on Biodiversity and Law* (Edward Elgar Publishing, 2016).

[125] International Covenant on Civil and Political Rights (adopted 16 December 1966, entered into force 23 March 1976) 999 UNTS 171 (ICCPR).

[126] *Legality of the Threat or Use of Nuclear Weapons* (n 43) para 25.

The Court affirmed that the law of armed conflict is specifically designed for armed conflict, and, therefore, it must prevail as the *lex specialis* law to the extent there is a normative conflict with the provisions of human rights law during an armed conflict.[127] The International Court of Justice circumvented to establish a general priority between the legal areas.[128] In addition, the International Criminal Tribunal for the former Yugoslavia (ICTY) has established the applicability of human rights law in times of armed conflict.[129] Hence, regarding the law of armed conflict as applying as the *lex specialis* in a situation of war does not suggest that human rights law, as one entire legal area of law, is displaced in such situations.

In addition, the suspension of all peacetime law is contradicted by the inclusion of derogation clauses in peacetime instruments because they indicate their continued applicability during armed conflicts. These would not have any function if they were considered to be automatically suspended during wartime.[130] For instance, Article 4 ICCPR and Article 15 of the European Convention on Human Rights (ECHR)[131] provide for derogation by state parties in an officially proclaimed public emergency that threatens the life of the nation. However, the articles only relate specifically to these human rights law instruments. MEAs rarely address the situations as armed conflict, although there are exceptions – as previously discussed, such as the World Heritage Convention, 1997 UN Convention on International Watercourses, and the African Convention on the Conservation of Nature and Natural Resources – that include provisions related to armed conflict. With regard to the 1997 UN Convention in International Watercourses, Roberts argues that it is drafted with Protocol I in mind.[132] The provision reads:

> International watercourses and related installations, facilities and other works shall enjoy the protection accorded by the principles and rules of international law applicable in international and non-international armed conflict and shall not be used in violation of those principles and rules.[133]

In conclusion, the *lex specialis* rule cannot be used to categorically displace the application of an entire legal field in situations of war. Consequently, the application of the law of armed conflict as the *lex specialis*, in accordance with the first take on the rule, is not a well-founded position within contemporary international law.

[127] ibid.
[128] M Koskenniemi, 'The Fate of Public International Law: Between Technique and Politics' (2007) 70 *Modern Law Review* 5.
[129] *Kunarac*, IT-96-23-T, Judgment of 22 February 2001, para 467.
[130] Milanovic (n 119) 25.
[131] European Convention for the Protection of Human Rights and Fundamental Freedoms, as amended by Protocols Nos 11 and 14 (adopted 4 November 1950, entered into force 3 September 1953) ETS 5 (ECHR).
[132] Roberts (n 30) 63.
[133] Article 29 Convention on International Watercourses.

ii. The Lex Specialis *Rule as Partially Displacing Other Areas of Law*

As proposed by Milanovic, the second take on the *lex specialis* rule is perceived in the literature as a rule that partially displaces peacetime law or as a rule of conflict solution. According to this view, the *lex specialis* rule prevails in case two rules are in conflict with each other. In other words, this take on the *lex specialis* rule is applied to resolve a conflict of rules, but only in so far as there is a concrete conflict to deal with. The International Court of Justice has established such a view of the rule in the *Nuclear Weapons* Advisory Opinion, the *Legal Consequences of the Construction of a Wall in the Occupied Palestinian Territory* (*Wall* Advisory Opinion), as well as in the *Armed Activities* case.[134] In these cases, the Court affirms that the law of armed conflict and human rights law could apply simultaneously. The Court recognised that these are two specialised fields of law: the human rights law concerns the rights of human beings to be protected against the abusive power of their state at all times and the law of armed conflict deals with the permissive conduct of parties to an armed conflict. Both areas of law apply in the same situations, 'but can also outlaw the same conduct', as expressed by Orakhelashvili.[135] However, the Court has not explained what the factors are that determine the qualification of one law as the being the *lex specialis* in comparison to the other.

In the *Nuclear Weapons* Advisory Opinion, the International Court of Justice merely stated that the law of armed conflict was specifically designed for armed conflict and thus it prevails based on the *lex specialis* rule in cases where there is an inconsistency in the application of the two legal areas.[136] Moreover, the Court explained that the law of armed conflict and human rights law could complement each other. For instance, while human rights law applies exclusively to some matters that fall outside the scope of the law of armed conflict, other matters would be exclusively dealt with under the law of armed conflict. In the *Wall* Advisory Opinion, the Court formulates it in this way:

> As regards the relationship between international humanitarian law and human rights law, there are thus three possible situations: some rights may be exclusively matters of international humanitarian law; others may be exclusively matters of human rights law; yet others may be matters of both these branches of international law. In order to answer the question put to it, the Court will have to take into consideration both these branches of international law, namely human rights law and, as *lex specialis*, international humanitarian law.[137]

[134] See *Legality of the Threat or Use of Nuclear Weapons* (n 43) 226; *Legal Consequences of the Construction of a Wall in the Occupied Palestinian Territory* (n 43) 136; *Armed Activities on the Territory of the Congo (Democratic Republic of the Congo v Uganda)* (n 122) 168. *Kunarac* (n 129) para 467.

[135] A Orakhelashvili, 'The Interaction Between Human Rights and Humanitarian Law: Fragmentation, Conflict, Parallelism, or Convergence?' (2008) 19 *European Journal of International Law* 163.

[136] *Legality of the Threat or Use of Nuclear Weapons* (n 43) para 25.

[137] *Legal Consequences of the Construction of a Wall in the Occupied Palestinian Territory* (n 43) para 106.

This take on the *lex specialis* rule does not generally exclude the application of peacetime treaties, but it may displace the application of a particular rule that conflicts with a rule under the law of armed conflict.[138]

The International Court of Justice has affirmed that human rights law continues to apply during armed conflicts and cannot unconditionally be overridden by the law of armed conflict.[139] The rules that are set aside maintain some legal effect. This take on the *lex specialis* rule, providing that the law of armed conflict in times of wartime partially displaces rules of peacetime law to solve normative conflicts, is widely accepted in the doctrine and in state practice.[140] I therefore consider that this take represents the correct legal definition of the rule.

iii. The Lex Specialis *Rule as an Interpretative Tool*

The third view of the *lex specialis* rule, as identified by Milanovic, is as a tool for interpretation. In such a case, it is not necessarily applied to solve a normative conflict but to interpret a rule in the light of another rule regulating the same subject matter, but in a more specific manner.[141] Mus has described the *lex specialis* rule to be a rule of interpretation rather than a rule to solve normative conflicts.[142] It is recognised under international law that human rights law can influence the interpretation of the law of armed conflict during armed conflicts. For instance, the ICTY has taken a comparable view by deciding that human rights law and the law of armed conflict are mutually complementary and can be used to inform the content and scope of each other's rules.[143] It has been expressed that human rights law

> is generally a welcome and needed assistance to determine the content of customary international law in the field of humanitarian law. With regards to certain of its aspects, international humanitarian law can be said to have fused with human rights law.[144]

For instance, Article 14 ICCPR, dealing with due process guarantees, informs the content of the right to a fair and regular trial under the 1949 Geneva Conventions, which is silent in regard to the meaning and requirements of such a trial.[145] In addition, the law of armed conflict could assist to interpret rules in the human rights law instruments. Milanovic suggests, as an example, that

[138] Vöneky, 'A New Shield' (n 31) 25.
[139] Lindroos (n 117) 43.
[140] Green (n 46) 226; Koppe (n 46).
[141] Milanovic (n 119).
[142] JB Mus, 'Conflicts Between Treaties in International Law' (1998) 45 *Netherlands International Law Review* 218.
[143] *Kunarac* (n 129) para 467.
[144] ibid, para 471.
[145] For further discussion, see O Ben-Naftali and Y Shany, 'Living in Denial: The Application of Human Rights in the Occupied Territories' (2003) 17 *Israel Law Review* 17, 105–06.

rules in the law of armed conflict can be applied to interpret the arbitrariness standard in Articles 6 (right to life) and 9 ICCPR (right to liberty and security) during armed conflicts.[146]

According to Tignino, concerning the *Armed Activities* case, the International Court of Justice adopts an approach that aims at promoting coherence between the law of armed conflict and human rights law. The Court did not refer to the *lex specialis* rule, but stated that the occupying power has a duty to comply with both regimes. Concerning this issue, Tignino also points out that both the Commission of Inquiry on Lebanon and the UN fact-finding mission in Gaza have employed similar reasoning. In these cases, a consistent interpretation was applied that concluded that the rules of the law of armed conflict must be read in the broader context of general law.[147] However, the practice referred to above merely regards the application of human rights law in relation to the law of armed conflict, and without applying the *lex specialis* rule.

According to Milanovic, this practice has been described in legal scholarship as applying the *lex specialis* rule in a similar manner as interpreting rules to achieve harmonisation.[148] These examples provide for the possibility of applying other legal areas in a complementary manner in relation to the law of armed conflict. The referred examples are examples of conducting an evolutionary interpretation of the treaty provisions, and not an application of the *lex specialis* rule. An evolutionary approach can be applied in an interpretation process, according to Article 31(1) VCLT, by using the language of international law as expressed in treaties to establish the ordinary meaning, or by using Article 31(3)(c) VCLT (also referred to as the principle of systemic integration), considering other relevant rules when conducting an interpretation. Thus, I do not agree that the examples are supporting the take on the *lex specialis* rule being referred to as a harmonising tool of interpretation. However, there are cases where it is unclear whether the *lex specialis* rule or the principle of systemic integration has been applied. As argued by d'Aspremont and Tranchez, the International Court of Justice in the *Wall* Advisory Opinion used the *lex specialis* rule and the principle of systemic integration 'in tandem' to harmonise when different standards of behaviour were provided under the law of armed conflict and human rights law. They described it as an 'unorthodox use' of the *lex specialis* rule.[149]

[146] Milanovic (n 119) 27.

[147] M Tignino, 'The Legal Regime of Natural Resources in Times of Armed Conflict and its Weaknesses' in Y Kerbrat and S Maljean-Dubois (eds), *The Transformation of International Environmental Law* (Hart Publishing and Editions A Pedone, 2011) 206. See also *Armed Activities on the Territory of the Congo (Democratic Republic of the Congo v Uganda)* (n 122) para 178.

[148] Milanovic (n 119) 27.

[149] J D'Aspremont and E Tranchez, 'The Quest for a Non-Conflictual Coexistence of International Human Rights Law and Humanitarian Law: Which Role for the *Lex Specialis* Principle?' in R Kolb and G Gaggioli (eds), *Research Handbook on Human Rights and Humanitarian Law* (Edward Elgar Publishing, 2013) 239–42.

iv. What to Make of the Different Takes of the Lex Specialis *Rule?*

I argue that the correct take on the *lex specialis* rule is a conflict solution technique applicable to resolve existing normative conflicts and that other takes on the rule are insufficiently grounded. In fact, to use the *lex specialis* rule as both a conflict solution technique as well as a rule of interpretation to harmonise between rules is contradictory because it gives the same rule different meanings. To sum up, while the first take on the *lex specialis* rule has been more or less abandoned in the modern doctrine, both the other two have support. This leads to some misunderstandings and confusion on what the *lex specialis* rule stands for and how it should be applied in international law. In both cases, the result is to allow a more special rule to prevail over another, either through establishing a priority between the rules or to provide for an interpretation to incorporate the more specialised rule into the general one. However, a rule of interpretation is exclusively used to establish the content in a certain treaty provision with an unclear 'ordinary meaning' and an interpretation process does not include the application of the *lex specialis* rule. It cannot be regarded as providing interpretation in a technical sense if it partly displaces the content of one of the two inconsistent rules, even if the purpose is to allow these to complement each other. Such an application of the *lex specialis* rule goes beyond treaty interpretation because its aim is in fact to establish a priority between the rules, even though the ambition is to harmonise them.

Albeit that the rules of interpretation offer methods to harmonise between rules – for instance, Article 31(3)(c) VCLT – these are limited. If Article 31(3)(c) VCLT is applied in an interpretation process, it is not a matter of applying the *lex specialis* rule but the rules of interpretation. In an interpretation process, once the ordinary meaning has been established, the options for various ways to interpret a rule have been exhausted. If a normative conflict persists, such a situation has to be resolved by using the legal techniques of conflict solutions because the rules of interpretation cannot establish a different meaning with the sole purpose of solving the conflict. If facing two alternative interpretations, however, interpretation using the context to choose the alternative that coheres with other relevant rules of international law can be done in accordance with Article 31(3)(c) VCLT.

In sum, the *lex specialis* rule applies as a conflict solution technique, even in cases where the normative value of the overridden rule is not completely displaced. It can only apply after an interpretation of a rule has been conducted with the result of an unsolved normative conflict. This view is supported by d'Aspremont and Tranchez. They claim that using the *lex specialis* rule as an interpretative tool is 'not only pointless, but also comes at the cost of the integrity and the clarity of the principle *lex specialis derogat generali.*[150] Thus, I think it is a misconception for the *lex specialis* rule to be conceived as a legal tool

[150] ibid, 242.

for interpretation. Reasonably, the *lex specialis* rule is a conflict solution technique that can be applied with various degrees of interference with regard to the general overridden rule depending on the type of normative conflict.[151]

B. Challenging the Application of the *Lex Specialis* Rule

The established view within international legal scholarship, and also as confirmed by the International Court of Justice, is that the law of armed conflict is considered to apply as the *lex specialis* in times of armed conflict in relation to inconsistent rules of peacetime law.[152] Such a view affirms international law as one system. While the law of armed conflict is specially designed to deal with situations of armed conflict, it can be questioned if all peacetime rules are considered as being the 'general law' in relation to the law of armed conflict in all circumstances during an armed conflict.

In the *Nuclear Weapons* Advisory Opinion, the International Court of Justice stated that environmental considerations have to be taken into account while assessing what is necessary and proportionate when verifying legitimate military objectives.[153] This statement reflects the view that the Court views the application of the law of armed conflict as the *lex specialis* applicable during armed conflicts and international environmental law (as well as human rights law) as the general law However, in this Advisory Opinion, the Court only dealt with international environmental law on an overall basis.

International environmental law can be specialised in its scope, in particular, if considering MEAs. They deal with the protection of specific components of the environment (such as the ozone layer, biodiversity, wetlands, certain species etc), or address a specific environmental problem (such as climate change, desertification, oil spills, etc). Whereas the rules of the law of armed conflict protect all types of objects and regulate all types of issues (including weapons, the treatment of prisoners of war, and the rules of military conduct), MEAs are restricted in their scope to a specific issue. From such a perspective, the rules of MEAs must be considered more specialised rules. On the other hand, the law of armed conflict requires an outbreak of an armed conflict to be activated and applicable, which makes the law of armed conflict more specific with regard to the temporal scope, in comparison with MEAs that apply at all times.[154]

There is no guidance that supports that the temporal scope of a legal regime would make an area of law, or a certain rule, more special or specific. In the

[151] A conflict that cannot be solved through harmonisation is usually referred to as a 'strict conflict' or 'genuine conflict'. See Lindroos (n 117) 39.

[152] W Jenks, 'The Conflict of Law-making Treaties' (1953) 30 *British Yearbook of International Law* 401, 446.

[153] *Legality of the Threat or Use of Nuclear Weapons* (n 43) para 30.

[154] See A O'Donoghue, 'Splendid Isolation: International Humanitarian Law, Legal Theory and the International Legal Order' (2011) 14 *Yearbook of International Humanitarian Law* 107, 116.

Nuclear Weapons Advisory Opinion, the Court determined that the applicable standard of killing was more specific in the law of armed conflict, designed for wartime, and therefore prevailed at the cost of Article 6 ICCPR. However, the Court did not describe how it reached the conclusion that the law of armed conflict is more special than human rights law. In fact, the *lex specialis* rule lacks a normative content to provide criteria to decide whether one area of law is more special.[155] The generality and specificity always relate to each other. For this reason, it must be determined within a system or structure that can provide a scale for the level of specification.

In a situation where two rules originate from two different specialised areas of law and apply to the same subject matter, some scholars question the usefulness of the *lex specialis* rule.[156] As expressed by Lindroos, while the *lex specialis* rule might be an appropriate tool to resolve 'norm conflicts within a single treaty or between treaties which are part of the same system or a system of treaties', it is difficult to apply it to establish priority between norms of different bodies of law.[157] According to Koskenniemi, the choice of what should constitute the *lex specialis* law depends on the perspective from which the issue is viewed.[158] Koskenniemi claims:

> The choice of one among several applicable legal regimes refers back to what is understood as significant in a problem. And the question of significance refers back to what the relevant institution understands as its mission, its structural bias.[159]

One of the examples that Koskenniemi provides regards the occupation of Iraq that can be addressed through the lens of 'human rights' as well as 'security' and thus points to diverse legal frameworks. The choice between these depends, according to Koskenniemi, on how occupation should be assessed – as an issue of security or human rights.[160] Hence, in the case where two norms apply to the same subject matter and they both may be regarded as special depending on which perspective is adopted, the *lex specialis* rule cannot determine which of the special norms prevails.[161]

As described by Lindroos, '[t]o settle priority to a special norm within the system of unclear norm relations, the decision will rely on political or other

[155] Lindroos (n 117) 66; Koskenniemi (n 128) 5.

[156] Lindroos (n 117) 41–44; J Pauwelyn, *Conflict of Norms in Public International Law: How WTO Law Relates to Other Rules of International Law* (Cambridge University Press, 2009) 388; I Scobbie, 'Principle or Pragmatics? The Relationship between Human Rights Law and the Law of Armed Conflict' (2010) 14 *Journal of Conflict & Security Law* 449 453; Eden and Happold (n 118) 3; F Hampson, 'Other Areas of Customary Law in Relation to the Study' in E Wilmshurst and S Breau (eds), *Perspectives on the ICRC Study on Customary International Humanitarian Law* (Cambridge University Press, 2007) 66–68.

[157] Lindroos (n 117) 41.

[158] Koskenniemi (n 128) 6–7.

[159] ibid, 6.

[160] ibid.

[161] Lindroos (n 117) 66.

considerations rather than on *lex specialis*'.[162] According to this view, the choice of which rule is to be given priority between norms of specialised regimes is a biased decision that is made outside the legal sphere and not by legal reasoning.[163] This makes the application of the *lex specialis* rule uncertain in its general application. However, as the international legal system is a single one, I argue that the specialised systems belong to one system, which facilitates the application of the *lex specialis* rule.

In opposition to what Koskenniemi argues regarding the application of the *lex specialis* rule in general, such a choice does not necessarily have to be based on a political preference. The choices that are offered to the law-applier can also be legally justified even if the law-applier has a certain discretionary power. The law-applier ought to take into account the bigger system of international law, because no legal area exists in a vacuum. Indeed, there is a well-established view among states, as well as scholars, that the law of armed conflict applies as the *lex specialis* in times of armed conflict in relation to peacetime law. The justification of this position is based on the will of the legislator (the states). As put by Milanovic, 'the legislator could not possibly have intended to legislate two hierarchically equal norms that are ultimately contradictory'.[164] Therefore, the principal international lawmakers – the states – could not have intended to create rules of peacetime law that would apply during armed conflicts and at the same time be more restricting than the rules of the law of armed conflict. States have historically acted in a manner that provides fewer restrictions on their behaviour during armed conflicts.[165] States have adopted the law of armed conflict to provide for exceptions to peacetime law under the exceptional circumstances prevailing during armed conflicts. This signals that it is one international legal system with a scale of speciality and generality, at least in relation to times of war and times of peace. Therefore, to determine that the law of armed conflict applies as the *lex specialis* during war is not a biased decision, but a logical application of international law in accordance with the legislator's (the states') intention.

Nevertheless, even if the law of armed conflict is regarded as the *lex specialis* during armed conflicts, it does not exclude rules of other legal areas from applying, as discussed above. In addition, it is of limited use because of the disagreements on how it applies. It does not prescribe exactly how overlaps between two areas of law should be dealt with.[166] Applicable MEAs have a normative value because they may inform and complement the application of the law of armed conflict in accordance with the prevailing view of the application of the *lex specialis* rule and an evolutionary interpretation approach.

[162] ibid, 42.
[163] ibid, 66.
[164] Milanovic (n 119) 29.
[165] ibid.
[166] Eden and Happold (n 118) 2.

The international environmental law instruments can assist in informing the broader body of law applicable to environmental protection during armed conflicts.[167] Such an application of the law is not made based on politically biased views, but on the rules of international law. As discussed in chapters three, four and five, the law of armed conflict contains vague rules in relation to environmental protection, leaving room for the law-applier's discretion. Such discretion can be narrowed by allowing international environmental rules to clarify these vague rules. MEAs can support and give specificity to the rules that are vague in the law of armed conflict.

VI. MEANINGLESS MEAs?

MEAs have a reputation among international lawyers as consisting of framework conventions that lack enforceable content. In fact, international environmental law is repeatedly criticised for being nothing more than a 'negotiation system' with a poor implementation record, even in peacetime.[168] Legal scholars, in particular those with a background in the law of armed conflict, question the ability of MEAs to put any constraints on the belligerent parties during an armed conflict.

Liebler discusses the potential of environmental treaties to address deliberate wartime air pollution. With regard to LRTAP (Convention on Long-Range Transboundary Air Pollution) and the Convention for the Protection of the Ozone Layer,[169] he states: 'In practice, however, these conventions do not impose real restrictions on deliberate wartime air pollution'.[170] He describes the terminology used in the conventions as 'extremely weak' by referring to the fact that state parties have to 'endeavour' to restrict the air pollution 'as far as possible' and take 'appropriate measures'. Furthermore, Liebler argues that the treaties do not provide for any measures to enforce state responsibility in case of a breach.[171]

Similarly to Liebler, Bunker acknowledges that MEAs may be applicable during armed conflicts, but she finds that the 'flexible and ambiguous' worded language in the provisions cannot provide any meaningful environmental protection during armed conflicts.[172] Hence, in the few cases in which specific MEAs are

[167] Bruch mentioned this in relation to non-international armed conflict, but it could also be used in relation to international armed conflict. C Bruch, 'All's Not Fair in (Civil) War: Criminal Liability for Environmental Damage in Internal Armed Conflict' (2000) 25 *Vermont Law Review* 695, 715.

[168] Bodansky (n 5) 226.

[169] Convention for the Protection of the Ozone Layer (adopted 22 March 1985, entered into force 22 September 1988) 1513 UNTS 323 (Vienna Convention).

[170] A Leibler, 'Deliberate Wartime Environmental Damage' (1992) 23 *California Western International Law Journal* 67, 80.

[171] ibid, 80–81.

[172] A-L Bunker, 'Protection of the Environment During Armed Conflict: One Gulf, Two Wars' (2004) 13 *Review of European, Comparative & International Environmental Law* 201, 211.

analysed in the literature, they are dismissed on the grounds of being unable to provide any tangible obligations during armed conflicts, because of their loosely worded provisions. However, there are exceptions. For instance, Hulme analyses the 'co-application' of the Biodiversity Convention and the World Heritage Convention in relation to armed conflict and investigates how these may provide protection on a general level.[173] Yet, the majority of the research overlooks how MEAs can operate in wartime to strengthen environmental protection because MEAs are not regarded as effective during armed conflicts.[174]

On the other hand, and interestingly enough, there seems to be a contrasting view among a few scholars on how MEAs could apply during armed conflicts. For instance, Loets states that if it can be established that environmental treaties apply during armed conflicts, 'they would thus significantly improve the lot of the environment compared to the prevailing legal situation'.[175] Bothe et al state that international environmental law

> provides a well-established body of norms, standards, approaches, and mechanisms preventing and redressing – including through responsibility and, increasingly, liability – damage to the environment during times of peace. With the development, maturation, and application of a substantial body of law governing environmental use and protection, the question is whether and to what extent these provisions of [international environmental law] continue to apply during armed conflict and whether they provide a meaningful protection against the specific risks of warfare.[176]

However, in a footnote in the same article, the authors say:

> We have seen that, although environmental treaties can be applied to situations of armed conflict, their provisions are often too flexible and ambiguous to provide any real guidance to commanders on the battlefield or to be enforced after the event.[177]

In addition, no commentators go into detail on how such instruments could apply to improve environmental protection.

The conflicting views in the legal doctrine indicate that there is a knowledge gap regarding how MEAs can contribute to enhance environmental protection in times of armed conflict. Hence, the current section seeks to remedy such a knowledge gap. I argue that MEAs are not meaningless instruments, but that they are constructed in a different way compared with instruments of the law of armed conflict. Therefore, a lawyer specialising in the law of armed conflict may at first glance perceive MEAs as vague frameworks without enforceable

Bunker does notice that MEAs protecting particular areas of environmental significance may be able to sustain some protection – defined areas can be avoided and protected in situations of armed conflict.

[173] Hulme, 'Armed Conflict and Biodiversity' (n 124).

[174] HH Almond, 'Weapons, War and the Environment' (1990) 3 *Georgetown International Environmental Law Review* 117, 131.

[175] Loets (n 58) 128.

[176] Bothe et al (n 31) 579.

[177] See Bothe et al 582, fn 46.

obligations and real constraints. However, MEAs establish entire treaty systems in which their provisions continuously develop, mainly through their treaty bodies. There is an absence of understanding on how such treaty systems function in the literature analysing wartime environmental damage.

The establishment of treaty systems are related to the fact that MEAs often represent the result of compromises from negotiations between states.[178] Because of the difficulties in achieving political consensus on global environmental issues – not serving any self-interest, but a common interest of all state parties – states are reluctant to express such commitments in explicit binding rules. It is often easier to persuade states to agree on adopting a plan of action or a declaration that expresses a political will to solve a particular problem, rather than to adopt a binding document.[179] Thus, quickly adjustable and non-binding acts are highly influential in MEAs and in international environmental law in general, to a much greater extent than in many other areas of international law. Consequently, MEAs replicate half steps agreed on by the negotiators and the treaty systems provide platforms for continued dialogue on these unsettled issues, putting an emphasis on the future process of developing the rules.

In the treaty systems, the treaty bodies play an essential role.[180] Given that MEAs largely build from frameworks – consisting of provisions that are often described as containing vague, open-ended, or flexible language[181] – the treaty bodies have a mandate to develop the content of the treaty provisions into more detailed obligations by adopting protocols, decisions, guidelines, recommendations, etc. Thus, the treaties are characterised by a 'dynamic approach' because they install a form of continuous negotiation among the state parties within the treaty system. As described by Maljean-Dubois:

> At the cost of legal insecurity, the set of rules is not rigid but evolving and perfectible depending on current scientific knowledge and its improvements as well as the gravity of the attacks against the natural environment. In practice, as far as revision is concerned a distinction is often made between general provisions and technical or scientific provisions of a treaty.[182]

Thus, even after a treaty text is adopted, the treaty bodies continue to develop the content.[183] The treaty texts are just the starting point of a normative process.

[178] M Kampto, 'Normative Uncertainties' in Y Kerbrat and S Maljean-Dubois (eds), *The Transformation of International Environmental Law* (Hart Publishing and Editions A Pedone, 2011) 57.

[179] T Koivurova, *Introduction to International Environmental Law* (Routledge, 2014) 58.

[180] R Churchill and G Ulfstein, 'Autonomous Institutional Arrangements in Multilateral Environmental Agreements: A Little-Noticed Phenomenon in International Law' (2000) 94 *American Journal of International Law* 623, 628; Kampto (n 178) 57.

[181] Birnie, Boyle and Redgwell (n 19) 17.

[182] Maljean-Dubois, 'The Making of International Law' (n 29) 37.

[183] Kampto (n 178) 57. See also Churchill and Ulfstein (n 180) 639 ff; A Wiersema, ''The New International Law-makers? Conferences of the Parties to Multilateral Environmental Agreements' (2009) 31 *Michigan Journal of International Law* 231.

To examine the contribution of MEAs in times of armed conflict, all the activities taking place within the treaty system have to be considered.

International environmental law can be described as partly 'organisational' in its nature, meaning that MEA treaty bodies form part of a broader institutional structure. Such a structure is created to facilitate states' cooperation in environmental matters.[184] The institutional structure can be defined as a collaboration or a network, with various actors involved formally or informally in the production and implementation of rules, policies and practices to respond to environment-related demands.[185] In other words, it constitutes the collective efforts of the environmental protection work undertaken by treaty bodies, states, international organisations, non-governmental organisations, companies etc. The collective work of all these actors is becoming increasingly influential in the policy-making and implementation of international environmental law, meaning that actors other than states are also influential in a process that is not purely legal.[186]

Boisson de Chazournes explains that the environmental instruments, 'allow for normative interaction between States and other players. They cause the [interaction] to commit themselves to attain objectives defined at international level'.[187] For instance, private companies develop 'codes of conduct', which are often created through collaboration with environmental organisations, on how the business sector can create and comply with environmental standards.[188] Another example is that environmental non-governmental organisations can have official roles under environmental treaties. For instance, the IUCN has an official advisory role to the executive treaty organ under the World Heritage Convention in selecting natural sites to be inscribed on the World Heritage List.[189] The institutional system of such collective efforts is related to the fact that the environment poses problems that cannot be solved by one state or by the law alone. A crucial factor in whether an environmental treaty is complied with and how well it can address environmental issues depends largely on the body of actors engaged to implement a certain instrument.[190] This is another factor

[184] Dupuy and Viñuales (n 3) 32.

[185] See UNEP, 'Environmental Governance' (2009), available at: www.unep.org/pdf/brochures/EnvironmentalGovernance.pdf.

[186] LJ Kotzé, *Global Environmental Governance: Law and Regulation for the 21st Century* (Edward Elgar Publishing, 2012) 7.

[187] Boisson de Chazournes (n 24) 10. She mentioned the ISO 26000 norms (standards adopted for specific needs) as an example of the effects that, other than classic sources of international law, could be of equal importance.

[188] An early example is the Coalition for Environmental Responsible Economies (CERES) principles for corporate environmental conduct. Corporations sign the principles voluntarily and submit annual reports on their progress. There are several newer examples of these types of initiative. See A Smith 'The CERES Principles: A Voluntary Code for Corporate Environmental Responsibility' (1993) 18 *Yale Journal of International Law* 307, 307–08.

[189] Article 14(2) World Heritage Convention. The IUCN is also implementing projects related to the Convention.

[190] Koivurova (n 179) 22.

that is disregarded if only examining the treaty text of MEAs in order to analyse their role in wartime.

To sum up, MEAs should be described as progressive instruments, rather than as meaningless instruments, for two reasons. First, MEA provisions are not toothless but formulated in a manner to be further developed under the treaty system. Often MEAs provide for continued dialogue and negotiation.[191] Second, MEAs are part of a bigger system of global structure relying on other actors besides its state parties to apply its content. Thus, the operation of MEAs in their larger context has to be examined when assessing their potential during armed conflicts, instead of only looking at the treaty provisions that may appear to be rather meaningless at first sight.

VII. CONCLUSIONS

The view that an outbreak of an armed conflict would displace the entire corpus of peacetime law is outdated. The International Law Commission's Draft Articles on Effects of Armed Conflict on Treaties has established a presumption that MEAs continue to apply during armed conflicts. However, the applicability of each MEA needs to be determined, on a case-by-case basis, because factors regarding the nature of the treaty, as well as the characteristics of the armed conflict, may affect the continued operation. As formulated by Parson: 'Two nations can be at war, and still follow norms that protect the environment'.[192] The question is to what extent and how the environmental norms can apply.

Moreover, even though the law of armed conflict is considered to apply as the *lex specialis* in times of armed conflict, it does not mean that it prevents other areas of law from applying at the same time. Instead, even if the rules in the law of armed conflict prevail in case of a normative conflict, the rules in MEAs may still maintain a normative impact. They can address issues that are not regulated under the law of armed conflict and inform the application of the law of armed conflict with regard to environmental protection. The MEAs' parallel application during armed conflicts and their possible influence on the law of armed conflict should therefore be explored, because there are opportunities to complement and ascertain the obligations under the law of armed conflict related to environmental protection.

In addition, the claim that MEAs are poorly tailored to apply in the context of armed conflict is misleading. They are simply constructed in a different way from the instruments of the law of armed conflict. Instead of seeing them as having vague provisions that lack enforceable content, they are progressive instruments providing for continued normative development. Once a state has

[191] Maljean-Dubois (n 29) 30.
[192] Parson (n 40).

ratified an environmental treaty, it has agreed to become part of a treaty system in progress. In order to dismiss the impact of an MEA during an armed conflict, one has to assess its whole treaty system.

To sum up, there are no longer any valid reasons to overlook the application of environmental treaties in times of armed conflict. They need to be carefully examined before they can be labelled as meaningless treaties unable to restrict belligerents' behaviour during armed conflicts. Consequently, the lack of examination of the environmental treaties in relation to wartime environmental damage constitutes a missed opportunity.

7

*New Approach: Reconciling International Environmental Law and the Law of Armed Conflict**

I. INTRODUCTION

THIS CHAPTER EXPLORES the application of MEAs (Multilateral Environmental Agreements) during wartime. The usefulness of the environmental treaties in relation to armed conflict raises two questions of a normative and operational nature. First, at the normative level, even though it is established that environmental treaties can apply during war, the interrelation between these and the law of armed conflict is unclear. The types of normative conflicts that may arise, as well as the extent that environmental treaties may be superseded by the rules of the law of armed conflict in accordance with the *lex specialis* rule, call for additional investigation. Second, at an operational level, MEAs often depend on domestic state organs to be applied because they frequently require the state parties to take active measures.

A domestic institutional structure may be seriously curtailed or even non-existent due to reasons related to the armed conflict. Nonetheless, I argue in this chapter that MEAs can play a potential role in relation to armed conflict because they provide a certain discretion within their provisions and establish treaty bodies, which facilitates adopting a 'reconciliatory approach'. Such an approach aims at reconciling the obligations in MEAs with other international obligations, such as those in the law of armed conflict. Also, the environmental treaty bodies can initiate cooperation with other treaty bodies, states, international organisations, non-governmental organisations, etc, which can contribute to applying the environmental treaties even in states with weak institutional structures, as well as to coordinate the action with other international obligations.

The current chapter starts in section II by identifying which MEAs are relevant to address wartime environmental damage. I focus mainly on the World

* Parts of this chapter were published in B Sjöstedt, 'The Reconciliatory Approach: How Multilateral Environmental Agreements Can Harmonize International Legal Obligations' in A Jakubowski and K Wierczyńska (eds), *The Arguments on Fragmentation and Constitutionalisation: An Inquiry into the Practice of International Law* (Routledge, 2016).

Heritage Convention and the Ramsar Convention. In section III, I examine how the obligations in the MEAs may interfere with the rules of the law of armed conflict when applied during armed conflicts. Thereafter, I introduce how such interference could be resolved by adopting a reconciliatory approach in section IV. Section V explores why a reconciliatory approach can be adopted in relation to environmental treaties to overcome possible normative interference. In section VI, I investigate what a reconciliation of norms could mean in practice, and, in section VII, I look at the environmental treaty bodies' role to enhance wartime environmental protection. Section VIII provides conclusions on the possibilities for MEAs to address environmental damage in relation to armed conflict by adopting a reconciliatory approach.

II. THE WORLD HERITAGE CONVENTION AND THE RAMSAR CONVENTION

There are over 1,300 MEAs and even more bilateral environmental agreements.[1] Each MEA focuses on a particular environmental issue. Several MEAs could be highly relevant in relation to armed conflict. For instance, the Transboundary Watercourses and International Lakes Convention could enhance the protection for important international waters during armed conflicts and prevent them from severe damage by military operations; or the Convention on International Trade in Endangered Species (CITES) could prevent the trade in international wildlife, which is frequently occurring in war-torn states that lack the means to control such activities.

I have, however, limited this study to examine the application of two conventions that establish protection for certain areas of environmental importance – the World Heritage Convention and the Ramsar Convention. The choice is based on three reasons. The first reason is related to the contribution of these protected areas as a tool to identify and preserve biological 'hot-spots' of international significance. These areas are selected for important environmental interests because they may safeguard particular ecosystems, species, landscapes, biological processes, etc.[2] Thus, by offering the areas protection, it contributes to preserving endangered species and rare ecosystems, and prevents the loss of biodiversity on a global scale.

The second reason for choosing the two conventions is related to the fact that a designated protected area constitutes a defined geographical space. The obligation to safeguard these areas is therefore perhaps more tangible in comparison

[1] The IEA (International Environmental Agreements) Database project website: iea.uoregon.edu.

[2] R Tarasofsky, 'Protecting Specifically Important Areas During International Armed Conflict: A Critique of the IUCN Draft Convention on the Prohibition of Hostile Military Activities in Protected Areas' in JE Austin and CE Bruch (eds), *The Environmental Consequences of War* (Cambridge University Press, 2000).

to protecting the environment in a broad sense or an environmental component of a more abstract nature, such as the climate or biodiversity. A clearly demarcated area facilitates establishing a protection in accordance with an area's particular needs and stipulates the types of measures that are necessary to safeguard it. In addition, similar types of protection mechanisms are already in place under the law of armed conflict. These are focused on protecting certain delimited geographical areas that take the form of demilitarised zones, neutrality zones and hospital and safety zones.[3] Thus, such mechanisms are already employed during armed conflicts, demonstrating that it is feasible to protect certain areas in wartime to avoid harmful action when planning military operations in these areas. The provision of special protection for certain environmental areas has been proposed in several fora as a measure to improve the environmental protection in relation to armed conflict, including by the negotiators of Protocol I,[4] the International Law Commission,[5] and the environmental organisation IUCN (International Union for Conservation of Nature and Natural Resources),[6] as discussed in chapter four.

The third reason for selecting the two conventions refers to the particular exposure of protected areas during armed conflicts. National Parks, nature reserves and other protected environmental areas are frequently affected during and after armed conflicts because of their richness in natural resources, dense vegetation, and, at times, isolated locations.[7] They can function as hiding places, be used to camouflage equipment and/or weapons, and provide shelter, food, fuel and incomes for armed groups and, often, the large number of displaced persons fleeing the hostilities.[8] Thus, due to this exposure, these protected areas are in particular need of protection during armed conflicts.

Considering the three reasons above, I argue that the World Heritage Convention and the Ramsar Convention can be applied to improve environmental

[3] Demilitarised zones are regulated in Article 60 of Protocol I; hospital and safety zones in Article 14 of the Geneva Convention IV; and neutralised zones in Article 15 of Geneva Convention IV.

[4] Article 48 *ter* was proposed during the negotiations of Protocol I to protect 'publicly recognized nature reserves'. The article was not adopted in the end. Y Sandoz, C Swinarski and B Zimmerman (eds), *Commentary on the Additional Protocols of 8 June 1977* (ICRC, Geneva, 1987) 664.

[5] The Special Rapporteur suggests this in a draft principle. See Special Rapporteur M Jacobsson, Second Report on the Protection of the Environment in Relation to Armed Conflicts, UN Doc A/CN.4/685, 28 May 2015, para 227. Two draft principles referring to protected zones were later adopted by the Drafting Committee of the International Law Commission on the first reading. See Draft Principles 4 and 17 in International Law Commission, 'Protection of the Environment. Text and Titles of the Draft Principles Provisionally Adopted by the Drafting Committee on First Reading' (Protection of the Environment, First Reading) UN Doc A/CN.4/L.937 (2019).

[6] Article 40(3) IUCN Draft International Covenant on Environment and Development (IUCN Draft Covenant), IUCN, 'Draft International Covenant on Environment and Development – Implementing Sustainability', 5th edn, IUCN Environmental Policy and Law Paper No 31 Rev 4 (IUCN, Gland).

[7] ILPI 2014, 'Protection of the Natural Environment in Armed Conflict: An Empirical Study', International Law and Policy Institute, Report 12/2014.

[8] JE Austin and CE Bruch, 'Legal Mechanisms for Addressing Wartime Damage to Tropical Forests' (2003) 16 *Journal of Sustainable Forestry* 161.

protection during armed conflicts, given that they offer area-based protection for clearly demarcated biological hot spots located in war-torn states. Area-based protection is also offered under other environmental treaties, including the Biodiversity Convention[9] and the Convention for the Protection and Development of the Marine Environment of the Wider Caribbean Region.[10] I have omitted these conventions in my research, however, because they lack a system of putting protected areas on a specific list, unlike the World Heritage Convention and the Ramsar Convention. The advantage of having a system with listed protected sites is that they are clearly marked and objectively identifiable, making the World Heritage Convention and the Ramsar Convection potential candidates to safeguard the environment in relation to armed conflict.

My primary focus lies on the World Heritage Convention. This is because I have identified it as the MEA that has the best potential to apply and provide protection during armed conflicts. The explicit reference to an 'outbreak of an armed conflict' in its provisions strengthens the notion that the World Heritage Convention continues to apply in times of armed conflict. Several scholars share this view.[11] However, scholars have also noted that the World Heritage Convention does not contain any specific provisions or mechanisms to protect world heritage sites during armed conflicts, which they claim may obstruct its application in such situations.[12] This claim is unfounded, and I will address later in this chapter.

The World Heritage Convention is negotiated under UNESCO, an organisation that is, to some extent, engaged in the application of the Convention, which I perceive as an advantage. This is because UNESCO is already involved in the wartime protection of cultural property, as the 1954 Hague Convention and its two protocols protecting cultural property during armed conflicts have appointed UNESCO to provide assistance to the state parties on how to safeguard cultural property in wartime.[13] Consequently, the World Heritage

[9] The Biodiversity Convention provides for in-situ conservation in accordance with its Article 8. Hulme explores the application of the article in relation to armed conflict. See K Hulme, 'Armed Conflict and Biodiversity' in M Bowman, P Davies and E Goodwin (eds), *Research Handbook on Biodiversity and Law* (Edward Elgar Publishing, 2016).

[10] See Article 10, Convention for the Protection and Development of the Marine Environment of the Wider Caribbean Region (adopted 24 March 1983, entered into force 11 October 1986) 1506 UNTS 157.

[11] See M Bothe et al, 'International Law Protecting the Environment During Armed Conflict: Gaps and Opportunities' (2010) 92 *International Review of the Red Cross* 569, 582; S Vöneky, 'Peacetime Environmental Law as a Basis of State Responsibility for Environmental Damage Caused by War' in JE Austin and CE Bruch (eds), *The Environmental Consequences of War* (Cambridge University Press, 2000) 224–25; Austin and Bruch (n 8) 171–72.

[12] See W Burhenne, 'The Prohibition of Hostile Military Activities in Protected Areas' (1997) 27 *Environmental Policy and Law* 373; W Verwey, 'Protection of the Environment in Times of Armed Conflict: In Search of a New Legal Perspective' (1995) 7, 8 *Leiden Journal of International Law* 15; Tarasofsky (n 2) 568.

[13] In Article 23 of the 1954 Hague Convention, UNESCO is authorised to assist the state parties to organise the protection of their cultural property. UNESCO is also authorised to make, on its own initiative, proposals on this matter to the state parties.

Convention, being supported by UNESCO with previous 'war experience', may be better equipped than many other MEAs to provide environmental protection during armed conflicts.

In addition, the World Heritage Convention protects what is referred to, in the Preamble, as sites of 'outstanding interest and therefore need to be preserved as part of the world heritage of mankind as a whole'. A site recognised as a world heritage site receives a certain status under international law, which is often connected with the national pride of the territorial state. Those states with world heritage sites situated within their territory are the most likely states to be concerned with the preservation and maintenance of them as world heritage, even in times of armed conflict.[14] Thus, the World Heritage Convention has a different position from many other MEAs to protect the environment during armed conflicts.

Nevertheless, if the natural world heritage sites receive protection during armed conflicts under the Convention, a similar protection may be transferred to other MEAs, in particular if they protect – similar to the World Heritage Convention – areas of environmental significance, for example, wetlands protected under the Ramsar Convention. The wetlands are recognised as having international importance. Thus, if it is accepted under international law that natural sites of outstanding interest require special protection in times of armed conflict, other environmental areas of comparable environmental prominence could also be granted wartime protection. The mechanism to provide protection is already in place under the Ramsar Convention.

The World Heritage Convention and the Ramsar Convention share many elements with regard to their structure, operation and purpose. Both conventions protect certain areas of international environmental importance that are included on specific lists. If the World Heritage Convention can play a meaningful role in protecting natural world heritage during armed conflicts, the Ramsar Convention may also be able to safeguard wetlands of international importance in similar situations.

A. The Aims of the Protection

The World Heritage Convention protects cultural and natural world heritage sites of outstanding interest. The Convention has 193 state parties.[15] Pursuant to Article 4 of the World Heritage Convention, the state parties are under an

[14] However, world heritage sites can also be directly targeted for their value as heritage during armed conflicts. For instance, in Syria in 2015, ISIS directly attacked the cultural heritage of Palmyra Archaeological Museum. See S Jeffries, 'Isis's destruction of Palmyra: "The heart has been ripped out of the city"' *The Guardian* (2 September 2015), available at: www.theguardian.com/world/2015/sep/02/isis-destruction-of-palmyra-syria-heart-been-ripped-out-of-the-city.

[15] See ratification on World Heritage Convention's web page: whc.unesco.org/en/statesparties.

obligation to ensure the identification, protection, preservation, presentation and transmission, for future generations of world heritage situated in their territory. Article 6(3) of the World Heritage Convention requires state parties to refrain from deliberately causing damage to the world heritage sites situated in the territory of other state parties, whether directly or indirectly. To enhance the protection, pursuant to Article 11(2), state parties can nominate sites in their territory to be inscribed on the World Heritage List. For designation to that list, a site has to fulfil the requirements set out in Articles 1 and 2 of the Convention.[16] A natural world heritage is defined in Article 2 in the World Heritage Convention as having:

> [N]**atural features** consisting of physical and biological formations or groups of such formations, which are of outstanding universal value from the aesthetic or scientific point of view;
>
> **geological and physiographical formations** and precisely delineated areas which constitute the habitat of threatened species of animals and plants of outstanding universal value from the point of view of science or conservation;
>
> **natural sites** or precisely delineated natural areas of outstanding universal value from the point of view of science, conservation or natural beauty.

The World Heritage Convention confers international recognition on precious protected areas hosting the most extraordinary ecosystems in the world that contain highly threatened species and exceptional biodiversity.[17] There are currently 213 natural world heritage sites on the list and 39 mixed sites.[18] When a site is put onto the World Heritage List, a management strategy has to be developed and funds, as well as other resources, allocated to maintain the integrity of the site.[19] The World Heritage List is supported by a separate 'Danger List' provided for in Article 11(4) of the Convention. Seventeen natural world heritage sites are currently inscribed on the Danger List.[20] These are prioritised for international assistance under the World Heritage Convention, according to Article 21(2). The 'outbreak of an armed conflict' is expressly identified as such a danger, as previously mentioned.[21]

[16] In accordance with Articles 1 and 2, these sites must all have elements that are of outstanding universal value.

[17] World Heritage Papers 17, Proceedings and Preserving Congolese Heritage, Linking Biological and Cultural Diversity, Proceedings of the Conference and Workshops, UNESCO, 13–17 September 2004, 96, available at: whc.unesco.org/en/documents/6411.

[18] See the World Heritage List on the World Heritage Convention's web page: whc.unesco.org/en/list.

[19] World Heritage Papers 17 (n 17) 96.

[20] See the World Heritage Danger List on the World Heritage Convention's web page: whc.unesco.org/en/list/?type=natural&danger=1.

[21] Other serious and specific dangers listed in Article 11(4) of the World Heritage Convention include: 'threat of disappearance caused by accelerated deterioration; large-scale public or private projects or rapid urban or tourist development projects; destruction caused by changes in the use or ownership of the land; major alterations due to unknown causes; abandonment for any reason

The Ramsar Convention protects wetlands and waterfowl of international significance. These are defined in Article 1 of the Convention, which reads:

1. For the purpose of this Convention wetlands are areas of marsh, fen, peatland or water, whether natural or artificial, permanent or temporary, with water that is static or flowing, fresh, brackish or salt, including areas of marine water the depth of which at low tide does not exceed six metres.
2. For the purpose of this Convention waterfowl are birds ecologically dependent on wetlands.

The protection is motivated on the 'fundamental ecological functions of wetlands as regulators of water regimes and as habitats supporting a characteristic flora and fauna, especially waterfowl', as stated in the Preamble to the Convention. In addition, the Preamble expresses that 'the wetlands constitute a resource of great economic, cultural, scientific, and recreational value, the loss of which would be irreparable'. The Ramsar Convention promotes the 'wise use' of the wetlands.[22] The concept of 'wise use', 'equates to the maintenance of ecosystem benefits/services to ensure long term maintenance of biodiversity as well as human well-being and poverty alleviation'.[23] The 'wise use' concept is meant to allow the state parties to use the wetlands in a sustainable way so that they are preserved for future generations. Thus, it takes interests other than purely conservation interests into account.

The Ramsar Convention has a similar system to the World Heritage Convention that encourages state parties to designate wetlands within their territory onto the 'List of Wetlands of International Importance' (the 'Ramsar List').[24] According to Article 2(2) of the Convention, the wetlands are selected 'on account of their international significance in terms of ecology, botany, zoology, limnology or hydrology'. In addition, the Convention has a list for wetlands requiring additional protection called the 'Montreux Record', which is comparable to the Danger List of the World Heritage Convention. The Montreux Record is not mentioned in the Convention's text, but it is a development by the treaty bodies established under the Ramsar Convention in order to improve compliance with the instrument.[25] The types of events that would trigger an inscription on the Montreux Record are not expressed. Instead an inscription of a wetland on the list occurs in cases where the wetland has an 'adverse change

whatsoever; calamities and cataclysms; serious fires, earthquakes, landslides; volcanic eruptions; changes in water level, floods and tidal waves'.

[22] Convention on Wetlands of International Importance Especially as Waterfowl Habitat (adopted 2 February 1971, entered into force 21 December 1975) 996 UNTS 245 (Ramsar Convention), Articles 1 and 3.

[23] Resolution IX.1, Annex A, A Conceptual Framework for the Wise Use of Wetlands and the Maintenance of their Ecological Character. 9th Meeting of the Conference of the Parties, Kampala, Uganda, 8–15 November 2005.

[24] Article 2 Ramsar Convention.

[25] A 'Conference of the Parties' (COP) is established in accordance with Article 6 of the Ramsar Convention.

in ecological character', which would create a 'need of priority conservation attention'.[26] Potentially, an outbreak of an armed conflict could cause such an adverse ecological change and invoke an inscription on the Montreux Record.

B. The Operation

As mentioned in chapter six, the provisions in MEAs are constructed in a particular manner. They use loosely formulated language, often containing wording such as 'as appropriate' or 'as far as possible', providing for context-based obligations. The World Heritage Convention and the Ramsar Convention utilise the same type of terminology in their provisions. For instance, Article 4 of the World Heritage Convention requires that state parties to do all they can to protect world heritage sites, 'to the utmost of [their] own resources'. Similarly, the Ramsar Convention promotes the wise use of wetlands in Article 3. In other words, both provisions give the state parties some discretionary power in their application of the instruments. It is up to the state party, in the first instance, to assess what the action should consist of to comply with the conventions.

The terminology may be perceived as providing imprecise obligations because they lack expressed tangible requirements.[27] Indeed, it may be difficult to establish the appropriate response that fulfils an obligation with such a terminology. However, the discretionary power that is allocated to the state parties can be assessed in relation to the parameters given in the provisions. It does not mean that the state parties are free to choose whatever measures they like, in particular, because the treaty bodies can evaluate the appropriateness of the measures. Still, the loosely formulated context-based obligations can complicate the establishment of a relationship between the provisions of the MEAs and the rules of the law of armed conflict, as I will discuss in section III.

Furthermore, the World Heritage Convention and the Ramsar Convention, like many other environmental treaties, establish a treaty system with treaty bodies and compliance mechanisms as a 'package deal'. The Ramsar Convention has established a 'Conference of the Parties' (COP) to be the decision-making treaty body. The World Heritage Convention has a General Assembly that corresponds to a COP.[28] In many cases, the treaty bodies have a broad mandate to ensure the effective application of the conventions by defining and developing

[26] See para 3.1. Guidelines for Operation of the Montreux Record, Adopted by the Conference of the Contracting Parties in Resolution VI.1, Brisbane, 1996, accompanying the Guidelines for Operation of the Montreux Record.

[27] G Carducci, 'Articles 4–7, National and International Protection of Cultural and Natural Heritage' in F Francioni (ed), *The 1972 World Heritage Convention: A Commentary* (Oxford University Press, 2008) 145.

[28] The General Assembly corresponds to a conference of the parties, which is usually the supreme decision-making organ in MEAs. See D Zacharias, 'The UNESCO Regime' for the Protection of World Heritage as Prototype of an Autonomy-Gaining International Institution' in A von Bogdandy et al (eds), *The Exercise of Public Authority by International Institutions* (Springer, 2010) 311–12.

the provisions in the form of decisions, recommendations and guidelines.[29] As opposed to the law of armed conflict, an environmental treaty's application is dependent on its treaty bodies and not only on the state parties.[30]

The environmental treaties operate differently from most international treaties, focusing on supportive measures to remedy the inability of state parties to protect their sites. The World Heritage Convention and the Ramsar Convention provide for different types of measures or tools to facilitate compliance among its state parties.[31] Examples of such measures are the manual drafted by the World Heritage Committee (WH Committee) containing operational guidelines to support state parties in their implementation of the Convention,[32] and the possibility for a state party to the Ramsar Convention to request a Ramsar Advisory Mission, which enables global expertise and advice for problems and threats that could lead to a loss in ecological character to a wetland.[33] It is also possible under both conventions to acquire funds to protect the designated protected areas on the lists.

The supportive compliance mechanisms described above may be of particular interest during and after armed conflict, which may be the occasion when states are facing particular difficulties to adequately safeguard the protected environmental areas within their territory. Nevertheless, it also depends much on the type of ongoing conflict. For instance, if the United States is engaged in an armed conflict taking place in Iraq or Afghanistan, it would probably not affect the ability to protect the world heritage sites or Ramsar sites situated on its territory. At the same time, a state like the DRC, which is affected by armed conflicts that have lasted over 20 years, lacks the domestic institutions as well as financial means to maintain a high level of protection of its sites. In such a case, the application of MEAs may be reliant on how effective and active the treaty bodies are of the conventions.

In conclusion, the World Heritage Convention and the Ramsar Convention focus on supportive measures to remedy the inability of state parties to protect areas of international environmental importance. In addition, they can rely on treaty bodies and other actors, besides the state parties, to apply the treaties. These elements are characteristic of MEAs in general and I will develop the elements' particular influences on the potential for MEAs to apply in relation to armed conflict in section V.

[29] The World Heritage Committee meets at least once a year. See *The Operational Guidelines for Implementation of the WHC* (November 2011), available at: whc.unesco.org/archive/opguide11-en.pdf (*WHC Operational Guidelines*).

[30] R Churchill and G Ulfstein, 'Autonomous Institutional Arrangements in Multilateral Environmental Agreements: A Little-Noticed Phenomenon in International Law' (2000) 94 *American Journal of International Law* 623.

[31] See D Bodansky, *The Art and Craft of International Environmental Law* (Harvard University Press, 2011) 226–27. On the WHC compliance mechanism in particular, see E Goodwin, 'The World Heritage Convention, the Environment, and Compliance' (2009) 20 *Colorado Journal of International Environmental Law and Policy* 157.

[32] *WHC Operational Guidelines*.

[33] This mechanism was formally adopted by the Ramsar Convention Recommendation 4.7 in 1990.

III. POTENTIAL NORMATIVE TENSIONS

In this section, I examine the potential normative problems that may arise when the World Heritage Convention and the Ramsar Convention apply concurrently with the law of armed conflict. I start by investigating the difficulties attached to determining the existence of conflicts between international norms (or normative tensions as I refer to them). Thereafter, I briefly touch on the differences when dealing with normative problems in an international armed conflict compared with a non-international armed conflict.

A. The Meaning of Normative Tensions

At the creation of new international rules, the legislator (the states) may not have foreseen that rules of separate legal areas could be applicable to the same subject matter concurrently. Therefore, they may not be compatible with each other because the application of one norm might be affected in order for a state to obey the other. Such a scenario is commonly referred to as a 'normative conflict', as discussed in chapter six. As stated by Lindroos, 'the notion of a normative conflict can be theoretically difficult to conceptualise'.[34] Thus, normative conflicts are perceived and defined differently in the doctrine. For instance, Jenks speaks of a normative conflict in a 'strict sense of direct incompatibility', which refers to the situation whenever two valid norms cannot be applied at the same time without one of the norms being violated.[35] However, as pointed out by Vranes, such a definition does not encompass the situation of incompatibilities when dealing with norms of a permissive nature.[36] Instead, he advocates a definition that reads, 'There is a conflict between norms, one of which may be permissive, if in obeying or applying one norm, the other norm is necessarily or potentially violated'.[37] Similarly, Pauwelyn describes a normative conflict as 'a situation where one norm breaches, has led to or may lead to breach of, another norm'.[38]

As pointed out by Mus, the difficulty attached to conceptualising normative conflicts can lead to confusion because the definitions are often 'ambiguous and not clearly defined'.[39] The problem with conceptualising normative conflicts is

[34] A Lindroos, 'Addressing Norm Conflicts in a Fragmented Legal System: The Doctrine of *Lex Specialis*' (2005) 74 *Nordic Journal of International Law* 27, 45.

[35] W Jenks, 'The Conflict of Law-making Treaties' (1953) 30 *British Yearbook of International Law* 401, 426.

[36] E Vranes, 'The Definition of "Norm Conflict" in International Law and Legal Theory' (2006) 17 *European Journal of International Law* 395, 395–96.

[37] ibid, 418.

[38] J Pauwelyn, *Conflict of Norms in Public International Law: How WTO Law Relates to other Rules of International Law* (Cambridge University Press, 2009) 199.

[39] JB Mus, 'Conflicts Between Treaties in International Law' (1998) 45 *Netherlands International Law Review* 208, 211.

partly because rules within the international legal system are of different types, and consequently, the conflicts between them will also differ. For instance, as briefly touched on, there is a distinction between 'mandatory norms' and 'permissive norms'.[40] A mandatory norm is an obligation to do something (an obligatory norm) or not to do something (prohibitive norm). A permissive norm is an invitation to do or not to do something. To act or not to act in accordance with the permissive norm cannot be seen as a violation of that norm, since the state has a choice to act or not to act. Consequently, there could be two definitions of a norm conflict only when looking at the application of these types of norms.

The first type of norm conflict deals with two conflicting mandatory norms that are applicable to the same subject matter in the same context. In cases where they proscribe different acts that cannot be fulfilled at the same time, it is impossible to comply with all the requirements of the two norms. This type of conflict that Jenks refers to is unlikely to occur between the rules of the law of armed conflict and environmental treaties. This is because most of the rules of the law of armed conflict that are relevant for environmental protection are of a permissive nature, in the sense that they enable states to harm the environment in their military operations, but they do not proscribe action requiring environmental harm.

The second type of normative conflict deals with a permissive norm and a mandatory norm that are applicable to the same subject matter in the same context. In this scenario, as pointed out by Vranes, it is impossible to make use of the permissive norm and at the same time comply with all the requirements of the mandatory norm (assuming that these are contradictory).[41] This is the most likely type of conflict to occur when the law of armed conflict and MEAs are concurrently applied.

Consider the following example of this type of normative conflict with a permissive norm and a mandatory norm. Article 6 of the World Heritage Convention requires that a state party does not harm a specific area that represents a world heritage site. But the law of armed conflict may allow military operations that harm the site if the site can be classified as a military target and the damage to the environment is proportional (compared with the anticipated military advantage) or does not reach the threshold detailed in Articles 35(3) and 55(1) of Protocol I.[42] There is, however, *no obligation* (an obligatory norm) to destroy the environment under the law of armed conflict. Article 6 in the

[40] See SA Sadat-Akhavi, *Methods of Resolving Conflicts Between Treaties* (Brill Academic Publishers, 2003) 5–6.

[41] ibid.

[42] However, Protocol I is only applicable in international armed conflicts, but the principle of distinction applies also to non-international armed conflict. So if the world heritage site represents a military target, it can be attacked under the law of armed conflict (and the same in non-international armed conflicts).

World Heritage Convention is, on the other hand, a mandatory obligation, requiring the state parties to not harm a world heritage site.

If the case, described above, was regarded as a normative conflict, the *lex specialis* rule would apply to determine the prevailing norm, the rule of the law of armed conflict. However, it could also be assumed that there is no normative conflict at all, since the state can comply with both norms without violating either. It can fulfil its obligations under the World Heritage Convention by refraining from conducting military operations inside a world heritage site without breaching the rules of the law of armed conflict. Nevertheless, the law of armed conflict is intended to enable exceptions from peacetime law and therefore it permits harm, even to a world heritage site, if it constitutes a military objective. Depending on how the example is viewed, it could be perceived as a normative conflict if taking the view of Vranes, but not necessarily if adopting Jenks' definition. To avoid getting stuck in definitional problems, and for the purpose of this chapter, I use the operational term of 'normative tension' to describe a broad range of scenarios where two norms that apply to the same subject matter at the same time have incompatible content at a prima facie level. Thus, the term is intended to encapsulate all types of strained norm relations, where the rights or obligations in two norms cannot be exercised and fully applied at the same time.

B. Impact of the Classification of the Armed Conflict

Depending on how an armed conflict is classified (international or non-international), the types of normative tensions may vary because different sets of rules of the law of armed conflict apply. For instance, Protocol I and the Convention on the Prohibition of Military or Any Other Hostile Use of Environmental Modification Techniques (ENMOD Convention) are applicable to international armed conflicts but not to non-international armed conflicts. However, in practice these instruments are rarely relevant to wartime environmental damage, as concluded in chapter three. Instead, it is more likely that the general rules of protection under the law of armed conflict may create normative tensions with the rules in MEAs. The general rules of protection in the law of armed conflict apply as customary international law in international as well as non-international armed conflicts. Hence, in relation to environmental protection under the law of armed conflict, the classification of an armed conflict does not involve any major change in practice with regard to the potential occurrence of normative tensions. However, the type of environmental harm, as well as the ability of a state to comply with MEAs, may differ depending on the character of the armed conflict.

The intensity of violence, the amount of destruction, the types of weapons used, the organisation of the parties of the conflict, the level of control over the territory, etc, are probably factors that would influence the ability of a state to fulfil its obligations in an MEA at the same time as it is involved in armed conflict. These factors are related to the factual circumstances and not the legal classification of the armed conflict.

IV. ADOPTING A RECONCILIATORY APPROACH

In this section, I suggest that norms can be reconciled when facing normative tensions between the rules of MEAs and the law of armed conflict.[43] I have coined the term 'reconciliatory approach' to describe the process under MEAs of avoiding determining whether a normative conflict exists, which forces the law-applier to prioritise between two incompatible norms. Instead, the law-applier should seek a way for overlapping and incompatible rules to be interpreted and applied in a harmonious manner that permits the consideration of each rule in order to overcome potential normative tensions.[44]

MEAs provide for collective measures to respond to global environmental problems, which mean they frequently interfere and intermingle with obligations of other areas of international law; for instance, as with human rights law, trade law and investment law.[45] Therefore, MEAs arguably have certain elements – with regard to their character, structure and operation – that facilitate a norm reconciliation with other international obligations to overcome normative tensions (as I will elaborate in the next section, section V).

A reconciliatory approach may only be useful in relation to MEAs because it makes use of the MEA provisions and their treaty bodies' ability to harmonise with other areas of international law and at the same time ensure continued operation of their instruments. The approach can be invoked in two ways: first, through complementary and harmonious application of the loosely formulated

[43] For further reading on the use of the reconciliatory approach within MEAs, see B Sjöstedt, 'The Reconciliatory Approach: How Multilateral Environmental Agreements Can Harmonize International Legal Obligations' in A Jakubowski and K Wierczyńska (eds), *The Arguments on Fragmentation and Constitutionalisation: An Inquiry into the Practice of International Law* (Routledge, 2016).

[44] Similar tendencies can also be seen in the human rights law area, see L Lixinski, 'Treaty Interpretation by the Inter-American Court of Human Rights: Expansionism at the Service of the Unity of International Law' (2010) 21 *European Journal of International Law* 585.

[45] For further reading, see M Tignino, 'The Legal Regime of Natural Resources in Times of Armed Conflict and its Weaknesses' in Y Kerbrat and S Maljean-Dubois (eds), *The Transformation of International Environmental Law* (Hart Publishing and Editions A Pedone, 2011); R Pavoni, 'Mutual Supportiveness as a Principle of Interpretation and Law-making: A Watershed for the "WTO-and-Competing Regimes" Debate?' (2010) 21 *European Journal of International Law* 649; H van Asselt, F Sindico and MA Mehling, 'Global Climate Change and the Fragmentation of International Law' (2008) 30 *Law & Policy* 423; WA Shutkin, 'International Human Rights Law and the Earth: The Protection of Indigenous Peoples and the Environment' (1990) 31 *Virginia Journal of International Law* 479; D Shelton, 'Human Rights, Environmental Rights, and the Right to Environment' (1991) 28 *Stanford Journal of International Law* 103; L Boisson de Chazournes, 'Features and Trends in International Environmental Law' in Y Kerbrat and S Maljean-Dubois (eds), *The Transformation of International Environmental Law* (Hart Publishing and Editions A Pedone, 2011) 14.

provisions in the MEAs by their treaty bodies, as well as their state parties; and second, through the treaty bodies' cooperation with other actors in different fields of law, for example, other treaty bodies, international organisations, states and state authorities, companies, or non-governmental organisations.

The first method of invoking a reconciliatory approach is where the state parties and the MEA treaty bodies are empowered with some discretion to apply and adapt the provisions set out in the treaties; therefore, they can circumvent clashes with other legal areas.[46] The context-based provisions enable the state parties and the MEA treaty bodies to achieve compromises between the MEA provisions and other legal obligations. Such compromises go beyond an interpretation exercise and could also consider non-binding commitments, not merely 'rules of international law' as provided in Article 31(3)(c) of the Vienna Convention on the Law of Treaties (VCLT).[47]

The second method of invoking the reconciliatory approach is where MEA institutions are authorised under their treaties to cooperate with other actors to launch specific measures or projects. Such cooperation could take place with actors outside the realm of international environmental law and may thereby have a harmonising effect on other international obligations of the state. Thus, a reconciliatory approach allows for adjustments of the application of MEAs to adapt to the prevailing conditions of factual, normative and operational character. Nevertheless, in cases where reconciliation is not possible, the *lex specialis* rule applies as a last resort, to establish a priority between the norms of the law of armed conflict and MEAs, with the law of armed conflict applying as the *lex specialis* (as explained in chapter six).

In the following subsections, I will explain how to justify the adoption of a reconciliatory approach from a broader perspective of international law (subsection VII.A). Thereafter in subsection VII.B, I look at how a reconciliatory approach relates to other tools to solve normative tensions in the international legal system.

A. The Need for Norm Reconciliation

A reconciliatory approach is not an expressed rule, principle, or concept of international law; it departs from legal reasoning grounded on the idea that international law is one system. Nevertheless, similar ideas of harmonious interpretation have been expressed by other scholars. For instance, Pavoni uses the term 'mutual supportiveness' to describe a tool for solving normative tensions between competing regimes. According to Pavoni, mutual supportiveness

[46] Bodansky (n 31) 155.

[47] See P Weil, 'Towards Relative Normativity in International Law' (1983) 77 *American Journal of International Law* 413; J Klabbers, 'The Redundancy of Soft Law' (1996) 65 *Nordic Journal of International Law* 167.

harmonises and reconciles competing obligations, mainly in regard to World Trade Organization (WTO) law.[48] According to van Damme, there exists a customary principle of harmonious interpretation that has not yet been codified in international law.[49] Matz-Lück acknowledges the use of 'harmonisation' as a tool to solve conflicts of norms through interpretation. She argues that 'the principle of harmonisation', 'systemic integration' and 'mutual supportiveness' are all reflecting a similar approach to solve conflicts based on legal reasoning and to achieve harmonisation but without applying the 'ordinary' rules of interpretation. She explains that the principle of harmonious interpretation is based on the idea of coherence within the international legal system.[50] Thus, there is support among other scholars to reconcile norms to avoid normative conflicts. However, a reconciliatory approach does not only operate on a normative level but also on an institutional one. Therefore, I describe it as a 'reconciliatory approach' to distinguish it from other tools, although I acknowledge that it has a resemblances to these tools.

Similarly, Matz-Lück describes in relation to the principle of harmonious interpretation that the reconciliatory approach operates on the basis of the inherent coherence of international law to achieve harmonisation among the norms and apply them in a manner to ensure their function in the legal system. Being one system, the law-applier should seek to achieve coherence between the rules within the international legal system.[51] As the Study Group on Fragmentation of the International Law Commission stresses:

> International law is a legal system. Its rules and principles (ie its norms) act in relation to and should be interpreted against the background of other rules and principles. As a legal system, international law is not a random collection of such norms. There are meaningful relationships between them.[52]

The Study Group on Fragmentation of the International Law Commission expresses that rules of international law share a 'systemic objective' that should be understood as all norms are connected to each other and have a function within it.[53] As international law develops and generates more diversified areas,

[48] Pavoni (n 45) 649.

[49] See I Van Damme, 'Some Observations About the ILC Study Group Report on the Fragmentation of International Law' (2006) 17 *Finnish Yearbook of International Law* 38.

[50] See N Matz-Lück, 'Harmonization, Systemic Integration, and Conflict-Solution Techniques' (2006) 17 *Finnish Yearbook of International Law* 39. Furthermore, the International Law Commission, as well as other scholars, have used the term 'harmonization principle' with regard to Article 31(3)(c) VCLT, which is also referred to as the systemic integration principle.

[51] Theories of the systematisation of legal norms work within the postulations of legal positivism and operate with logic. As described by Carty, such theories impound values that can be argued as immanent to the legal system of binding norms. A Carty, *Philosophy of International Law* (Edinburgh University Press, 2007) 1–2.

[52] International Law Commission, 'Fragmentation of International Law: Difficulties Arising from the Diversification and Expansion of International Law', Report of the Study Group of the International Law Commission, UN Doc A/CN.4/L.702, 18 July 2006, para 14(1).

[53] Pauwelyn, *Conflict of Norms* (n 38) 5.

the risk of arising normative tensions increases. The phenomenon is referred to as fragmentation of international law and is occasionally described as a threat to its unity by some scholars, whereas other scholars consider it as development of the system.[54] Regardless of how the phenomenon should be regarded, the international legal system needs to address these normative tensions.

The development of new norms and specialised areas of international law can result in isolating, as well as connecting, norms. The specialised areas have horizontal relations with each other, but there is no overarching structure to ensure that these functions operate in a coordinated and coherent manner.[55] This is because the international legal system lacks a centralised legislative body and a unified judicial system. Therefore, newly created rules may develop randomly and not always be coherent with the already existing rules.[56] Consequently, rules that were not intended to be applied in relation to other areas of law may be incompatible with each other if they apply to the same subject matter within the same time frame. Milanovic describes it as:

> When state representatives (often individuals, depending on the subject area) sit down to draft treaties, they do not have in their minds a comprehensive list of all possible applications of that treaty to concrete problems, and even less so how the treaty would interact with other norms of international law in every conceivable permutation.[57]

Given the fact that the international legal order is not centralised, states may draft and ratify treaties that conflict with other rules. Of course, it is a result that should be avoided; nevertheless, it occurs.[58] In such a case, to impose the systematic objective of international law means that the rules of these areas should, as far as possible, be interpreted and applied in a harmonious manner. The reasoning originates from the fact that all rules of international law are equally binding, as confirmed in Article 26 VCLT. Thus, states have to consider all its obligations on an equal basis. However, states can 'contract out' from

[54] For further reading on the debate on fragmentation/development of international law, see J Pauwelyn, 'Bridging Fragmentation and Unity: International Law as a Universe of Inter-Connected Islands' (2004) 25 *Michigan Journal of International Law* 903; A Fischer-Lescano and G Teubner, 'Regime-Collisions: The Vain Search for Legal Unity in the Fragmentation of Global Law' (1999) 25 *Michigan Journal of International Law* 999; P-M Dupuy, 'A Doctrinal Debate in the Globalisation Era: On the "Fragmentation" of International Law' (2007) 1 *European Journal of Legal Studies* 1; M Koskenniemi and P Leino, 'Fragmentation of International Law? Postmodern Anxieties' (2002) 15 *Leiden Journal of International Law* 553; N Krisch, *Beyond Constitutionalism: The Pluralist Structure of Postnational Law* (Oxford University Press, 2010); M Prost, *The Concept of Unity in Public International Law* (Hart Publishing, 2012).

[55] Lindroos (n 34) 31.

[56] X Hanqin, 'Fragmented Law or Fragmented Order? (2006) 17 *Finnish Yearbook of International Law* 58.

[57] M Milanovic, 'The Lost Origins of *Lex Specialis*: Rethinking the Relationship Between Human Rights and International Humanitarian Law' in JD Ohlin (ed), *Theoretical Boundaries of Armed Conflict and Human Rights* (Cambridge University Press, 2016).

[58] ibid.

the rules of the international legal system (with the exception of the *jus cogens* norms)[59] by using derogation or conflict solution clauses in treaties.[60]

The intention of the parties is the decisive element for determining the norm relation. Nevertheless, in the absence of such a decisive element, all norms should be respected. Applying the same reasoning, parties to an armed conflict that are also parties to certain MEAs should try to fulfil their obligations of both frameworks as far as possible. Although there appears to be an agreement among states that the law of armed conflict should apply as the *lex specialis* during armed conflicts (as discussed in chapter six), states should still try to comply with other obligations as far as possible. This is particularly important because there is no consistent view on how the *lex specialis* rule applies and how to establish the existence of a normative conflict. Thus, by endorsing a reconciliatory approach allowing conflicting norms to be applied in the light of other international norms could be a way to preserve the systemic objective of the international legal system, and to enhance environmental protection during armed conflicts.

A reconciliatory approach may have limited use when involving instruments other than MEAs, given that these are designed in a particular way with loosely formulated provisions and established treaty systems with treaty bodies. Nevertheless, some underlying justifications for reconciling norms may be found in the international legal system, because there is a need for solutions that harmonise international obligations.

B. Reconciliatory Approach versus Other Tools

The International Law Commission's Study Group on Fragmentation of International Law has suggested a set of legal tools to respond to normative tensions.[61] The tools consist of: interpretation according to Articles 31 and 32 VCLT, in particular Article 31(3)(c), which is referred to as the principle of systemic integration;[62] and the conflict solution rules of *lex superior*, *lex specialis* and *lex posterior*.[63] This subsection explains how a reconciliatory approach relates to these other tools in order to respond to normative tensions.

[59] The *jus cogens* norms are considered as peremptory norms and cannot be set aside. The least controversial examples of *jus cogens* norms include prohibition of the use of force, genocide, crimes against humanity, slavery and piracy. See I Brownlie, *Principles of Public International Law*, 7th edn (Oxford University Press, 2008) 510–11.

[60] One example of such a clause is provided in Article 103 of the UN Charter that provides that obligations of the UN Charter prevail over other treaty obligations.

[61] According to the International Law Commission, the relationship between two or more legal norms is determined by either interpretation or conflict resolution. In the first case, a norm can assist in the interpretation of the other norm and both norms can be applied in conjunction. In the latter case, the norms are incompatible and a choice has to be made between them. See International Law Commission, 'Fragmentation of International Law' (n 52) para 2.

[62] International Law Commission, 'Fragmentation of International Law' (n 52) paras 17–23.

[63] See ibid.

Article 31(3)(c) VCLT reflects, to some extent, the idea of a reconciliatory approach, although it is subject to several limitations. The article permits that 'any relevant rules of international law applicable in the relation between the parties may be considered while interpreting a treaty provision.[64] It provides for consideration of external material sources in treaty interpretation, including other treaties, customary rules, or general principles of law. Pauwelyn describes the use as when a treaty provides a possibility for interpretation, an effort must be made to understand it in a manner that reconciles it with other relevant rules applicable between the parties, as prescribed by Article 31(3)(c) VCLT.[65]

Sands expresses that, 'Article 31(3)(c) reflects a "principle of integration". It emphasises both the "unity of international law" and the sense in which rules should not be considered in isolation of general international law'.[66] In addition, he states that it 'appears to be the only tool available under international law to construct a general international law by reconciling norms arising in treaty and custom across different subject matter areas'.[67]

The Study Group of the International Law Commission refers to Article 31(3)(c) VCLT as the principle of systemic integration because it affirms the unity and systemic objective within international law.[68] According to such an understanding, the principle of systemic integration is an expression of the idea that the international legal order is one system permitting parties to adopt a uniform interpretation of certain terms and concepts, as formulated in other international rules. This reading of the article contributes to ensure coherence within the international legal system.

The Study Group of the International Law Commission on Fragmentation has even described Article 31(3)(c) as 'a "master key" to the house of international law'.[69] However, I do not agree that Article 31(3)(c) VCLT can be regarded as a 'master key' because the article is limited as a tool to achieve harmonisation across different specialised legal areas. More specifically, I argue that it has three limitations that diminish its usefulness at preserving coherence and unity within the international legal system.[70]

The first limitation is that, because Article 31(3)(c) VCLT is a rule of interpretation, it can only be used in an interpretation process. It applies if the

[64] See Study Group on Fragmentation of the International Law Commission, 'Fragmentation of International Law: Difficulties Arising from the Diversification and Expansion of International Law', Report of the Study Group of the International Law Commission, Finalised by Martti Koskenniemi, UN Doc A/CN.4/L.682, 13 April 2006.

[65] Pauwelyn, 'Bridging Fragmentation' (n 54) 906–07.

[66] P Sands, 'Treaty, Custom and the Cross-fertilization of International Law' (1998) 1 *Yale Human Rights & Development Law Journal* 85, 95.

[67] ibid, 87.

[68] 'Fragmentation of International Law: Difficulties Arising From the Diversification and Expansion of International Law', Report of the Study Group of the International Law Commission, Finalised by Martti Koskenniemi (n 64) para 413.

[69] ibid, para 420.

[70] Van Damme supports the view of the limited use of Article 31(3)(c) VCLT as the principle of systemic integration. See Van Damme (n 49) 38.

ordinary meaning in a provision is unclear and consequently requires interpretation. Rules of interpretation cannot be used to substitute, displace, or modify provisions, only to establish the meaning of unclear terms. The treaty that is being interpreted maintains the principal position, while the other rules that are used for assisting in the interpretation process have a secondary role as a means to interpret the provisions in the principal treaty.[71] An interpretation rule is not able to reconcile two overlapping and inconsistent provisions of separate instruments and harmonise them on an equal footing.

The rules on treaty interpretation are limited to interpret one treaty at the time. If the treaty provision text is clear, according to its ordinary meaning, then there is no possibility to initiate an interpretation process to reconcile the provision because the meaning has already been established. Hence, a conflict between two inconsistent obligations of equal authority in different treaties that have clear meanings cannot be resolved through treaty interpretation. This is a considerable restriction on treaty interpretation for harmonising incoherent norm relations and thus to apply Article 31(3)(c) VCLT for such a purpose.[72] However, it does reflect the possibility of adopting elements of harmonisation within the parameters of an interpretation process.

The second limitation of Article 31(3)(c) VCLT concerns the fact that it is a part of the larger interpretation process set out in the remainder of Article 31, as well as in Article 32 VCLT. Therefore, it is just one means of interpretation among others. According to Articles 31 and VCLT, an interpretation process starts with examining the ordinary meaning of a treaty provision. Then, and only if there is some vagueness or ambiguity, may the interpreter continue to consider other means of interpretation, such as the treaty's context, object and purpose, subsequent practice and, lastly, the preparatory work and other circumstances at the conclusion of the treaty. Consequently, Article 31(3)(c) VCLT cannot be taken out of the larger interpretation process to deal with a general application of treaties and resolve inconsistency between two overlapping rules.

The third limitation of Article 31(3)(c) VCLT concerns the identity of the parties to different treaties in the interpretation process, leaving international customary law aside. According to Article 31(3)(c) VCLT, 'the relevant rules' that are taken into consideration in the interpretation process have to be 'applicable in the relations between the parties'. However, it is unclear to which 'parties' the article refers. The plausible view is that Article 31(3)(c) VCLT requires that the parties to the treaty that is the subject of interpretation are also bound by the rules that are used for the interpretation.[73] If this is the correct view, it constitutes a significant restraint of Article 31(3)(c) VCLT for achieving the systemic objective of international law. In fact, it might deconstruct the

[71] Pauwelyn, *Conflict of Norms* (n 38) 254.
[72] N Matz and R Wolfrum, *Conflicts in International Environmental Law* (Springer, 2003) 139–44.
[73] For a further examination on this matter, see U Linderfalk, 'Who are "The Parties"? Article 31, Paragraph 3(c) of the 1969 Vienna Conventions and the Principle of Systemic Integration Revised' (2008) 55 *Netherlands International Law Review* 343.

international legal system into smaller inter-systems between states that are parties to certain treaties. Used in such a manner, Article 31(3)(c) VCLT can only be used to reconcile norms in certain constellations of parties to treaties, and not in a wider sense across specialised fields of law. Given these limitations, Article 31(3)(c) VCLT cannot be seen as the master key that is able to open the doors between the norms within the house of international law.

A reconciliatory approach, on the other hand, differs from Article 31(3)(c) VCLT because it is not limited to making sense of the wording of provisions within a specific treaty, but to making sense of the meaning with regard to the conflicting norms set out in separate treaties. It could harmonise norms across legal areas by applying a norm in consideration of other applicable norms. However, there is no legal obligation to strive for coherence within the international legal system, but there is legal reasoning for such an aspiration.

In this book, I advocate that a reconciliatory approach can and should be used by the treaty bodies to harmonise the MEA norms with other international obligations. MEA treaty bodies can overlook the limitations of the interpretation tools because they are empowered to perform tasks beyond treaty interpretation in their application of the MEA provisions. The treaty bodies can apply the provisions in a manner that considers the other norms and interests set out in other treaties and fields of law. Such an application functions on the view of the international rules as being a part of a bigger system.

Moreover, the conflict solution techniques address normative tensions by prioritising one norm over another. Typically, in times of armed conflict, a normative conflict is solved with the conflict solution rule of the *lex specialis*, as discussed in chapter six. It prescribes that the rules of the law of armed conflict prevail at the expense of peacetime rules. The other conflict techniques suggested by the International Law Commission include the *lex superior* rule, providing the precedence of *jus cogens* rules over other rules of international law because these are peremptory norms and supersede other rules. This conflict solution technique is only of relevance when dealing with *jus cogens* norms and I will not further discuss it as the protection of environment in times of armed conflict rarely involves such norms.[74] In addition, the *lex posterior* rule, which is codified in Article 30 VCLT addresses norm conflicts. It deals with the situation where successive treaties relate to the same subject matter and enjoy priority over earlier treaties.

There are particular problems connected with the application of the *lex posterior* rule with regard to multilateral agreements, such as MEAs and the instruments of the law of armed conflict. The conflicting norms may derive from treaties that do not have the same state parties.[75] In addition, the time factor is

[74] 'Fragmentation of International Law: Difficulties Arising From the Diversification and Expansion of International Law', Report of the Study Group of the International Law Commission, Finalised by Martti Koskenniemi (n 64) paras 361–73.

[75] For further reading, see Matz and Wolfrum (n 72) 129.

difficult to establish since it is not expressed whether it is the time of negotiation, the entry into force, or the ratification that determines when a treaty is successive in relation to the other. Thus, the *lex posterior* rule is not further analysed in this thesis. Furthermore, when dealing with MEAs and the law of armed conflict, it might not be so straightforward to determine whether a normative tension is in fact a normative conflict that needs to be solved by establishing priority between the norms, as discussed in the previous section. Most of the provisions in the environmental treaties, as well as in the law of armed conflict, are framed in a way that gives states a discretionary power in the application.

In addition, conflicting solution tools are often avoided when dealing with MEAs. This is because MEAs protect interests shared by the state parties and require compliance from all of them to achieve the common treaty objective.[76] As discussed earlier, environmental challenges, such as climate change or protection of the ozone layer, cannot be remedied if only one state cuts its carbon emissions or usage of ozone depleting substances, while the rest of the states maintain or increase theirs. To be effective, a larger group of states has to contribute together.[77] State parties have to do what they can to prevent or at least minimise environmental harm. To allow state parties to derogate from these types of obligations would impede the efficiency of MEAs. Consequently, the conflict resolution techniques are not desirable methods when dealing with environmental treaties established to achieve a common objective shared by all state parties, and sometimes even shared by the international community as a whole.[78]

Moreover, the tools suggested by the Study Group on Fragmentation of the International Law Commission do not offer the appropriate means to deal with normative tensions in a satisfactory manner when involving MEAs. They do not provide for non-binding acts to be taken into account in the interpretation, which may be problematic when dealing with MEAs. As discussed in chapter six, non-binding instruments play a prominent part in advancing strategies within MEAs. The treaty bodies develop the provisions through decisions, declarations, recommendations, resolutions, activities, projects, etc, that are not necessarily legally binding, but still influential of the state parties' behaviour. These acts have unclear legal status. As the conflict resolution rules and Article 31(3)(c) VCLT operate mainly among legal rules, without allocating non-binding instruments any particular significance, they thereby fail to fully address the normative processes taking place under the MEAs.[79] Nevertheless, the practice of the treaty

[76] Boisson de Chazournes (n 45) 11.

[77] Matz and Wolfrum (n 72) 160.

[78] ibid, 131–33; K Bannelier-Christakis, 'International Law Commission and Protection of the Environment in Times of Armed Conflict: A Possibility for Adjudication?' (2013) 20 *Journal of International Cooperation Studies* 129.

[79] C McLachlan, 'The Principle of Systemic Integration and Article 31(3)(c) of the Vienna Convention' (2005) 54 *International & Comparative Law Quarterly* 279, 290–91. See also Weil (n 47) 413; Klabbers (n 47) 167.

bodies can impact the interpretation process under certain conditions as subsequent practice in accordance with Article 31(3)(b) VCLT, among other means of interpretation, as mentioned in chapter one.[80] However, in the *Whaling* case, the International Court of Justice rejected Australia's claim that the resolutions adopted by the International Whaling Commission (a treaty body of the International Convention for the Regulation of Whaling (1946 Whaling Convention))[81] comprised subsequent practice or subsequent agreements in accordance with Article 31(3)(a) and (b) VCLT. According to the Court, many of the resolutions were adopted without the support of all state parties to the Convention and, in particular, without the concurrence of Japan (accused of breaching the Convention). Therefore, the recommendatory resolutions and Guidelines adopted by the International Whaling Commission could not be regarded as subsequent practice or subsequent agreements between the parties regarding the interpretation of the treaty within the meaning of subparagraphs (a) and (b), respectively, of Article 31(3) VCLT.[82]

V. THE ELEMENTS THAT ENABLE MEAs TO RECONCILE

MEAs have an ability inherent within their construction to reconcile with rules of other legal areas. MEAs do not form a homogeneous group; nonetheless, most of them share four elements with regard to their character, structure and operation that facilitate the adoption of a reconciliatory approach. These elements are: (1) treaty provisions providing for a wide discretionary power in their application; (2) establishment of treaty institutions; (3) the use of compliance systems focusing on supportive measures; and (4) the ability of the treaty institutions to cooperate with each other and with other actors, including international organisations, non-governmental organisations, states and private actors. The elements are linked to the objectives of MEAs, addressing complex international environmental issues as a shared concern of the state parties that require context-based responses and international cooperation.

In the following subsections, I use the World Heritage Convention and the Ramsar Convention as examples in order to describe the four elements and how they facilitate the use of a reconciliatory approach for MEAs.

[80] A Arato, 'Subsequent Practice and Evaluative Interpretation: Techniques of Treaty Interpretation Over Time and their Diverse Consequences' (2010) 9 *The Law and Practice of International Courts and Tribunals* 443.

[81] International Convention for the Regulation of Whaling (adopted 2 December 1946, entered into force 10 November 1948) 161 UNTS 72 (1946 Whaling Convention).

[82] *Whaling in the Antarctic (Australia v Japan: New Zealand Intervening)*, Judgment, ICJ Reports 2014, 226, paras 83, 257.

A. The First Element: Provisions Designed for Discretionary Application

MEAs address environmental problems that change rapidly, and the process to identify what needs to be done to protect the environment is highly dependent on updated scientific knowledge.[83] These complex problems are best dealt with by using a less fixed application of rules that can offer context-based measures.[84] Therefore, most MEAs are framework conventions drafted with the intention to formulate provisions that give the law-applier (state parties) a wide discretionary power in their application.[85] The MEA provisions provide the state parties with a certain amount of flexibility to adapt the responses accordingly to the geographical, economic and social factors of the state parties, as well as the evolution of science.[86]

This applies to the World Heritage Convention and the Ramsar Convention, as mentioned in section II. For instance, Article 5 of the World Heritage Convention requires that each state party

> shall endeavour, in so far as possible, and as appropriate for each country … to take the appropriate legal, scientific, technical, administrative and financial measures necessary for the identification, protection, conservation, presentation and rehabilitation [of its world heritage sites].

Similarly, the Ramsar Convention uses flexible obligations. Article 3 of the Ramsar Convention requires that state parties 'formulate and implement their planning so as to promote the conservation of the wetlands' and to make 'as far as possible the wise use of the wetlands in their territory'. The wording used in both these treaties allows the state parties a certain amount of discretion to adapt the measures to the specific challenges within the national context, taking into account geographic and biological differences or the nature of the environmental problems.[87]

B. The Second Element: Treaty Bodies

MEAs establish treaty bodies empowered to develop the provisions by adopting decisions, resolutions, and/or recommendations. They also initiate activities, programmes and projects to ensure the implementation of the treaties.[88]

[83] T Koivurova, *Introduction to International Environmental Law* (Routledge, 2014) 55.

[84] D Shelton, 'Comments on the Normative Challenge of Environmental "Soft Law"' in Y Kerbrat and S Maljean-Dubois (eds), *The Transformation of International Environmental Law* (Hart Publishing and Editions A Pedone, 2011) 71.

[85] P Birnie, A Boyle and C Redgwell, *International Law & the Environment* (Oxford University Press, 2009) 17.

[86] Boisson de Chazournes (n 45) 10–11.

[87] Carducci (n 27) 145.

[88] A Wiersema, 'The New International Law-makers? Conferences of the Parties to Multilateral Environmental Agreements' (2009) 31 *Michigan Journal of International Law* 231, 284–85.

The institutional architecture among the MEAs varies, although there are some shared fundamental attributes.

In general, all state parties are represented in the main decision-making treaty bodies, for instance, the COP of the Ramsar Convention.[89] Some MEAs have separate executive treaty bodies, like the World Heritage Convention,[90] which has established the WH Committee. In contrast to most other MEAs, the World Heritage Convention has assigned a large amount of the decision-making competencies to the WH Committee as opposed to its General Assembly.[91]

The mandate of the executive body is generally set out in the treaty provisions and formulated in a broad manner without clear limits.[92] Often, the executive treaty body has a general authorisation to carry out activities to accomplish the object and purpose of the MEA.[93] This means that it can undertake internal procedural actions, such as deciding on meeting agendas, adopting procedural rules for itself and its subsidiary bodies, and creating new subsidiary bodies. The body can also make decisions with regard to the substantive obligations concerning the application and operation of the treaty.[94] The executive body also usually monitors compliance and decides on measures in cases of non-compliance.[95] In the case of the World Heritage Convention, the WH Committee has a broad mandate – ensuring the application of the Convention, and defining and developing the provisions by adopting decisions, recommendations and guidelines.[96] The executive organ of an MEA, being a Committee or the COP, is in many cases assisted by a secretariat dealing with administrative matters, and sometimes also by expert subsidiary bodies.[97] Both the World Heritage Convention and the Ramsar Convention have secretariats and subsidiary bodies to assist their executive bodies.

The establishment of the treaty bodies and the empowerment of them to adopt wide-reaching measures to apply the Convention limits the discretionary power granted to the state parties of the MEAs. In the case of the Ramsar Convention, with the COP being the executive treaty body, all the state parties

[89] Zacharias (n 28).

[90] This is the case in the Convention on Long-Range Transboundary Air Pollution (adopted 13 November 1979, entered into force 16 March 1983) 1302 UNTS 217 (LRTAP); Convention on the Protection of the Marine Environment of the Baltic Sea Area (adopted 9 April 1992, entered into force 17 January 2000) 1507 UNTS 167 (Helsinki Convention); and the Convention for the Protection of the Marine Environment of the North-East Atlantic (adopted 22 September 1992, entered into force 25 March 1998) 2354 UNTS 67 (OSPAR Convention).

[91] Matz and Wolfrum (n 72) 166.

[92] G Ulfstein, 'Treaty Bodies' in D Bodansky, J Brunnée and E Hey (eds), *Oxford Handbook of International Environmental Law* (Oxford University Press, 2007).

[93] Churchill and Ulfstein (n 30) 639 ff.

[94] Matz and Wolfrum (n 72) 166–67.

[95] Churchill and Ulfstein (n 30) 626.

[96] The WH Committee meets at least once a year. See *WHC Operational Guidelines*.

[97] Churchill and Ulfstein (n 30) 623. The authors list over 20 international and regional MEAs that are constructed in this manner.

are represented in the executive treaty body and can continuously influence decision-making. Thereby, they are involved in the normative process, setting the direction for how the treaty should develop. With regard to the World Heritage Convention, the executive body of the WH Committee has only 21 state parties, which means that the decision-making power is not allocated to all the state parties but a limited group of state parties. This could make the decision process faster.

The wide-reaching mandate of the MEAs' bodies injects a political component into their application of the treaties. Given that they are empowered to ensure the general goals of the MEAs, within the limits of the treaty provisions, they can adopt decisions guided by pragmatic considerations that have more of a political than a legal character. Such decisions can be aimed at achieving compromises between different interests and may vary from different albeit similar cases. The content of the decisions can be more diverse and nuanced. In that way, these decisions differ from legal decisions, which must maintain predictability and stability, and are therefore more rigid.[98] Consequently, the activities under the MEAs blur the line between political decision-making and treaty interpretation, and also between binding and non-binding commitments. The solutions can be more context-based and adjusted to the particular problem that a state party faces, and can consider the resources and ability of that state. Additionally, other legal interests that may interfere with the application of the treaty could also be taken into account.

The establishment of MEA institutions with degrees of decision-making authority can enable compromises that characterise a reconciliatory approach. Such an approach can solve normative tensions by going beyond 'pure' treaty interpretation and conflict solution techniques, to seek more politically oriented solutions that can consider the other international obligations of the state party concerned.[99]

C. The Third Element: Non-confrontational Compliance Mechanisms

The majority of MEAs share a third element of having supportive non-confrontational compliance mechanisms. The primary aim of the mechanisms is to assist and motivate state parties to comply and secure the MEA objective.[100] They are designed to facilitate state parties' fulfilment of their obligations, rather than punishing failures to do so.[101] The mechanisms build on the idea

[98] M Cerer, 'The Relationship Between Law and Politics' (2009) 15 *Annual Survey of International & Comparative Law* 19, 33–34.

[99] On the need for a political process to respond to fragmentation, see Matz-Lück (n 50) 50.

[100] N Goeteyn and F Maes, 'Compliance Mechanisms in Multilateral Environmental Agreements: An Effective Way to Improve Compliance?' (2011) 10 *Chinese Journal of International Law* 791, 815.

[101] Churchill and Ulfstein (n 30) 629; Goeteyn and Maes (n 100) 797–99.

that state parties are unable rather than unwilling to comply.[102] The reason why the compliance mechanisms of most MEAs are designed in this manner is that the protection measures can only have effect if the parties work together. As opposed to many other areas of international law, rules on state responsibility are of limited use for enforcing international environmental treaties, unless it concerns transboundary environmental damage. Similarly, using the means provided under the VCLT – such as withdrawal, suspension and termination – is not helpful to advance the aims of the MEAs either.[103] In addition, MEAs rarely provide for traditional dispute settlements.[104] Such dispute settlements have often limited effect in these types of treaties, in which the goal is to protect a concern shared by the parties, rather than to exchange performances.

An example is if a state does not protect its wetlands, all states will be affected in the sense that an important ecosystem – a shared concern – will be damaged. Therefore, unless it regards transboundary environmental damage, dispute settlements are often avoided in MEAs, because they may not put the disputing parties into compliance with the MEAs and the injury will be done to all state parties alike. Both the World Heritage Convention and the Ramsar Convention lack dispute settlement procedures, which may weaken their means to influence environmental protection during armed conflicts, as pointed out by several scholars.[105] Nevertheless, it does not mean that these conventions (or in fact other MEAs) do not have mechanisms to ensure compliance.

MEA institutions collect and share information on the parties' implementation record in order to analyse causes of non-compliance. Almost all MEAs, including the World Heritage Convention and the Ramsar Convention, use a self-reporting system that requires 'State parties to submit national reports to the MEA bodies to be evaluated on how they fulfil the commitments'.[106] The reports are also the basis for the MEA bodies to provide guidance for decisions, recommendations, and/or initiate activities for enhanced compliance. This could be achieved through establishing action plans, providing financial and technical support, and implementing capacity-building measures, including workshops, consultations, and training, etc.[107] Brunnée has described it as a 'tailor-made approach' to respond to cases of non-compliance of the state parties.[108] The purpose is to strengthen the capacity and to change behaviour in the state parties, rather than to achieve a specified result.

[102] Goeteyn and Maes (n 100) 799.
[103] Churchill and Ulfstein (n 30) 646.
[104] Such a mechanism is provided in Article 18 of the Convention on the Conservation of European Wildlife and Natural Habitats (adopted 19 September 1979, entered into force 1 June 1982) 1284 UNTS 209 (Bern Convention).
[105] See Burhenne (n 12) 373; Verwey (n 12) 15; Tarasofsky (n 2) 568.
[106] Goeteyn and Maes (n 100) 811.
[107] Ulfstein (n 92); Goeteyn and Maes (n 100) 814.
[108] J Brunnée, 'Enforcement Mechanisms in International Law and International Environmental Law' in U Beyerlin, PT Stoll and R Wolfrum (eds), *Ensuring Compliance with Multilateral Environmental Agreements: A Dialogue Between Practitioners and Academia* (Martinus Nijhoff, 2006) 16.

There are MEAs that employ coercive enforcement measures.[109] Such punitive components could consist of naming and shaming, warnings, sanctions and financial penalties.[110] The World Heritage Convention provides for penalising non-compliance through 'international exposure and embarrassment'.[111] In exceptional cases, delisting of a site from the World Heritage List may occur.[112] This would happen if the site has lost its outstanding value due to wilful mistreatment, neglect, or accident, and if the site no longer constitutes a world heritage as a result.[113] Deletion from the World Heritage List is an unwanted measure to adopt under the World Heritage Convention, because its main objective is to make sure that world heritage is preserved. The Ramsar Convention functions in an equivalent manner. Furthermore, under the World Heritage Convention, state parties can request international assistance from the WH Committee for securing the protection, conservation, presentation, or rehabilitation of the world heritage sites.[114] International assistance can be offered in terms of studies, the provision of experts, skilled labour, training of staff and specialists, supply of equipment, low-interest or interest-free loans, or the granting of non-repayable subsidies under the World Heritage Convention.[115]

Funding is frequently provided under the MEAs because many developing state parties need financial assistance and technology to comply with the treaties. The World Heritage Convention has established a World Heritage Fund that provides financial support.[116] The text of the Ramsar Convention does not express that it provides for international assistance or funds to its state parties to protect the wetlands identified on the Ramsar List. However, its treaty institutions have established three assistance programmes for small projects (or parts of larger projects) for the conservation and wise use of wetlands with direct

[109] See Bodansky (n 31) 226–27. On the WHC compliance mechanism in particular, see Goodwin (n 31) 157.

[110] The Convention on International Trade in Endangered Species (adopted 3 March 1973, entered into force 1 July 1975) 993 UNTS 243 (CITES) provides for economic inducements such as trade sanctions for the non-compliant party. See also Goeteyn and Maes (n 100) 800.

[111] Goodwin (n 31) 157.

[112] The Committee suggested starting a process to delist the cultural site – Cologne cathedral – in Germany, unless Germany reconsidered its building projects. Germany halted the building plans and Cologne cathedral was kept on the World Heritage List. In 2007, the Committee decided to remove the 'Arabian Oryx Sanctuary', because hydrocarbon exploration activities inside the world heritage site reduced its outstanding value. See T Scovazzi, 'Articles 8–11, World Heritage Committee and World Heritage List' in F Francioni (ed), *The 1972 World Heritage Convention: A Commentary* (Oxford University Press, 2008) 170–71.

[113] This happened in the case of the Dresden Waldschlosschen Bridge and Elbe Valley Cultural Landscape in Germany. For further reading on this issue, see S von Schorlemer, *Compliance with the UNESCO World Heritage Convention: Reflections on the Elbe Valley and the Dresden Waldschlösschen Bridge* (Duncker & Humblot, 2009).

[114] The WH Committee grants the requests in accordance with Article 13(1) of the World Heritage Convention.

[115] Article 22 World Heritage Convention.

[116] ibid, Article 15.

assistance, funds, capacity building, etc.[117] For instance, the Ramsar Convention can provide for funds and plans for the restoration of wetlands.[118]

Other MEAs also have similarly established funds[119] or received funding from the Global Environment Facility to finance compliance activities. The Global Environment Facility is the world's largest public financer of global environmental issues and provides funds to support developing states to ratify and implement key international environmental agreements. For instance, it is funding several projects for applying the Biodiversity Convention and its two protocols.[120]

Another measure carried out under the World Heritage Convention for effective implementation is the establishment of the Danger List for world heritage sites under threat, so that these sites can receive strengthened protection.[121] The Danger List demonstrates how the World Heritage Convention proactively seeks to ensure protection for the sites, rather than punishing the state parties for not adequately protecting them. The Ramsar Convention has the similar Montreux Records, as described in section II.

As a result, the opportunities to adopt measures to help state parties to be in compliance provide further degrees of flexibility on how to apply the treaties. The measures can be undertaken in a manner that ensures that they do not interfere with other obligations of the state. They could even be combined with other interests. For instance, programmes and projects can be initiated with the goal to develop a state's capacity to protect its wetlands and at the same time benefit the development of local communities. In case of a Ramsar site located in Cambodia, threatened by over-fishing, a project aimed at ensuring the wise use of the site by providing alternative livelihoods to the local communities, to reduce their dependence on natural resources, has been initiated under the Convention.[122] Such a project seeks to advance the Ramsar Convention's objec-

[117] The Small Grants Fund supports projects from around the world, both through direct assistance and by seeking donors for additional proposals. The Wetland for the Future initiative, funded by the US State Department and Fish and Wildlife Services, supports small capacity-building projects in Latin America. The Swiss Grant for Africa assists the Secretariat's Africa regional team in facilitating specific activities in that region. See Ramsar web page: www.ramsar.org /cda/en/ramsar-activities-grants/main/ramsar/1-63-68_4000_0__.

[118] P Griffin, 'The Ramsar Convention: A New Window for Environmental Diplomacy?', The Institute for Environmental Diplomacy and Security (2013), available at: www.uvm.edu/ieds/sites/default/files/Ramsar_IEDSResearchSeries.pdf, 18.

[119] For instance, the COP of Climate Change Convention recently created a new fund, the Green Climate Fund, for financing the implementation of the Convention. See: www.dlapiper.com/~/media/Files/Insights/Publications/2012/12/Green%20Climate%20Fund%20GCF/Files/Climate_Change_Alert_Renewables_Dec_2012/FileAttachment/Climate_Change_Alert_Renewables_Dec_2012.pdf.

[120] See the Global Environment Facility website: www.thegef.org/gef/Press_release/ GEF_establishes_NPIF 195.

[121] Article 11(4) World Heritage Convention.

[122] Ramsar Convention, 'Investing in Wetlands' (2014), available at: www.ramsar.org/sites/default/files/documents/library/ramsar_sgf_portfolio_2014_20.pdf.

tive, but at the same time also consider other interests that may be linked to the compliance of the Convention. The wide variety of supportive compliance measures that can be invoked move MEAs away from being pure legal instruments and provide them with tools for pragmatic solutions, which could involve reconciliation across legal fields – if needed – to ensure compliance.

D. The Fourth Element: Institutional Cooperation

The fourth element relates to how the MEA institutions are often encouraged in the treaty provisions to cooperate with other stakeholders, such as other treaty bodies, states, international organisations, non-governmental organisations and private companies. The element is closely related to the character of environmental problems, which requires a collective response to achieve a higher level of efficacy for the MEAs.[123] Thus, cooperation is an established form of applying MEAs.[124] The cooperation may consist of exchange of information, partnerships and joint activities, but there is no set template.[125] In addition, given that there are many environmental treaties adopted at various times and having different parties, the environmental legal field is difficult to overview.[126] Therefore, MEAs seem to overcome issues of inconsistency by establishing cooperation and coordination between each other's treaty organs, as well as with other institutions or organisations.

Cooperation can mutually reinforce efforts made by various institutions under the MEAs to accomplish coherence within the international environmental sphere.[127] For example, a Joint Liaison Group of the 'Rio Conventions', including the Climate Change Convention, the Biodiversity Convention, and the UN Convention to Combat Desertification[128] has been established to coordinate application. In addition, the five biodiversity-related conventions – the Biodiversity Convention, CITES, the Convention on Migratory Species, the Ramsar Convention, and the World Heritage Convention – have a joint website, initiated in March 1999, for the purpose of coordination between the five conventions. Similar cooperation could be imitated to accomplish coherence with other areas

[123] Matz and Wolfrum (n 72) 119 and 170.

[124] Churchill and Ulfstein (n 30) 626.

[125] For instance, the UN Environmental Programme promotes and coordinates cooperation between MEAs. UNEP has held several conferences to coordinate the secretariats of the MEAs, as confirmed by the UN General Assembly. See General Assembly, International Institutional Arrangements Related to Environment and Development, UN Doc A/54/468, 15 October 1999.

[126] Koivurova (n 83) 8.

[127] Matz and Wolfrum (n 72) 203.

[128] UN Convention to Combat Desertification in Those Countries Experiencing Serious Drought and/or Desertification, Particularly in Africa (adopted 14 October 1994, entered into force 6 December 1996) 1954 UNTS 3 (UNCCD).

of international law, given that the MEA treaty bodies can cooperate with other actors outside the environmental field by entering into partnerships or joint projects.[129]

MEAs can either explicitly or implicitly empower its institutions to instigate cooperation with other actors. Cooperation can be launched by invitation of the executive treaty body or the secretariat.[130] The WH Committee is authorised to cooperate with other stakeholders pursuant to Article 13(7) of the World Heritage Convention. It reads:

> The Committee shall co-operate with international and national governmental and non-governmental organizations having objectives similar to those of this Convention. For the implementation of its programmes and projects, the Committee may call on such organizations, particularly the International Centre for the Study of the Preservation and Restoration of Cultural Property (the Rome Centre), the International Council of Monuments and Sites (ICOMOS) and the International Union for Conservation of Nature and Natural Resources (IUCN), as well as on public and private bodies and individuals.

For instance, the WH Committee cooperates with the Earth Watch Institute, Panasonic, the *International New York Times*, Norwegian Foreign Ministry of Affairs, Deutsche Gesellschaft für Technische Zusammenarbeit, Belgian Federal Science Policy, etc.[131] Thus, it is a mix of actors involving states, non-governmental organisations and companies. With regard to the Ramsar Convention, because it is not expressed in the treaty, there is implicit empowerment to cooperate with other actors. For instance, the treaty bodies of the Ramsar Convention cooperate with six global non-governmental organisations, namely BirdLife International, the IUCN, the International Water Management Institute, Wetlands International, Wildfowl and Wetlands Trust, and the World Wide Fund for Nature.[132] The Ramsar Convention has also established cooperation with private companies, including the Danone Group and Evian Water Company.[133] In addition, cooperation is conducted under the Convention with five other international environmental treaties,[134] a number of regional

[129] Matz and Wolfrum (n 72) 191.

[130] M Young, 'Regime Interaction in Creating, Implementing and Enforcing International Law in M Young (ed), *Regime Interaction in International Law: Facing Fragmentation* (Cambridge University Press, 2012) 99; Matz and Wolfrum (n 72) 167.

[131] On the World Heritage Convention's website the different actors who are partners with the Convention are listed, see: whc.unesco.org/en/partners/.

[132] Ramsar Convention Resolution VII.3 (1999), where four NGOs were confirmed in the formal status of International Organization Partners of the Convention. In Resolution IX.16 (2005), the parties judged that IWMI meets the qualifications for Ramsar IOP status that was outlined in 1999. See: ramsar.rgis.ch/cda/en/ramsar-about-partners/main/ramsar/1-36-57_4000_0__.

[133] See partnership on Ramsar Convention web page: ramsar.rgis.ch/cda/en/ramsar-about-private/main/ramsar/1-36-50_4000_0__.

[134] These include the World Heritage Convention, the UN Framework Convention on Climate Change, the UN Convention to Combat Desertification, the Convention on Conservation of Migratory Species of Wild Animal (adopted 23 June 1979, entered into force 8 October 1991) 1651 UNTS

conventions and basin commissions,[135] UN Environment, and the UN Food and Agriculture Organization.[136] An example of such collaboration is a joint project by the Swiss Grant Fund for Africa, administered by the Ramsar Secretariat since 1989 and funded by Switzerland to support wetland conservation and the implementation of the Ramsar Convention in Africa. The collaboration has financed specific activities in areas of wetland in need of conservation and also promoted the Convention in Africa.[137]

Neither the World Heritage Convention nor the Ramsar Convention specify what form the collaborations should take. Generally, the provisions set out in the MEAs provide for flexibility as to how to conduct the cooperation.[138] As it is not restricted to certain forms or actors, cooperation could be undertaken with actors engaged in other areas of international law. Collaborating with other actors is a way of finding innovative solutions to achieve conservation of the environment. The official website of the Ramsar Convention states that collaboration contributes to

> bringing together experts and policy makers to develop guidance and guidelines together; tapping expertise and knowledge at a broader level; leveraging resources at all levels; seeking creative or innovative solutions of mutual interest collectively; and forging new linkages and alliances between capacity-building needs and cooperative actions.[139]

Hence, the involvement of MEA institutions in such collaborations strengthens the capacity of state parties to comply, and can contribute to reconciling tensions with the other legal obligations.[140]

(CMS); and the Biodiversity Convention. See: ramsar.rgis.ch/cda/en/ramsar-about-synergy/main/ramsar/1-36-192_4000_0__.

135 For instance, with UNEP's Convention for the Protection and Development of the Marine Environment of the Wider Caribbean Region and with the Coordinating Unit of the Mediterranean Action Plan of the Convention for the Protection of the Marine Environment and the Coastal Region of the Mediterranean. A Memorandum of Cooperation was signed with the Convention on the protection and sustainable development of the Carpathians in December 2006. The Pacific Regional Environment Programme is a partner with the Ramsar Convention under a Joint Work Plan that began in 2002 and now includes the basing of a Ramsar officer for the Oceania region in Samoa. The International Commission for the Protection of the Danube river cooperates under the terms of an agreement first signed in November 2000. Furthermore, the Ramsar Convention is closely involved in the work of the Lake Chad Basin Commission and the Niger Basin Authority, and the Ramsar Secretariat signed a memorandum of cooperation with both of these in November 2002. A new agreement was finalised with the Commission Internationale du Bassin Congo-Ougangui-Sang in March 2006. See: ramsar.rgis.ch/cda/en/ramsar-about-synergy/main/ramsar/1-36-192_ 4000_0__.

136 See Ramsar Convention website: ramsar.rgis.ch/cda/en/ramsar-about-synergy/main /ramsar/1-36-192_4000_0__.

137 ibid.

138 Matz and Wolfrum (n 72) 161.

139 See Ramsar web page: www.ramsar.org/cda/en/ramsar-activities-partnershipindex/ main/ramsar/1-63-506_4000_0__.

140 In relation to cooperation between the WTO and Climate Change Convention institutions, there are no legal obstacles, only political obstacles, if anything. See van Asselt, Sindico and Mehling (n 45) 437 and 440.

In sum, most MEAs have a similar structure that accommodates the four elements, enabling them to develop and respond to global environmental challenges by adopting innovative strategies. The elements allow MEAs to reconcile and interact with other areas of law by adopting strategies that combine political decision-making with legal interpretation and law-making. Bringing a political component into the legal domain of applying and interpreting MEAs facilitates a reconciliatory approach, because it builds on context-based pragmatism to overcome tensions between legal norms.[141]

VI. RECONCILIATION: IS IT POSSIBLE?

This section explores the meaning of reconciling rules by examining three hypothetical examples of normative tensions between the law of armed conflict and three MEAs. The examples were partly discussed in section III, in relation to the conceptualisation of normative conflicts.

> **Example 1:** Article 6 of the World Heritage Convention prohibits any deliberate activities that may directly or indirectly damage sites recognised as world heritage. Under the law of armed conflict, the same site constitutes a military objective because armed groups are hiding inside the site. The world heritage site may be lawfully attacked in accordance with the law of armed conflict, as long as the damage is proportional in relation to the anticipated military advantage or does not reach the absolute threshold detailed in Articles 35(3) and 55(1) of Protocol I (in case of an international armed conflict). Such an attack would clearly be contrary to Article 6 of the World Heritage Convention, but lawful according to the law of armed conflict. Thus, this is a situation involving a normative tension – where a state cannot fully act in accordance with the rules of both legal frameworks without possibly violating one. Can the norms can be reconciled in this situation?

One way for the norms to be reconciled, in the situation described above, could be for the law-applier to allow the norms of the World Heritage Convention to complement the law of armed conflict, in the sense that the world heritage site remains protected even if it constitutes a military objective. In such a case, any military operation that could damage or harm the site would be prohibited. Hence, a state that refrains from conducting military operations in the site would not be violating any of the relevant norms under the law of armed conflict

[141] For the discussion on law and politics, see Cerer (n 98) 32.

or the World Heritage Convention. This could be a form of reconciliation where environmental protection is reinforced by permitting the MEA norms to inform the interpretation of the provisions under the law of armed conflict in order to safeguard areas protected under the World Heritage Convention. On the other hand, this view would only restrict the application of the law of armed conflict, while the World Heritage Convention applies fully. Hence, the approach – in this case – may not reflect a *reconciliation* of the norms.

> **Example 2**: Assuming that armed groups are hiding inside a wetland site protected under the Ramsar Convention, and consequently constitutes a military objective. An attack on the site would then be lawful in accordance with the law of armed conflict, as long as the attack is proportional in relation to the anticipated military advantage or does not result in damage reaching the absolute threshold detailed in Articles 35(3) and 55 of Protocol I. This case is also an example of a normative tension. However, the question is how should such an attack be viewed under the concept of wise use of the site, pursuant to Article 3 of the Ramsar Convention? Would a norm reconciliation be possible in this example?

An attack resulting in harming the wetland would be contrary to the wise use of the site and therefore would constitute a violation of Article 3 of the Ramsar Convention. However, if a military attack is necessary in order to regain control over the wetland and to protect it, it could then be argued that the attack would be in conformity with the wise use concept. For instance, if the armed group occupies the site and uses it in an unsustainable way by engaging in overexploitation of natural resources, an attack could be the only feasible way to safeguard the site from the rebels in the wetland area. Although such an attack may harm the site, it might be considered a measure consistent with the wise use concept because it contributes to stabilising the area and thereby enabling conservation work from a long-term perspective.

Having control over its territory could be seen as a precondition for a state to be able to safeguard its protected areas. Conceivably, therefore, if certain precautionary measures were undertaken prior to the attack – for instance, by using ammunition with little environmental impact or avoiding targeting certain parts of the wetland that has endangered species – then such an action could be regarded as a *reconciliation* of norms. By applying the principle of proportionality and the principle of precaution under the law of armed conflict in a manner that minimises the adverse impacts on the wetland, the law-applier would have applied its obligations in a reconciliatory manner and fulfilled its obligations to the furthest extent under both the Ramsar Convention and the law of armed conflict.

> **Example 3**: A petrochemical complex, which constitutes a military objective under the law of armed conflict, is placed close to a lake that is protected under the Transboundary Watercourses and International Lakes Convention. An attack on the complex would result in adverse impacts on the lake and cause damage to the environment of the neighbouring state. According to Article 1 of the Convention, state parties 'shall take appropriate measures' to prevent transboundary damage. To launch an attack on the petrochemical complex is probably not regarded as such an 'appropriate measure' and would therefore be considered a violation of the Convention. At the same time, such an attack is permissive under the law of armed conflict, as long as the collateral damage of the attack is proportionate in relation to the military advantage anticipated, as prescribed by the proportionality principle and not reaching the damage threshold in Articles 35(3) and 55(1) Protocol I.

In this example, similar problems will arise as those discussed in relation to the first example with the world heritage site. This means that abstaining from attacking the petrochemical complex would ensure that the state fully complied with the MEA without violating any norms under the law of armed conflict. However, the inclusion of the word 'appropriate' in Article 1 of the Convention could imply that a state's action may be assessed in the light of the particular circumstances existing in an armed conflict. Under such circumstances, the attack may be considered as an 'appropriate measure', if precautionary measures are undertaken to minimise the environmental impacts – thus not violating the Convention. For instance, assuming that the attacking state made a choice to attack the petrochemical complex instead of another military target that could have caused even worse adverse transboundary impacts on the same lake, the attack may be considered appropriate and therefore not a violation of the Transboundary Watercourses and International Lakes Convention.

The fact that an attack may harm a lake or a wetland that is protected under an international environmental treaty may influence the assessment of collateral damage under the proportionality principle and what is a 'feasible measure' to minimise collateral damage under the principle of precaution according to the law of armed conflict. The law-applier in such a case would have to correlate what is considered appropriate under the Transboundary Watercourses and International Lakes Convention with what is proportional collateral damage and feasible measures to minimise it. Hence, the discretionary power provided under the MEAs, but also the law of armed conflict, may offer opportunities to reconcile the MEA norms in relation to the law of armed conflict, which also narrows the discretion.

To conclude, there is no clear assertion on the permissible level of environmental damage in the law of armed conflict. In addition, there is no clear guidance of what measures are considered appropriate or adequate under an

MEA. The law-applier is provided with discretion to apply the instruments and should try to comply with the applicable international obligations in a reconciliatory manner, as far as possible. Consequently, there are some possibilities to elaborate on reconciliation between the norms of the law of armed conflict and the MEAs, but there is little guidance on how it can be made. However, the MEA treaty bodies could offer clarification of the appropriate measures to comply with an MEA in relation to armed conflict, which I will address in the next section (section VII).

VII. ROLE OF TREATY INSTITUTIONS

The treaty bodies could play a key role in advancing a reconciliatory approach when applying and developing the provisions under the MEAs, as well as through cooperation with other actors. In times of armed conflict, the treaties bodies could recommend measures that are adapted to respond to the specific environmental problems arising from the armed conflict situation. In addition, they can endorse measures that are feasible for a state to undertake, even if it is involved in hostilities. As the treaty bodies have a discretionary power, they can consider both the factual circumstances that a war-torn state party is facing (which may involve curtailed domestic institutions, damaged infrastructure, lack of control over parts of its territory, etc) as well as the legal situation with the application of other international obligations, including the law of armed conflict, to respect military necessity and minimise human harm. It could also be that a state party affected by an armed conflict has commitments in accordance with decisions by the UN Security Council under the UN Charter to address a situation threatening international peace and security.

In this sense, the norms of the MEAs can be interpreted in a manner that is consistent with the law of armed conflict, but still addresses the environmental issues protected under the treaty. For instance, the loose language used in Article 5 of the World Heritage Convention requires a state party to take measures to protect world heritage 'as far as possible' and 'as appropriate'. Thus, the WH Committee could recommend that a belligerent state party undertake measures appropriate within an armed conflict context.

There may be problems related to the environmental treaties' dependence for their application on an institutional structure that may no longer be in place in war-torn states. In many cases, such states may have inadequate infrastructure and non-functional state organs in place, which would obstruct any type of environmental protection work. However, as the environmental treaties apply supportive measures, they have an ability to reinforce the institutions of a weak state party but also engage other actors in the conservation work. They can apply the treaties with limited state involvement by relying on cooperation with a range of actors, including other treaty bodies, UN agencies, non-governmental organisations, or private enterprises.

Although the cooperating actors cannot substitute for domestic organs, they can minimise environmental destruction by providing funding, capacity building, equipment support, data analysis, consultation on national regulation, and coordination of international and local actors outside the state organs involved in protection work. For instance, funds can be given to support the project of a non-governmental organisation carried out in the territory of a state party to further the aims of an MEA.[142] The supportive measures can be carried out during, as well as after, armed conflict, at the same time as the law of armed conflict applies. The possibility to adopt measures to help state parties to be in compliance allows MEAs to be applied in a manner that can find pragmatic solutions adapted to particular challenges posed by armed conflict. Therefore, the assessment of the role of an MEA requires an analysis that takes into account the full operation of it, including the activities taking place within its institutional structure.[143]

Nevertheless, the environmental treaty bodies act in a manner to further a treaty's objective and purpose. Institutions may not consider the interests protected under other areas of law, because they will actively guard their interests to enable compliance with their conventions. Unlike MEAs, the law of armed conflict does not depend on any institutional arrangement to ensure compliance.[144] This may weaken the application of the law of armed conflict in relation to MEAs. However, an MEA will only be able to further its aims to the extent that is tolerated by its state parties. To be able to operate during armed conflicts, MEAs probably have to adjust to the armed conflict context and consider the norms of the law of armed conflict to be able to adopt decisions and recommendations that are feasible for the party and will be respected. If state parties do not accept the treaty decisions/recommendations, there are few sanctions within MEAs. Adopting a reconciliatory approach in relation to the law of armed conflict could contribute to ensure that state parties accept the recommendations and decisions under the MEAs.

VIII. CONCLUSIONS

Normative tensions between the rules of MEAs and the law of armed conflict can be resolved by applying a reconciliatory approach that could strengthen environmental protection during armed conflicts. If it is not possible to reconcile the norms, the *lex specialis* rule applies to solve the normative tension by allowing derogation from the MEA provisions for the precedence of the rules of the law of armed conflict.

[142] Churchill and Ulfstein (n 30) 623 ff.

[143] Bodansky (n 31) 158.

[144] A O'Donoghue, 'Splendid Isolation: International Humanitarian Law, Legal Theory and the International Legal Order' (2011) 14 *Yearbook of International Humanitarian Law* 107, 112.

MEAs are constructed in a manner that enables a reconciliatory approach in their application, which can serve to bridge the areas of international environmental law and the law of armed conflict. Such an approach is useful because the focus is on how the obligations of the two frameworks can be fulfilled at the same time and to the furthest extent. It does this by avoiding determining the existence of normative conflicts and, hence, the application of the *lex specialis* rule. A reconciliatory approach builds from two strategies. First, addressing the normative problem by using the ability of the law-applier, due to his/her discretionary power, to take other international obligations into consideration when applying the international obligations of the MEA. Second, the institutional cooperation between MEA treaty bodies and other actors that can combine the objectives of the treaties with other interests protected under international law.

The first strategy of the reconciliatory approach involves the fact that overlapping and incoherent norm relations, at a prima facie level, can be solved by regarding other legal commitments in the application of MEA provisions. In many instances, there may not even be any contradiction between the rules after an interpretation is made; rather they may regulate different aspects of a situation. Therefore, the rules may complement and reinforce each other.[145] The second strategy of the reconciliatory approach addresses the institutional problem through cooperation between different institutions, which can have a reconciliatory effect. Such a cooperative arrangement could take place between the institutions connected to different treaties. It could involve certain types of partnerships or joint projects with the purpose of achieving several of the treaty aims of those involved in the cooperation.

Nonetheless, there are limitations connected with adopting a reconciliatory approach. Such an approach represents an ongoing process to merge the norms of international law. A reconciliatory approach cannot provide exact guidance on how to reconcile rules on a general basis, since it has to be done in a concrete case and considering all the circumstances. Hence, the adoption of a reconciliatory approach that lacks firm direction may create some unpredictability in the application.[146] Such unpredictability may even jeopardise the stability of the legal system to some extent.

Additionally, in a reconciliation process, there will always be a certain risk of biased decisions in the application. This is because there is no established procedure on how to go about it. However, any conflict resolution undertaken to solve a normative conflict involves a certain element of decision-making based on preferences that may be partial. By applying a reconciliatory approach, the law-applier has to adopt the meaning that best reconciles the norms in accordance

[145] See Droege's analysis regarding the law of armed conflict and human rights law: C Droege, 'The Interplay Between International Humanitarian Law and International Human Rights Law in Situations of Armed Conflict' (2007) 40 *Israeli Law Review* 310, 344.

[146] G Hafner, 'Pros and Cons Ensuing from Fragmentation of International Law' (2004) 25 *Michigan Journal of International Law* 849, 856.

with the legal standards stipulated in the rules. Hence, an effort to reconcile conflicting norms may in fact be less biased than prioritising one rule over another. However, in the case of MEAs, there are, in most cases, treaty bodies in place that can conduct the reconciliation, given that they have a mandate to apply the treaty with a certain level of discretion.

As demonstrated in this chapter, there are opportunities, as well as deficiencies, with a reconciliatory approach in relation to MEAs and the law of armed conflict. To allow MEAs to complement environmental protection during armed conflicts and to reinforce those rules in the law of armed conflict may not always involve a reconciliation of the norms. To just add the obligations of MEAs onto states on top of the rules of the law of armed conflict cannot be considered as a norm reconciliation. However, a reconciliatory approach focuses on achieving compliance with both frameworks. The normative tensions that may occur between MEAs and the law of armed conflict need to be examined in concrete cases – which will be the focus of the next chapter – in order to analyse the potential of the environmental treaties in an armed conflict context.

8

Protection of World Heritage in Relation to Armed Conflict: The Case of the DRC[*]

I. INTRODUCTION

TO BE ABLE to further evaluate the role of MEAs in relation to armed conflict and to also explore the usefulness of a reconciliatory approach, this chapter examines the application of the World Heritage Convention in relation to the armed conflicts taking place in the Democratic Republic of the Congo (DRC) between 2000 and 2015. During this time period, the hostilities do not reach a constant level of intensity in violence and the organisation of the parties do not continuously fulfil the conditions to be defined as an armed conflict. Thus, this chapter also deals with the application of the Convention during the unstable phase of post-conflict.

The DRC is ranked fifth in the world regarding its biodiverse flora and fauna. It hosts large mammals that only exist in the region, including okapis, eastern lowland gorillas, mountain gorillas and bonobos.[1] In accordance with Articles 2 and 11(3) of the World Heritage Convention, the DRC has five natural world heritage sites that are inscribed on the World Heritage List due to their exceptional biological diversity and astonishing beauty.[2] I have focused on the case of the DRC because all five of its natural world heritage sites are on the Danger List because of the threat posed by the armed conflicts taking place inside and

* Parts of this chapter have been published in B Sjöstedt, 'The Role of Multilateral Environmental Agreements in Armed Conflict: "Green-keeping" in Virunga Park. Applying the UNESCO World Heritage Convention in the Armed Conflict of the Democratic Republic of the Congo' (2013) 82 *Nordic Journal of International Law* 129; and B Sjöstedt, 'Protecting the Environment During and After Armed Conflict Through Multilateral Environmental Agreements' in C Stahn, J Iverson and JE Easterday (eds), *Environmental Protection and Transitions from Conflict to Peace* (Oxford University Press, 2017). The author acknowledges the kind support of Forskraftstiftelsen Theodor Adelswärds Minne, who funded a field trip to the DRC, where research for this chapter was carried out.

[1] ILPI 2014, 'Protection of the Natural Environment in Armed Conflict: An Empirical Study', International Law and Policy Institute, Report 12/2014, 34.

[2] The DRC ratified the World Heritage Convention on 23 September 1974. See: whc.unesco.org/en/statesparties. The DRC now has five natural world heritage sites protected under the World Heritage Convention, including Salonga National Park, the Okapi Faunal Reserve, Kahuzi-Biega National Park and Garamba National Park.

around the sites. This makes these sites eligible for strengthened protection under the Convention in accordance with Article 11(4).

In addition, in 2000, it was decided by the executive treaty body of the Convention, the World Heritage Committee (WH Committee), to launch a project titled 'Biodiversity Conservation in Regions of Armed Conflict: Conserving World Heritage Sites in the Democratic Republic of the Congo'.[3] The project consists of a partnership including the World Heritage Centre (the administrative treaty body of the Convention) and the Congolese state organ entrusted with the management of the world heritage sites. Other UN agencies and UN programmes, states and international and national governmental and non-governmental organisations active in the DRC are also involved in the project.[4] The project's ambition is to guarantee that a basic protection of world heritage sites is maintained under international law, even in times of armed conflict, and to prepare the actors in the international arena to respond to such situations.[5]

The activities that are undertaken under the auspices of the project exemplify how the World Heritage Convention can play a role in protecting the environment during armed conflicts and how its obligations may interact with other applicable legal regimes. The case study examines the decisions, recommendations, international assistance, cooperative relationships and other actions carried out by UNESCO and the WH Committee. It considers how these actions can advance environmental protection during armed conflicts. The case study is intended to shed some light on how inconsistency between the norms of the World Heritage Convention and the law of armed conflict are dealt with in practice. In particular, the case study may disclose if the co-application of the two legal frameworks creates any tension or synergy between them. However, as the application is context based, it cannot provide any conclusive answers on how the World Heritage Convention applies during armed conflicts in general. It merely represents a starting point to explore how environmental treaties can address wartime environmental damage.

[3] See UNESCO World Heritage Committee, Decision 23.COM.X.A4, adopted at 23rd Session on 29 November–4 December 1999, UN Doc WHC-99/CONF.209/22, 2 March 2000, 22.

[4] The partnership consists of UNESCO's World Heritage Centre and Division of Ecological Sciences in cooperation with the Congolese Wildlife Authority, IUCN, Deutsche Gesellschaft für Zusammenarbeit, and a task force of conservation non-governmental organisations, including the International Rhino Foundation; the International Gorilla Conservation Programme; the Wildlife Conservation Society; the WWF; and the Gilman International Conservation. Also, other UN agencies or programmes (ie, UNDP and UNEP), as well as the United Nations Mission to DRC (MONUC), collaborate with the World Heritage Centre to address issues relating to the safeguarding of world heritage properties in the DRC. See L Patchett, 'Articles 17–18 Activities to Support the World Heritage Fund' in F Francioni (ed), *The 1972 World Heritage Convention: A Commentary* (Oxford University Press, 2008) 298; World Heritage website: whc.unesco.org/en/congobiodiversity.

[5] UNESCO World Heritage Committee, Report of the Rapporteur on the 23rd Session of the Bureau of the World Heritage Committee, Doc WHC-99/CONF.209/4, 11 October 1999, 5. See also UNESCO World Heritage Committee, State of Conservation of the Properties Inscribed on the List of World Heritage in Danger, UN Doc WHC-12/36.COM/7A.Add, 1 June 2012, 6.

The current chapter is structured as follows. Section II provides a background to the armed conflicts taking place in the DRC. Thereafter, in section III, I look at the environmental damage that has been caused by these armed conflicts. In sections IV and V, I examine the application of the World Heritage Convention in the DRC, and how it has contributed to protect the world heritage sites in the context of an armed conflict. In section VI, I conclude with some reflections on the use of the Convention and what it may imply in a broader context.

II. THE ARMED CONFLICTS

Since 1996, a number of armed conflicts, both of international and non-international character, have taken place in the DRC. The DRC, formerly named Zaire, covers over 2,260,000 sq km and has a population of 58 million. The State has major wealth in natural resources, including the world's largest deposits of cobalt, coltan and tantalum, as well as huge reserves of copper, gold, diamonds and other minerals.[6] In addition, the DRC is one of the African states with the richest biodiversity. The tropical forest is the second largest after the Amazon rainforest and it has been referred to as the 'world's second lung'.[7] However, notwithstanding all of its natural resources, the DRC is one of the poorest states in the world. An estimated 150,000 people die every year from hunger, disease and other causes related to the unstable situation.[8] Approximately 20 armed groups operate in the eastern DRC.[9] The provinces of North and South Kivu, Eastern Orientale, and Ituri have been affected by the hostilities the most.[10]

The armed conflicts in the DRC have a political as well as an economic side. Many of the armed groups are dependent on exploiting natural resources to receive an income; therefore, the economic motives are very strong.[11] Armed conflicts of this kind are more likely to occur in weak and ineffectively governed states, rich in natural resources. The parties to the armed conflicts frequently change identity, often involving former state forces, leading to confusion.[12] Rebel armed groups, foreign occupying forces, criminal networks and private companies have all been involved in resource exploitation in the DRC.[13]

[6] W Cdr and UC Jha, *Armed Conflict and Environmental Damage* (Vij Books, India, 2014) 104.
[7] ibid.
[8] ibid.
[9] ILPI 2014 (n 1) 35.
[10] UNEP, 'The Democratic Republic of the Congo Post-Conflict Environmental Assessment United Nations Environment Programme Synthesis for Policy Makers' (UNEP, Kenya, 2011) 24.
[11] ILPI 2014 (n 1) 35.
[12] S Haines, 'The Nature of War and the Character of Contemporary Armed Conflict' in E Wilmshurst (ed), *International Law and the Classification of Conflicts* (Oxford University Press, 2012) 9.
[13] P Okowa, 'Sovereignty Contests and the Protection of Natural Resources in Conflict Zones' (2013) 66 *Current Legal Problems* 33, 40.

The First Congo War broke out in 1996. The war involved the DRC, Rwanda, Uganda and Angola. The war ended in 1998, when the Congolese leader, Mobutu Sese Seko, was defeated in a coup d'état led by Laurent Kabila, who seized power. The Second Congo War followed, which lasted from 1998 until 2003 and involved – to varying degrees – the DRC, Rwanda, Uganda, Zimbabwe, Burundi, Angola, Namibia, Chad, Eritrea and Sudan. A peace agreement was signed between the warring parties in 2002. Still, even after the official peace agreement was concluded, the hostilities continued – at times to such a degree that the hostilities reached the definition of being an armed conflict in a legal sense.

Hostilities in the DRC have been going on for several decades – there have been periods of intense violence, as well as periods of calm.[14] Several states have made interventions that have supported as well as fought against the Congolese army forces. Foreign troops have also fought against non-state actors on Congolese territory.[15] Even the multinational forces under the UN flag that are deployed in the region to ensure peace have been involved in the hostilities on occasion. At times, this has been to such a degree that they, themselves, have been considered to be parties to the armed conflict.[16]

In most cases, the fighting in the DRC, when being classified as an armed conflict, has been regarded as having a non-international character. The lines are blurred, however, with regard to the fighting being an armed conflict at all, or being an international or a non-international armed conflict.[17] For instance, in the summer of 2014, clashes arose between the Congolese and Rwandan governmental forces, turning the hostilities into an international armed conflict.[18] Bruch describes this type of conflict as follows:

> Frequently, it is a complex – if not impossible – task to ascertain into which category a particular conflict falls within. An internal conflict may wane so many times it may be characterized more as internal disturbance, only to flare up again.[19]

Such a conflict cycle raises questions as to which set of rules under the law of armed conflict applies and whether the peacetime rules are applicable without risking being superseded by the law of armed conflict. Nevertheless, the

[14] For instance, in 2009, a peace agreement was signed between the Congolese government and the armed group CNDP. Again in 2013, the DRC signed a peace agreement with the armed group M23. The peace agreements have been followed by a period of calm but the hostilities have nevertheless continued.

[15] C Bruch, 'All's Not Fair in (Civil) War: Criminal Liability for Environmental Damage in Internal Armed Conflict' (2000) 25 *Vermont Law Review* 695, 708.

[16] A Arimatsu, 'The Democratic Republic of the Congo 1993–2010' in E Wilmshurst (ed), *International Law and the Classification of Conflicts* (Oxford University Press, 2012) 193–95.

[17] OCHA, Democratic Republic of the Congo Mapping Exercise (2010) 8–10, documenting the most serious violations of human rights and international humanitarian law 1993–2003, available at: www.ohchr.org/Documents/Countries/ZR/DRC_MAPPING_REPORT_FINAL_EN.pdf.

[18] ILPI 2014 (n 1) 35.

[19] Bruch (n 15) 707.

application of the World Heritage Convention does not change because of the existence or the classification of the conflicts. It rather adapts to the prevailing protection needs of the world heritage sites, regardless of the legal definition of the fighting.

III. THE IMPACT OF ARMED CONFLICTS ON WORLD HERITAGE SITES

All five of the world heritage sites in the DRC have been affected by conflict. The rich fauna has been threatened. For instance, among other species, the endangered white rhinos and the mountain gorillas, are both close to extinction.[20] The world heritage sites' richness in natural resources has made control over these sites an important feature in the armed conflicts, for both strategic and economic reasons. The sites function as hiding places and bases to launch attacks, as well as an income generator for funding the conflict.[21] There are also indirect environmental impacts on the sites that are related to the large number of people fleeing from the hostilities. The world heritage sites offer shelter, foodstuffs, water and charcoal for cooking and heating, therefore it is not only armed groups taking refuge inside the sites, but also persons displaced by the fighting.[22] The collapse of domestic institutions and infrastructure, as well as the ability to uphold the rule of law, has put further stress on the sites.

In the following subsections, I will address the direct and indirect impacts of the armed conflicts, although these cannot be separated from each other completely.

A. Direct Environmental Impacts

Armed groups have used the inaccessible nature of the sites to hide and to perform military operations.[23] The presence of the rebel groups in the sites

[20] Since 1975, the mountain gorilla has been included in Appendix I of the 1973 Convention on International Trade in Endangered Species (adopted 3 March 1973, entered into force 1 July 1975) 993 UNTS 243 (CITES). Appendix I lists species that are the most endangered among CITES-listed animals and plants (see Article 2(1) of the Convention). See CITES website: www.cites.org/eng/app/appendices.php.

[21] A Crawford and J Bernstein, *MEAs, Conservation and Conflict: A Case Study of Virunga National Park, DRC* (International Institute for Sustainable Development, Winnipeg, 2008) 17–18.

[22] A massive influx of approximately 800,000 Rwandan refugees arrived in Goma in eastern DRC after the Rwandan genocide in 1994. See Crawford and Bernstein (n 21) 15–16. See also UNESCO World Heritage Committee, State of Conservation of the Properties Inscribed on the List of World Heritage in Danger, UN Doc WHC-08/32.COM/7A, 22 May 2008, 10.

[23] See UNESCO World Heritage Committee, Report distributed 8 February 2002 (UN Doc WHC-01/CONF.208/24) 17. For example, between 2008 and 2009, armed rebel groups occupied the sector with the gorilla habitat in Virunga Park. See also UNESCO World Heritage Committee, State of Conservation of the Properties Inscribed on the List of World Heritage in Danger, distributed 11 May 2009 (UN Doc WHC-09/33.COM/7A) 12.

has also resulted in the corresponding conduct of military operations by the Congolese army aimed at defeating the rebel groups.[24] To deny the rebel groups their cover, the army has entered the world heritage sites. Its operations have jeopardised the integrity of the sites by cutting down trees and placing army posts, as well as training camps, inside the sites, for example.[25] Consequently, one of the main environmental impacts of the military operations is the fast and uncontrolled deforestation.[26]

As economic motives have been influential in attracting armed groups to the world heritage sites, members of armed groups have been involved in the illegal[27] exploitation of the sites' natural resources. Mining activities, fishing and charcoal production are conducted both for sustaining the military operations and for personal gain.[28] Such activities have caused, for instance, deforestation, the pollution of streams by silt from the washing process, the debarking of trees to make panning trays for washing coltan, and declining biodiversity.[29] In addition, wildlife poaching has accelerated. As a consequence of weapons and ammunition circulating in the area, armed groups use automatic weapons in large-scale poaching on the sites.

Poaching is directed at the protected animal species for food purposes and for a war sustaining trade in ivory, trade with exotic species and bush meat.[30] The increased consumption of bush meat is partly explained by the destruction of the infrastructure and the lack of security in the region, which makes

[24] UNESCO World Heritage Committee, State of Conservation of the Properties Inscribed on the List of World Heritage in Danger, UN Doc WHC-07/31.COM/7A, 10 May 2007, 9.

[25] In 2006, it was reported that four brigades, totalling 12,000 soldiers, were deployed inside or close to one of the world heritage sites, some of them with their families. See UNESCO World Heritage Committee, State of Conservation of the Properties Inscribed on the List of World Heritage in Danger, UN Doc WHC-06/30.COM/7A, 26 May 2006, 27; State of Conservation of the Properties Inscribed on the List of World Heritage in Danger, 22 May 2008 (n 22) 10. See also J Kalpers, *Overview of the Armed Conflict and Biodiversity in Sub-Saharan Africa: Impact, Mechanisms and Responses* (Biodiversity Support Program, Washington DC, 2001) 13.

[26] ILPI 2014 (n 1) 35.

[27] The term 'illegal' in this book is used in the same sense as in the 'Report of the Panel of Experts on the Illegal Exploitation of Natural Resources and Other Forms of Wealth in the Democratic Republic of the Congo'. It means all activities including extraction, production, commercialisation, and exports occurring in the DRC without being approved by the DRC government. It also includes activities that are not in accordance with existing national regulations; not in accordance with accepted practices in trade and business, as conducted in the DRC; and/or in violation of international law. For further explanation, see UN Security Council, 'Report of the Panel of Experts on the Illegal Exploitation of Natural Resources and Other Forms of Wealth in the Democratic Republic of the Congo', UN Doc S/2001/357, 21 April 2001, para 15.

[28] See UNESCO World Heritage Committee, State of Conservation of the Properties Inscribed on the List of World Heritage in Danger, 26 May 2006 (n 25) 27; State of Conservation of the Properties Inscribed on the List of World Heritage in Danger, 10 May 2007 (n 24) 9; State of Conservation of the Properties Inscribed on the List of World Heritage in Danger, 22 May 2008 (n 22) 8. See also Crawford and Bernstein (n 21) 17–18.

[29] Cdr and Jha (n 6) 109–11.

[30] See UNESCO World Heritage Committee, State of Conservation of the Properties Inscribed on the List of World Heritage in Danger, 10 May 2007 (n 24) 9; State of Conservation of the Properties Inscribed on the List of World Heritage in Danger, 22 May 2008 (n 22) 8.

this meat the only accessible protein source in many places.[31] Poaching has led to serious consequences for the wildlife of the world heritage sites where, for example, the endangered hippopotamus population[32] has now been taken to the brink of extinction in the site of Virunga National Park.[33] The only remaining wild population of white rhinoceros in the world, as well as the buffalo population, has dropped considerably in the site of Garamba National Park.[34] The same applies to the elephant population in all the sites because these are killed to feed the armed forces, as well as for their valuable ivory.

In the site of the Okapi Faunal Reserve, elephant meat was sold in the park's administrative centre, with the park rangers being forced by rebel groups to guard the poached ivory.[35] On one occasion – as revenge aimed at the park rangers for regaining control over the park station of the Okapi Faunal Reserve – several of the okapis that were held in captivity were killed. Similarly, the gorilla population has been put at risk because of the armed conflicts. In 1994 and 1995, it was estimated that about 8,000 gorillas lived in the world heritage site of Kahuzi-Biega National Park. The population was reduced to 126 by August 2000 at the peak of the Second Congo War. Salonga National Park, which is the largest Congolese world heritage site, became a poacher's nest thanks to its navigable rivers. However, this park never become fully under rebel control, as was the case with the other world heritage sites.

In addition, poor discipline, irregular pay and lack of food have resulted in the growing participation of the Congolese army personnel in these illegal activities, including artisanal mining, charcoal production and wildlife poaching.[36] In the Okapi Faunal Reserve, deserters from the army set up poaching camps on a large scale.[37] Several army members have collaborated with the rebels in the illegal charcoal trade in Virunga National Park.[38] Even though the Congolese army has agreed to cooperate with the park rangers to protect the world heritage sites, the army's involvement in illegal activities has made such cooperation difficult. Violent confrontations have occurred between the DRC army and the park staff, resulting in the deaths of several park rangers.[39] In one particularly noteworthy

[31] ILPI 2014 (n 1) 35.

[32] Hippopotamuses have been listed in Appendix II of the CITES since 1995. *See* CITES website: cites.org/eng/app/appendices.php.

[33] Crawford and Bernstein (n 21) 20.

[34] After 1996, the elephant population inside Garamba National Park went from 11,000 to less than 5,500. The buffalo population went from 25,000 to less than 8,000. See Cdr and Jha (n 6) 108.

[35] Cdr and Jha (n 6) 108–09.

[36] See UNESCO World Heritage Committee, State of Conservation of the Properties Inscribed on the List of World Heritage in Danger, UN Doc WHC-04/28.COM/15A Rev, 21 June 2004, 8; UNESCO World Heritage Committee, State of Conservation of the Properties Inscribed on the List of World Heritage in Danger, UN Doc WHC-10/34.COM/7A, 1 June 2010, 11.

[37] Cdr and Jha (n 6) 109.

[38] UN Security Council, Final Report of Groups of Experts on the DRC, UN Doc S/2008/773, 12 December 2008, para 113.

[39] See UNESCO World Heritage Committee, State of Conservation of the Properties Inscribed on the List of World Heritage in Danger, 21 June 2004 (n 36) 8; State of Conservation of the Properties

incident in November 2006, the head of one of the park ranger stations was tortured by the commander of the Congolese army camp in Rutshuru, located inside Virunga National Park, probably in order to discourage the efforts of the park rangers to control the charcoal activities involving members of the army.[40]

Members of the park staff have been accused of corruption and involvement in illegal activities themselves. In the summer of 2007, the chief warden of Virunga National Park, Honoré Mashagiro, was arrested for his involvement in the charcoal trade and in an incident concerning the killing of 10 gorillas.[41] Allegedly, the killing of the gorillas was conducted with the purpose of denying Virunga National Park its value as a world heritage site and thereby the reason to protect it.[42]

The job of the park rangers – monitoring and controlling the world heritage sites – has become extremely dangerous because of the hostilities and has led to the park rangers being themselves targeted.[43] Between 1996 and 2008, more than 190 park rangers were reportedly killed while performing their duties.[44] In Virunga National Park, in all the world heritage sites, the park stations were looted and park rangers' weapons and ammunition stolen, which resulted in poorly equipped park rangers who lacked morale and were unable to patrol and thereby protect the sites. As a result, the world heritage sites became open for poaching and unsustainable exploitation.[45]

B. Indirect Environmental Impacts

Besides the direct environmental impacts of the warfare, there are knock-on effects. The DRC has experienced a disruption in its governmental structure followed by an 'institutional vacuum' and lack of governance, which influences environmental conservation work.[46] The governance collapse fosters corruption among public officials who then prioritise personal interests, leading to uncontrolled exploitation of natural resources and wildlife poaching, not only

Inscribed on the List of World Heritage in Danger, 26 May 2006 (n 25) 27; State of Conservation of the Properties Inscribed on the List of World Heritage in Danger, 1 June 2010 (n 36) 11; State of Conservation of the Properties Inscribed on the List of World Heritage in Danger, UN Doc WHC-10/34.COM/7A.Add, 22 June 2010, 82–83.

[40] Following an international protest, the Minister of Defence in the DRC ordered an investigation of this event. See UNESCO World Heritage Committee, State of Conservation of the Properties Inscribed on the List of World Heritage in Danger, 10 May 2007 (n 24) 9.

[41] Crawford and Bernstein (n 21) 22.

[42] ILPI 2014 (n 1) 36.

[43] UNESCO World Heritage Committee, State of Conservation of the Properties Inscribed on the List of World Heritage in Danger, UN Doc WHC-98/CONF.203/7, 30 September 1998, 4.

[44] UNEP, The Last Stand of the Gorilla, Environmental Crime and Conflict in the Congo Basin (2010) 21, available at: www.unep.org/pdf/GorillaStand_screen.pdf.

[45] Cdr and Jha (n 6).

[46] UNEP, 'From Conflict to Peacebuilding: The Role of Natural Resources and the Environment' (UNEP, Switzerland, 2009) 17.

by rebel groups and the army, but also by civilians.[47] The Congolese army uses its official position to facilitate the exploitation of the dealers, bypassing any official controls.[48] Without efficient environmental regulations and legal authority with enforcement powers, belligerents, as well as civilians, can engage in unsustainable and prohibited acts towards the environment without risking any punishment.[49] Thus, the exploitation of natural resources and wildlife, having severe environmental impacts, can continue without being addressed by the authorities. For instance, the unregulated mining activities have polluted soil, water and air.[50]

Moreover, damage to infrastructure affects a state's ability to handle waste and sewage, as well as its ability to provide basic services, such as sanitation and water. Due to the absence of investment in the infrastructure in war-torn societies, the problems continue and accelerate,[51] which is noticeable in the DRC. This is, in particular, evident when dealing with the great number of displaced persons. Pollution, like water contamination, is often caused by large concentrations of displaced persons living without sanitary facilities or waste removal services.[52]

After the Rwandan genocide in 1994, approximately 720,000 displaced persons were permitted by the UN High Commissioner for Refugees (UNCHR) to settle in and around Virunga National Park.[53] The UNCHR allowed the displaced population to cut firewood inside the site due to the lack of fuel. The cutting of firewood, as well as the wildlife poaching, by the displaced population adversely affected the environment,[54] leading to the deforestation of a 300 sq km area that imperilled the unique ecosystem of the park and threatened the mountain gorillas.[55] In addition, Kahuzi-Biega National Park, located at the border with Rwanda, was adversely affected by the Rwandan war and the establishment of camps for displaced persons near the park. The growing population put stress on the natural resources of the park in particular, because the DRC did not have the means to provide for these persons. The displaced persons, as well as the armed groups, got involved in unregulated mining activities for gold, coltan and castorite in Kahuzi-Biega National Park.

One of the main challenges in undertaking environmental work in armed conflict, as well as post-conflict situations, is the absence of human and financial resources, as well as technical capacity. As a result, much of the environmental

[47] ibid.

[48] UNEP, 'The Democratic Republic of the Congo' (n 10).

[49] UNEP, 'From Conflict to Peacebuilding' (n 46) 17.

[50] J Oglete, J Shambaugh and R Kormos, 'Parks in the Crossfire: Strategies for Effective Conservation in Areas of Armed Conflict' 14 War and Protected Areas (2004) *International Journal for Protected Areas Managers* 3, available at: cmsdata.iucn.org/downloads/14_1.pdf.

[51] UNEP, 'From Conflict to Peacebuilding' (n 46) 17.

[52] Oglete, Shambaugh and Kormos (n 50) 3.

[53] Crawford and Bernstein (n 21) 15–16.

[54] ibid, 15.

[55] UNEP, 'The Democratic Republic of the Congo' (n 10) 26.

protection work terminates. Furthermore, in the aftermath of an armed conflict, most stakeholders involved in the rehabilitation and restoration are focused on humanitarian assistance and democracy issues, and the environment is not a prioritised concern.[56] This has also been the case in the DRC.

Managing natural resources has been highlighted as an important aspect to meet the basic needs of the population, such as providing water, food, shelter and livelihoods, and to reconstruct the financial system and rebuild the governmental structure.[57] States that are unable to give their populations the support they require, may create additional environmental degradation and foster further conflicts. In the DRC, a large number of public officials benefit from the wars on a personal level and therefore the revenues from natural resources do not enrich the state. The DRC remains unable to build strong governmental institutions and the environmental degradation continues. As a result, the population suffers.[58] Thus, the environmental damage caused in relation to the armed conflicts, as well as the lack of environmental protection, impede the outlook for peace and for Congolese society to recover.[59]

IV. THE APPLICATION OF THE WORLD HERITAGE CONVENTION

The DRC is a state party to several MEAs that could be of interest for addressing the environmental damage caused during the armed conflicts. Besides the World Heritage Convention, it has ratified the Convention for International Trade in Endangered Species (CITES); the Biodiversity Convention; the Convention on Migratory Species; the Ramsar Convention; and the 2003 African Convention on the Conservation of Nature and Natural Resources. However, due to the armed conflicts, governmental officials have been unable to enforce the international environmental treaties.[60] Nevertheless, because of the launch of the UNESCO project, several activities have been undertaken to enforce the World Heritage Convention despite the hostilities.

The project has its roots in a request directed to UNESCO. In 1999, the Director-General of the Institut Congolais pour la Conservation de la Nature (Congolese Wildlife Authority) – the organ assigned to manage the national parks in the DRC, including the world heritage sites – informed the UNESCO World Heritage Centre (the secretariat for the World Heritage Convention) that his office in Kinshasa could no longer access four world heritage sites that were under rebel control in the eastern DRC. The Congolese Wildlife Authority

[56] Oglete, Shambaugh and Kormos (n 50) 3–4.

[57] CE Bruch et al, 'Post-conflict Peace Building and Natural Resources' (2009) 19 *Yearbook of International Environmental Law* 58, 67.

[58] Okowa (n 13), 33, 40–42.

[59] UNEP, 'The Democratic Republic of the Congo' (n 10); UNEP, 'From Conflict to Peacebuilding' (n 46) 19.

[60] ILPI 2014 (n 1) 39.

requested the World Heritage Bureau (a treaty body established to assist the WH Committee)[61] and the WH Committee to support the park staff in the four sites. The Director-General suggested that this could be done by assisting the park rangers through the non-governmental organisations and other stakeholders still present in the rebel controlled regions.[62] In 2000, in response to the request and as an available strategy to apply the Convention, the WH Committee launched the project of Biodiversity Conservation in Regions of Armed Conflict: Conserving World Heritage Sites in the Democratic Republic of the Congo (the World Heritage project).[63]

The project had four aims: (1) to provide specific and collaborative support to the Congolese sites, including the payment of salaries and salary supplements linked to the performance of anti-poaching and surveillance duties; (2) to raise awareness and support of international and regional diplomatic and political communities dealing with conflict in the DRC and in neighbouring states to the conservation of the sites; (3) to disseminate information of the critical role of the park staff in the protection of the sites, involving risk to their lives and property, and developing sustainable financing mechanisms to support the staff and the conservation of the sites; and (4) to identify, document and disseminate the lessons learnt in the conservation of the sites in the DRC, to improve preparedness of the actors in the international arena to meet conservation problems of natural world heritage sites in areas of armed conflict.[64]

The project was launched in 2000 and was divided into three phases. The first phase took place between 2000 and 2004 and focused on retaining conservation activities in all the five world heritage sites and establishing a 'Diplomacy of Conservation' (political and diplomatic support for the sites' conservation). Using the World Heritage Convention as a vehicle, the project has actively sought to attain the cooperation of the different parties involved in the armed conflicts, in order to achieve the protection of the world heritage sites. During the project's second phase, between 2005 and 2010, conservation diplomacy was continuously conducted. In a context of high-security risks linked to the presence of armed groups in the eastern DRC, emergency action plans have been established for three of the world heritage sites – Kahuzi-Biega National Park, Virunga National Park, and the Okapi Faunal Reserve. In Garamba National

[61] The Bureau consists of seven state parties elected annually by the Committee: a chairperson, five vice-chairpersons, and a rapporteur. The Bureau of the Committee coordinates the work of the Committee and fixes the dates, hours and order of business of meetings. See: whc.unesco.org/en/committee/.

[62] UNESCO World Heritage Committee, State of Conservation of the Properties Inscribed on the List of World Heritage in Danger, UN Doc WHC-99/CONF.209/13, 18 October 1999, 3–5.

[63] World Heritage Papers 17, Proceedings and Preserving Congolese Heritage, Linking Biological and Cultural Diversity/Promouvoir et Préserver le patrimoine congolais, Lier diversité biologique et culturelle, Proceedings of the Conference and Workshops, UNESCO, 13–17 September 2004, 110, available at: whc.unesco.org/en/documents/6411.

[64] UNESCO World Heritage Committee, Decision 23.COM.X.A4 (n 3) 22; State of Conservation of the Properties Inscribed on the List of World Heritage in Danger, 18 October 1999 (n 62) 3–5.

Park, a similar plan of 'community conservation' has been settled. The third phase of the project took place between 2010 and 2013. It was directed at setting conditions for the recovery of all five sites, mainly through the completion of emergency action plans and by reinforcing the component of conservation diplomacy.[65]

The activities that have been carried out under the project show how UNESCO and the WH Committee have undertaken the leading role to prevent, or at least minimise, damage to the natural world heritage sites in relation to the armed conflicts through the application of the World Heritage Convention.[66] The expressed ambition of the project is to 'provide important lessons that may be applicable elsewhere in the world for the protection [of] World Heritage sites in times of armed conflict'.[67] To protect the sites, UNESCO and the WH Committee have enacted conservation diplomacy between the parties to the conflicts, to advocate the neutrality of the world heritage sites and their park staff. They have also provided support and equipment to the park management and attracted other stakeholders to endorse the project's aims.[68] In the following subsections, I will analyse how these measures have contributed to protect the sites in relation to the armed conflicts.

A. Conservation Diplomacy

To protect and preserve the world heritage sites, the UNESCO project has sought to keep park rangers in their posts. Due to the lack of security and governmental control, the job of the park rangers in the DRC has become extremely dangerous. The conflicts have partly taken place in the remote areas of the world heritage sites, where the park rangers patrol. Thus, the rangers have ended up in the war zone and they have been exposed to risks, particularly because they carry weapons while on duty.[69] Being employees of a Congolese state organ, the park rangers have not been trusted by the rebel groups who associate them with the government and the Congolese army. At the same time, the Congolese army has been suspicious of the park rangers, because they have often continued to engage in protection work in the rebel controlled areas.[70] As a result, the park

[65] See the World Heritage Convention web page: whc.unesco.org/en/congobiodiversity/.

[66] For further reading on the application of the WHC during the armed conflicts in the DRC, see B Sjöstedt, 'The Role of Multilateral Environmental Agreements in Armed Conflict: "Green-keeping" in Virunga Park. Applying the UNESCO World Heritage Convention in the Armed Conflict of the Democratic Republic of the Congo' (2013) 82 *Nordic Journal of International Law* 129.

[67] UNESCO World Heritage Committee, Report of the Rapporteur on the 23rd Session of the Bureau of the World Heritage Committee, 11 October 1999 (n 5) 5.

[68] World Heritage Papers 17 (n 63) 110.

[69] Interview with Planning Officer, Virunga National Park, Congolese Wildlife Authority, Goma, DRC, 4 April 2015, interview with Director, Congolese Wildlife Authority, Kinshasa, DRC, 30 March 2015.

[70] Interview with Planning Officer, Virunga National Park, Congolese Wildlife Authority, 4 April 2015 (n 69); interview with Country Director for the DRC, Wildlife Conservation Society, Kinshasa,

rangers have been targeted from several sides of the conflicts, and, as mentioned earlier, several have been killed while on duty. In some cases, the rangers were even taken to the front line to fight for the rebel groups.[71] Due to the insecure situation and the fact that their salaries were not paid, many rangers left their posts. Consequently, the world heritage sites were, in some cases, left without protection.

To enhance the park rangers' situation, UNESCO and the WH Committee have endorsed conservation diplomacy to try to convey the neutral status of the world heritage sites and the park rangers. In November 2000, UNESCO and the WH Committee organised a meeting in Nairobi with representatives from the Congolese government and two rebel groups that controlled parts of the world heritage sites in eastern DRC at the time. The meeting focused on how to ensure the continuation of the work of the park rangers during the ongoing hostilities, in order to maintain the protection of the world heritage sites.[72] UNESCO and the WH Committee acted as mediators to convince the parties to the conflict to respect the integrity of the world heritage sites and, more importantly, the park rangers. Thus, UNESCO and the WH Committee have advocated that the park rangers should be considered as neutral in the conflict and as having immunity from attack, similar to medical staff.[73] Further diplomacy measures consisted of conducting diplomatic missions to meet the rebel groups; organising tripartite meetings; carrying out targeted missions to the world heritage sites, including those under rebel control; and having individual contacts with high-level authorities.[74] UNESCO and the WH Committee sent two diplomatic missions to all five of the Congolese world heritage sites during the armed conflicts in 1999 and 2000.[75]

It has been acknowledged that, as a result of the diplomatic efforts of UNESCO and the WH Committee, rebel groups did respect the sites to some extent. Statements by the rebel groups claim that they stopped engaging in bush meat and ivory trades, although the enactment of such commitments is difficult to verify.[76] However, at a conference in Paris in 2004, it was expressed by Henri Djombo – former president of the Conference of Ministers in Charge of Forests in Central Africa – that UNESCO and the WH Committee's diplomatic missions contributed to securing the Mikeno sector of Virunga National

1 April 2015. The County Director also has experience of working for the Congolese Wildlife Authority in the world heritage site of the Okapi Faunal Reserve.

[71] Interview with Planning Officer, Virunga National Park, Congolese Wildlife Authority, 4 April 2015 (n 69).

[72] C Wilunga Balongelwa, *Patrimoine Naturel et Conflicts Armés* (Harmattan, 2013) 112.

[73] World Heritage Papers 17 (n 63) 112.

[74] ibid, 112.

[75] For instance, in May 2000, a UNESCO delegation visited Kahuzi-Biega National Park. The delegation visited the gorilla family of Mugaruka. The delegation had meeting with the military leaders in the region to keep a safety distance at 200 metres from the Park. See C Schuler, *Leben und Überleben im Kongo, Gorillaschutz und Familienleben im Krieg* (BfT Verlag, 2013) 233–34.

[76] Interview with Director, Congolese Wildlife Authority, 30 March 2015 (n 69).

Park, which is an area that encompasses the important habitat of the mountain gorillas. This was described as an achievement of the mediation of UNESCO between the belligerent parties.[77]

Although, the park rangers remained in a vulnerable position – with several rangers being killed in the hostilities, despite the diplomatic efforts – their claimed neutral status did contribute to improve their working conditions and to develop a new practice around conservation of the world heritage sites. For instance, during 2006–07, when the rebel group National Congress for the Defence of the People (CNDP) took control of the Mikeno sector of Virunga National Park, all governmental authorities, including the Congolese Wildlife Authority, left the rebel controlled areas of the park. However, some of the park rangers decided to stay and continue to protect the park, and in particular the gorilla population, acting outside their official capacity. At this time, they received equipment and salaries from non-governmental organisations active in the area, such as the International Gorilla Conservation Programme, through the UNESCO project.

In the above example, rebel groups accepted that the park rangers were performing conservation work in the areas under their control. The rebel leader, Laurent Nkunda, even declared that he had plans to organise gorilla excursions for tourists in the park. In an interview with *National Geographic News*, he stated, '[i]n other places they have petrol. We have the gorillas. The park is like our petrol; the gorillas are our fuel. These gorillas will remain and the national park will remain forever. We have to protect them'.[78] This statement indicates that there was also an economic motivation for the rebel groups to preserve both the park and the gorilla population, which probably contributed to them permitting the conservation work of the park rangers in the area.

Similarly, in 2012, the rebel group of the March 23 Movement (M23) took control of parts of Virunga National Park. This time, the Congolese Wildlife Authority stayed and supported the park rangers' continued work to patrol the park. Even though the park rangers were still involved in hostilities, overall the cooperation with the rangers and rebel groups was functioning. While the facts are difficult to verify in an armed conflict context, it seems like the Mikeno sector in Virunga National Park remained well monitored and protected during the time the rebels controlled the sector.[79] Reportedly, tourist excursions were made to the gorillas with the permission of M23. The Congolese Wildlife Authority claims that the excursions were undertaken outside its involvement.[80]

[77] World Heritage Papers 17 (n 63) 103, 120.

[78] S Lovgren, 'Congo Warlord's Arrest Puts Gorillas' Future in Turmoil' *National Geographic News* (23 January 2009), available at: news.nationalgeographic.com/news/2009/01/090123-nkunda-arrested.html.

[79] Interview with DRC Country Coordinator, International Gorilla Conservation Programme, Goma, DRC, 20 March 2015.

[80] P Jones, 'Congolese Rebels Cash in on Gorilla Tourism to Fund Insurgency' *The Guardian* (19 October 2012), available at: www.theguardian.com/world/2012/oct/19/congo-rebels-gorilla-tour-insurgency.

Nevertheless, the fact that the Congolese Wildlife Authority could stay at the site, even though it was taken over by the rebels, shows that it was regarded as a neutral organisation and that its presence was largely tolerated by the parties of the armed conflict. Thus, UNESCO and the WH Committee's conservation diplomacy has been crucial to maintaining some kind of protection work during the armed conflicts, in particular in the rebel controlled gorilla habitats of Virunga National Park.[81]

Moreover, park rangers have witnessed how international attention has affected the rebel groups' attitude towards them. Several rebel groups did express their commitment to protect the sites and respect the park rangers' neutral status. For instance, in Kahuzi-Biega National Park, the rebel group controlling the site, allegedly influenced by international opinion, announced that the gorillas must receive protection and granted the rangers permission to monitor the sites.[82] In Virunga National Park, rebels made similar announcements during the conflicts.[83] Also, in the Okapi Faunal Reserve, the park rangers described how the acknowledgment of their neutral status made it possible for them to continue their work and to keep their weapons and equipment for this purpose.[84] In most of the world heritage sites, the park rangers could move freely around the rebel controlled areas for protection purposes. The park rangers would advise the rebels to let them know when and where they patrolled the sites to avoid confrontations. The park rangers were even allowed to travel to Kinshasa to coordinate their work at the headquarters of the Congolese Wildlife Authority.[85] The diplomacy of UNESCO and the WH Committee attained the cooperation of the army and the rebel groups for conservation and re-established the links between the Congolese Wildlife Authority's headquarters in Kinshasa and the park rangers at the sites, including those under rebel control.[86]

[81] World Heritage Papers 17 (n 63) 110–12. Also the Deutsche Gesellschaft für Zusammenarbeit directly negotiated with rebel groups in Kahuzi-Biega National Park. World Heritage Papers 17 (n 63) 117.

[82] For instance, to convince the rebel leaders to protect the gorillas, the park rangers in the world heritage site of Kahuzi-Biega National Park brought them to see the gorilla populations. Interview with Park Director and Chief Warden, Kahuzi-Biega National Park, Congolese Wildlife Authority, Bukavu, DRC, 24 March 2015.

[83] In January 2007, an agreement was made between Virunga Park Senior Warden Paulin Ngobobo and Rebel Group leader Colonel Makenga for the National Congress for the Defence of the People (CNDP). The agreement sought to spare the gorillas during the ongoing armed conflict. J Owen, 'Congo Rebels Agree to End the Gorilla Slaughter' *National Geographic News* (25 January 2007), available at: news.nationalgeographic.com/news/2007/01/070125-gorillas-congo.html. Interview with DRC Country Coordinator, International Gorilla Conservation Programme, 20 March 2015 (n 79); Interview with Planning Officer, Virunga National Park, Congolese Wildlife Authority, 4 April 2015 (n 69).

[84] Interview with Country Director for the DRC, Wildlife Conservation Society, 1 April 2015 (n 70).

[85] ibid; Interview with Park Director and Chief Warden, Kahuzi-Biega National Park, Congolese Wildlife Authority, 24 March 2015 (n 82).

[86] World Heritage Papers 17 (n 63) 111.

The political and diplomatic support for protecting the sites has been described as an innovative characteristic of the UNESCO project to engage the different rebel groups and the Congolese army. Conducting conservation diplomacy could be seen as the WH Committee acting under Article 13(3) of the World Heritage Convention. It reads:

> The Committee shall decide on the action to be taken with regard to these requests [for international assistance], determine where appropriate, the nature and extent of its assistance, and authorize the conclusion, on its behalf, of the necessary arrangements with the government concerned.

The loose wording in the provisions may not have been intended to enable the WH Committee together with UNESCO to conduct conservation diplomacy as an 'action' to respond to a request of international assistance. Nevertheless, it is an 'appropriate' action for protecting world heritage in the context of meeting the challenges facing the DRC.

B. Strengthening the Role of the Park Rangers

As mentioned earlier, many park rangers regularly left their posts due to a number of reasons, including the non-payment of salaries, the lack of equipment, and the insecure situation in general. In response, the UNESCO project has provided funding for salaries, equipment and training activities for the park rangers.[87] Over 60 per cent of the budget of the project's first phase was allocated to the payment of salaries to the park rangers.[88] Prior to the project, many of them working in the rebel controlled areas had not received a salary for several years, because they were cut off from the Congolese Wildlife Authority.[89] At the beginning of the project, UNESCO provided salaries directly to the park rangers. The salaries were paid in the form of bonuses to replace the absent salaries. Although, there were some practical problems attached to this system, it did contribute to establishing a new work ethic among the park rangers. This type of support has been described as essential for the park rangers to continue their work despite the armed conflicts.[90]

[87] During the first phase of the pilot project (2001–05), approximately $US900,000 was spent on salaries, equipment, etc. See UNESCO World Heritage Committee, State of Conservation of the Properties Inscribed on the List of World Heritage in Danger, 26 May 2006 (n 25) 26.

[88] World Heritage Papers 17 (n 63) 110.

[89] As the Kinshasa-based Congolese Wildlife Authority was not in contact with the four rebel-controlled sites in the eastern DRC, salaries could not be provided. Therefore, it requested the WH Bureau and the Committee to help the park rangers in these sites by providing assistance. The Bureau approved the request and funds were distributed via contracts established with conservation non-governmental organisations and other partners of UNESCO that remained in the field. The Bureau approved a total sum of $US105,000 for the four sites. See UNESCO World Heritage Committee, State of Conservation of the Properties Inscribed on the List of World Heritage in Danger, 18 October 1999 (n 62) 4.

[90] World Heritage Papers 17 (n 63) 110.

International assistance can be granted under Article 22 of the World Heritage Convention. It reads:

> Assistance granted by the World Heritage Committee may take the following forms:
>
> 1. studies concerning the artistic, scientific and technical problems raised by the protection, conservation, presentation and rehabilitation of the cultural and natural heritage, as defined in paragraphs 2 and 4 of Article 11 of this Convention;
> 2. provisions of experts, technicians and skilled labour to ensure that the approved work is correctly carried out;
> 3. training of staff and specialists at all levels in the field of identification, protection, conservation, presentation and rehabilitation of the cultural and natural heritage;
> 4. supply of equipment which the State concerned does not possess or is not in a position to acquire;
> 5. low-interest or interest-free loans which might be repayable on a long-term basis;
> 6. the granting, in exceptional cases and for special reasons, of non-repayable subsidies.

In accordance with Article 22(4) of the Convention, the park rangers received equipment, including trucks, pick-ups, speed boats and an aeroplane.[91] Facilities at the park stations and the patrol posts were repaired and reconstructed because many of them were looted during the hostilities.[92] In 2011, it was reported that all park stations in Virunga National Park had mobile phone coverage, which enabled coordination of the park activities.[93] The supply of equipment was granted under the World Heritage Convention, albeit that much of it was financed by the other partners in the project.[94] The WH Committee underscored in its decisions the importance of ensuring that the rangers were properly equipped and, in particular, that they had adequate arms and ammunition; although the military equipment was provided through the Congolese army and was, therefore, not directly under the Convention.

The WH Committee called for improved staff training among the park rangers.[95] Training constitutes an essential element in international assistance,

[91] During the first phase of the pilot project (2001–05) approximately $US900,000 was spent on salaries, equipment, etc. See UNESCO World Heritage Committee, State of Conservation of the Properties Inscribed on the List of World Heritage in Danger, UN Doc WHC-11/35. COM/7A.Add, 27 May 2011, 4.

[92] UNESCO World Heritage Committee, State of Conservation of the Properties Inscribed on the List of World Heritage in Danger, UN Doc WHC-11/35.COM/7A.Add, 27 May 2011, 4.

[93] See UNESCO World Heritage Committee, State of Conservation of the Properties Inscribed on the List of World Heritage in Danger, 1 June 2010 (n 36) 12.

[94] According to Article 22(4) of the WHC, assistance in the form of supply of equipment should be of such nature that the state party does not possess or is not in a position to acquire it – which seems to be the case here.

[95] See UNESCO World Heritage Committee, Decision 30 COM 7A.7 adopted at the 30th Session 8–16 July 2006, UN Doc WHC-06/30.COM/19, 23 August 2006, 17. See also State of Conservation of the Properties Inscribed on the List of World Heritage in Danger, 1 June 2010 (n 36) 12.

as provided in Article 22(3) under the World Heritage Convention. In 2011, a major training effort was reported to be under way, consisting of high-level paramilitary training by specialists of the Belgian Special Forces.[96] The park rangers have indeed received training from the Belgian Special Forces and French Special Forces. There is no explanation in the report issued to the WH Committee of the context in which park rangers are expected to make use of the training. However, it can be inferred that the paramilitary training may be useful when the rangers take part in disarming operations, dealing with poachers or persons engaged in illegal exploitation of the natural resources in the sites.

Reportedly, all the military training of the rangers has been conducted under the supervision of the Congolese army because training would not be permitted without the army's consent.[97] Consequently, an advanced park ranger force was fully operational in 2007 in Virunga National Park and has been effective in securing parts of the park that were occupied by the rebels.[98] The Congolese Wildlife Authority has its own surveillance mechanism, security system and a security force to monitor and protect the world heritage sites. The security force has been described as having a paramilitary structure.[99] The ability of the park rangers' security force was demonstrated when it managed to clear the volcano sector of Virunga National Park from rebel groups without assistance from the Congolese army or the UN peacekeeping mission deployed in the DRC. As a result, since October 2014, tourist excursions have been conducted to visit the volcano.[100]

Nevertheless, the park rangers are not employed to combat militias but to perform conservation work. Although rebels groups are present in the sites, it is the army's responsibility to respond to such threats.[101] Yet, as the park rangers have become a strong actor in the region, with a paramilitary force able to secure areas, they also bring safety to the local population. This is putting pressure on the conservation work of the sites, however, because the local communities move closer to the secure sites controlled by the park rangers, while, at the same time, the ambition of the park management is to limit the number of persons living inside the sites for conservation purposes.

To sum up, the UNESCO project has endorsed the important role of the park rangers. At a conference in Paris in 2004, Natjaran Ishwaran, Director of the Divisions of Ecological Science of UNESCO at the time, expressed that 'without the guards the parks would have never survived'.[102] Enabling salaries, equipment

[96] See UNESCO World Heritage Committee, State of Conservation of the Properties Inscribed on the List of World Heritage in Danger, 27 May 2011 (n 92) 4.

[97] Interview with Country Director for the DRC, Wildlife Conservation Society, 1 April 2015 (n 70).

[98] UNESCO World Heritage Committee, State of Conservation of the Properties (n 28) 10.

[99] Interview with Director, Congolese Wildlife Authority, 30 March 2015 (n 69).

[100] Interview with Planning Officer, Virunga National Park, Congolese Wildlife Authority, 4 April 2015 (n 69).

[101] Interview with Director, Congolese Wildlife Authority, 30 March 2015 (n 69).

[102] World Heritage Papers 17 (n 63) 108.

and training have contributed to the fact that park rangers in the DRC are relatively well paid, respected and adequately equipped, even though there are some differences between the sites. Moreover, although the material support in the form of equipment and monetary compensation has been essential for the park rangers to continue their work, allegedly, the moral support from international actors has been of equal importance. Altogether, it has created a more secure environment for the park rangers, which has encouraged them to perform their jobs, even during the hostilities.

C. Call for Non-military Activities in the Sites and Assistance from the Congolese Army

As discussed above, the presence of rebel groups and the DRC army have had negative environmental impacts on the world heritage sites. Therefore, the WH Committee has urged the DRC to remove all the armed groups and to halt all military activities inside the sites.[103] The WH Committee has also requested that the DRC reduce the number of military posts inside the world heritage sites, suggesting that they place them at a satisfactory distance away.[104]

A call to remove all military activity from the world heritage sites may be justified on the basis of Article 5(4) of the World Heritage Convention, when seen from a strictly environmental perspective. Article 5(4) of the Convention states that each party shall endeavour, 'to take the appropriate legal, scientific, technical, administrative and financial measures necessary for the identification, protection, conservation, presentation and rehabilitation of this heritage'. However, the call for the removal of the army from the sites clearly has the capacity to interfere with the ability of the DRC to conduct its military operations against armed groups hiding in or operating from the sites. For example, the settlement of military camps in the sites by the Congolese army and the decision to cut down trees to locate the rebels are permissible acts taken against military objectives in accordance with the law of armed conflict. This runs, however, contrary to the obligation in Articles 4 and 6(3) of the World Heritage Convention that prohibits acts that directly or indirectly harm the world heritage sites. Article 4 states that:

> Each State Party to this Convention recognizes that the duty of ensuring the identification, protection, conservation, presentation and transmission to future generations of the cultural and natural heritage referred to in Articles 1 and 2 and situated on its

[103] See UNESCO World Heritage Committee, Decision 27 COM 7A.2, adopted at the 27th Session on 30 June–5 July 2003, UN Doc WHC-03/27.COM/24, 10 December 2003, 10; Decision 28 COM 15A.3 adopted at the 28th Session on 28 June–7 July 2004, UN Doc WHC-04/28/COM/26, 29 October 2004, 52.

[104] See UNESCO World Heritage Committee, Decision 28 COM 15A.3 (n 103), 52; Decision 31 COM 7A.7 adopted at the 31st Session on 23 June–2 July 2007, UN Doc WHC-07/31.COM/24, 31 July 2007, 11.

> territory, belongs primarily to that State. It will do all it can to this end, to the utmost of its own resources and, where appropriate, with any international assistance and co-operation, in particular, financial, artistic, scientific and technical, which it may be able to obtain.

In addition, the immediate removal of the army, as requested by the WH Committee, could also obstruct the efforts of the DRC to protect the civilian and displaced population inside the world heritage sites. The position adopted by the WH Committee, however, does not inevitably mean that there is a clash between the obligations in the World Heritage Convention and the law of armed conflict. This is because the DRC could avoid taking action that would harm the sites without breaching any obligation in the law of armed conflict, as discussed in chapter seven. Nevertheless, it raises the question of whether the actions suggested by the WH Committee imply that the outstanding interests of world heritage to humankind should take precedence over military necessity in an armed conflict context.

Furthermore, given the ongoing hostilities within the sites, the WH Committee has seen cooperation with the army as an alternative measure to protect the sites – a request for military support for the park rangers has been directed to the Congolese army. For its part, the WH Committee has acknowledged the role of the military to ensuring security in the world heritage sites, which is important for park rangers to be able to perform their conservation work. The army has assisted in monitoring the sites and taken measures to disarm and evacuate armed groups inside them. Through military operations, the Congolese army has succeeded, as required by the WH Committee, to drive rebel groups out from several of their positions in and around the sites. As a result, park rangers have been able to regain control over their park stations and the site areas.[105] In addition, when the sites are not under rebel control, the park rangers and the Congolese army have collaborated and performed joint patrols inside the sites, exchanged information, and rangers have received military training as well as weapons from the army. In rebel controlled areas, the park rangers could obviously not collaborate with the Congolese army, if wishing to be considered neutral. The collaboration in the governmental controlled areas may thus be an obstruction for the rangers to be respected for having neutral status. In addition, the WH Committee has seemingly tried to influence the DRC in its military decisions and planning. It is questionable if the WH Committee is in the position to determine the best strategy for how the DRC should conduct its warfare and protect the park rangers.

Although the cooperation between the army and the park rangers is presently well established, it has not been formalised. It takes place on an ad hoc and short-term basis, depending on the location of the rebel groups and the

[105] UNESCO World Heritage Committee, State of Conservation of the Properties Inscribed on the List of World Heritage in Danger, 1 June 2010 (n 36) 10.

security needs of the sites.[106] A special environmental brigade has been installed in Garamba National Park. In the central sector of Virunga National Park, a mixed brigade consisting of both members of the Congolese army and park rangers has been set up to secure the area. The cooperation with the army has been somewhat problematic, not only by the fact that it may affect the neutral status of the park rangers, but also because many of the army members are underpaid, if paid at all. The army members have been involved in illegal activities, harming the world heritage sites, as described in section III. Thus, there have been some violent confrontations between the park rangers and the army. Such confrontations have contributed to the WH Committee demanding that the Congolese army should relocate its military posts away from the sites.[107] However, in the case with the mixed brigade in Virunga National Park, the park authority has provided salaries to the brigade's army members and, hence, there have not been any reported instances of illegal activities from the army's side. In this case, the cooperation between the army and the park rangers has functioned well overall.

Nonetheless, the collaboration between the army and the park rangers is complicated. As noted above, the involvement of the army in illegal resource exploitation within the sites has resulted in the deaths of several park rangers. Therefore, the WH Committee has urged the DRC to follow up on the illegal activities of the army soldiers.[108] At the same time, some success has been noted with the Congolese army and the park rangers conducting joint operations to prevent poaching and the illegal exploitation of the natural resources by the rebels.[109]

The law of armed conflict does not directly address the issue of exploitation of natural resources, but under certain circumstances, such exploitation for personal profit, could amount to pillage, which is prohibited under the law of armed conflict.[110] The prohibition of pillage concerns destruction and seizure of civilian state-owned or private property. Whether natural resources could constitute civilian property was dealt with in the judgment of the International Court of Justice in the *Armed Activities* case. The State of Uganda was held internationally responsible under the law of armed conflict for looting, plundering and exploiting the DRC's natural resources by failing to prevent members of its army from committing these acts during the armed conflicts when Uganda

[106] Interview with Director, Congolese Wildlife Authority, 30 March 2015 (n 69).

[107] See UNESCO World Heritage Committee, Decision 28 COM 15A (n 103) 52; Decision 31 COM 7A.7 (n 104) 11.

[108] See UNESCO World Heritage Committee, Decision 34 COM 7A.4, adopted at the 34th Session on 25 July–3 August 2010, UN Doc WHC-10/34.COM/20, 3 September 2010, 20. See also State of Conservation of the Properties Inscribed on the List of World Heritage in Danger, 1 June 2010 (n 36) 11–12.

[109] UNESCO World Heritage Committee, State of Conservation of the Properties Inscribed on the List of World Heritage in Danger, 26 May 2006 (n 25) 27.

[110] The prohibition of pillage is discussed in ch 5.

was occupying areas of the DRC.[111] The Court stated that the exploitation of natural resources constitutes plunder or pillage, as set out in the law of armed conflict.[112] In this context, the recommendation of the WH Committee to call for preventing and punishing the illegal exploitation activities is both consistent with and strengthens the law of armed conflict.

Overall, the WH Committee is divided over the question as to how the army should behave with regard to the world heritage sites. On the one hand, the WH Committee wants the army to refrain from entering the sites at all, but on the other, it requests that the army should demobilise and disarm rebel groups in the sites and cooperate with the park rangers. The WH Committee seems to be unclear as to how to balance security and conservation needs, in particular, since the needs appear to be interrelated. Given that the Congolese army has other tasks than assisting the park rangers to remove rebels inside the world heritage sites, it may be debatable if it is appropriate for an environmental treaty body to attempt to influence the Congolese army in its warfare.

The army has a right to fight rebels inside the world heritage sites under the law of armed conflict. If the army does not have such a right, would this mean that conservation of world heritage, at least in part, contradicts and supersedes the law of armed conflict? At the same time, the decisions and recommendations of the WH Committee seem to imply an obligation for the Congolese army to protect the sites. However, the request from the WH Committee does not express any consideration of the need for the Congolese army to defend its territory through military operations that may have to be conducted inside the world heritage sites. The restriction on military operations, as imposed under the World Heritage Convention, could impede performance of the law of armed conflict by denying the application of the doctrine of military necessity.

At the very least, in the specific case described above, and if taking the decisions of the WH Committee seriously, the practical outcome is one where the provisions of the World Heritage Convention inform the interpretation and application of the law of armed conflict to a certain degree. This suggests that although there is no existing obligation in the law of armed conflict to spare world heritage sites, such an obligation could be read into the rules when interpreting the law of armed conflict in the light of the obligations set out in the World Heritage Convention. In particular, as the rules of the law of armed conflict are often considered vague and weak with regard to environmental protection, to interpret them using the obligations set out in international environmental law could clarify the law to some extent.

[111] *Armed Activities on the Territory of the Congo (Democratic Republic of the Congo v Uganda)*, Judgment of 19 December 2005, ICJ Reports 2005, paras 242–46.

[112] ibid, paras 219 and 242–46. The International Court of Justice based its decision on customary international law corresponding to Article 47 of the Hague Regulations and Article 33 of the 1949 Geneva Convention IV. The Hague Regulations have become part of customary law and are binding on both parties in the conflict, in this case Uganda and the DRC.

D. Collaboration with the UN Peacekeeping Forces

In the case of the DRC, the World Heritage Convention is not only applied through the Congolese state organs but also through other actors, such as the stakeholders involved as partners in the World Heritage project. In addition to the project partners, the WH Committee has invited the UN peacekeeping forces that are deployed in the DRC to provide assistance to disarm and evacuate armed rebel groups from the world heritage sites.[113] The UN peacekeepers operate under the UN Organization Stabilization Mission in the DRC (MONUSCO), which in 2010 replaced the UN Organization Mission in the DRC (MONUC).[114] MONUC/MONUSCO are deployed in accordance with Chapter VII of the UN Charter, because the situation in the DRC constitutes a threat to international peace and security.[115] The Security Council has authorised MONUC/MONUSCO to use all necessary – including military – means to support the DRC in protecting civilians and humanitarian workers, disarming belligerents or armed groups, collecting arms, preventing entry of military materiel, and enhancing the security situation in the region where the world heritage sites are located.[116]

Pursuant to Article 13(7) of the World Heritage Convention, the WH Committee is empowered to cooperate with other organisations, bodies and individuals to implement projects and programmes funded with international assistance. On this basis, since October 2003, MONUC/MONUSCO has collaborated with the WH Committee. It has performed military operations putting an end to some of the hostilities in and around the Congolese world heritage sites.[117] The cooperation demonstrates the potential of the overlapping application of the World Heritage Convention and the UN Charter with the Security Council decisions with regard to disarming rebels and restoring security in the eastern DRC.

MONUC/MONUSCO has helped the park rangers to monitor some of the world heritage sites through helicopter reconnaissance flights.[118] The peacekeepers have also agreed to conduct disarmament operations of rebel groups, in cooperation with the park rangers.[119] Although the cooperation between

[113] See UNESCO World Heritage Committee, Decision 27 COM 7.A.2 (n 103) 10. See also Decision 30 COM 7A.7 (n 95) 18.

[114] Since the end of June 2010, MONUC operates under the name MONUSCO, with a decreased number of personnel. See UN Security Council Resolution, UN Doc S/RES/1925, 28 May 2010, para 1.

[115] UN Security Council Resolution, UN Doc S/RES/1493, 28 July 2003 in the Preamble, para 12.

[116] See UN Security Council Resolutions UN Doc S/RES/1493 (2003) paras 17–20 and 25–26; UN Doc S/RES/1565, 1 October 2004, paras 4–6; UN Doc S/RES/1592, 30 March 2005, para 7; UN Doc S/RES/1756, 15 May 2007, paras 2–4; UN Doc S/RES/1856, 22 December 2008, paras 3–5; UN Doc S/RES/1906, 23 December 2009, paras 5–6; UN Doc S/RES/1925 (2010) paras 11–12; UN Doc S/RES/1991, 28 June 2011, para 1.

[117] UNESCO World Heritage Committee, Decision 28 COM 15A.3 (n 103) 52.

[118] UNESCO World Heritage Committee, State of Conservation of the Properties Inscribed on the List of World Heritage in Danger, 1 June 2010 (n 36) 13.

[119] UNESCO World Heritage Committee, State of Conservation of the Properties Inscribed on the List of World Heritage in Danger, 21 June 2004 (n 36) 7.

MONUC/MONUSCO and the WH Committee is not formal, mixed patrols with the peacekeeping forces and park rangers have been organised in some of the world heritage sites. This has allowed the park rangers to access areas previously unreachable due to security concerns.[120] However, the Congolese Wildlife Authority and the local park authorities have expressed dissatisfaction with regard to the cooperation with the peacekeepers. In 2011, it was reported that the WH Committee remained in contact with the UN peacekeeping troops, but that little direct support was actually provided to the sites.[121]

In accordance with Security Council Resolution 1493, all states, including the DRC, are legally bound to prevent the direct and indirect supply of weapons and related material, and to prevent any advice or training related to military activities being provided to all armed groups operating in the territory in the eastern DRC.[122] The weapons embargo does not apply to supplies for MONUC/MONUSCO or the integrated DRC army and police forces or to the supplies of non-lethal equipment for humanitarian purposes only.[123] Thus, the weapons, ammunition and military training that the park rangers have received complicate the maintenance of the weapons embargo, even if it has been done with the consent and supervision of the Congolese army.

If the park rangers were viewed as an integrated part of the army, there would not be a breach of the weapons embargo to speak of. However, the park rangers would then be considered belligerents, in accordance with the law of armed conflict, if they take a direct part in the hostilities as members of the armed forces on a continuing basis.[124] On this analysis, the park rangers are legitimate military objectives pursuant to the law of armed conflict and may be the subject of an attack. If, however, the park rangers are not an integrated part of the Congolese army, but act as an independent group, then the weapons, ammunition and military training provided to the park rangers would constitute a violation of the weapons embargo, even with the consent of the DRC.

[120] UNESCO World Heritage Committee, State of Conservation of the Properties Inscribed on the List of World Heritage in Danger, 11 May 2009 (n 23) 14.

[121] See UNESCO World Heritage Committee, State of Conservation of the Properties Inscribed on the List of World Heritage in Danger, 27 May 2011 (n 92) 5.

[122] UN Security Council Resolution, UN Doc S/RES/1493 (2003) paras 20–21. The weapons embargo has been reaffirmed in UN Security Council Resolutions UN Doc S/RES/1533, 12 March 2004, para 1; UN Doc S/RES/1807, 31 March 2008, para 5; UN Doc S/RES/1896, 7 December 2009, para 1; UN Doc S/RES/1952, 29 November 2010, para 1; UN Doc S/RES/2021, 29 November 2011, para 1.

[123] UN Security Council Resolution, UN Doc S/RES/1493 (2003) paras 20–21.

[124] Membership of a national guard, customs, or police force can qualify as armed forces if they assume the function of armed forces in a non-international armed conflict. Also, just as in an international armed conflict, membership of irregular state armed forces includes members of militia, volunteer, or paramilitary groups if having a continuous combat function. See N Melzer, 'Interpretive Guidance on the Notion of Direct Participation in Hostilities Under International Humanitarian Law, Adopted by the Assembly of the International Committee of the Red Cross on 26 February 2009' (2008) 90 *International Review of the Red Cross* 991, 1005.

Thus, the Security Council's decision to adopt a weapons embargo is likely to apply to the park rangers. The decisions and recommendations of the WH Committee could therefore be inconsistent with the Security Council's decision. In addition, according to Article 103 of the UN Charter, obligations under the UN Charter prevail in relation to obligations stemming from other instruments. The Security Council's decision should, therefore, supersede the WH Committee's request for weapons, ammunition and military training for the park rangers.

The informal collaboration between the park rangers and the UN peacekeeping forces is surprising, particularly given that it is not within the ordinary tasks of UN peacekeepers to participate in conservation operations in world heritage sites. However, the Security Council has acknowledged that there is a link between the illegal exploitation of natural resources and the outbreak, escalation, or continuation of armed conflict.[125] In the case of the DRC, the Security Council has noted that the exploitation of natural resources is one of the main elements fuelling the armed conflicts, which often take place inside the sites.[126] Hence, there is an impetus for the Security Council to engage in security issues related to exploitation of the environment.

UN Environment has recommended that the UN peacekeeping forces should be more involved in the monitoring of exploitation of natural resources to support peace and stabilisation in general.[127] In 2000, the Security Council established a Panel of Experts to examine the illegal exploitation of natural resources and its connection to the continuation of the armed conflicts in the DRC and to inform the mandate of peacekeeping forces.[128] The Panel recommended increased institutional capacity of the Congolese authority to control and govern the natural resources.[129] The recommendation was considered in the revised mandate and, consequently, from 2008, the Security Council has empowered MONUC/MONUSCO to fight the illegal exploitation and trade of natural resources using military means. It should be noted that the mandate of MONUC/MONUSCO is limited to dealing with the armed rebels only and excludes unlawful exploitation and/or trade activities carried out by the Congolese army.[130] The mandate does not include protection of the world heritage sites per se, only where such

[125] UN Security Council Resolution, UN Doc S/RES/1625, 14 September 2005, para 6.

[126] UN Security Council Resolution, UN Doc S/RES/1457, 24 January 2003, paras 3 and 8, which has been reaffirmed in several of the following resolutions adopted by the Security Council.

[127] See UNEP, 'Greening the Blue Helmets, Environment, Natural Resources and UN Peacekeeping Operations' (2012) 81–82, available at: postconflict.unep.ch/publications/UNEP_greening_blue_helmets.pdf.

[128] See 'Report of the UN Panel of Experts on the Illegal Exploitation of Natural Resources and Other Forms of Wealth of the Democratic Republic of the Congo' (n 27).

[129] Final Report of the Groups of Experts on the DRC, Pursuant to Security Council Resolution 1698 (2006), UN Doc S/2007/423, 18 July 2007, 11, para 40. See also UNEP, 'Greening the Blue Helmets' (n 127) 53.

[130] See UN Security Council Resolution, UN Doc S/RES/1856 (2008) paras 3 (j) and 5; UN Doc S/RES/1906 (2009) para 21(d); UN Doc S/RES/1925 (2010) para 12(r); UN Doc S/RES/1991 (2011) para 1.

sites are directly linked to the security threats.[131] However, in March 2015 there was a proposal initiated by MONUSCO and UN Environment to include the protection of the world heritage sites as an expressed mandate of the UN peacekeeping mission in the DRC. Although the protection of the world heritage sites was included in a draft decision, it did not end up in the Security Council's final decision.[132] As a result, the protection of world heritage remains outside the scope of the UN peacekeepers' mandate.

Nevertheless, the informal institutional arrangement of the WH Committee and MONUC/MONUSCO enables the WH Committee to acquire assistance from an external actor to secure and protect the environment in world heritage sites. In this way, the WH Committee and MONUC/MONUSCO can buttress the competence of the other to address common goals and balance security and conservation needs. The UN peacekeeping forces can secure safety in the sites and enable the park rangers to monitor the world heritage sites, while the peacekeeping forces can be assisted by the park rangers to control the exploitation of resources. Undoubtedly, the WH Committee would have preferred that military activities did not occur in the sites at all. However, given the reality of the situation and the ongoing military activity in the sites, the cooperation with MONUC/MONUSCO represents an interesting, albeit not entirely uncomplicated, approach to dealing with the situation.

E. Relocating the Refugee Camps

After the Rwandan War 1994, a large number of displaced persons fleeing the genocide in Rwanda entered the DRC and camps were installed near and inside two of the world heritage sites, namely Virunga National Park and Kahuzi-Biega National Park. With regard to Virunga National Park, it was reported that since July 1994, the threats to the park have been aggravated because almost one million refugees had settled in and around the southern parts of the park. The fuel wood demand of the refugees living in the park, estimated

[131] UNESCO World Heritage Committee, Reflection on the Trends of the State of Conservation, UN Doc WHC-12/36.COM/7C, 15 June 2012, para 26.

[132] During the experts' meeting, the following statement was proposed for consideration by the UN Security Council during the upcoming review of MONUSCO's mandate: 'Authorizes MONUSCO to support national and regional efforts to investigate, prosecute and sanction members of armed groups and criminal networks engaged in national and transnational organized crime including, but not limited to, the illicit exploitation and trade in natural resources, such as gold and other minerals, wildlife, charcoal and timber, with special emphasis on addressing sources of conflict and safeguarding protected areas from armed groups, particularly, but not limited to, UNESCO World Heritage Sites'. UNEP MONUSCO, Final Report From Expert Meeting, 'Background Paper on Illegal Exploitation and Trade in Natural Resources Benefitting Organized Criminal Groups and its Implications on MONUSCO's Role in Fostering Stability and Peace in Eastern DR Congo', Goma, DRC, 21 March 2015, available at: postconflict.unep.ch/publications/UNEP_DRCongo_MONUSCO_OSESG_final_report.pdf.

at 600 metric tonnes/day, led to widespread depletion of the forest areas of the park. Consequently, Virunga National Park was inscribed onto the World Heritage Convention's Danger List in 1994. Furthermore, the WH Committee requested the World Heritage Centre to communicate with UNHCR and other agencies involved in the management of the refugee camps in and around Virunga National Park to express concern over the depletion of forest resources in the park, stressing that utmost care must be taken to avoid the establishment of refugee camps in or near the world heritage sites.[133]

With regard to Kahuzi-Biega National Park, in August 1994 the World Heritage Centre was informed that a UNHCR refugee camp for 50,000 people was going to be established near a three-kilometre strip of the park. The World Heritage Centre immediately contacted UNHCR to request for the relocation of the camp. With the relocation of the camp, Kahuzi-Biega National Park seems to be less threatened, whereas the situation at Virunga National Park remained critical[134] until it was also relocated by the efforts of the World Heritage Centre.

Nevertheless, in spite of the relocation of the camps, the entire region, particularly Virunga National Park, has been destabilised by the uncontrolled arrival of refugees causing deforestation and poaching in the sites. In order to assist the DRC (at the time, Zaire) to stabilise the situation, the chairperson of the WH Committee approved a total of $US50,000 emergency assistance for the world heritage sites.[135] Albeit, the UNCHR camps have been relocated, other camps, often unofficial camps were established close to the sites. The World Heritage Centre has continued to aim for the relocation of the refugee camps at a greater distance from the parks.

F. Attracting International Attention

The UNESCO project did make efforts for the political mobilisation of the actors on the international arena for protecting the natural world heritage in war-torn DRC.[136] In 2004, UNESCO organised a conference in Paris with the dual purpose of getting international attention for the situation in the DRC and the damage caused to the world heritage sites by the armed conflicts and to attract donors to support and protect the sites. At the conference, it was noted that major funding for conservation projects, to encourage the respect of international

[133] UNESCO World Heritage Committee, Monitoring of the State of Conservation of the World Heritage Cultural and Natural Properties, UN Doc WHC-94/CONF.OOJ/6 Paris, 28 October 1994, 27; UNESCO World Heritage Committee, Report, UN Doc WHC-94/CONF.003/16, 31 January 1995, 21.

[134] World Heritage Convention's web page on Virunga National Park: whc.unesco.org/en/soc/1793.

[135] UNESCO World Heritage Committee, Decision 18COMIX adopted at the 18th Session on 12–17 December 1994, WHC-94/CONF.003/16, 31 January 1995.

[136] World Heritage Papers 17 (n 63) 103.

environmental treaties, is possible even in times of armed conflict.[137] However, the role of UNESCO and the WH Committee have become less significant since 2000, as more international organisations, non-governmental organisations and other stakeholders have returned to the DRC to engage in environmental protection work.

Nonetheless, the World Heritage Convention remains crucial as a tool to safeguard the world heritage sites. This is mainly because world heritage site status attracts international attention that enables cooperation and financial support. Thus, the recognition of being a world heritage site and having rare species, such as mountain gorillas and okapis, facilitates international aid. It gives access to funds not only from UNESCO and the UN system but also from other states, international organisations and non-governmental organisations. As the governmental institutions of the DRC are weak and without sufficient financial means, stakeholders involved in the protection work have contributed to strengthen capacity building and provide funding. The protection work of the world heritage sites in the DRC has largely been funded by international aid since the outbreak of the armed conflicts.

Furthermore, most of the management of the world heritage sites is conducted by non-governmental organisations, private actors, etc, and with limited involvement of the government of the DRC. A management plan of the sites has been developed in cooperation with national and international agencies and an institutional structure has been set up to facilitate the application of the World Heritage Convention. It consists of a general management plan for all sites, the 'Congo Conservation Coalition', and a management plan for each world heritage site, the 'Site Coordination Committees'. These are forums to coordinate between the partners and donors funding the sites.[138] Each site has its own donors and partners.[139] Several of the sites are under the direct management of so-called Private–Public Partnerships or non-governmental organisations collaborating with the Congolese Wildlife Authority. The Private–Public Partnership is a common feature within international environmental law to engage with the private sector to incorporate certain environmental conservation aims.[140] Consequently, as the Congolese government is financially challenged, most of the funding to perform the management activities of the world heritage sites is coming from outside the Congolese state budget.[141]

[137] ibid.

[138] ibid, 110.

[139] Interview with Senior Planning Officer, Deutsche Gesellschaft für Technische Zusammenarbeit, Kinshasa, DRC, 1 April 2015.

[140] See, for instance, P Glasbergen (ed), *Co-operative Environmental Governance: Public–Private Agreements as a Policy Strategy* (Kluwer Academics, 1998); LB Andonova, 'Public–Private Partnerships for the Earth: Politics and Patterns of Hybrid Authority in the Multilateral System' (2010) 10 *Global Environmental Politics* 25.

[141] The involvement of UNESCO has made it possible to generate additional funds for the world heritage sites. World Heritage Papers 17 (n 63) 111.

To conclude, the UNESCO project has managed to engage stakeholders involved in environmental protection work in the DRC to protect the world heritage sites. Even if it is presently less involved, it was the instigator and the organisation taking the first measures to protect the sites during the war. It has facilitated collaboration between the Congolese Wildlife Authority and its governmental and non-governmental partners.[142] The collaborations with other stakeholders have managed to apply the World Heritage Convention with little involvement from the Congolese state organs.

V. CONTRIBUTION OF THE WORLD HERITAGE CONVENTION

The World Heritage Convention has enabled various stakeholders to collaborate and contribute to protecting natural world heritage sites during and after armed conflicts in the DRC. However, Congolese world heritage remains under threat, mainly because of reasons connected to the hostilities and a weak domestic institutional structure.[143] Nevertheless, the World Heritage project has provided alternative protection strategies that have complemented the existing legal environmental protection under the law of armed conflict. The measures have been undertaken thanks to the treaty bodies of the Convention and their partners.

Particularly with respect to the sites on the Danger List, the WH Committee has an extensive mandate to decide on the appropriate action needed. While this may result in disagreement between a state party and the WH Committee with regard to the action required under the World Heritage Convention, it should be remembered that a state party has, by ratifying the World Heritage Convention, agreed to restrict its sovereignty with respect to sites inscribed on the World Heritage List. Thus, the WH Committee is permitted to act in the interest of all its state parties to protect world heritage in accordance with the Convention. In the case of the DRC, the WH Committee has acted to ensure the protection of the world heritage sites. Although the DRC has not implemented all the decisions and recommendations of the WH Committee fully, neither has the DRC expressly opposed them.

The tension between respect for state sovereignty and the international interest in protecting world heritage sites is embodied in Article 6(1) of the World Heritage Convention, which establishes a duty of the international community to cooperate to protect world heritage while 'fully respecting' state sovereignty. The protection of a collective or an international interest of the state parties and the non-reciprocal character of Articles 6(1) and 7 of the Convention

[142] World Heritage Papers 17 (n 63) 110.

[143] On 2 March 2015, unnamed UN officials stated that Virunga National Park was clear of rebels. Nevertheless, the park was still under threat from potential oil exploration. The government permitted Soco International, a British oil company, to explore the possibility to exploit oil from Lake Edward, situated in the heart of Virunga Park. See K Heath, 'Virunga Cleared of Rebels Claim' *Wildlife News* (2 March 2015), available at: wildlifenews.co.uk/2015/03/virunga-cleared-of-rebels-claim/.

can be distinguished from other obligations of a reciprocal character owed to another state. All the state parties therefore have a legal interest in protecting such a concern.[144] Similarly, the protection of the world heritage sites represents a shared interest that all state parties to the World Heritage Convention have a legal obligation to uphold. Article 7 establishes a system for international cooperation under the World Heritage Convention, enabling international assistance to protect this common interest. It reads:

> For the purpose of this Convention, international protection of the world cultural and natural heritage shall be understood to mean the establishment of a system of international co-operation and assistance designed to support States Parties to the Convention in their efforts to conserve and identify that heritage.

Thus, international assistance embodies the protection of a common concern of the state parties by the international community.[145] Therefore, Articles 6(1) and 7 of the World Heritage Convention constitute *erga omnes partes* obligations.[146] This may imply that the protection of a collective interest in a world heritage site may, in some situations, supersede state sovereignty. State parties have, after all, agreed to constrain their sovereignty in relation to the world heritage sites, in accordance with the binding obligations in the World Heritage Convention.[147] Nevertheless, Article 4 of the World Heritage Convention acknowledges that

[144] Compare *Case Concerning the Barcelona Traction, Light and Power Company Limited (Belgium v Spain)*, Judgment of 5 February 1970, ICJ Reports 1970, para 33.

[145] G Carducci, 'Articles 4–7, National and International Protection of Cultural and Natural Heritage' in F Francioni (ed), *The 1972 World Heritage Convention: A Commentary* (Oxford University Press, 2008) 119–20. See also UNESCO World Heritage Committee, Legal Considerations Concerning the Inscription of Properties on the List of World Heritage in Danger and the Deletion of Properties From the World Heritage List, UN Doc WHC-02/CONF.202/8, 21 May 2002, paras 34–35.

[146] *Erga omnes partes* obligations must be distinguished from *erga omnes* obligations. *Erga omnes partes* obligations are established to protect a common interest of a group of state parties to a specific regime. These 'collective obligations' are binding for the group of states and are often concerned with extra-state interests of a non-reciprocal character. *Erga omnes* obligations are owed to the international community as a whole. The distinction between the two categories is blurred in practice, because *erga omnes partes* obligations may also have *erga omnes* effects, in some cases if they have been recognised as customary law. Therefore, obligations with the same content may concurrently belong to both categories. See International Law Commission, Commentary on Draft Article 48 in Draft Articles on Responsibility of States for Internationally Wrongful Acts, with commentaries; Draft Articles on Responsibility of States for Internationally Wrongful Acts, Report of the International Law Commission, adopted at the 65th Session (2001) *Yearbook of the International Law Commission*, Volume II, Part Two, 126, paras 6–9. See also LA Sicilianos, 'The Classification of Obligations and the Multilateral Dimension of the Relations of International Responsibility' (2002) 13 *European Journal of International Law* 1125, 1136; E de Wet, 'The International Constitutional Order' (2006) 55 *International & Comparative Law Quarterly* 51, 55.

[147] GP Buzzini and L Condorelli, 'Article 11, List of World Heritage in Danger and Deletion of a Property from the World Heritage List' in F Francioni (ed), *The 1972 World Heritage Convention: A Commentary* (Oxford University Press, 2008) 178. See also UNESCO World Heritage Committee, Legal Considerations Concerning the Inscription of Properties on the List of World Heritage in Danger and the Deletion of Properties from the World Heritage List (n 145) para 33.

the duty to protect world heritage belongs, primarily, to the territorial state. It states that:

> Each State Party to this Convention recognizes that the duty of ensuring the identification, protection, conservation, presentation and transmission to future generations of the cultural and natural heritage referred to in Articles 1 and 2 and situated on its territory, belongs primarily to that State. It will do all it can to this end, to the utmost of its own resources and, where appropriate, with any international assistance and co-operation, in particular, financial, artistic, scientific and technical, which it may be able to obtain.

Article 13(3) of the Convention requires the WH Committee to make the necessary arrangements with the territorial state to carry out international assistance. Accordingly, once the WH Committee approves an international assistance request, the World Heritage Centre concludes an agreement with the concerned state defining the conditions for how the international assistance is to be performed pursuant to Article 26 of the World Heritage Convention. Article 26 states:

> The World Heritage Committee and the recipient State shall define in the agreement they conclude the conditions in which a programme or project for which international assistance under the terms of this Convention is provided, shall be carried out. It shall be the responsibility of the State receiving such international assistance to continue to protect, conserve and present the property so safeguarded, in observance of the conditions laid down by the agreement.

In accordance with Article 4 in the Convention, however, the state receiving the assistance retains the primary obligation to continue to safeguard the site.[148] In this respect, international assistance is only a supplement to national resources and is only given to enable a state party to meet its obligations under the World Heritage Convention.[149] If a state party is unwilling to receive international assistance, the WH Committee cannot intervene. This was graphically illustrated in March 2001, when the Taliban government of Afghanistan destroyed the sculptures of the Buddhas of Bamiyan, despite the efforts made by the Director-General of UNESCO and the WH Committee to prevent the act.[150] Furthermore, a state party that does not approve the measures adopted by the WH Committee has the option to denounce the World Heritage Convention in accordance with Article 35 of the Convention.

[148] A Lemaistre and F Lenzerini, 'Articles 19–26, International Assistance' in F Francioni (ed), *The 1972 World Heritage Convention: A Commentary* (Oxford University Press, 2008) 323.

[149] AF Vrdoljak, 'Article 14, the Secretariat and Support of the World Heritage Committee' in F Francioni (ed), *The 1972 World Heritage Convention: A Commentary* (Oxford University Press, 2008) 226–27.

[150] For further reading, see F Francioni and F Lenzerini, 'The Destruction of the Buddhas of Bamiyan and International Law' (2003) 14 *European Journal of International Law* 619.

To conclude, the World Heritage Convention, like many other MEAs, protects a shared concern, which allows it to adopt measures to protect the concern for the sake of all its state parties. Nevertheless, in cases where the territorial state disagrees with the action, the World Heritage Convention has few sanctions to force the state to comply. The key seems to be to ensure that the actions to protect the shared concern are undertaken with the approval of the concerned state.

VI. CONCLUSIONS

During the hostilities, four out of the five Congolese world heritage sites have fallen under rebel control. It has been difficult for the DRC to fulfil its obligations under the World Heritage Convention, given the fact that the state lacked control over the sites. In addition, as parts of the world heritage sites, on various occasions, fulfilled the requirements of being legitimate military targets, the military situation did not always permit that the obligations could be fully respected under the World Heritage Convention. Nevertheless, the ability of the treaty bodies of the World Heritage Convention to adopt measures to provide environmental protection to world heritage in an armed conflict context has been demonstrated by the action undertaken under the World Heritage project.

Under the evaluation of the first phase of the project, it was noted that it was crucial to attract international support, instead of solely relying on the state party's ability to act. The support was provided by other states, international organisations and non-governmental organisations. The importance of donors contributing to the support of the park rangers and to the training of Congolese organs has been the essential part of the project.[151] The World Heritage Convention has enabled commitments of the actors in the international arena to engage to rebuild the capacity of the DRC to ensure conservation work in the world heritage sites.[152] To some extent international organisations, non-governmental organisations and other actors are filling the 'institutional vacuum' that has occurred in the DRC because of the armed conflicts. Although, the world heritage sites in the DRC are still in danger because of the insecure situation, the World Heritage project has contributed to maintaining the park rangers at their posts and facilitated the conservation work that may have prevented further damage. The efforts cannot replace domestic governance, but they can provide some institutional reinforcement during armed conflicts, as well as the transition phase from armed conflict to peace.

The WH Committee has managed to provide alternative measures to the natural world heritage sites, during and after the armed conflicts, in a manner

[151] World Heritage Papers 17 (n 63) 106.
[152] ibid.

that can complement the law of armed conflict and strengthen environmental protection. By using the loosely worded provisions in the Convention and the broad mandate to adapt the measures to the national context of the DRC, UNESCO and the WH Committee have made an effort to preserve the world heritage sites. They have minimised the damage to the sites by providing funds; by adopting recommendations and decisions on how the sites should be protected in the light of the particular challenges that the DRC is facing; by supporting the development of national institutions and associated regulations; and by assisting in monitoring and controlling the sites by supporting the park rangers with salaries, equipment and training.

Arguably, some of the decisions and recommendations that have been adopted by the WH Committee constrain the ability of the DRC to engage in lawful military operations as permitted under the law of armed conflict. However, it is suggested that the law of armed conflict should be interpreted in a manner that construes consistency with the legal obligations in the World Heritage Convention. Interpreting the law of armed conflict in the light of the obligations set out in the World Heritage Convention (and other MEAs) could help to achieve harmonisation in the application of obligations to overcome the vague rules of the law of armed conflict relating to protection of the environment.

The outstanding interest of world heritage constitutes a common concern and a collective interest of the international community. However, the interest must be balanced with other concerns, such as the need for the DRC to conduct military operations to defend and protect its territory and population, or with the UN peacekeepers' task of restoring international peace and security in the DRC and elsewhere. As demonstrated above, at both the institutional level and the operational level, the WH Committee has made significant efforts to collaborate with other relevant actors to overcome conflicting interests. The collaboration with the peacekeepers represents an attempt to reconcile the interests and mandates of the WH Committee and the UN Security Council. It can be viewed as a bridge between the legal regimes of the UN Charter and the World Heritage Convention. This interaction is an interesting, albeit controversial, attempt to overcome the problems of normative tensions in international law, in order to create solutions for addressing the specific problem of protection of the environment in relation to armed conflict.

9

Protection of the Ramsar Sites in Relation to Armed Conflict: The Case of Mali

I. INTRODUCTION

THIS CHAPTER CONCERNS the application of the Ramsar Convention during the non-international armed conflict taking place between 2012 and 2015 in Mali. The conflict has generated at least 2,000 deaths and over 200,000 displaced persons.[1] This study focuses on the continued protection work of the conflict-affected Ramsar site Delta Intérieur du Niger (the Inner Niger Delta) during the conflict.[2]

Mali is a dry, landlocked state situated in north-western Africa. The capital Bamako is located in south-eastern Mali along the Niger River. The Niger River is an essential source of food, drinking water, irrigation and transportation. The majority of Mali's 19 million inhabitants live along the Niger River, of which over one million live in the Inner Niger Delta area. The delta area is situated in the centre of Mali and in the heart of the Sahel area.[3] Nearly one million people depend on the resources that the Inner Niger Delta provides.[4] It ensures water services and produce food. It is often described as a lifeline in the otherwise dry climate of the Sahel area.

In 2012, an armed conflict broke out and Tuareg separatists in alliance with Islamist jihadist groups, occupied northern Mali, including parts of the Inner Niger Delta.[5] The conflict has had severe impacts on the wetlands due to lack of

[1] L Ferrini and L Benavides, 'The Inner Niger Delta/Nexus Dynamics at the Heart of the Sahel' (2018), *Nexus – The Water, Energy and Food Security, Resource Platform*, available at: www.water-energy-food.org/resources/resources-detail/the-inner-niger-delta-nexus-dynamics-at-the-heart-of-the-sahel/.

[2] Mali currently has four Ramsar sites. However, the last three were added to the Ramsar List on 22 March 2013 and were thus not protected during the whole time of the conflict. See Ramsar Convention website: www.ramsar.org/news/mali-names-three-new-ramsar-sites.

[3] WA Holthuijzen and JR Maximillian, 'Dry, Hot, and Brutal: Climate Change and Desertification in the Sahel of Mali' (2011) 13 *Journal of Sustainable Development in Africa*, available at: www.jsd-africa.com/Jsda/Vol13No7-Winter2011A/PDF/Dry%20Hot%20and%20Brutal.Wieteke%20Holthuijzen.pdf.

[4] Factsheet of Inner Niger Delta, Ramsar Convention website, available at: www.ramsar.org/sites/default/files/documents/library/wwd2004_rpt_mali_press_e.pdf.

[5] B Lecocq and G Klute, 'Tuareg Separatism in Mali' (2013) 68 *International Journal* 424, 430.

security and inability to maintain effective conservation work and institutional services. However, the main threat to the wetlands is caused by other factors including environmental degradation, weather changes, increased population as well as the construction of dams upstream of the Niger River.[6] The cumulative effects of frequent drought, hostilities and overall insecurity have contributed to a progressive worsening of livelihoods in Mali resulting in a food security crisis in the already poor and vulnerable state.[7]

This case study differs in several aspects from the first case study on the Democratic Republic of the Congo (DRC) and the application of the World Heritage Convention. First, the Inner Niger Delta is an economic centre in the region, and not a protected area as in the case of the world heritage sites in the DRC. Because of the importance of the economic activities in the delta area, as in many other wetlands, the Ramsar Convention does not require its state parties to completely abstain from activities with negative effects on the wetlands inscribed on the Ramsar List. Instead, the state parties are under the obligation to apply the concept of 'wise use' of the wetlands, which enables consideration for economic, social and cultural activities in the sites (as discussed in chapter seven). Thus, the type of protection measures in Ramsar sites differs from those in the world heritage sites. Second, while studying the application of the Ramsar Convention during armed conflicts, it is evident that it has a more limited capacity to address military activities and armed conflicts in comparison to the World Heritage Convention. The Ramsar Convention has no explicit references to armed conflict in the treaty text. There are no decisions or recommendations by the treaty bodies that refer to armed conflicts in general or specifically in Mali, and there is no project in place in Mali with the expressed aim of protecting Ramsar sites in wartime, similar to the World Heritage project in the DRC. This means that this case study cannot provide a detailed study of how the law of armed conflict and the Ramsar Convention can be reconciled. Also, most of the projects are mainly managed by partners of the Ramsar Convention. Thus, the treaty bodies are not as active in the implementation as in the case of the World Heritage Convention. Third, the main threats to the Inner Niger Delta site are not directly linked to the hostilities. Therefore, the activities undertaken to apply the Ramsar Convention do not address the conflict as such but aim at sustaining the conservation work despite the insecure situation. There is no clear picture of how the treaty bodies of the Ramsar Convention relate to the context of an armed conflict. Nevertheless, the projects in Mali indicate the Ramsar Convention can play a role in armed conflict in Mali and the Convention has the potential to strengthen wartime environmental protection of wetlands.

[6] Food and Agricultural Organization of the UN (FAO), 'Project Resource' (2017), available at: www.fao.org/3/a-i7626e.pdf.

[7] OC Ajayi et al, 'Rapid assessment of the inner Niger Delta of Mali' (2012) World Agroforestry Working Paper, available at: www.worldagroforestry.org/downloads/Publications/PDFS/WP17336.pdf.

This chapter will first give a brief background of the armed conflict from 2012 to 2015 in Mali. Thereafter, the environmental impacts and threats to the Inner Niger Delta will be explained. In section IV, I address the application of the Ramsar Convention in Mali during the conflict and in section V, I will analyse its potential role to address wartime environmental damage, also considering other cases. The last section, section VI, will provide my conclusions.

II. THE ARMED CONFLICT

In early 2012, an armed conflict broke out in Mali. Even though conflicts and coup d'états have occurred on several occasions in Mali in the past decades, the war in 2012 was somewhat of a surprise. Mali was at the time considered a stable state and a 'model democracy' in West Africa. The war can partly be explained as a result of the overthrow of Prime Minister Muammar al-Qaddafi in neighbouring Libya and the chaos that followed, which destabilised the whole region of North Africa. With the influx of weapons and mercenaries from Libya, a coalition of separatist and Islamic rebel groups including the secular Tuareg separatists National Movements for the Liberation of Azawad and the jihadist groups Ansar Dine and the Movement for Oneness and Jihad in West Africa took control over northern Mali. The violence in the north provoked protests in Bamako, as a reaction to how the government had been dealing with the rebellion. A military coup ousted President Amadou Toumani Touré from his post. The weakened Malian army and the coup d'état led to quick advancement of the rebellion into the regions of Kidal, Gao and Timbuktu, taking control of two-thirds of the Malian territory.[8] Clashes between the different rebel groups and against the Malian army continued.[9] Civilians were also attacked. The coalition between the jihadist groups and the secular Tuaregs eventually dissolved with jihadist groups including the al-Qaeda in the Islamic Maghreb (AQIM) taken over large parts of the formally coalition-controlled areas. The jihadist groups introduced a strict form of Sharia law, with harsh punishments for violations of law including beating, amputation and stoning. The attacks on civilians and the strict sharia law forced hundreds of thousands to flee.[10]

After the passing of the UN Security Council Resolution in December 2012[11] and an official request by the Malian interim government, a French military intervention and an African-led mission were launched. The operations sought to gain control of northern Mali from AQIM and affiliated groups. In July 2013, a UN peacekeeping force – Multidimensional Integrated Stabilization Mission

[8] Lecocq and Klute (n 5) 430–31.

[9] Ajayi et al (n 7).

[10] Human Rights Watch report, 'La Paix – Mali Conflict and Aftermath. Compendium of Human Rights Watch Reporting 2012–2017' (2017) 32, 146–47, available at: www.hrw.org/sites/default/files/report_pdf/malicompendium0217.pdf.

[11] UN Security Council Resolution, UN Doc S/RES/2085, 20 December 2012.

in Mali (MINUSMA) – acting under Chapter VII of the UN Charter was deployed.[12] Also, other European states in the European Training Mission (EUTM) Mali have been militarily present from 2013 and onwards. These troops were first deployed to fight against Islamist extremists throughout the Sahel region, and later to focus on building local security capacity.[13] In addition, a G5 Sahel joint force is present in Mali and planned to take over the responsibility for upholding regional security. The G5 Sahel joint force is a UN-supported joint force between Mauritania, Burkina Faso, Mali, Niger and Chad. The aim of joint force is to fight terrorism and drug trafficking, reinstate state authority, and enable humanitarian operations and development programmes. Despite the international elements, the conflict in Mali has remained non-international in character.

In June 2015, a peace agreement was signed in Bamako by an alliance of Tuareg rebel groups and the Malian government and allied militias to formally end the conflict.[14] Nevertheless, the situation in northern Mali is still subject to violence between armed groups. The jihadist groups are still strong and the situation for the civilian population is difficult. The three international forces still operate in north and central Mali to help stabilise the region, protect civilian populations, and alleviate the threat of terrorism.[15] Despite substantial efforts to ensure medical aid, food and drinking water, local communities lack many rudimentary services and live in constant fear of being attacked.[16] The implementation of the peace agreement has stagnated and Mali has entered a post-conflict phase of unrest. As a result of conflict and instability, more than three million people are in need of humanitarian assistance, 120,000 are internally displaced and nearly 139,000 Malians are refugees in asylum states.[17]

III. ENVIRONMENTAL IMPACTS AND RISING TENSIONS IN THE RAMSAR SITES

Mali has four inscribed Ramsar sites.[18] The Inner Niger Delta is the site most affected by the war. It is the largest site in Mali and the third largest Ramsar site

[12] UN Security Council Resolution, UN Doc S/RES/2100, 25 April 2013.

[13] European Union Training Mission Mali website: eutmmali.eu/en/eutm-mali-mission/.

[14] YI Ibrahim and M Zapata, 'Regions at Risk – Preventing Atrocities in Mali', Early Warning Country Report (2018), the Simon-Skjodt Center for the Prevention of Genocide, available at: www.ushmm.org/m/pdfs/Mali_Report_English_FINAL_April_2018.pdf.

[15] Initially, the Economic Community of West African States (ECOWAS) organised the African-led International Support Mission to Mali (AFISMA), which was supported by the African Union and the UN Security Council. However, the French intervened and when AFISMA deployed earlier than planned it was criticised for lack of capabilities and resources. MINUSMA quickly took charge and coordinated military operations, overshadowing ECOWAS and the African Union.

[16] Ferrini and Benavides (n 1).

[17] World Food Programme (WPF), Mali, WFP website: www1.wfp.org/countries/mali.

[18] The other Ramsar sites are Lac Wegnia, Plaine Inondable du Sourou and Lac Magui, see Ramsar Convention website: www.ramsar.org/wetland/mali.

in the world covering a surface of more than four million hectares. It is also the largest reservoir of biological diversity in Mali and the richest wetland regarding birdlife in West Africa. More than 350 different bird species, including migratory and waterfowl species, use it as their breeding site.[19] The Inner Niger Delta is located in the south of the Sahara Desert in the Sahel. The Sahel area is one of the most challenging places in the world to live due to droughts causing food and water scarcity. The Inner Niger Delta is essential for providing food and water. In Mali, 30 per cent of the rice production and 80 per cent of the fish production comes from the Inner Niger Delta, as well as 60 per cent of the cattle.[20]

During the armed conflict from 2012 to 2015, armed groups took control of parts of northern Mali, including parts of the Inner Niger Delta. The conflict resulted in some direct environmental impacts. For instance, anti-personnel mines have polluted the soil, oil spills have occurred from attacks, and waste is produced by the thousands of fighters as well as the international forces present in the area.[21] The most serious consequence is the food security crisis and the rising tensions between the population in the Inner Niger Delta, which conflict and insecurity have contributed to and intensified. The various armed groups have prevented pastoral activities and obstructed nomadic movement of inhabitants and cattle. Many of the animals died as their movement was restricted, which hindered access to pasture and animal care. Also, cattle have been repeatedly stolen. Fertile land in the Inner Niger Delta has been abandoned due to the insecurity generated by the armed conflict. As a result, food production has been severely disrupted in the region.[22] Due to the fact that the armed groups controlled the major roads and communication lines, the food trade with the south was disrupted. Moreover, many of the public servants fled the conflict areas and infrastructure was abandoned, plundered or destroyed.[23] The population of the Inner Niger Delta was cut off from basic services normally provided by public authorities, such as access to water facilities. In December 2013, the Comité Permanent Inter-Etats contre la Sécheresse dans le Sahel (Permanent Interstate Committee for drought control in the Sahel) stated that several areas in the Inner Niger Delta were in food security crisis. Mali had been struggling to provide basic services even before the war due to recurrent droughts and

[19] Factsheet of Inner Niger Delta (n 4). For instance, the endangered West African black-crowned crane uses the site for breeding.

[20] B Liggitt, 'Inner Niger Delta threatened by Fomi Dam construction', The Royal Society for the Protection of Birds (RSPB), available at: community.rspb.org.uk/getinvolved/b/specialplaces/posts/inner-niger-delta-threatened-by-fomi-dam-construction.

[21] Délégation de l'Union Européenne au Mali, 'Révision du profil environnemental du Mali – Rapport final' (2014), available at: eeas.europa.eu/sites/eeas/files/profil_environnemental_du_mali_0.pdf.

[22] Concern Worldwide and Welthungerhilfe, 'Country Case Studies, Coping with armed conflict and hunger Mali and South Sudan' (2015), available at: www.concernusa.org/wp-content/uploads/2015/03/global_hunger_index_2015_-_case_studies.pdf.

[23] FAO, 'The 2012 crisis in Mali and its implications on resilience and food security' (2017) FAO Agricultural Development Economics Working Paper, available at: www.fao.org/3/a-i7560e.pdf.

dehydration of water points. However, the armed conflict, the lack of agricultural products and high prices for basic food have turned the situation into a crisis.[24]

The existing tensions and conflicts between farmers, pastoralists and fishermen over the use of land, water and pasture in the Inner Niger Delta have increased due to the conflict together with extreme weather and ecological changes. For centuries, these groups have used the same natural resources to conduct diverse economic activities by using them at different times of the year. However, more frequent extreme climatic conditions have increased desertification, deforestation, soil erosion, water scarcity and biodiversity loss. For instance, water grass (bourgoutières), which provides essential food for cattle, and the water grass fields which serve as a nursery habitat for juvenile fish, have been lost in many areas. Also, the forest areas in Mali are being reduced by 0.8 per cent each year, which is one of the highest deforestation rates in West Africa.[25] The area of grazing land had diminished and the periods of drought have forced the herders to bring their animals to the wetlands earlier in the year, before the farmers' crops have been harvested. This means that farmers and herders have started to compete over the same land at the same time. For instance, farmers occupy corridors that were used by herders for their animals to reach water. Therefore, the herders have begun to take their animals through the farms to access water, causing significant damage to crops. Farmers have accused herders of intentionally bringing their animals into the farms to destroy crops and herders have complained that the farmers have encroached the pastoral land leaving no choice for herders but to enter the farms either for passage or for grazing.

Whereas a certain level of tension between herders and farmers is inevitable, the proliferation of arms and jihadist influence has transformed these tensions into conflict often framed around ethnicity. For instance, the jihadist groups have clearly taken the side of the pastoralists. They have removed the fees for access to grazing areas and opened corridors for animal passage. These efforts have been widely endorsed by herders who see them as correcting years of unfair treatment. At same time, farmers in the Delta have been disfavoured by these efforts. In addition, there have been claims that the jihadist groups have directly attacked farmers.[26]

The Inner Niger Delta wetland is created by annual flooding of the Niger River between June and December resulting in floods covering up to three million hectares.[27] However, the critical water flow is under threat from existing

[24] ibid.

[25] Swedish International Development Cooperation Agency (SIDA) website: www.sida.se/English/where-we-work/Africa/Mali/examples-of-results/inner-niger-delta-mali/facts-inner-niger-delta/.

[26] UN Office for West Africa and the Sahel (UNOWAS), 'Pastoralism and Security in West Africa and the Sahel – Towards Peaceful Coexistence', UNOWAS Study (2018) 45–49, available at: unowas.unmissions.org/sites/default/files/rapport_pastoralisme_eng-2.pdf.

[27] J Klemm, 'Lifeline for Over 1 Million in Mali Under Threat by World Bank Dam Plans' (*International Rivers* Blog post), available at: www.internationalrivers.org/blogs/352/lifeline-for-over-1-million-in-mali-under-threat-by-world-bank-dam-plans.

as well as planned dams, hydropower plants and irrigation installations endangering livelihoods and food production, perhaps even more than the conflict or changes in the climate.[28] There are several dams installed upstream along the Niger River that have already decreased water flow in the Inner Niger Delta. For instance, the Sélingué reservoir and the irrigation scheme of the Office du Niger, a government agency in Mali administrating irrigation, have lowered the water level in the Inner Niger Delta by 20 to 25 cm. The flooded area of the delta has been decreased by 90,000 hectares. The impact of these dams in adjacent areas is overall positive. Hydropower plants produce energy and with the irrigation new agricultural land has been created increasing the food production.[29] In some cases wetlands have been created which some waterfowl populations are now dependent on. In addition, the means to control water flow is needed to avoid heavy flooding going beyond the 'normal' flooding. However, in other areas, the impact of dams has been devastating. Water levels have dropped and the area of annually inundated floodplain has been reduced. The fisheries, navigation and grazing area for the cattle and agriculture have been negatively affected. Also, millions of waterfowl have lost their important breeding areas.[30]

Furthermore, a new project to construct a dam and a hydropower station – known as the Fomi dam – is being built with support from the World Bank.[31] Located upstream in Guinea, it is intended to facilitate regulation of the flow of the Niger River and ensure irrigation all year round.[32] Mali is supposed to benefit from the project by doubling the size of its agricultural land, which is desirable considering Mali's food security crisis. However, the impacts of the Fomi dam project on the Inner Niger Delta will be severe. Studies conducted by Wetlands International show that the construction of the Fomi dam in combination with expansion of the irrigated area would reduce the average amount of water flowing into the Inner Niger Delta by 23 per cent.[33] Water levels in the Inner Niger Delta will drop by 45 cm and the inundated area will be further reduced by 140,000 hectares diminishing the area of the Inner Niger Delta.[34] The lower water level would also reduce the important water grass fields by 62 per cent.[35] As a consequence, decline in rice cultivation would follow, fish

[28] J Kortlandth, 'An environmental flow for the Inner Niger Delta' (*Wetlands International* Blog post), available at: www.wetlands.org/blog/an-environmental-flow-for-the-inner-niger-delta/.

[29] The Markala dam has created large areas of new agricultural land. The Selingué dam has generated a large energy supply.

[30] Wetlands International, 'Impact of dams on the people of Mali', available at: archive.wetlands.org/Portals/0/publications/Count%20Form/Brochure/WI%20Upper%20Niger%20brochure.pdf.

[31] World Bank, Niger River Basin Management Project (P149714), Implementation Status & Results Report, available at: documents.worldbank.org/curated/en/911111559857546894/pdf/Disclosable-Version-of-the-ISR-Niger-River-Basin-Management-Project-P149714-Sequence-No-09.pdf.

[32] Programme for Infrastructure Development in Africa (PIDA), 'Fomi Multi-purpose Dam (Niger River Basin)', available at: www.au-pida.org/view-project/1013/.

[33] Liggitt (n 20).

[34] Wetlands International (n 30).

[35] ibid.

stocks will drop, and rivalry among herders, fishermen and farmers is likely to be further exaggerated.[36] In addition, displacement of approximately 45,000 people and the encroachment of parts of the wetland is expected to occur.[37] The Fomi dam might also lead to significantly lower population levels in water birds and the last remaining large breeding colonies of cormorants, ibises, herons and egrets in West Africa could be endangered.

To sum up, the armed conflict taking place in Mali has had some negative impacts on the Inner Niger Delta. However, due to the nature of the conflict, no major environmental destruction by directly attacking sensitive infrastructure or the environment itself or parts of it have been reported. In fact, the major threats are due to development projects and extreme weather. Nevertheless, the armed conflict has spurred existing tensions and interferes in the protection work, mainly due to the knock-on effects involving institutional collapse and the inability to maintain the rule of law in the region. For instance, the irregular supply of fuel became worse after the conflict broke out, which hampered electricity production.[38] Due to the insecure situation, it has been difficult to carry out protection work and to mobilise internal financial resources in Mali to protect the wetlands. There is also a lack of specialised staff to manage the wetlands. The impacts of the conflict together with a breakdown of institutions and the rule of law in the region have heightened and radicalised natural resource-related tensions.[39] In addition, the hostilities have led to a great number of displaced persons being left in dry infertile areas. Lacking basic infrastructure and sanitation services, they put pressure on natural resources. Most of the displaced people are however not located in the Inner Niger Delta, but in the south, mainly in and around Bamako.[40]

IV. APPLICATION OF THE RAMSAR CONVENTION

The Ramsar Convention has remained in operation during the non-international conflict in Mali. Several projects have been carried out to ensure compliance with the Convention in the Inner Niger Delta. The majority of these projects are managed, funded and/or designed by other state parties or the official partners of the Ramsar Convention. Most of the funding is aid from developed states notably from Sweden, the Netherlands and Japan, with a broader aim than protecting the Ramsar site Inner Niger Delta. GEF (the Global Environment Facility), the World Bank and International Fund for Agricultural Development (IFAD) are also funding several projects, mainly

[36] Klemm (n 27).
[37] PIDA (n 32).
[38] FAO, 'The 2012 crisis in Mali' (n 23).
[39] UNOWAS Study (n 26).
[40] Délégation de l'Union Européenne au Mali (n 21).

with the objective of implementing other environmental conventions or other development aims. Among the official partners of the Ramsar Convention, Wetlands International, the International Union for Conservation of Nature and Natural Resources (IUCN) and the World Wide Fund for Nature have been the main actors in Mali during 2012 to 2015.[41]

In this section, I describe some of the major projects aimed at implementing the Ramsar Convention in the Inner Niger Delta during the conflict, namely the Small Grants Fund project and the Sustainable Development Programme. Other projects are also of importance, but these are either of smaller scale or have not included protection of the Ramsar site as a part of their objectives. None of the projects address the conflict as such and they are not developed to respond to typical wartime environmental damage. Instead, they aim at protecting the ecological character of the Inner Niger Delta, increasing climate change resilience and to contributing to sustainable development. The conflict is rarely mentioned in the project documents, and if it is, it is merely acknowledged as a 'crisis' or a 'situation of insecurity' that affects the implementation of the projects.[42]

A. Small Grants Fund

As mentioned in chapter seven, there are three funds that approve grants for implementing the Ramsar Convention. These are the Small Grants Fund (formerly the 'Wetland Conservation Fund'), the Swiss Grants for Africa, and the United States-supported Wetlands for the Future Fund. While the two latter funds are funded by one state party respectively (Switzerland and the United States), the Small Grants Fund is a multi-donor fund open for any state party to voluntarily contribute. It is intended to assist developing countries to implement the Convention to ensure the conservation and sustainable use of their wetland resources while maintaining a strong human and social dimension. The Small Grants Fund is administered by the Ramsar Secretariat. To facilitate the project selection and implementation, a set of Operational Guidelines have been developed under the Ramsar Convention. According to the Operational Guidelines, project funding can be applied for, inter alia: (a) 'activities that clearly contribute to the implementation of the Convention's Strategic Plan'; (b) 'emergency assistance related to maintaining the ecological character of designated Ramsar sites'; or (c) for preparatory assistance to allow non-state parties to prepare for

[41] See ch 7 for more information on the official partners of the Ramsar Convention.

[42] In the FODESA project the conflict is described as a 'socio-political crisis'. See GEF website: www.thegef.org/sites/default/files/project_documents/GEF%25201152_TER_IFAD_MALI_English%2520Translation_0.pdf. Another GEF-funded project mentioned that some activities had to be cancelled due to the insecure situation in the Inner Niger Delta, but that the activities had been carried out in the following year.

accession to the Convention.[43] Emergency assistance can be applied for wetlands that 'have suffered damage or are in imminent danger of damage as the result of technological developments, pollution, other human interference or natural phenomena such as hurricanes or drought'. Thus, armed conflicts are not explicitly mentioned as a reason to apply for emergency assistance but could be included as 'other human interference'.[44]

Between 2009 and 2014, a Ramsar Small Grants Fund project titled 'Sauvons le delta intérieur du fleuve Niger' ('Saving the Inner Niger Delta')[45] was carried out to assist Mali's compliance with the Ramsar Convention regarding the site of the Inner Niger Delta.[46] The aim of the project was to mitigate the effects of human activities in the Inner Niger Delta and to find solutions by involving the local communities. It was, however, launched before the outbreak of the conflict and was therefore not designed to respond to wartime damage. The fund financed a wide range of activities that were implemented partly during the conflict. The main activities focused on spreading knowledge about the wise use concept and restoring forests in the region. For instance, local radio stations and networks of researchers broadcast messages conveying the need to apply the wise use concept and protect the wetlands by addressing the causes and consequences of the degradation of the delta. The messages were communicated in several of the local languages in the Inner Niger Delta, including Peulh, Bozo, Bamanan, Sonrhai and French. More than 30 meetings involving 170 villages in the region have been arranged to promote awareness of the need to protect the ecosystems of the wetlands.

These activities aim at invoking Article 3(1) of the Ramsar Convention that specifies that 'Contracting Parties shall formulate and implement their planning so as to promote the conservation of the wetlands included in the List' as well as promoting the wise use of all the wetlands in their territory. To guide state parties on the meaning of this provision, recommendations and guidelines have been adopted by the Ramsar treaty bodies. For instance, in the Ramsar Handbook, one aspect of the 'wise use' concept is to carry out public awareness and engage in education.[47] Furthermore, meeting with members in the villages is also incorporating the guidelines adopted under the Ramsar Convention to make sure that local communities and indigenous peoples participate in the management of wetlands and to ensure that the wise use of the wetlands also

[43] Small Grants Fund (SGF) Operational Guidelines 2019, available at: www.ramsar.org/document/ramsar-small-grants-fund-for-wetland-conservation-and-wise-use-sgf-operational-guidelines-0.

[44] SGF Operational Guidelines, section III.

[45] Project SGF/ML/2009 approved in Decision SC30-12: The Standing Committee approved Small Grants Fund allocations to the A1 list found in DOC. SC30-11 addendum 1, 5, and agreed to fund the A2 list (six, with Mali listed second and Zambia removed) if additional resources should become available. 30th Meeting of the Standing Committee Gland, Switzerland, 13–16 January 2004.

[46] Ramsar Convention website: www.ramsar.org/news/small-grants-fund-project-for-the-protection-of-the-inner-niger-delta-completed.

[47] Ramsar Convention Secretariat, 'An Introduction to the Ramsar Convention on Wetlands', 5th edn (previously The Ramsar Convention Manual) (2016), Gland, Switzerland, 38.

benefits the quality of life of local and indigenous people.[48] The application of the Ramsar Convention from this aspect does not appear to conflict with any of the provisions under the law of armed conflict but rather complements it.

Moreover, approximately 10 hectares of the Inner Niger Delta have been planted with around 5,000 native trees to protect the severely affected river banks. The new plants have been protected with fences around them. Members of the local communities have been trained and equipped to monitor the development of the conservation efforts in order to guarantee that the results of the project continue.[49] Under Article 4(5) of the Ramsar Convention, state parties are under an obligation to promote training of personnel competent to manage and warden wetlands. In the case of the Inner Niger Delta, Mali lacks the resources to fulfil this obligation. Thus, the Small Grants Fund can be used to assist Mali in this respect. In an armed conflict, similar to the discussion in relation to the training of park rangers in the DRC, there are possibilities that such training may interfere in the warfare. The Small Grants Fund project does not state how the training should be conducted and what it consists of. Thus, no conclusions can be drawn of how training of members in the community may be incompatible with other rules of international law. It seems to be training on how to look after restored areas rather than arming guards to defend them, as in the case of the DRC and the world heritage sites. Nevertheless, it indicates that there are also possibilities under the Ramsar Convention to employ more 'hands-on' measures to protect Ramsar sites, that could interfere with other rules of international law.

B. Sustainable Development Programme of the Inner Niger Delta

As a follow-up to the Small Grants Project and another restoration project of the Inner Niger Delta,[50] a 10-year project titled 'Programme de développement durable du delta intérieur du Niger' (the Sustainable Development Programme) was launched in 2013. The programme divided into two phases: a transitional phase (planned for four years);[51] and a phase II (planned for six years). Despite the project commencing after the outbreak of armed conflict, the activities do not address the conflict as such. The Sustainable Development Programme links

[48] According to the 'Guidelines for establishing and strengthening local communities' and indigenous peoples' participation in the management of wetlands' Recommendation 6.3, 1996; Handbook 7. See also Handbook, 41.

[49] Ramsar Convention website: archive.ramsar.org/cda/en/ramsar-activities-grants-rsgf-sgf-mali-2009/main/ramsar/1-63-68-159%5E26581_4000_0__.

[50] The Rehabilitation of Degraded Ecosystems of the Inner Niger Delta (REDDIN) implemented from 2009 to 2014 by IUCN and Wetlands International and financially supported by Sweden.

[51] The transitional phase was the subject of a Specific Agreement for the financing of the Sustainable Development of the Inner Niger Delta (PDD-DIN) signed on 24 October 2013, between the government of Mali and the Kingdom of Sweden. An amendment to the Specific Financing Agreement was then signed on 9 December 2015, extending the transition phase until 30 June 2018.

protection of biodiversity and ecosystems with socio-economic development, poverty eradication, and humanitarian issues. The programme aims at promoting sustainable use of the natural resources and supporting adaptation to the effects of climate change, in which the wetland plays a key role. Ensuring that the environmental protection work also contributes to humanitarian issues, such as strengthening resilience and security as well as decreasing the need for humanitarian assistance in the conflict affected region, may however be a result of the armed conflict. Thus, the programme addresses several interrelated and interdependent issues and challenges, including security aspects, to ensure wise use of the Inner Niger Delta site. However, as support for the programme is not provided by funds under the Ramsar Convention, the activities go beyond implementing the scope of the Convention.

The programme consists of four main components. These are: (1) institutional development and capacity building for implementation of the programme; (2) infrastructure and equipment priority; (3) the protection of resources and ecosystems in the Inner Niger Delta; and (4) rural development. Each component is accompanied by the support of a ministerial department in the Malian government having the mandate to implement it with support from other actors. The main actors are the Ministry of Environment in Mali, with the National Forests Directorate responsible for daily operations, and Sweden as the main donor.[52] Dividing the programme into several components to be fulfilled by different actors has made the implementation of the programme fragmented and difficult to overview. There are overlaps between the components and actors as well as between the two phases. Due to differences in financing and priorities, the components have reached different stages in terms of implementation.

The implementation of the transitional phase finished in 2018. The purpose of the phase was to set priorities for investment and prepare strategic and technical conditions for the second phase. A large part of the transitional phase was carried out in the context of the armed conflict, which has negatively affected the implementation of the first phase. For instance, jihadist attacks have occurred in the region and the insecurity has made certain parts difficult to perform, including: the ability to monitor activities; the timetable by causing delays and changes in intervention strategies; the governance of natural resources and forest management, which were at times inoperative; access to certain sites of high ecological value; and difficulties in setting up and upholding rules for managing restored perimeters.

Yet, with the support of local and international non-governmental organisations, the programme could be carried out and managed to fulfil some of its objectives.[53] The programme has, for instance, been able to build sustainable infrastructures such as boreholes, water tanks and water pumps working

[52] SIDA website: www.sida.se/English/where-we-work/Africa/Mali/examples-of-results/inner-niger-delta-mali/facts-inner-niger-delta/.

[53] PDD-DIN project, available at: pdd-din.org/documents/PDD-DIN-II.pdf.

with solar energy as well as providing equipment and storage for agricultural products. The use of solar dryers has improved the quality of food products and their availability for the communities. In the field of hygiene and sanitation, 30 public latrines have been built in local villages. These activities have contributed to ensuring access to water as well as food, which has contributed to improve food security. These activities may not be directly connected to preserving the ecological character of the Ramsar site. However, these activities can be joined with the concept of wise use. According to the Changwon Declaration on human well-being and wetlands, a resolution adopted for 'relevant implementation commitments' for the wise use of wetlands,[54] calls for co-management of human health and wetlands. The Declaration states:

> Wetland and water managers must identify and implement interventions that benefit both wetland ecosystem 'health' and human health. It is already clear that many of the continuing pressures on wetlands that are driving trends in human health are rooted in issues of water, as for example waterborne transmission of diseases and vectors and/or dwindling supplies of water of suitable quality for food production, sanitation, and drinking water.[55]

Thus, the implementation of the wise use of wetlands under the Ramsar Convention can go well beyond the treaty text and also be adapted to address pressing needs in an area, such as Mali, fighting food deprivation and sanitation problems. Indirectly, as the food security crisis is partly caused by the armed conflict, the Ramsar Convention can contribute to a remedy for wartime environmentally related issues.

The programme has specifically targeted the education and empowerment of women. For instance, the training of almost 400 women to improve their knowledge of resource management in general, and strengthen their abilities in material manufacturing techniques of soap in particular, have resulted in women's financial, social and nutritional status improving.[56] Small businesses and local farmers have also received direct support. Almost 600 local farmers have also been supported with poultry farming, beekeeping, and sheep and goat fattening.[57] Implementing the Ramsar Convention by providing support for local businesses may not be directly deduced from interpretation of the treaty text of the wise use of the Ramsar site. However, according to the revised definition of the concept of 'wise use', it should be implemented in a context

[54] Ramsar Convention Secretariat, 'Handbook 1 – Wise Use of Wetlands', Ramsar Handbooks, 4th edn (2010) 7.

[55] The Changwon Declaration, Resolution X.3 adopted by the 10th meeting of COP (2008) 5, available at: www.ramsar.org/sites/default/files/documents/library/cop10_changwon_english.pdf.

[56] SIDA website: www.sida.se/English/where-we-work/Africa/Mali/examples-of-results/inner-niger-delta-mali/facts-inner-niger-delta/.

[57] P Chalmers, 'Managing Mali's Wetland Wealth', Wetlands International, available at: archive.wetlands.org/Portals/0/publications/Strategy%20paper/WI_Managing%20Malis%20Wetland%20Wealth_WEB.pdf.

of sustainable development.[58] The Changwong Declaration also endorses such a reading as it supports action 'to maintain the benefits provided by the wetlands for economic development and the livelihoods of the people specially the poor'.[59]

The programme has also restored several hundred hectares of forest as well as recovering the habitats of the fish population.[60] State parties are not required to restore sites under the Ramsar Convention, although it is recommended.[61] Local fisheries councils developed in partnership with municipalities[62] ensure sustainable use of the fish stocks in accordance with the wise use concept under Article 3(1) of the Ramsar Convention.

Furthermore, a Plan for Sustainable Development of the Inner Niger Delta to be used for future interventions to ensure the wise use of the wetlands has been adopted[63] and organs of government and management of the programme at national, regional and local level have been established.[64] The plan and the newly established bodies assist Mali in complying with Article 6(3) of the Ramsar Convention, namely to ensure that 'those responsible at all levels for wetlands management shall be informed of, and take into consideration, recommendations of such Conferences concerning the conservation, management and wise use of wetlands and their flora and fauna'.

The transitional phase of the programme has been described as a success despite the difficulties due to insecurity.[65] The implementation of the second phase was approved in February 2019, and is expected to run until 2022. A contribution from Sweden of 9.8 million euros has been secured. The second phase will continue the work of the first phase focusing on sustainable resource management and conservation of ecosystems, building the resilience of local communities to respond to challenges linked to climate change and the promotion of new and renewable energies. In addition, the programme will increase efforts in the areas of sanitation, by constructing collective sanitation facilities; food security, through developing market gardens and field irrigation and investing in fish and poultry farms; and conflict reduction related to the use of

[58] A Conceptual Framework for the wise use of wetlands and the maintenance of their ecological character, Resolution IX.1 Annex A, adopted by the 9th meeting of COP (2005) Kampala, available at: www.ramsar.org/sites/default/files/documents/pdf/res/key_res_ix_01_annexa_e.pdf.

[59] The Changwon Declaration (n 55) 4.

[60] Chalmers (n 57).

[61] Wetland restoration, Recommendation 4.1, adopted by the fourth meeting of the COP, Montreux (1990), available at: www.ramsar.org/sites/default/files/documents/library/key_rec_4.01e.pdf.

[62] Chalmers (n 57).

[63] ibid.

[64] ibid.

[65] Maliweb.net, 'Programme de développement durable du delta intérieur du Niger: Après le succès de la première phase, la seconde lancée' (13 October 2018), available at: www.maliweb.net/economie/programme-de-developpement-durable-du-delta-interieur-du-niger-apres-le-succes-de-la-premiere-phase-la-seconde-lancee-2781498.html.

natural resources in the Inner Niger Delta, through developing good governance initiatives.[66]

None of the activities that have been carried out are in direct conflict with the rules under the law of armed conflict. However, the provisions of the Ramsar Convention have maintained the protection work and probably contributed to lessening the tensions between groups in the Inner Niger Delta.

V. CONTRIBUTION OF THE RAMSAR CONVENTION

None of the Ramsar Convention-related projects in Mali specifically address wartime damage or the armed conflict. They rather strive to promote sustainable development and to limit negative impacts on the ecosystems in the Inner Niger Delta in a general manner. The activities of the projects have contributed to preventing unsustainable exploitation of resources by controlling the use of and spreading knowledge about the wise use of the wetlands; by minimising pollution through taking measures to improve sanitation; by providing channels for participation in decision-making; and by creating business opportunities in the local communities. The projects have supported and even developed some basic services and institutional functions and have thereby contributed to infrastructure maintenance, food production support programmes and land use monitoring. Without addressing the conflict as such, the projects appear nevertheless to have reacted to the threats posed by the conflict and limited the gravity of its consequences. For instance, by endorsing small businesses and supporting alternative livelihoods, competition over natural resources is likely to be reduced. As the impacts of the conflict along with a weakening of the rule of law have intensified natural resource-related tensions already aggravated by climate-related conditions, the projects may have had some stabilising effects. Thus, the projects appear to have had a positive influence to some extent, preventing the situation escalating by maintaining an international, national, regional and local presence in the Inner Niger Delta to prevent institutional collapse. Overall, the case shows that the Ramsar Convention has opportunities through its partners to address wartime environmental damage.

Nevertheless, the treaty bodies of the Ramsar Convention could be even more active. For instance, in Mali, since 2018, the UN peacekeeping force has requested several UN Security Council Resolutions to consider the environmental impacts of its operations when fulfilling its mandated tasks.[67] MINUSMA also has a mandate to protect cultural and historic sites, being the first peacekeeping

[66] Afrik21, 'Mali: Close to €11 million to be invested to protect Inner Niger Delta' (20 February 2019), available at: www.afrik21.africa/en/mali-close-to-e11-million-to-be-invested-to-protect-inner-niger-delta/.

[67] UN Security Council Resolution, UN Doc S/RES/2423, 28 June 2018, paras 67–68 and; UN Security Council Resolution, UN Doc S/RES/2480, 28 June 2019, para 61.

operation with such a mandate. There may have been overlaps with the environmental work from which the treaty bodies of the Ramsar Convention could have profited in a similar manner to the DRC.

The question is whether the Ramsar Convention as such has played a role given the broad objectives of the projects. Other projects similar to the Sustainable Development Programme and Small Grants Fund project have been implemented in the Inner Niger Delta during the Malian conflict as well, with a clear focus on development, the resilience of local communities and environmental protection. Without aiming at implementing the Ramsar Convention, much of the activities that have been carried out resemble those in the Ramsar projects. For instance, the project 'Integrating climate resilience into agricultural production for food security in rural areas of Mali' was implemented between 2012 and 2016. The project was funded by the Food and Agricultural Organization of the UN (FAO) and GEF (Global Environment Facility). The project's objective was to strengthen the capacity of Mali's agricultural sector to be able to cope with climate change, by incorporating climate change adaptation strategies into agricultural practices. The project's activities were organised into three main components: (1) piloting of improved climate-resilient agricultural practices; (2) capacity building and promotion of improved agricultural practices; and (3) climate change considerations mainstreamed into agricultural sector policies and programmes. The project was implemented in the Inner Niger Delta, but also in other regions in the south and centre of Mali.

Also, the Sahelian Areas Development Fund Programme (FODESA) 3 project funded by GEF, IFAD and the Malian government and implemented between 2007 and 2013 consisted of a restoration programme combining poverty reduction with environmental protection in the Inner Niger Delta. The project had a strong environmental dimension to ensure sustainable management of resources in the delta. The project has remained in operation with the agreement of the Malian government despite some difficulties with regard to the implementation relating to the breakout of armed conflict. In sum, FODESA 3 is a micro project focused on pastoralists and farmers as well as fishermen. It involved approximately 57,000 persons, of which 49 per cent were women. The project was implemented through local organisations. In essence, the project contributed to reducing conflict over resources, secured income, and empowered members of the local communities. It also improved protection of ecosystems and biodiversity in the Inner Niger Delta. Some of the concrete results of the projects included: the restoration and farming of 2,000 hectares of water grass pastures; the setting up of 27 market garden plots with fruit trees of almost 40 hectares; the recovery of 900 hectares of degraded land to be used for agriculture; the construction of nine pastoral wells; the dissemination of modern fish smoking technologies; and animal, plant and fish species that had become scarce, such as the vulnerable hippopotamus, reappeared and are now better protected. FODESA 3 has been described as having 'extremely positive impacts on the populations and on the environment of the Inner Niger Delta'.[68]

Despite the clear focus on protecting and developing the Inner Niger Delta in both of these projects, no explicit reference was made to the Ramsar Convention or the commitments of Mali under the treaty. However, the resemblance is not a coincidece. The Sustainable Development Programme was indeed a result of the consolidated achievements of FODESA 3. Thus, many of the actors and donors involved in the work of the Ramsar projects are also involved in these and other projects. This can be explained by the fact that environmental work under MEAs is carried by a network of actors and that the complexity of environmental issues can rarely be addressed in isolation. Thus, the impacts of MEAs are not always easy to establish. In fact, it can be seen as a major advantage that the projects in Mali were implemented with the government and its cooperation with the partners and other state parties of the Ramsar Convention.

Nonetheless, the role of the Ramsar Convention in armed conflict is context based and in other conflicts, the projects are likely to have a different design. In some armed conflict, it may be impossible to implement any type of project to endorse compliance with the Ramsar Convention. For instance, in 1993, the Croatian Ramsar site Kopacki Rit was inscribed on the Montreux Record as a site under threat due to ecological changes in its character caused during the occupation of the site by Serbian rebels. There were reports of severe damage to the site through deforestation for firewood and an indication of plans to construct a military transport road across the site. The Ramsar Secretariat were in touch with the UN Protection Force in Zagreb (UNPROFOR) advising against a visit of the Ramsar Advisory Mission to the site due to the unmapped minefields in the area. The Ramsar Secretariat decided to not pursue application of the Monitoring Procedure by referring to the practical and political problems at time, ie, the armed conflict.[69] This indicates that the treaty bodies of the Ramsar Convention regarded themselves as unable to take measures to protect the site in the armed conflict context in Croatia at the time.

In regard to the armed conflict in the DRC, the Ramsar Advisory Mission acted differently and conducted a field operation in 2014 to provide technical advice on how to protect the Ramsar site at Virunga National Park (addressed in the previous chapter being also a world heritage site). In its report drafted together with representatives from the World Heritage Centre/UNESCO and IUCN, the Mission advised the DRC to take measures to disarm armed groups inside the site in cooperation with MONUSCO, to prevent the illegal

[68] IFAD, Sahelian Areas Development Fund Programme (FODESA) Project Completion Report, Main report, 2013, available at: www.thegef.org/sites/default/files/project_documents/GEF%25201152_TER_IFAD_MALI_English%2520Translation_0.pdf.

[69] Ramsar Advisory Mission No 55: Croatia (2005) 1–2, available at: www.ramsar.org/sites/default/files/documents/library/ram55_croatia_kopacki_rit_2005.pdf.

exploitation of natural resources also involving the Congolese army, and to stop the licence of oil exploration inside the site.[70]

In many ongoing armed conflicts, there are no activities reported from the affected state parties to the Ramsar Convention. For instance both Syria and Yemen are state parties with Ramsar sites but no reports have been submitted since conflicts broke out. Overall, the operation of the Ramsar Convention is more likely to continue with projects if the state party has approved the activities and the conflict is less intense. Furthermore, the strategy of not highlighting the conflict as such may be a way of remaining operational in a conflict-affected region by formulating the responses under the Ramsar Convention as only addressing the changes in the ecological character of the wetlands regardless of the cause.

VI. CONCLUSIONS

The objective of the Ramsar Convention is described as 'the conservation and wise use of all wetlands through local and national actions and international cooperation, as a contribution towards achieving sustainable development throughout the world'.[71] The dual objective to protect and to contribute to sustainable development may enhance the chances of remaining operational during armed conflicts compared with environmental treaties having a more clear-cut conservation purpose. This is because it can be combined with providing humanitarian assistance as the human dimension is a part of the objective of the Ramsar Convention. In the case of Mali, the preservation of the Inner Niger Delta is linked to solving Mali's food security crisis with a long-term perspective and to assist Mali in adapting and mitigating challenges linked to climate change. The international cooperation around wetlands and the Ramsar Convention is important to maintain services that a war-torn state no longer can provide by mobilising funding as well as competent staff, similar to that in the DRC and the protection of the world heritage sites.

Even though the Ramsar Convention has managed to remain operational and influential during armed conflicts by addressing the ecological state of a Ramsar site and the surrounding communities, it has not taken an active role in protecting the Inner Niger Delta. The Ramsar Convention has the potential to explicitly provide protection in times of armed conflict, similar to the World

[70] Ramsar Advisory Mission, Rapport De Mission, Mission de suivi réactif de l'Etat de Conservation du parc national des Virunga, République démocratique du Congo (RDC) (2014) 4–7, available at: www.ramsar.org/sites/default/files/documents/library/ram78_e_drcongo.pdf. However, Virunga National Park is not included in the Montreux Record, which lists Ramsar sites under threat due to changes in their ecological character. See the List Of Wetlands of International Importance Included in the Montreux Record, 2016, available at: www.ramsar.org/sites/default/files/documents/library/montreux_list_2016_efs.pdf.

[71] See Ramsar Convention website: www.ramsar.org/about/the-ramsar-convention-and-its-mission.

Heritage Convention. The Inner Niger Delta in Mali is extremely important in creating a buffer for climate change in the dry climate of Sahel. Thus, it is crucial for the Malian population as well for the international community that the Inner Niger Delta also remains protected during armed conflicts. To allow attacks damaging such important areas in times of armed conflict is likely to become less justifiable. Wetlands contribute a disproportionally large share in comparison to other types of ecosystem to adapt to climate change. This is because wetlands store a surplus of water during periods of highest rainfall that can be used in drier seasons.[72] With climate change and rising temperatures, it is likely that it will become even more important to maintain wetlands in the future to regulate water storage, prevent forest fires and conserve important key biodiversity. Therefore, the COP of the Ramsar Convention could also make use of this knowledge to promote and enhance the protection of Ramsar sites in wartime.

[72] A van Dam, 'Wetlands: Important for Nature and for People', 2019, available at: www.un-ihe.org/stories/world-wetlands-day-2019-ramsar-convention-wetlands-remains-important.

10

The Way Forward

I. INTRODUCTION

THE AIM OF this study has been to examine the environmental protection provided under the law of armed conflict and international environmental law in times of war and how these can be reconciled and complement each other.

This chapter is divided into six sections. In section II, I outline the shortcomings of the law of armed conflict to address environmental protection. In section III, I explore alternative approaches to enhance wartime environmental protection under international law. In section IV, I discuss the potential application of a reconciliatory approach, which can enable a parallel application of the law of armed conflict and MEAs by reconciling their norms. The two remaining sections of this chapter, sections V and VI, suggest a way forward. Section V analyses the factors contributing to the successful operation of MEAs and suggests how these factors can strengthen environmental protection during armed conflicts. In the final section, section VI, I provide my suggestions on the future use of MEAs in times of armed conflict.

II. SHORTCOMINGS OF THE LAW OF ARMED CONFLICT

The ENMOD Convention, together with Articles 35(3) and 55 of Protocol I, provide direct environmental protection during international armed conflict. The ENMOD Convention exclusively applies to the intentional manipulation of environmental forces for hostile use having transboundary adverse implications. It has, therefore, a very limited scope, because these techniques are rarely employed during warfare. Articles 35(3) and 55 of Protocol I set an absolute limit on the permissive level of environmental damage, even if the environment or parts of it constitute a military target. However, in most cases the extensive environmental damage caused by military operations would not be covered by either the rules in the ENMOD Convention or Protocol I.

The indirect protection offered to the environment as a civilian object under the general rules of protection applies to both international and non-international armed conflicts, and is reflected in customary international law. The indirect protection is broader because it does not require a threshold for its application. Nevertheless, indirect protection has limitations. One such limitation of indirect protection is that the rules fail to address the special characteristics of the environment. They apply to the environment as a civilian object, without bearing in mind that some environmental areas may be more vulnerable to an attack, potentially leading to unforeseeable and even irreparable damage with adverse effects on human health.

In sum, military operations causing environmental damage are lawful under the law of armed conflict as long as they do not involve the manipulation of environmental forces in accordance with the ENMOD Convention; as long as they do not reach the high thresholds of Articles 35(3) or 55(1) of Protocol I; or, as long as the military advantage anticipated from the attacks outweighs the environmental damage according to the proportionality principle. The result is that, even though environmental protection exists under the law of armed conflict, much – if not most – of the environmental damage resulting from warfare is permitted.

Conclusion 1:
The law of armed conflict can be clarified to a certain degree by interpreting its rules in the light of customary international environmental law. Yet, the direct protection remains inapplicable in most cases of wartime environmental damage and the overall environmental protection under the law of armed conflict is vague and does not cover all issues occurring in a war context.

III. EXPLORING OTHER OPTIONS

The law of armed conflict does not regulate environmental issues that are not directly caused by warfare. For instance, the unsustainable exploitation of natural resources that finances combat is not addressed at all under the law of armed conflict, unless it falls under the definition of pillage. Similarly, the indirect environmental damage caused by displaced persons or collapsed governmental structures is not dealt with under this legal framework. The knock-on effects can at times be of even greater environmental harm than the warfare itself. The need for alternative legal measures has been noted elsewhere in the literature, in particular, in the phase between peace and war.[1] In this regard, the work of the

[1] This issue has been explored under the concept of *jus post bellum*. The concept of *jus post bellum* is described in various ways and it appears that there is no agreed or unified view of what the concept is or should be. For further reading, see E de Brabandere, 'The Concept of Jus Post Bellum in International Law, A Normative Critique' in C Stahn, JS Easterday and J Iverson, (eds), *Jus Post Bellum: Mapping the Normative Foundations* (Oxford University Press, 2014); C Stahn, '*"Jus ad bellum", "jus in bello" … "jus post bellum"*? – Rethinking the Conception of the Law of Armed Conflict' (2007) 17 *European Journal of International Law* 921. For a discussion, in particular,

International Law Commission has provisionally adopted draft principles that go beyond the traditional sphere of the law of armed conflict to address these issues and that are intended to apply in the context of armed conflict to enhance environmental protection. Draft Principle 10 addresses corporate due diligence with the respect to the protection of the environment. It calls for states to adopt appropriate legislative and other measures to ensure that natural resources are used in a sustainable manner.[2] Draft Principle 11 calls for states to take appropriate legislative and other measures to ensure that corporations can be held accountable for environmental harm.[3] These principles were adopted at the first reading. Despite the fact that they are not formulated to reflect existing customary law, as the wording 'should' is used instead of 'shall', they represent an important step to show that environmental protection in armed conflict must go beyond the law of armed conflict to also include other arrangements, such as environmental governance network and voluntary codes of conduct.

Similarly, the International Law Commission adopted at the first reading Draft Principle 8 that applies to human displacement.[4] It addresses the clear link between displacement and environmental degradation. It builds from the Environmental Guidelines adopted by the UNHCR that aims at mitigating adverse environmental impacts on displaced persons.[5] In addition, Article 40 of the IUCN Draft Covenant on Environment and Development as well as Article 9(2)(j) of the 2009 African Union Convention for the Protection of Internally Displaced Persons in Africa (Kampala Convention) address the issue. All these instruments are referred to as the basis of the adoption of this draft principle.[6] The adoption of these draft principles acknowledge the complexity of environmental protection and how it is interlinked with socio-economic and humanitarian issues as seen in the case of Mali and the Democratic Republic of the Congo (DRC).

The International Law Commission also adopted Draft Principles 4 and 17 suggesting that 'areas of major environmental and cultural importance as protected zones' should be designated by states by entering agreement or otherwise as discussed in chapter five.[7] However, it may be difficult to conclude the agreements on a voluntarily basis to safeguard environmental areas in times of war, particularly because many states are reluctant to agree to any new regulations that restrict their warfare.

on the environment and *jus post bellum*, see C Payne, 'The Norm of Environmental Integrity in Post-Conflict Legal Regimes' in C Stahn, JS Easterday and J Iverson (eds), *Jus Post Bellum: Mapping the Normative Foundations* (Oxford University Press, 2014).

[2] International Law Commission, 'Protection of the Environment. Text and Titles of the Draft Principles Provisionally Adopted by the Drafting Committee on First Reading' (Protection of the Environment, First Reading), UN Doc A/CN.4/L.937 (2019).

[3] ibid.

[4] ibid.

[5] UNHCR, UNCHR Environmental Guidelines (Geneva, 2005).

[6] Special Rapporteur M Lehto, Second Report on the Protection of the Environment in Relation to Armed Conflicts, UN Doc A/CN.4/728, 27 March 2019, paras 41–49.

[7] International Law Commission, 'Protection of the Environment, First Reading'.

Instead of venturing into new regulations, the World Heritage Convention and the Ramsar Convention could be used to adopt such a protection of certain areas of environmental and cultural importance. The designation of areas of particular environmental importance to conserve and protect important biodiversity is frequently conducted under existing international environmental treaties.[8] To use these treaties in warfare follows the trend of how peacetime rules can influence the development of the law of armed conflict.[9] For instance, Bruch points out that: 'Increasingly, broader international humanitarian law norms – including human rights law and even peacetime international environmental law – may be deemed to constrain the action of belligerents'.[10] As protection for certain environmental areas is in place in peacetime under international law, the World Heritage Convention and the Ramsar Convention could inform and complement the rules of armed conflict to safeguard important key areas of biodiversity in wartime. They could invoke the proposals of designated areas to enhance environmental protection during armed conflicts without the need to conclude agreements on demilitarised zones or adopt an entirely new treaty.

The advantage with these existing conventions is that they have a legal framework in place, as well as treaty bodies with a mandate to apply the instruments. In addition, the environmental areas have already been identified and inscribed on certain lists, in accordance with an international standard that is set out in the conventions. Hence, environmental protection under the law of armed conflict could be reinforced by applying the World Heritage Convention and the Ramsar Convention, thus bringing international environmental law closer to the law of armed conflict. As seen in the case of the DRC, the treaty bodies of the World Heritage Convention have called for withdrawing all military operations from the world heritage sites in a manner that resembles protected zones as suggested by the International Law Commission.

Conclusion 2:
Environmental treaties as well as existing initiatives of non-binding guidance can complement and reinforce environmental protection under the law of armed conflict.

IV. NEW OUTLOOK: FROM *LEX SPECIALIS* TO RECONCILIATION

In this section, I suggest that the provisions of environmental treaties can apply concurrently, and be reconciled with the law of armed conflict, in case of a

[8] For instance, Article 8 of the Biodiversity Convention encourages state parties to establish protected areas to conserve biodiversity.

[9] A Bouvier, 'Protection of the Natural Environment in Time of an Armed Conflict' (1991) 31 *International Review of the Red Cross* 438.

[10] CE Bruch, 'All's Not Fair in (Civil) War: Criminal Liability for Environmental Damage in Internal Armed Conflict' (2000) 25 *Vermont Law Review* 695, 701.

normative tension between them. Such an application challenges the traditional view of the law of armed conflict, as being the *lex specialis* in wartime, to prevail if facing conflicting peacetime norms by reconciling the norms to avoid normative tensions. As discussed in chapter six, there are certain problems with the application of the *lex specialis* rule, which are connected to the difficulties in determining the existence of a normative conflict. Given that the perception, as well as the definition, of a normative conflict can vary, the *lex specialis* rule has been applied differently. The rule has been applied to solve conflicts by prescribing the precedence of one rule over another and also to provide a complementary interpretation of the other rule.

The inconsistent application of the *lex specialis* rule creates confusion that can result in a biased application of the rule. Thus, in line with what I suggested in chapter seven, instead of focusing on which rule should prevail over another, a reconciliatory approach could be adopted to solve such situations that involve environmental treaties. The MEAs have, in most cases, the advantage of being assisted in their application by treaty bodies. These treaty bodies can apply MEA provisions to avoid normative conflicts and reconcile other rules, as illustrated in the application of the World Heritage Convention in the DRC in chapter eight. For instance, although the Convention has been applied in relation to ongoing hostilities that at times amounted to an armed conflict, the WH Committee has not acknowledged that there could be a potential clash between its decisions and the rules of the law of armed conflict. Instead of addressing the possibility of a normative tension that could imply that the rules of the law of armed conflict prevail as the *lex specialis* during armed conflicts, the WH Committee adopted measures adjusted to the current circumstances in the DRC to respond to the factual protection needs of the world heritage sites.

MEA provisions can apply in a manner that harmonises with the law of armed conflict, which also avoids being superseded as prescribed by the *lex specialis* rule. A reconciliatory approach operates on the basis that the international legal system is one system and that all of its rules are part of it. Thus, neither the law of armed conflict nor international environmental law are isolated frameworks – they belong to the international legal system and have to be applied in relation to the other rules within it. If the rules of the law of armed conflict and the MEAs apply in the same context and to the same subject matter in an incoherent manner, such tensions can be resolved by reconciling the norms. A reconciliatory approach can contribute to infuse the requirements under MEAs into the application of the law of armed conflict. Such an application would contribute to a coherent, but also a broader environmental protection that unites the law of armed conflict and international environmental law in wartime.

A reconciliatory approach can be applied by the treaty bodies thanks to the four elements that I discuss in chapter seven. The first element is that of having provisions offering a wide discretionary power in the application of the MEAs to state parties, to consider other interests when applying the treaty. The second element is that treaty bodies can assist the state parties to suggest such context-based measures as considering other interests and legal requirements. The third element is that of tailored compliance measures that can address the needs of the state parties. The fourth and final element that can help overcome normative tensions is that treaty bodies can initiate cooperation with other stakeholders.

> **Conclusion 3:**
> Instead of focusing on the determination of normative conflicts, obligations under MEAs can avoid being superseded by the law of armed conflict by adopting a reconciliatory approach, thanks to four structural elements that most MEAs share.

Looking closer at the treaty bodies' application of the World Heritage Convention in the DRC, the WH Committee urged the Congolese army to remove the rebel groups that were hiding and operating in the sites as a measure to safeguard the world heritage sites. At the same time, it also advised the DRC to remove its army forces from the sites because their presence had adverse impacts on the world heritage sites. As argued in chapter eight, such actions, to some extent, interfere with the DRC's ability to fully make use of the means and methods of warfare that are permitted under the law of armed conflict.

Lawful behaviour under the law of armed conflict may include destroying irreplaceable and unique biodiversity of world heritage on the condition that the area constitutes a military objective or proportional collateral damage. To restrict such conduct, the WH Committee suggested that the Congolese army cooperate with the park rangers to safeguard the world heritage sites. For instance, the army contributed to protecting the world heritage sites and support the park rangers by the establishment of the special brigade in Garamba National Park and the mixed brigade in Virunga National Park. In case of the mixed brigade, the Congolese army received salaries from the park authority of Virunga National Park, which solved both the problem of illegal exploitation by the army and ensured that the world heritage site received protection from the army.

The measures adopted by the WH Committee also incorporated and supported the army's interest to disarm the rebel groups and protect Congolese territory. Thus, the cooperation between the army and the park rangers partly overcame the normative tensions and reconciled the two frameworks of the World Heritage Convention and the law of armed conflict. In addition, the WH Committee called for the Congolese government to take action against army members who were engaged in the illegal exploitation of the natural resources, as well as poaching of the protected wildlife inside the sites. Such acts constitute pillage and violate the law of armed conflict, as confirmed by the International Court of Justice in the *Armed Activities* case.[11] Consequently, these measures

[11] See ch 8, section IV for further analysis on this issue.

would buttress the application of the law of armed conflict, as well as the World Heritage Convention.

Furthermore, the measures undertaken by the WH Committee advocating for neutrality of the world heritage sites may be seen as a way to apply the law of armed conflict in a manner that ensures respect of the World Heritage Convention. The law of armed conflict provides for belligerents to conclude agreements on establishing demilitarised zones according to Article 60 of Protocol I or protected zones as proposed by the International Law Commission. Thus, the call from the WH Committee to demilitarise the sites could be regarded as informing the interpretation of Article 60 of Protocol I in the light of the World Heritage Convention.

Even though Protocol I only applies to international armed conflicts, demilitarised zones can also be established in non-international armed conflicts because there is nothing preventing the parties from entering agreements on such matters. The call for the neutral status of world heritage sites could reconcile the rules of the law of armed conflict with those of the World Heritage Convention by using the mechanism of demilitarised zones under the law of armed conflict to protect the world heritage sites and thereby combining the two legal frameworks. A similar approach could also be made under the Ramsar Convention, in cases where the Ramsar sites or parts of them are protected as nature reserve in accordance with Article 4(1) of the Convention.

The WH Committee's appeal to invoke immunity for the park rangers during armed conflicts may however be a more controversial call. The park rangers are armed and will take action against poachers and persons involved in the illegal exploitation of natural resources in a conflict zone. They may therefore act with force against the armed groups and members of the Congolese army if they engage in activities that harm the world heritage sites. This means that the park rangers may use force not only for the purpose of self-defence. Thus, they may be seen as participating directly in the hostilities, which means that they lose their status as civilians and thereby their immunity from attacks according to the rules of the law of armed conflict.[12] Under the World Heritage Convention, the WH Committee has requested the rangers to perform such acts, including using force, to protect the world heritage sites, but it has also called for them to be neutral and immune from attacks.

Calling for the neutral status of park rangers, even though they carry weapons and use force, could be another attempt to reconcile the obligations of the World Heritage Convention, and is inspired by the rules of protection for medical staff under the law of armed conflict.[13] These rules grant a neutral status to medical personnel, even though they carry light weapons for self-defence and

[12] Article 51(3) of Protocol I and Article 13(3) of Protocol II provide that civilians can lose their protection against attack when, and for such time as, they take a direct part in hostilities.

[13] For the protection of medical staff and the right to carry light weapons, see for instance Articles 13(2)(a) and 15 of Protocol I.

for patients' security. Similarly, the park rangers could be considered neutral and permitted to carry light weapons to protect both themselves and the security of the world heritage sites. Thus, initiating conservation diplomacy to make the parties agree on immunity for the armed park rangers could be a novel approach that reconciles the tensions between the necessity for the rangers to carry (and use, if needed) weapons to protect the sites listed under the World Heritage Convention, and the possibility to provide for immunity of certain categories of persons under the law of armed conflict. In this case, the category has been expanded to include environmental protection workers, even though this category is not incorporated under the law of armed conflict.

The WH Committee's calls for neutral status for both the world heritage sites and for the park rangers is indeed a progressive use of its mandate to apply the Convention. To be able to act in this manner, the WH Committee has to acknowledge that the DRC may be faced with a conflict of interests consisting of, on the one hand, preserving the world heritage sites and, on the other, fighting the rebels and protecting its territory and civilian population. Ensuring that the fighting does not take place inside the relatively unpopulated areas of the world heritage sites may in fact have the effect of endangering villages and cities, if it results in the hostilities moving closer to populated areas.

Moreover, the UN peacekeeping mission employed in the DRC in accordance with the Security Council's decisions, has conducted operations that adversely affect the world heritage sites. The WH Committee has therefore urged the peacekeeping mission to avoid such behaviour. Similar to the decisions directed at the Congolese army, the WH Committee has requested that the UN peacekeepers protect the sites as well as the park staff. This is another way to reconcile the interests of the peacekeepers to control and stabilise the areas around the world heritage sites, as well as to provide security inside the sites for the park rangers. As reported, cooperation between the UN peacekeeping mission and the park rangers has taken place in a limited form on an ad hoc basis. Furthermore, in Mali the UN peacekeepers are already under the obligation to not cause environmental damage in accordance with its mandate. This follows the International Law Commission's Draft Principle 7 that requires states and international organisations to consider the impact of their peace operations on the environment and take measures to prevent, mitigate and remedy any negative environmental consequences of the operations.

The proposal for an expressed mandate of the peacekeepers to protect the world heritage sites indeed signifies a joint interest of the WH Committee and the Security Council to prevent the illegal exploitation of natural resources. Thus, there are shared concerns between the two regimes of the UN Charter and the World Heritage Convention that can be advanced through the cooperation of their treaty bodies. Instead of disarming park rangers, as they may not be permitted to receive arms according to the weapons embargo issued by the Security Council, the peacekeepers have directly cooperated with them to stop illegal resource exploitation and wildlife poaching. I have coined the interaction with the peacekeepers as a 'green-keeping' operation.[14] For example, the mechanism of 'green-keeping' could be used to reconcile the otherwise apparent incompatible decisions of the WH Committee with those of the Security Council. Admittedly, such collaboration may be controversial, but it is not contrary to international law, provided of course that both the Security Council and the WH Committee act within their mandates.

Collaboration between international institutions established under different international regimes may also provide some reconciling effects on their operational activities, and may also expand the possibilities of action under either or both regimes.[15] As the UN Charter's obligations have precedence in accordance with Article 103 of the Charter, it means that obligations deriving from the World Heritage Convention may be superseded by the decisions of the Security Council. However, in this case, the WH Committee has ignored the normative clashes between the regimes and searched for a solution that addresses the common interests of the regimes in order to reconcile them. Such behaviour embodies a reconciliatory approach that endorses the unity of the international legal system.

In sum, when applying the World Heritage Convention in relation to the Congolese armed conflicts, the WH Committee has adjusted its actions to the context of the hostilities and considered needs other than those set out in the Convention, at least to some degree. For instance, the WH Committee has adopted decisions that are suitable during armed conflicts, including trying to change the Congolese army's behaviour inside the sites; conducted conservation diplomacy; provided international assistance, including equipment and training, to the park rangers; and collaborated with the UN peacekeeping mission. The adjustment of the measures to the armed conflict context probably contributes to ensuring that the DRC accepts the recommendations, decisions and other measures adopted under the Convention. The case of the DRC illustrates how reconciliation could be achieved, in a concrete case with the World Heritage Convention, to address wartime environmental destruction.[16] Moreover, in many cases MEAs can remain in operation without interfering with the application of the law of armed conflict, in particular to address knock-on effects. For instance, in the case of Mali, the Ramsar-related projects have not interfered with any military operations but still ensure that protection work of the Inner

[14] See B Sjöstedt, 'The Role of Multilateral Environmental Agreements in Armed Conflict: "Green-keeping" in Virunga Park. Applying the UNESCO World Heritage Convention in the Armed Conflict of the Democratic Republic of the Congo' (2013) 82 *Nordic Journal of International Law* 129.

[15] See JL Dunhoff, 'A New Approach to Regime Interaction' in M Young (ed), *Regime Interaction in International Law Facing Fragmentation* (Cambridge University Press, 2012) 166–67.

[16] For a discussion on how the World Heritage Convention may apply specifically in a post-conflict context, see B Sjöstedt, 'Protecting the Environment During and After Armed Conflict Through Multilateral Environmental Agreements' in C Stahn, J Iverson and JE Easterday (eds), *Environmental Protection and Transitions from Conflict to Peace* (Oxford University Press, 2017).

Niger Delta is carried out. Small businesses have been invested in, forest areas have been restored and capacity-building measures have been carried out. The WH Committee has also provided alternative protection measures to address the environmental knock-on effects of the war. For instance, the World Heritage project provided alternative fuel sources to the refugees in the camps close to the world heritage sites to prevent deforestation of the sites. The World Heritage Project and the Ramsar projects have addressed several pressing needs in the context of armed conflict without any interference with other rules of international law.

Conclusion 4:
The World Heritage Convention as well as the Ramsar Convention have the ability to provide substantial environmental protection during armed conflicts on a normative level, as well as an operational level.

V. FACTORS CONTRIBUTING TO THE OPERATION OF MEAs IN RELATION TO ARMED CONFLICT

In this section, I identify the factors – inferred from the empirical case studies and confirmed by the doctrinal analysis – that contribute to determine whether an MEA will operate successfully during armed conflicts to provide meaningful measures that enhance wartime environmental protection.

To facilitate the discussion, I have divided the factors into two categories. The first relates to the nature of the treaty, and the second relates to the characteristics of the armed conflict.[17]

A. The Nature of the Treaty

This section examines the factors affecting the operation related to the nature of the treaty, namely the treaty's scope of application, the types of obligations, the formulation of the provisions, the existence of treaty bodies, the types of compliance mechanisms, and the capacity to initiate cooperation with other actors. The last four factors correspond to the four elements that enable the adoption of a reconciliatory approach.

The first factor concerns the scope. For an MEA to apply, a subject matter regulated under the treaty must trigger its application. For instance, if a certain species, protected area, watercourse, etc, has been imperilled or a prohibited substance used, then an MEA regulating the issue applies. In the case of Mali,

[17] The division of the factors replicates the approach adopted by the International Law Commission in its work on the topic of the Effects of Armed Conflicts on Treaties, as discussed in ch 6.

the Inner Niger Delta is a Ramsar site and applies despite the outbreak of the armed conflict. In the case of the DRC, the world heritage site was adversely affected by the armed conflict that called for inclusion on the Danger List and special measures under the World Heritage Convention.

An MEA must also have a defined and clear scope. For instance, both the World Heritage Convention and the Ramsar Convention have defined and clear scopes, because they apply to specific sites that are geographically demarcated and are put on lists administrated by their treaty bodies. Other MEAs that employ area-based protection mechanisms, such as the Biodiversity Convention and the Convention for the Protection and Development of the Marine Environment of the Wider Caribbean Region, could be applicable in a similar manner during armed conflicts (although they have a wider scope of protection that goes beyond certain areas).

There are a large number of MEAs, besides those providing area-based protection, that are applicable to other environmental issues of relevance during and in the aftermath of armed conflicts. For instance, the Convention for International Trade in Endangered Species (CITES) could prohibit the trade of ivory and other valuable wildlife products that in many cases finances warfare. CITES uses a listing system to determine which species it protects. In addition, the Convention on Conservation of Migratory Species of Wild Animals protects migratory species threatened with extinction, which are listed in an appendix of the Convention.[18] To respond to threats to migratory species, the Convention adopts new instruments, such as the Gorilla Agreement adopted in 2007. The agreement has the specific objective to protect gorillas in Central Africa, including in the war-torn states of the DRC and the Central African Republic.[19]

Similarly, other MEAs that have a clearly defined scope protecting geographic spaces like rivers, or prohibiting a certain activity or use of a particular substance, etc are also likely to be able to apply and to have an impact during an armed conflict. The scope must be specific enough so that the law-applier (military commanders) can clearly distinguish which objects are protected under the MEAs in order to avoid attacking targets or using methods or substances that would be in violation of the MEAs.

Another contributing factor is the type of obligations, which is related to the subject matter of the treaty. As discussed in chapter six, many of the MEAs protect a shared concern with obligations owed to all the state parties. These MEAs may even protect a concern that is shared by the whole international

[18] See Convention on Conservation of Migratory Species of Wild Animals, available at: www.cms.int/en/legalinstrument/cms.

[19] See the Gorilla Agreement (Convention on Conservation of Migratory Species of Wild Animals). See Grauer's Gorillas and Chimpanzees in Eastern Democratic Republic of Congo (Kahuzi-Biega, Maiko, Tayna and Itombwe Landscape) Conservation Action Plan 2012–2022, available at: www.cms.int/sites/default/files/document/IUCN%20Grauer%E2%80%99s%20Gorillas%20and%20Chimpanzees%20in%20Eastern%20Democratic%20Republic%20of%20Congo_2013.pdf.

community in order to respond to environmental problems on a global scale.[20] As these MEAs, often require that all state parties collaborate for the measures to be effective, to permit derogation from the obligations in wartime would undermine the operation of the treaties. This is because they do not work in a reciprocal way and would also affect third states that are not involved in the armed conflict. This would call for pressure by the other state parties to ensure that the MEA also continues to apply in times of armed conflict.

In addition to the scope and the types of obligations, the four structural elements of the MEAs play a role in their operation during armed conflicts. For the sake of clarity, the elements are significant for two reasons. First, they facilitate the adoption of a reconciliatory approach in the MEAs' application with other international obligations. Second, they constitute contributing factors for the MEAs' potential to operate during armed conflicts. In this section, I will discuss the latter.

A war-torn state party can comply with the treaty even under difficult conditions but in an adjusted manner thanks to the first element of the MEAs, because it provides a certain degree of discretion for the state parties. In addition, if the MEAs have treaty bodies, they can adopt context-based decisions/recommendations suitable for the state party to fulfil the treaty objective.[21] In the case of the World Heritage Convention and its application during the armed conflicts in the DRC, the loosely formulated provisions have been utilised to create novel approaches to accomplishing the object and purpose of the Convention. Hence, the fact that the treaty provisions have a general and flexibly formulated language does not mean that they lack significance or are unable to provide for substantive obligations, but that tailor-made measures can be suggested that can even enable a war-torn state party to comply. However, the loosely formulated provisions introduce a certain amount of vagueness in the application of the MEAs.

The second element, namely to have treaty bodies, is a crucial factor for an environmental treaty to be operational during armed conflicts. For instance, the World Heritage project was a creation of the treaty bodies of the World Heritage Convention. As a result of the efforts of the WH Committee, UNESCO, and the World Heritage Centre, the conservation work of the Congolese world heritage sites has continued during the armed conflicts. The treaty bodies can turn general and loosely worded provisions into substantive actions, and they can provide the necessary support for the state parties to comply, even under challenging circumstances, such as in the event of a war. Similarly, partners and state parties can also be engaged in protection work to ensure compliance as in the case of Mali and the application of the Ramsar Convention.

[20] J Brunnée, 'Common Areas, Common Heritage, and Common Concern' in D Bodansky, J Brunnée and E Hey (eds), *Oxford Handbook of International Environmental Law* (Oxford University Press, 2007) 553–55.

[21] D Bodansky, *The Art and Craft of International Environmental Law* (Harvard University Press, 2010) 155.

MEAs are created to operate in peacetime, but as seen in the case of the DRC and Mali, they can also function in wartime. There are several passages in the provisions of the World Heritage Convention that are dependent on further elaboration from the treaty bodies to be transformed into substantive obligations. Through its executive role, the WH Committee has developed these provisions to respond to the environmental problems related to the armed conflicts in the DRC. For instance, looking at the engagement as a mediator performing conservation diplomacy in the ongoing armed conflict or the military training provided to the park rangers by the Belgian and French special forces (as described in chapter eight), it seems that the WH Committee has favoured a progressive application when elaborating on the content of the international assistance provided in Article 22(3) of the Convention. The Ramsar Convention has an expansive view of what is considered 'wise use' of a Ramsar site, which enables the Convention to be applicable to various projects with far-reaching objectives. Numerous MEA treaty bodies have, like the WH Committee, a far-reaching mandate to act in a comparable manner to advance the object and purpose as set out in the treaty.

In most of the MEAs' executive treaty bodies – the COPs – the state parties are represented and have the possibility of directly influencing the application of the convention. Collectively the state parties remain in control of how the MEAs can be applied, because they represent the treaty bodies. Thus, the treaty bodies need to have state parties' support to be able to launch a project such as the one in the DRC. Having treaty bodies supported by the state parties is a central factor that determines the types of measures that can be undertaken under the MEAs. Through the treaty bodies, the state parties can – if they wish – adopt measures to ensure the application of the treaty in states affected by armed conflict.

Moreover, the third element of supportive mechanisms may be a factor of equal importance for MEAs to provide meaningful measures in an armed conflict context. Given that state parties affected by armed conflict often have a limited capacity to act to ensure environmental protection, support in the forms of funds, training and equipment provided under the MEAs can be an important contribution for conservation work to be conducted in these states. Not all MEAs have the same possibilities with regard to what kind of assistance can be provided. Thus, the capability of the MEAs to provide support to its state parties will have a significant impact on its role in preventing or minimising environmental damage in relation to armed conflict. On this aspect, the World Heritage Convention and the Ramsar Convention have a large array of different measures to choose from in order to support their state parties to stay in compliance. As an example, the international assistance granted under the World Heritage Convention has provided the park rangers with salaries, equipment and training. These are, indeed, very concrete measures offered to protect world heritage sites during armed conflicts. Being backed up with the financial means to enable assistance on such a scale is an essential factor that has contributed to the protection of the Congolese world heritage sites under the World Heritage Convention. Still, even if an MEA is not well funded, it may be able to attract funds or other forms of assistance from external actors, as in the case of the Ramsar Convention. Therefore, the fourth element of an MEA's treaty bodies' ability – to cooperate with other actors – also contributes to the treaty's capacity to operate in relation to armed conflict.

The ability to initiate cooperation with other actors in the international arena has profoundly contributed to the implementation of the World Heritage project and the Ramsar projects. Although, there was some funding available under the conventions, these projects were to a large extent funded by means of their external partners. In addition, UNESCO and the WH Committee have also attracted supplementary funding to support the Congolese world heritage sites from outside the project. Currently, the management of all five of the sites is mainly financed by external actors and not by the Congolese State.

Besides financial means, the WH Committee provided security for the park rangers in the form of the UN peacekeeping forces and directly engaged with the UNHCR to have refugee camps within the sites relocated. Thus, measures contributing to the safeguarding of the world heritage sites have been enabled through the cooperation of the treaty bodies with external actors. In general, many of the MEAs engage a broad spectrum of stakeholders. Various types of constellations can feed in from the competences and resources of other stakeholders to apply to MEAs. For instance, funds can be given to support a non-governmental project in a state that is a party to an MEA in order to further the aims of the treaty, because cooperation with other stakeholders is a strategy employed to apply the treaty. Thus, such measures can contribute to enhance the environmental protection both during and after armed conflict by relying on actors other than the state party.

These factors have also contributed to the operation of the World Heritage Convention in relation to other sites that are also inscribed on the Danger List due to armed conflict and/or civil unrest. This includes sites located in Côte d'Ivoire, Ethiopia, the Central African Republic[22] and Niger.[23] As an example, the outbreak of the armed conflict in Côte d'Ivoire in 2002 led to the world heritage site of Mount Nimba Strict Nature Reserve being added onto the Danger List. The site was occupied by rebel forces, which resulted in the suspension of all

[22] The Manovo-Gounda St Floris National Park in the Central African Republic was put on the Danger List because of civil unrest. The WH Committee recommended military training and improved arms and ammunition for the park rangers to help them control the situation. UNESCO World Heritage Committee, Decision 27COM7A.1, adopted at the 27th Session on 30 June–5 July 2003, UN Doc WHC-03/27.COM/24, 10 December 2003.

[23] Similarly, the WH Committee also included the world heritage site of Air and Ténéré Natural Reserves in Niger on the Danger List because of the outbreak of the armed conflict in 1991. Measures adapted to the situation have been undertaken, including drafting urgent action plans for the rehabilitation of the sites. UNESCO World Heritage Committee, Decision 16COMVIII, adopted at the 16th Session on 7–14 December 1992, UN Doc WHC-92/CONF.002/12, 14 December 1992.

conservation activities, including the Côte d'Ivoire Protected Areas Programme funded by the European Union. For security reasons, all staff involved in conservation were relocated to territory that was under governmental control. The park authority's equipment was looted and the park administration buildings and guard posts were taken over by the rebel groups.

In response to the site's occupation by rebel forces, in 2005, a long-term project titled 'Conservation of the Biodiversity of the Nimba Mountains Through Integrated and Participatory Management' was launched, with a budget of US$11 million. The project – supported by the UN Development Programme (UNDP), the World Heritage Centre, the Global Environmental Fund, Fauna and Flora International, and Guinea (which also bordered the world heritage site concerned) – aimed at preserving the natural resources of the site.[24]

The Simien Park in Ethiopia was put on the Danger List in 1985 due to armed conflict. The IUCN reported that the park staff had abandoned the site and that the area was under the control of armed groups. Until 2003, a total of $US233,171 was approved under the World Heritage Convention as international assistance, including training of the park rangers and equipment to protect the site.[25] Although the measures in these cases have not been as extensive as in the case of the DRC, the four elements have been important factors to enable action under the World Heritage Convention to protect the sites in war-torn states. The funding and cooperation with external actors appears, in particular, to be essential in order to address the wartime damage of the world heritage sites.

All these factors considered, the Ramsar Convention has the potential to provide meaningful protection to the sites included on the Ramsar List that are threatened by armed conflicts. The treaty has a defined scope, has the four elements of supportive compliance mechanisms, and has treaty bodies with a wide discretionary power and ability to cooperate. However, the Convention has not identified the outbreak of armed conflict as an expressed danger to the wetlands, as is the case in the World Heritage Convention. Nevertheless, the Ramsar Convention has established the Montreux Record in order for sites that are under threat to get strengthened protection under the Convention.

Although, the Ramsar Convention contains provisions that provide for measures that can adapt to the circumstances during an armed conflict, the treaty bodies established under the Ramsar Convention do not seem to have taken any particular action to address armed conflict in relation to sites that are located in conflict areas. However, the Ramsar Convention has still remained in operation in some conflict areas, often thanks to cooperation with other actors.

[24] UNESCO World Heritage Committee, Decision 29COM7A.3, adopted at the 29th Session on 10–17 July 2005, UN Doc WHC-05/29.COM/7A, 9 September 2005.

[25] See UNESCO World Heritage Committee, Decision 08COMXIII.40, adopted at 8th Ordinary Session on 29 October–2 November 1984, UN Doc SC/84/CONF0004/9, 2 November 1984.

As noted by Crawford and Bernstein, the Ramsar Convention could mitigate the environmental impacts of the conflicts in the DRC region, particularly with regard to the Lake Edward ecosystem. They suggest that the treaty bodies of the Ramsar Convention could adopt measures focused on endorsing sustainable fishing on Lake Edward.[26] In addition, as highlighted by Griffin, the treaty bodies could offer conservation diplomacy,[27] similar to the diplomacy offered under the World Heritage Convention. Nevertheless, it appears that the treaty bodies under the Ramsar Convention have – so far – failed to take the opportunity to specifically address wartime conservation issues.

Furthermore, the treaty bodies of CITES have launched several projects that aim to safeguard species from, inter alia, effects associated with armed conflicts. These have been implemented in war-torn states, including the DRC, Liberia and the Central African Republic to prevent the international trade in endangered species of wild animals and plants.[28] Such trade frequently occurs in states suffering from armed conflict. However, the CITES projects are not – in contrast to the World Heritage project – established with the express purpose of operating during armed conflicts.

The International Consortium on Combating Wildlife Crime project (ICCWC project) addresses wildlife crimes, such as poaching, illegal logging, and the illegal processing of animal and plant material, which are often connected with armed conflicts.[29] Therefore, the project is implemented in war-torn states, but also in other states.[30] The project attempts to enforce the enhanced protection of mountain gorillas by organising meetings with representatives from the DRC, Angola, Cameroon, the Central African Republic, the Republic of the Congo, Equatorial Guinea, Nigeria, Rwanda and Uganda, which are nine of the 10 states in Africa where gorillas can still be found in the wild. The project is a collaboration between CITES, the International Police (INTERPOL), the UN Office on Drugs and Crime, the World Bank, and the World Customs Organisation.[31]

In 2013, the ICCWC project delivered a two-day 'cutting-edge' training workshop for wildlife law enforcement officials from 21 states.[32] The training was

[26] A Crawford and J Bernstein, *MEAs, Conservation and Conflict: A Case Study of Virunga National Park, DRC* (International Institute for Sustainable Development, Winnipeg, 2008) 15–16.

[27] P Griffin, 'The Ramsar Convention: A New Window for Environmental Diplomacy?' The Institute for Environmental Diplomacy and Security (2013), available at: www.uvm.edu/ieds/sites/default/files/Ramsar_IEDSResearchSeries.pdf.

[28] CITES web page: www.cites.org/eng/disc/what.php.

[29] In the tool kit that CITES has developed to deal with poachers, insurgents and rebel groups are specially mentioned. See 'Wildlife and Forest Crime Analytic Toolkit', compiled by International Consortium on Combating Wildlife Crime (UN, New York, 2012) 147.

[30] See CITES web page: www.cites.org/eng/news/sundry/2013/20131104_iccwc_ training.php.

[31] The project is funded by the European Commission, the Netherlands, Sweden, the United Kingdom, the United States and the World Bank. See CITES web page: www.cites.org/eng/prog/iccwc.php/Donors.

[32] These included Botswana, Burundi, China, Congo Brazzaville, the Czech Republic, Ethiopia, Ghana, Indonesia, Kenya, Liberia, Malawi, Malaysia, Mozambique, Nepal, the Philippines, South Africa, Tanzania, Thailand, Uganda, Vietnam, and Zambia in Kenya.

intended to strengthen the skills of law enforcement officers from across Africa and Asia, in order to help them combat transnational organised wildlife crime more effectively using a broad range of innovative and specialised investigation techniques. Thus, the ICCWC project seeks to respond to poor governance of its state parties through the support of law enforcement. By building long-term capacity among the national agencies responsible for wildlife law enforcement, and providing these authorities with the tools and services they need, the goal is to achieve the competence to combat wildlife crime.[33]

CITES has launched another project to prevent the illegal killing of elephants. Killing elephants for the ivory trade is another common feature in relation to armed conflict.[34] The objective is to create systems to monitor the illegal killing of elephants and it is also incorporated in states affected by armed conflict.[35] The project is a collaboration between CITES, UN Environment, and the European Commission. Furthermore, CITES is also involved in the Chainsaw Project that aims at preventing illegal logging.[36] Logging of timber is a recognised high-value resource subject to unsustainable exploitation, often in relation to armed conflict.[37] CITES' treaty organs work together with INTERPOL and the World Bank to improve and enforce the law on this issue.[38] Overall, CITES is an environmental treaty characterised by having most of the crucial factors related to the nature of a treaty that is able to contribute to the continued operation during armed conflicts. It has a defined scope applying to species identified in its licence system; it has treaty bodies[39] with a wide discretionary power to apply the Convention; it has the ability to adopt supportive application measures; and it can initiate international cooperation.

In sum, MEAs with a clear scope for protecting certain areas or species, or prohibiting a certain substance or behaviour, have the potential to operate and strengthen environmental protection in relation to armed conflict. Having the four elements – in particular, active treaty bodies, wide discretionary powers that can tailor the protection measures to the prevailing circumstances, and access to funding, or the ability to attract funds or other support from external actors – all contribute to their role in enhancing wartime environmental protection.

[33] CITES web page: www.cites.org/prog/iccwc.php/Strategy.

[34] UNEP, 'Protecting the Environment During Armed Conflict: An Inventory and Analysis of International Law' (UNEP, Switzerland, 2009) 34.

[35] The project has been implemented in several states in Africa and Asia, including the DRC, CAR, Uganda, Liberia, etc. See 'Long Term System for Monitoring the Illegal Killing of Elephants, Phase II Final Evaluation Report', available at: www.cites.org/sites/default/files/common/prog/mike/prog_reports/1309_MIKE_ph2_final_EvaluationReport.pdf. See also CITES web page: www.cites.org/eng/prog/mike_etis.php.

[36] See 'Chainsaw Project, An INTERPOL Perspective on Law Enforcement in Illegal Logging', available at: www.illegal-logging.info/sites/default/files/uploads/WorldBankChainsawIllegalLoggingReport.pdf.

[37] UNEP, 'Protecting the Environment During Armed Conflict' (n 34) 52.

[38] See 'Chainsaw Project (n 36).

[39] CITES has established a COP, Standing Committee, and Secretariat. See CITES web page: www.cites.org/eng/disc/org.php.

B. The Characteristics of the Armed Conflict

In the present subsection, I discuss how the characteristics of the armed conflict may affect the operation of MEAs by looking at the following factors: intensity of violence; type of violence; organisation of the parties to the armed conflict; motives of the parties to the armed conflict; and type of environmental damage caused. Many of these factors are interrelated so they may not be fully separated in the discussion.

With regard to its work on the Effects of Armed Conflicts on Treaties, the International Law Commission has not distinguished between international and non-international armed conflict. Such a distinction does not appear to be of particular importance regarding environmental treaties because they apply in the same way in both types of conflict. However, the measures invoked under the MEAs may be different in different armed conflicts, but that would be because of the factual circumstances in the armed conflict rather than the legal classification of it, as established in chapter seven. These factual circumstances are the factors that I analyse in this subsection to determine how they influence the operation of environmental treaties in relation to armed conflict.

The intensity of violence has an immediate impact on the capability of a state party affected by an armed conflict to apply MEAs. In armed conflicts with highly intensive fighting, the belligerent parties would probably be limited in regard to the measures they can carry out in terms of environmental conservation work. Yet, they may be able to avoid certain behaviour in their warfare. State parties could avoid attacks in environmental areas directly protected under MEAs, or in areas hosting species protected by MEAs; they could refrain from using certain substances prohibited by MEAs; or carefully choose weapons, or targets, in order to minimise interference with the obligations under the MEAs.

A state party may, however, struggle to comply with positive and burdensome obligations proscribed under MEAs that would require active conservation measures during intense violent hostilities. For instance, setting up a breeding programme to conserve an endangered species or intentionally flooding an area to construct a wetland to ensure biodiversity may not be possible during intense hostilities. Nevertheless, as discussed in the previous subsection, the measures required under most MEAs can be adjusted to the context. Therefore, the treaty bodies could avoid calling for such burdensome obligations if a state party is involved in armed conflict with a high level of intense violence. Instead, they could advise the state parties on the types of measures that would be achievable in such situations. In contrast, if the intensity of violence is low, if the fighting is limited to a certain geographical area, or if the hostilities are taking place outside the territory, the state's compliance ability may not be affected at all, even in regard to the positive obligations under the MEAs.

The type of violence determines the amount, as well as the kind, of the material destruction that is caused as a result of the armed conflict. For instance, a war involving conventional bombing of military targets, including factories, electricity plants, weapon storages, and communication systems would often result in the large-scale destruction of buildings, infrastructure and other facilities, causing serious environmental damage with oil spills, toxic leakage from facilities and sewage systems, etc. The attacks could immobilise the state's capacity to take action. Office buildings might be demolished and abandoned, equipment could get broken or stolen, basic services might stop functioning, and the financial means of the state might be invested in military operations and/or humanitarian assistance, rather than engaging in environmental projects to implement environmental treaties. Thus, lack of functional state organs and financial means would have negative impacts on the ability of the state to comply with the MEAs.

Moreover, in a conflict with a low level of violence, presumably a larger number of external actors would be present in the state; for instance, UN organs and other international organisations, non-governmental organisations, companies, etc. As noted in the DRC and in Mali, external actors can be influential in applying MEAs and contributing to environmental protection work, even if the state party is restricted in complying. The MEA treaty bodies can directly cooperate with other actors to launch projects and programmes with the aim of restoring and protecting the environment. This may be of particular interest if the domestic infrastructure has been severely affected by warfare and the state is restricted in its capability to ensure law and order and to provide basic state functions. Thus, the presence of these external actors can affect the ability of MEAs to continue to operate as the cooperative initiatives can reinforce the institutional structure of the state and assist in performing environmental conservation work. For instance, the presence of UN peacekeepers could be influential. There are some precedents showing that UN peacekeepers have taken a role to prevent and minimise environmental damage. For instance, in 1992 in the former Yugoslavia, the Peruca dam was at risk of attack, which could have led to major destruction downstream. The commander of the UN Protection Force (UNPROFOR) took action to protect the dam. Subsequently, in Resolution 779 (1992), the UN Security Council stated that 'it approves the report of the Secretary General including the steps taken to ensure the control of the Peruca dam by UNPROFOR'.[40] As noted by Roberts, 'This ex post facto mandate illustrates the way in which environmental issues have entered into the work of peacekeeping forces in practice, in advance of formal legal provision for them'.[41] Although UN peacekeepers do not act to directly invoke MEAs, there is an interest in preserving the environment as a measure to protect civilians as well as to maintain the stability of the region, which is evidenced also in the DRC. Therefore, there are opportunities to engage UN peacekeepers in

[40] UN Security Council Resolution, UN Doc S/RES/779, 6 October 1992.

[41] A Roberts, 'The Law of War and Environmental Damage' in JE Austin and CE Bruch (eds), *The Environmental Consequences of War* (Cambridge University Press, 2000) 85.

environmental-related operations, in particular, because there are links between environmental protection and security.

Furthermore, the organisation of the parties involved in armed conflict plays a role in how the operation of MEAs can contribute to environmental protection. Two states that are involved in a conflict and that are also parties to MEAs have international obligations under these MEAs, while non-state actors are not directly obligated under international law to respect the MEAs. In a non-international armed conflict, it might be more challenging to engage non-state actors (armed groups) to fulfil environmental obligations. The armed groups would probably lack the incentive to comply with MEAs. Nevertheless, the MEAs may directly involve non-state actors to invoke environmental protection. In the case of the DRC, efforts were directly aimed at the rebel groups. They were invited to meetings and diplomatic missions were carried out in rebel controlled areas to promote the application of the World Heritage Convention.

Armed groups that have a high level of organisation, including a clear command structure and internal disciplinary system, would be better equipped to fulfil environmental obligations than a smaller less top-controlled armed group. Thus, the parties to the armed conflict that have a certain level of organisation, status and a reputation to care about would most likely be easier to influence to comply with environmental commitments. A plausible reason for why the armed groups in the DRC agreed to some of the measures proposed by the WH Committee is that these groups had the ambition to seize governmental power. The destruction of the world heritage sites would give them an unfavourable international reputation, which may have contributed to the fact that they were willing to comply with some of the decisions and recommendations stemming from the World Heritage Convention. Thus, the organisation and the motives of the armed groups are factors contributing to how the MEAs can operate.

In addition, the operation of the MEAs depends on the type of environmental damage that is caused during the armed conflict. The fact that the Congolese conflicts jeopardised the gorillas, being a flagship species loaded with regional pride and an international symbol for endangered species, may have contributed to mobilising the attention of the actors in the international arena and attracting funding. In addition, the gorillas represent economic value as a tourist attraction, therefore, the rebel groups could financially profit by protecting the gorillas by arranging tourist excursions. Hence, both international attention and economic motives may have facilitated the agreement with the rebels to allow park rangers to protect the habitat of the gorillas and thereby the world heritage sites (although for the same motive, some of the rebel groups directly attacked the gorillas to deprive the world heritage sites of their value and reason to be protected).

Conclusion 5:
Factors related to both the nature of the MEA and the characteristics of the armed conflict determine how MEAs can operate to enhance wartime environmental protection. These factors interact and must be studied on a case-by-case basis.

VI. THE WAY FORWARD

In this closing section, I will outline the contribution of the research to international scholarship and provide some suggestions on the future use of MEAs in relation to armed conflict.

The main contribution of my book is that I have not only shown that MEAs *can* operate both during and in the aftermath of armed conflict, but I have also exemplified *how* they can operate to enhance environmental protection. The case studies of the DRC and Mali can be used as a starting point that examines concrete cases on how environmental damage has been addressed under MEAs in relation to armed conflict. It provides new knowledge on the operation of MEAs that takes into account all the measures that have been conducted under the broader treaty system and international institutional structure that may not be deduced simply from a reading of the treaty text on its own. For instance, I have shown how the park rangers have received salaries, equipment and training to perform their work to protect the world heritage sites in the DRC; that the park rangers and the world heritage sites have been pledged to have neutral status; how cooperation has been initiated with the UN peacekeeping mission and the UNCHR to safeguard the sites; and how substantial funding has been awarded to manage the sites in both Mali and the DRC.

Environmental treaties are frequently applied using innovative strategies that reinforce the state parties' capacity to comply with the treaties and improve their environmental protection at times when a state party may be incapable of protecting the environment. As long as the state party is willing to comply, the treaty bodies can initiate projects and programmes to train state officials and provide equipment and funds, as well as other forms of assistance. By using a reconciliatory approach, the MEAs can minimise the discretionary power of the law-applier in its application of the law of armed conflict. A simultaneous application of environmental treaties and the law of armed conflict can augment environmental protection by adding to the protection of certain components covered by environmental treaties, such as world heritage sites, wetlands, endangered species and watercourses. In relation to these components, the belligerents could be forced to take reasonable steps to avoid or minimise environmental damage, guided by the treaty bodies in accordance with the MEAs.

Consequently, such a reading would prevent the law-applier from getting carte blanche to destroy unique biodiversity and endangered species that are protected under international law under the pretext that such actions are lawful under the rules of the law of armed conflict.

There may however still be room for some discretionary power for the law-applier, because MEAs also provide for such power in their application. Yet, the treaty bodies can limit the power by advising the law-applier in their decisions or recommendations that often consider other interests in order to ensure acceptance by the state party. In addition, the MEAs can provide alternative protection measures, which can be influential in maintaining some environmental protection work despite the general collapse of institutions that occurs in many of the war-torn states. The inventive strategies that are enabled under the MEAs can therefore strengthen the protection of the environment during armed conflicts at an institutional level to accompany the normative one.

My suggestion is that the actors under the international legal system should make more use of the existing mechanisms of the MEAs to address wartime environmental damage. States, international organisations, non-governmental organisations and private actors should encourage the treaty bodies of the MEAs to take an active role in relation to armed conflict. Besides their potential to inform the application of the law of armed conflict, I argue that the MEAs could contribute in the context of armed conflict to reinforce fragile and institutionally weak state parties that are struggling but are still willing to meet their environmental obligations. Consequently, the role of MEAs has the potential to complement environmental protection by offering practical and concrete measures, not only in peacetime, but also during armed conflicts and in the blurred phase between peace and armed conflict without separating these phases.

In addition, environmental treaty bodies can play a meaningful role by engaging in conservation diplomacy. They could be a starting point to initiate diplomatic discussions between the parties to an armed conflict. UNESCO/WH Committee's conservation diplomacy has had a prominent role as a mediator during the conflicts in the DRC to protect the world heritage sites. Other treaty bodies of MEAs could conduct comparable conservation diplomacy in relation to armed conflict. This could be particularly relevant in a transboundary conflict between two states. Conservation diplomacy has the advantage that the treaty bodies, with their scientific competence, can focus on conservation issues related to the transboundary environment, such as how to protect an international river or migrating endangered species, which both parties have an interest in.

As an example, the Ramsar List includes many areas that are shared between two state parties. Its treaty bodies could act as mediators in cases where a transboundary Ramsar site is involved in hostilities. Griffin explains it as:

> Environmental scientists as diplomatic actors may be able to shift dialogue to gathering data and developing a consensual knowledge base about a shared resource.

> Such work also builds capacity, especially when assisted by the myriad tools and resources of conventions like Ramsar and others.[42]

Given that diplomacy can focus on environmental concerns, it could make the parties to an armed conflict start negotiating and at the same time provide for environmental protection. Conservation diplomacy could have a stabilising effect because the treaty bodies of the MEAs can offer a neutral platform for dialogue – not focusing on solving the issues underlying the conflict, but discussing environmental protection. As the treaty bodies are also in place in peacetime, conservation diplomacy may also be invoked to avoid the outbreak of an armed conflict, because many conflicts concern transboundary environmental issues.

To sum up, MEAs have the potential to address some aspects of wartime environmental damage by complementing the law of armed conflict. They can adjust to the prevailing circumstances and adopt context-based measures. This may introduce an element of vagueness, but it is necessary in order to be able to adjust to the issues they are facing. Armed conflicts, as well as environmental problems, are always different, so there cannot be a 'one size fits' all answer. Thus, it is difficult to assess the MEAs' role on a general level, because they need to be studied in a concrete context where the activities of the treaty bodies, the cooperative initiatives between stakeholders, and the compliance measures can be taken into account to evaluate the function of an MEA. Several case studies are needed to provide a more conclusive analysis of how MEAs operate in armed conflict. Hence, further research is called for to fully assess the patchwork of MEAs in the context of coping with wartime damage to the environment. My contribution has shown that MEAs have a place to fill in relation to armed conflict, because they do have the potential to operate and enhance environmental protection in such situations. By providing both practical and theoretically constructed examples, this thesis has narrowed the existing knowledge gap on how environmental treaties can be applied in relation to armed conflict.

[42] Griffin (n 27).

Bibliography

Books

Alchourrón, CE and Bulygin, E, *Normative Systems* (Springer, 1971).

Beyerlin, U and Marauhn, T, *International Environmental Law* (Hart Publishing, 2011).

Birnie, P, Boyle, A and Redgwell, C, *International Law & the Environment* (Oxford University Press, 2009).

Bodansky, D, *The Art and Craft of International Environmental Law* (Harvard University Press, 2010).

Bothe, M, Partsch, KJ and Solf, W, *New Rules for Victims of Armed Conflicts: Commentary on the Two 1977 Protocols Additional to the Geneva Conventions of 1949* (Nijhoff, 1982).

Brownlie, I, *Principles of Public International Law*, 7th edn (Oxford University Press, 2008).

Carty, A, *Philosophy of International Law* (Edinburgh University Press, 2007).

Cdr, W and Jha, UC, *Armed Conflict and Environmental Damage* (Vij Books, India, 2014).

Dam-de Jong, DA, *International Law and Governance of Natural Resources in Conflict and Post-Conflict Situations* (EM Meijers Instituut, 2013).

Das, O, *Environmental Protection, Security and Armed Conflict* (Edward Elgar Publishing, 2013).

Desai, B, *Multilateral Environmental Agreements: Legal Status of the Secretariats* (Cambridge University Press, 2010).

Dinstein, Y, *The Conduct of Hostilities Under the Law of International Armed Conflict*, 3rd edn (Cambridge University Press, 2016).

Doswald-Beck, L, *1994 San Remo Manual on International Law Applicable to Armed Conflicts at Sea, Prepared by International Lawyers and Naval Experts at the International Institute for Humanitarian Law* (Cambridge University Press, 1995).

Dryzek, J, *The Politics of the Earth: Environmental Discourses* (Oxford University Press, 2005).

Dupuy, P-M and Viñuales, JE, *International Environmental Law*, 2nd edn (Cambridge University Press, 2018).

Frank, V, *The European Community and the Marine Environmental Protection in the International Law of the Sea: Implementing Global Obligations on a Regional Level* (Nijhoff, 2007).

Freeland, S, *Addressing the Intentional Destruction of the Environment During Warfare Under the Rome Statute of the International Criminal Court* (Intersentia, 2015).

Gardiner, R, *Treaty Interpretation* (Oxford University Press, 2008).

Gillespie, A, *Protected Areas and International Environmental Law* (Martinus Nijhoff Publishers, 2007).

Glasbergen, P (ed), *Co-operative Environmental Governance: Public–Private Agreements as a Policy Strategy* (Kluwer Academics, 1998).

Henckaerts, J-M and Doswald-Beck, L (eds), *Customary International Humanitarian Law Study*, Volume I: Rules (Cambridge University Press, 2005).

—— *Customary International Humanitarian Law Study*, Volume II: Practice (Cambridge University Press, 2012).

Hermerén, G, *God forskningssed* (Vetenskapsrådet, 2011).

Hulme, K, *War Torn Environment: Interpreting the Legal Threshold* (Nijhoff, 2004).

Koivurova, T, *Introduction to International Environmental Law* (Routledge, 2014).

Koppe, EV, *The Use of Nuclear Weapons and the Protection of the Environment During International Armed Conflict* (Gildeprint, 2006).

Kotzé, LJ, *Global Environmental Governance: Law and Regulation for the 21st Century* (Edward Elgar Publishing, 2012).
Krisch, N, *Beyond Constitutionalism: The Pluralist Structure of Postnational Law* (Oxford University Press, 2010).
Linderfalk, U, *On the Interpretation of Treaties* (Springer, 2007).
Louka, E, *International Environmental Law: Fairness, Effectiveness, and World Order* (Cambridge University Press, 2006).
Matz, N and Wolfrum, R, *Conflicts in International Environmental Law* (Springer, 2003).
Pauwelyn, J, *Conflict of Norms in Public International Law: How WTO Law Relates to Other Rules of International Law* (Cambridge University Press, 2009).
Pictet, J, *Commentary (I) Geneva Convention for the Amelioration of the Condition of the Wounded and Sick in Armed Forces in the Field* (ICRC, Geneva, 1952).
Plant, G, *Environmental Protection and the Law of War: A 'Fifth Geneva' Convention on the Protection of the Environment in Time of Armed Conflict* (Belhaven Press, 1992).
Prost, M, *The Concept of Unity in Public International Law* (Hart Publishing, 2012).
Sadat-Akhavi, SA, *Methods of Resolving Conflicts Between Treaties* (Brill Academic Publishers, 2003).
Sandoz, Y, Swinarski, C and Zimmerman B (eds), *Commentary on the Additional Protocols of 8 June 1977* (ICRC, Geneva, 1987).
Sands, P et al, *Principles of International Environmental Law*, 4th edn (Cambridge University Press, 2018).
Schuler, C, *Leben und Überleben im Kongo, Gorillaschutz und Familienleben im Krieg* (BfT Verlag, 2013).
Smith, JE, *Weather Warfare: The Military's Plan to Draft Mother Nature* (Adventure Unlimited Press, Kempton, US, 2006).
Trouwborst, A, *Evolution and Status of the Precautionary Principle in International Law* (Kluwer Law International, 2002).
von Schorlemer, S, *Compliance with the UNESCO World Heritage Convention: Reflections on the Elbe Valley and the Dresden Waldschlösschen Bridge* (Duncker & Humblot, 2009).
Westing, A, *Pioneer on the Environmental Impact of War* (Springer, 2013).
Wilunga Balongelwa, C, *Patrimoine Naturel et Conflicts Armés* (Harmattan, 2013).
Yin, RK, *Application of Case Study Research*, 2nd edn (Sage Publications, 2003).
—— *Case Study Method: Design and Methods*, 5th edn (Sage Publications, 2014).

Journal Articles and Chapters

Adede, AO, 'Protection of the Environment in Times of Armed Conflict: Reflections on the Existing and Future Treaty Law' (1994) 1 *Annual Survey of International and Comparative Law* 161.
Akande, D, 'Classification of Armed Conflicts: Relevant Legal Concepts' in E Wilmshurst (ed), *International Law and the Classification of Conflicts* (Oxford University Press, 2012).
Allukian, M and Atwood, P, 'Public Health and the Vietnam War' in BS Levy and VW Sidel (eds), *War and Public Health* (Oxford University Press, 1997).
Almond, HH, 'Weapons, War and the Environment' (1990) 3 *Georgetown International Environmental Law Review* 117.
Andonova, LB, 'Public–Private Partnerships for the Earth: Politics and Patterns of Hybrid Authority in the Multilateral System' (2010) 10 *Global Environmental Politics* 25.
Andresen, S, Lerum Boasson, E and Honneland, G, 'An International Environmental Policy Takes Shape' in S Andresen, E Lerum Boasson and G Honneland (eds), *International Environmental Agreements, An Introduction* (Routledge, 2013).
Andresen, S and Skjaerteth, JB, 'Science and Technology: From Agenda Setting to Implementation' in D Bodansky, J Brunnée and E Hey (eds), *Oxford Handbook of International Environmental Law* (Oxford University Press, 2007).

Arato, A, 'Subsequent Practice and Evaluative Interpretation: Techniques of Treaty Interpretation Over Time and their Diverse Consequences' (2010) 9 *The Law and Practice of International Courts and Tribunals* 443.

Arimatsu, A, 'The Democratic Republic of the Congo 1993–2010' in E Wilmshurst (ed), *International Law and the Classification of Conflicts* (Oxford University Press, 2012).

Austin, JE and Bruch, CE, 'Existing and Emerging Wartime Standards, Introduction' in JE Austin and CE Bruch (eds), *The Environmental Consequences of War* (Cambridge University Press, 2000).

—— 'Legal Mechanisms for Addressing Wartime Damage to Tropical Forests' (2003) 16 *Journal of Sustainable Forestry* 161.

Baker, B, 'Legal Protections for the Environment in Times of Armed Conflict' (1993) 33 *Virginia Journal of International Law* 351.

Bannelier-Christakis, K, 'International Law Commission and Protection of the Environment in Times of Armed Conflict: A Possibility for Adjudication?' (2013) 20 *Journal of International Cooperation Studies* 129.

Ben-Naftali, O and Shany, Y, 'Living in Denial: The Application of Human Rights in the Occupied Territories' (2003) 17 *Israel Law Review* 17.

Bethlehem, D, 'The Methodological Framework of the Study' in E Wilmshurst and S Breau (eds), *Perspectives on the ICRC Study on Customary International Humanitarian Law* (Cambridge University Press, 2007).

Beyerlin, U, 'Different Types of Norms in International Environmental Law Policies, Principles and Rules' in D Bodansky, J Brunnée and E Hey (eds), *Oxford Handbook of International Environmental Law* (Oxford University Press, 2007).

Bodansky, D, Brunnée, J and Hey, E, 'International Environmental Law: Mapping the Field' in D Bodansky, J Brunnée and E Hey (eds), *Oxford Handbook of International Environmental Law* (Oxford University Press, 2007).

Boisson de Chazournes, L, 'Features and Trends in International Environmental Law' in Y Kerbrat and S Maljean-Dubois (eds), *The Transformation of International Environmental Law* (Hart Publishing and Editions A Pedone, 2011).

Bothe, M, 'The Protection of the Environment in Times of Armed Conflict: Legal Rules, Uncertainty, Deficiencies and Possible Developments' (1991) 34 *German Yearbook of International Law* 54.

—— 'Customary International Humanitarian Law: Some Reflections on the ICRC Study' (2005) 8 *Yearbook of International Humanitarian Law* 143.

—— 'The Ethics, Principles and Objectives of Protection of the Environment in Times of Armed Conflict' in R Rayfuse (ed), *War and the Environment: New Approaches to Protecting the Environment in Relation to Armed Conflict* (Brill Nijhoff, 2014).

Bothe, M et al, 'International Law Protecting the Environment During Armed Conflict: Gaps and Opportunities' (2010) 92 *International Review of the Red Cross* 569.

Bouvier, A, 'Protection of the Natural Environment in Time of an Armed Conflict' (1991) 31 *International Review of the Red Cross* 438.

Boyle, A, 'Environmental Damage in International Law' in M Bowman and A Boyle (eds), *Environmental Damage in International and Comparative Law* (Oxford University Press, 2002).

—— 'Relationship between International Environmental Law and Other Branches of International Law' in D Bodansky, J Brunnée and E Hey (eds), *Oxford Handbook of International Environmental Law* (Oxford University Press, 2007).

Bruch, CE, 'All's Not Fair in (Civil) War: Criminal Liability for Environmental Damage in Internal Armed Conflict' (2000) 25 *Vermont Law Review* 695.

Bruch, CE et al, 'Post-conflict Peace Building and Natural Resources' (2009) 19 *Yearbook of International Environmental Law* 58.

Brunnée, J, 'Enforcement Mechanisms in International Law and International Environmental Law' in U Beyerlin, PT Stoll and R Wolfrum (eds), *Ensuring Compliance with Multilateral Environmental Agreements: A Dialogue Between Practitioners and Academia* (Martinus Nijhoff, 2006).

—— 'Common Areas, Common Heritage, and Common Concern' in D Bodansky, J Brunnée and E Hey (eds), *Oxford Handbook of International Environmental Law* (Oxford University Press, 2007).

Bunker, A-L, 'Protection of the Environment During Armed Conflict: One Gulf, Two Wars' (2004) 13 *Review of European, Comparative & International Environmental Law* 201.

Burger, J, 'Environmental Aspects of Non-International Conflicts: The Experience in Former Yugoslavia' in R Grunawalt, J King and R McClain, R (eds), *Protection of the Environment During Armed Conflict* (1996) 69 *International Law Studies* 333.

Burhenne, W, 'The Prohibition of Hostile Military Activities in Protected Areas' (1997) 27 *Environmental Policy and Law* 373.

Buzzini, GP and Condorelli, L, 'Article 11, List of World Heritage in Danger and Deletion of a Property From the World Heritage List' in F Francioni (ed), *The 1972 World Heritage Convention: A Commentary* (Oxford University Press, 2008).

Carducci, G, 'Articles 4–7, National and International Protection of Cultural and Natural Heritage' in F Francioni (ed), *The 1972 World Heritage Convention: A Commentary* (Oxford University Press, 2008).

Cassese, A, 'The Martens Clause: Half a Loaf or Simply Pie in the Sky?' (2000) 11 *European Journal of International Law* 187.

Cerer, M, 'The Relationship Between Law and Politics' (2009) 15 *Annual Survey of International & Comparative Law* 19.

Chinkin, C, 'Normative Development in the International Legal System' in D Shelton (ed), *Commitment and Compliance: The Role of Non-Binding Norms in the International Legal System* (Oxford University Press 2000).

Churchill, R and Ulfstein, G, 'Autonomous Institutional Arrangements in Multilateral Environmental Agreements: A Little-Noticed Phenomenon in International Law' (2000) 94 *American Journal of International Law* 623.

Cohan, JA, 'Modes of Warfare and Evolving Standards of Environmental Protection Under the International Law of War' (2003) 15 *Florida Journal of International Law* 481.

D'Aspremont, J and Tranchez, E, 'The Quest for a Non-Conflictual Coexistence of International Human Rights Law and Humanitarian Law: Which Role for the *Lex Specialis* Principle?' in R Kolb and G Gaggioli (eds), *Research Handbook on Human Rights and Humanitarian Law* (Edward Elgar Publishing, 2013).

Dam-de Jong, D, 'International Law and Resource Plunder: The Protection of Natural Resources During Armed Conflict' (2009) 19 *Yearbook of International Environmental Law* 27.

de Brabandere, E, 'The Concept of *Jus Post Bellum* in International Law, A Normative Critique' in C Stahn, JS Easterday and J Iverson (eds), *Jus Post Bellum: Mapping the Normative Foundations* (Oxford University Press, 2014).

de Wet, E, 'The International Constitutional Order' (2006) 55 *International & Comparative Law Quarterly* 51.

Deiderich, MD, 'Law of War and Ecology – A Proposal for a Workable Approach to Protecting the Environment Through the Law of War' (1992) 136 *Military Law Review* 137.

Desgagné, R, 'The Prevention of Environmental Damage in Time of Armed Conflict: Proportionality and Precautionary Measures' (2000) 3 *Yearbook of International Humanitarian Law* 109.

Dienelt, A, '"After War is Before the War" – The Environment, Preventative Measures Under International Humanitarian Law, and their Post-Conflict Impact' in C Stahn, J Iverson and JE Easterday (eds), *Environmental Protection and Transitions from Conflict to Peace* (Oxford University Press, 2017).

Dinstein, Y, 'Protection of the Environment in International Armed Conflict' (2001) 5 *Max Plank Yearbook of United Nations Law* 523.

Droege, C, 'The Interplay Between International Humanitarian Law and International Human Rights Law in Situations of Armed Conflict' (2007) 40 *Israeli Law Review* 310.

Droege, C and Tougas, M-L, 'The Protection of the Natural Environment in Armed Conflict – Existing Rules and Need for Further Legal Protection' (2013) 82 *Nordic Journal of International Law* 21.

Dunoff, JL, 'Levels of Environmental Governance' in D Bodansky, J Brunnée and E Hey (eds), *Oxford Handbook of International Environmental Law* (Oxford University Press, 2007).

—— 'A New Approach to Regime Interaction' in M Young (ed), *Regime Interaction in International Law: Facing Fragmentation* (Cambridge University Press, 2012).

Dupuy, P-M, 'A Doctrinal Debate in the Globalisation Era: On the "Fragmentation" of International Law' (2007) 1 *European Journal of Legal Studies* 1.

—— 'Formation of Customary International Law and General Principles' in D Bodansky, J Brunnée and E Hey (eds), *Oxford Handbook of International Environmental Law* (Oxford University Press, 2007).

Eden, P and Happold, M, 'Symposium: The Relationship between International Humanitarian Law and International Human Rights Law' (2010) 14 *Journal of Conflict & Security Law* 1.

Emerson, S, 'When Earth Takes the Hit' (1991) 21 *International Wildlife* 38.

Falk, R, 'The Environmental Law of War: An Introduction' in G Plant (ed), *Environmental Protection and the Law of War: A 'Fifth Geneva' Convention on the Protection of the Environment in Time of Armed Conflict* (Belhaven Press, 1992).

—— 'Evaluating the Adequacy of Existing International Law Standards' in JE Austin and CE Bruch (eds), *The Environmental Consequences of War* (Cambridge University Press, 2000).

Fischer-Lescano, A and Teubner, G, 'Regime-Collisions: The Vain Search for Legal Unity in the Fragmentation of Global Law' (2004) 25 *Michigan Journal of International Law* 999.

Fitzmaurice, G, 'The Law and Procedure of the International Court of Justice 1951–1954: Treaty Interpretation and Other Treaty Points' (1957) 33 *British Yearbook of International Law* 203.

Fleck, D, 'The Protection of the Environment in Armed Conflict: Legal Obligations in the Absence of Specific Rules' (2013) 82 *Nordic Journal of International Law* 7.

—— '*Jus Post Bellum* as Partly Independent Legal Framework' in C Stahn, JE Easterday and J Iverson (eds), *Jus Post Bellum: Mapping the Normative Foundations* (Oxford University Press, 2014).

Flyvbjerg, B, 'Five Misunderstandings About Case-Study Research' (2006) 12 *Qualitative Inquiry* 219.

Forrest, C, 'The Doctrine of Military Necessity and the Protection of Cultural Property During Armed Conflicts' (2007) 37 *California Western International Law Journal* 177.

Francioni, F and Lenzerini, F, 'The Destruction of the Buddhas of Bamiyan and International Law' (2003) 14 *European Journal of International Law* 619.

Frumkin, H, 'Agent Orange and Cancer: An Overview for Clinicians' (2003) 53 *A Cancer Journal for Clinicians* 245.

Ghérari, H, 'The Adaptation of International Economic Law to Environmental Issues: Regional Trade Agreements and Environmental Protection' in Y Kerbrat and S Maljean-Dubois (eds), *The Transformation of International Environmental Law* (Hart Publishing and Editions A Pedone, 2011).

Goeteyn, N and Maes, F, 'Compliance Mechanisms in Multilateral Environmental Agreements: An Effective Way to Improve Compliance?' (2011) 10 *Chinese Journal of International Law* 791.

Goodwin, E, 'The World Heritage Convention, the Environment, and Compliance' (2009) 20 *Colorado Journal of International Environmental Law and Policy* 157.

Green, LC, 'The Environment and the Law of Conventional Warfare' (1991) 29 *Canadian Yearbook of International Law* 222.

Greenwood, C, 'Historical Development and Legal Basis' in D Fleck (ed), *The Handbook of International Humanitarian Law* (Oxford University Press, 2008).

—— 'Scope of Application of Humanitarian Law' in D Fleck (ed), *The Handbook of International Humanitarian Law* (Oxford University Press, 2008).

Hafner, G, 'Pros and Cons Ensuing from Fragmentation of International Law' (2004) 25 *Michigan Journal of International Law* 849.

Haines, S, 'The Nature of War and the Character of Contemporary Armed Conflict' in E Wilmshurst (ed), *International Law and the Classification of Conflicts* (Oxford University Press, 2012).

Hampson, F, 'Other Areas of Customary Law in Relation to the Study' in E Wilmshurst and S Breau (eds), *Perspectives on the ICRC Study on Customary International Humanitarian Law* (Cambridge University Press, 2007).

Hanqin, X, 'Fragmented Law or Fragmented Order? (2006) 17 *Finnish Yearbook of International Law* 55.

Henckaerts, J-M, 'International Legal Mechanisms for Determining Liability for Environmental Damage Under International Humanitarian Law' in JE Austin and CE Bruch (eds), *The Environmental Consequences of War* (Cambridge University Press, 2000).

Henckaerts, J-M and Constantin, D, 'Protection of the Environment' in A Clapham and P Gaeta (eds), *The Oxford Handbook of International Law in Armed Conflict* (Oxford University Press, 2014).

Holthuijzen, WA and Maximillian, JR, 'Dry, Hot, and Brutal: Climate Change and Desertification in the Sahel of Mali' (2011) 13 *Journal of Sustainable Development in Africa*, available at: www.jsd-africa.com/Jsda/Vol13No7-Winter2011A/PDF/Dry%20Hot%20and%20Brutal.Wieteke%20Holthuijzen.pdf.

Huang, LY, 'Israel–Lebanese Conflict: A Case Study for Protection of the Environment in Times of Armed Conflict' (2006) 20 *Florida Journal of International Law* 103.

Hulme, K, 'Natural Environment' in E Wilmshurst and S Breau (eds), *Perspectives on the ICRC Study on Customary International Humanitarian Law* (Cambridge University Press 2007).

—— 'Taking Care to Protect the Environment Against Damage: A Meaningless Obligation?' (2010) 92 *International Review of the Red Cross* 675.

—— 'Armed Conflict and Biodiversity' in M Bowman, P Davies and E Goodwin (eds), *Research Handbook on Biodiversity and Law* (Edward Elgar Publishing, 2016).

Hunay, E, 'Black Rain in Turkey: Possible Environmental Effects of the Gulf War' (1992) 26 *Environmental Science & Technology* 873.

Jacoby, J, 'Introduction' in JE Austin and CE Bruch (eds), *The Environmental Consequences of War* (Cambridge University Press, 2000).

Jenks, W, 'The Conflict of Law-making Treaties' (1953) 30 *British Yearbook of International Law* 401.

Kampto, M, 'Normative Uncertainties' in Y Kerbrat and S Maljean-Dubois (eds), *The Transformation of International Environmental Law* (Hart Publishing and Editions A Pedone, 2011).

Kellman, B, 'The Chemical Weapons Convention: A Verification and Enforcement Model for Determining Legal Responsibility for Environmental Harm Caused by War' in JE Austin and CE Bruch (eds), *The Environmental Consequences of War* (Cambridge University Press, 2000).

Klabbers, J, 'The Redundancy of Soft Law' (1996) 65 *Nordic Journal of International Law* 167.

Koppe, E, 'The Protection of the Environment During International Armed Conflict' in W van Genugten et al (eds), *Criminal Jurisdiction 100 Years After the 1907 Hague Peace Conference* (TMC Asser Press, 2009).

—— 'The Principle of Ambiguity and the Prohibition against Excessive Collateral Damage to the Environment during Armed Conflict' in R Rayfuse (ed), *War and the Environment: New Approaches to Protecting the Environment in Relation to Armed Conflict* (Brill Nijhoff, 2014).

Koskenniemi, M, 'The Fate of Public International Law: Between Technique and Politics' (2007) 70 *Modern Law Review* 1.

Koskenniemi, M and Leino P, 'Fragmentation of International Law? Postmodern Anxieties' (2002) 15 *Leiden Journal of International Law* 553.

Leaning, J, 'War and the Environment: Human Health Consequences of Environmental Damage of War' (1993) *Critical Condition: Human Health and the Environment* 123.

—— 'Tracking the Four Horsemen: The Public Health to Approach the Impact of War and War-Induced Environmental Destruction in the Twentieth Century' in JE Austin and CE Bruch (eds), *The Environmental Consequences of War* (Cambridge University Press, 2000).

Lecocq, B and Klute, G, 'Tuareg Separatism in Mali' (2013) 68 *International Journal* 424.

Leibler, A, 'Deliberate Wartime Environmental Damage' (1992) 23 *California Western International Law Journal* 67.

Lemaistre, A and Lenzerini, F, 'Articles 19–26, International Assistance' in F Francioni (ed), *The 1972 World Heritage Convention: A Commentary* (Oxford University Press, 2008).

Linderfalk, U, 'Who Are "The Parties"? Article 31, Paragraph 3(c) of the 1969 Vienna Conventions and the Principle of Systemic Integration Revised' (2008) 55 *Netherlands International Law Review* 343.

Lindroos, A, 'Addressing Norm Conflicts in a Fragmented Legal System: The Doctrine of *Lex Specialis*' (2005) 74 *Nordic Journal of International Law* 27.

Lixinski, L, 'Treaty Interpretation by the Inter-American Court of Human Rights: Expansionism at the Service of the Unity of International Law' (2010) 21 *European Journal of International Law* 585.

—— 'Environment and War: Lessons From International Cultural Heritage Law' in R Rayfuse (ed), *War and the Environment: New Approaches to Protecting the Environment in Relation to Armed Conflict* (Brill Nijhoff, 2014).

Loets, A, 'An Old Debate Revisited: Applicability of Environmental Treaties in Times of International Armed Conflict Pursuant to the International Law Commission's "Draft Articles on the Effects of Armed Conflict on Treaties"' (2012) 21 *Review of European, Comparative & International Environmental Law* 127.

Low, L and Hodgkinson, D, 'Compensation for Wartime Environmental Damage: Challenges to International Law After the Gulf War' (1994) 35 *Virginia Journal of International Law* 405.

Maljean-Dubois, S, 'The Making of International Law Challenging Environmental Protection' in Y Kerbrat and S Maljean-Dubois (eds), *The Transformation of International Environmental Law* (Hart Publishing and Editions A Pedone, 2011).

Mann-Borgese, E, 'The Protection of the Marine Environment in the Case of War', The Future of the International Law of the Environment, Workshop (1984).

Marsh, J, '*Lex Lata* or *Lex Ferenda*? Rule 45 of the ICRC Study on Customary International Humanitarian Law' (2008) 198 *Military Law Review* 116.

Marauhn, T, 'Environmental Damage in Times of Armed Conflict – Not "Really" a Matter of Criminal Responsibility?' (2000) 82 *International Review of the Red Cross* 1029.

Matz-Lück, N, 'Harmonization, Systemic Integration, and Conflict-Solution Techniques' (2006) 17 *Finnish Yearbook of International Law* 39.

—— 'Norm Interpretation Across International Regimes: Competences and Legitimacy' in M Young (ed), *Regime Interaction in International Law: Facing Fragmentation* (Cambridge University Press, 2012).

McLachlan, C, 'The Principle of Systemic Integration and Article 31(3)(c) of the Vienna Convention' (2005) 54 *International & Comparative Law Quarterly* 279.

McNeeley, JA, 'War and Biodiversity: An Assessment of Impacts' in JE Austin and CE Bruch (eds), *The Environmental Consequences of War* (Cambridge University Press 2000).

Melzer, N, 'Interpretive Guidance on the Notion of Direct Participation in Hostilities Under International Humanitarian Law, Adopted by the Assembly of the International Committee of the Red Cross on 26 February 2009' (2008) 90 *International Review of the Red Cross* 991.

Meron, T, 'The Martens Clause, Principles of Humanity, and Dictates of Public Conscience' (2000) 94 *American Journal of International Law* 78.

Milanovic, M, 'The Lost Origins of *Lex Specialis*: Rethinking the Relationship Between Human Rights and International Humanitarian Law' in JD Ohlin (ed), *Theoretical Boundaries of Armed Conflict and Human Rights* (Cambridge University Press, 2016).

Mus, JB, 'Conflicts Between Treaties in International Law' (1998) 45 *Netherlands International Law Review* 208.

Ngo, A et al, 'Association Between Agent Orange and Birth Defects: Systematic Review and Meta-analysis' (2006) 35 *International Journal of Epidemiology* 1220.

Ngo, AD, Taylor, R and Roberts, C, 'Paternal Exposure to Agent Orange and Spina Bifida: A Meta-analysis' (2010) 25 *European Journal of Epidemiology* 37.

O'Donoghue, A, 'Splendid Isolation: International Humanitarian Law, Legal Theory and the International Legal Order' (2011) 14 *Yearbook of International Humanitarian Law* 107.

Oglete, J, Shambaugh, J and Kormos, R, 'Parks in the Crossfire: Strategies for Effective Conservation in Areas of Armed Conflict' War and Protected Areas (2004) 14 *International Journal for Protected Areas Managers*, available at: cmsdata.iucn.org/downloads/14_1.pdf.

Okowa, P, 'Sovereignty Contests and the Protection of Natural Resources in Conflict Zones' (2013) 66 *Current Legal Problems* 33.

Omar, SAS et al, 'The Gulf War Impact on the Terrestrial Environment of Kuwait: An Overview' in JE Austin and CE Bruch (eds), *The Environmental Consequences of War* (Cambridge University Press, 2000).

Orakhelashvili, A, 'The Interaction Between Human Rights and Humanitarian Law: Fragmentation, Conflict, Parallelism, or Convergence?' (2008) 19 *European Journal of International Law* 161.

Orellana, M, 'Criminal Punishment for Environmental Damage: Individual and State Responsibility at a Crossroad' (2005) 17 *Georgetown International Environmental Law Review* 673.

Pantazopoulos, S-E, 'Protection of the Environment during Armed Conflicts: An Appraisal of the ILC's Work' (2016) 43 *Questions of International Law* 7.

Parson, RJ, 'Fight to Save the Planet: US Armed Forces, Greenkeeping, and Enforcement of the Law Pertaining to Environmental Protection During Armed Conflict' (1997) 10 *Georgetown International Environmental Law Review* 441.

Patchett, L, 'Articles 17–18 Activities to Support the World Heritage Fund' in F Francioni (ed), *The 1972 World Heritage Convention: A Commentary* (Oxford University Press, 2008).

Pauwelyn, J, 'Bridging Fragmentation and Unity: International Law as a Universe of Inter-Connected Islands' (2004) 25 *Michigan Journal of International Law* 903.

Payne, C, 'The Norm of Environmental Integrity in Post-Conflict Legal Regimes' in C Stahn, JS Easterday and J Iverson (eds), *Jus Post Bellum: Mapping the Normative Foundations* (Oxford University Press, 2014).

Pavoni, R, 'Mutual Supportiveness as a Principle of Interpretation and Law-making: A Watershed for the "WTO-and-Competing Regimes" Debate?' (2010) 21 *European Journal of International Law* 649.

Plant, G, 'Introduction' in G Plant (ed), *Environmental Protection and the Law of War: A 'Fifth Geneva' Convention on the Protection of the Environment in Time of Armed Conflict* (Belhaven Press, 1992).

Pronto, A, 'The Effect of War on Law – What Happens to their Treaties when States go to War?' (2013) 2 *Cambridge Journal of International and Comparative Law* 227.

Roberts, A, 'Environmental Destruction in the 1991 Gulf War' (1992) 32 *International Review of the Red Cross* 538.

—— 'The Law of War and Environmental Damage' in JE Austin and CE Bruch (eds), *The Environmental Consequences of War* (Cambridge University Press, 2000).

Roch, P and Perrez, FX, 'International Environmental Governance: The Strive Towards a Comprehensive, Coherent, Effective and Efficient International Environmental Regime' (2005) 16 *Colorado Journal of International Environmental Law and Policy* 1.

Sand, PH, 'The Evolution of International Environmental Law' in D Bodansky, J Brunnée and E Hey (eds), *Oxford Handbook of International Environmental Law* (Oxford University Press, 2007).

Sands, P, 'Treaty, Custom and the Cross-fertilization of International Law' (1998) 1 *Yale Human Rights and Development Law Journal* 85.

Schafer, BK, 'The Relationship Between the International Laws of Armed Conflict and Environmental Protection: The Need to Reevaluate what Types of Conduct are Permissible During Hostilities' (1989) 19 *California Western International Law Journal* 287.

Schmitt, M, 'Green War: An Assessment of the Environmental Law of International Armed Conflict' (1997) 22 *Yale Journal of International Law* 1.

—— 'War and the Environment: Fault Lines in the Prescriptive Landscape' in JE Austin and CE Bruch (eds), *The Environmental Consequences of War* (Cambridge University Press, 2000).

—— 'Classification in Future Conflict' in E Wilmshurst (ed), *International Law and the Classification of Conflicts* (Oxford University Press, 2012).

Schwabach, A, 'Environmental Damage Resulting from the NATO Military Action Against Yugoslavia' (2000) 25 *Columbia Journal of Environmental Law* 117.

Scobbie, I, 'The Approach to Customary International Law in the Study' in E Wilmshurst and S Breau (eds), *Perspectives on the ICRC Study on Customary International Humanitarian Law* (Cambridge University Press 2007).

—— 'Principle or Pragmatics? The Relationship between Human Rights Law and the Law of Armed Conflict' (2010) 14 *Journal of Conflict & Security Law* 449.

Scovazzi, T, 'Articles 8–11, World Heritage Committee and World Heritage List' in F Francioni (ed), *The 1972 World Heritage Convention: A Commentary* (Oxford University Press, 2008).

Seacor, JE, 'Environmental Terrorism: Lessons From the Oil Fires of Kuwait' (1994) 10 *American University Journal of International Law and Policy* 481.

Shelton, D, 'Human Rights, Environmental Rights, and the Right to Environment' (1991) 28 *Stanford Journal of International Law* 103.

—— 'Comments on the Normative Challenge of Environmental "Soft Law"' in Y Kerbrat and S Maljean-Dubois (eds), *The Transformation of International Environmental Law* (Hart Publishing and Editions A Pedone, 2011).

Shutkin, WA, 'International Human Rights Law and the Earth: The Protection of Indigenous Peoples and the Environment' (1990) 31 *Virginia Journal of International Law* 479.

Sicilianos, LA, 'The Classification of Obligations and the Multilateral Dimension of the Relations of International Responsibility' (2002) 13 *European Journal of International Law* 1125.

Simonds, S, 'Conventional Warfare and Environmental Protection: A Proposal for International Legal Reform' (1992) 29 *Stanford Journal of International Law* 165.

Sjöstedt, B, 'The Role of Multilateral Environmental Agreements in Armed Conflict: "Green-keeping" in Virunga Park. Applying the UNESCO World Heritage Convention in the Armed Conflict of the Democratic Republic of the Congo' (2013) 82 *Nordic Journal of International Law* 129.

—— 'The Reconciliatory Approach: How Multilateral Environmental Agreements Can Harmonize International Legal Obligations' in A Jakubowski and K Wierczyńska (eds), *The Arguments on Fragmentation and Constitutionalisation: An Inquiry into the Practice of International Law* (Routledge, 2016).

—— 'Protecting the Environment During and After Armed Conflict Through Multilateral Environmental Agreements' in C Stahn, J Iverson and JE Easterday (eds), *Environmental Protection and Transitions from Conflict to Peace* (Oxford University Press, 2017).

Smith, A, 'The CERES Principles: A Voluntary Code for Corporate Environmental Responsibility' (1993) 18 *Yale Journal of International Law* 307.

Stahn, C, '"*Jus ad bellum*", "*jus in bello*" … "*jus post bellum*"? – Rethinking the Conception of the Law of Armed Conflict' (2006) 17 *European Journal of International Law* 921.

Talbot Jensen, E, 'The Intentional Law of Environmental Warfare: Active and Passive Damage During Armed Conflict' (2005) 38 *Vanderbildt Journal of Transnational Law* 145.

Tarasofsky, R, 'Protecting Specifically Important Areas During International Armed Conflict: A Critique of the IUCN Draft Convention on the Prohibition of Hostile Military Activities in Protected Areas' in JE Austin and CE Bruch (eds), *The Environmental Consequences of War* (Cambridge University Press, 2000).

Thirlway, H, 'Reflections on *lex ferenda*' (2001) 32 *Netherlands Yearbook of International Law* 3.

Thomas, C, 'Advancing the Legal Protection of the Environment in Relation to Armed Conflict: Protocol I's Threshold of Impermissible Environmental Damage and Alternatives' (2013) 82 *Nordic Journal of International Law* 83.

Tignino, M, 'The Legal Regime of Natural Resources in Times of Armed Conflict and its Weaknesses' in Y Kerbrat and S Maljean-Dubois (eds), *The Transformation of International Environmental Law* (Hart Publishing and Editions A Pedone, 2011).

Ulfstein, G, 'Treaty Bodies' in D Bodansky, J Brunnée and E Hey (eds), *Oxford Handbook of International Environmental Law* (Oxford University Press, 2007).

van Asselt, H, Sindico, F and Mehling, MA, 'Global Climate Change and the Fragmentation of International Law' (2008) 30 *Law & Policy* 423.

van Damme, I, 'Some Observations About the ILC Study Group Report on the Fragmentation of International Law' (2006) 17 *Finnish Yearbook of International Law* 21.

van den Herik, L and Dam-de Jong, D, 'Revitalizing the Antique War Crime of Pillage: The Potential and Pitfalls of Using International Criminal Law to Address Illegal Resource Exploitation during Armed Conflict' (2011) 22 *Criminal Law Forum* 237.

Verwey, W, 'Protection of the Environment in Times of Armed Conflict: In Search of a New Legal Perspective' (1995) 8 *Leiden Journal of International Law* 7.

von Heinegg, HW and Donner, M, 'New Developments in the Protection of the Natural Environment in Naval Armed Conflicts' (1994) 37 *German Yearbook of International Law* 281.

Vrdoljak, AF, 'Article 14, the Secretariat and Support of the World Heritage Committee' in F Francioni (ed), *The 1972 World Heritage Convention: A Commentary* (Oxford University Press, 2008).

Vranes, E, 'The Definition of "Norm Conflict" in International Law and Legal Theory' (2006) 17 *European Journal of International Law* 395.

Vöneky, S, 'A New Shield for the Environment: Peacetime Treaties as Legal Restraints of Wartime Damage' (2000) 9 *Review of European, Comparative & International Environmental Law* 20.

—— 'Peacetime Environmental Law as a Basis of State Responsibility for Environmental Damage Caused by War' in JE Austin and CE Bruch (eds), *The Environmental Consequences of War* (Cambridge University Press, 2000).

Weil, P, 'Towards Relative Normativity in International Law' (1983) 77 *American Journal of International Law* 413.

Weinstein, T, 'Prosecuting Attacks that Destroy the Environment: Environmental Crimes or Humanitarian Atrocities?' (2005) 17 *Georgetown International Environmental Law Review* 697.

Westing, A, 'Ecological Consequences of the Second Indochina War: A Case Study' (1975) 4 *Ambio: A Journal of Human Environment* 216.

Wiersema, A, 'The New International Law-makers? Conferences of the Parties to Multilateral Environmental Agreements' (2009) 31 *Michigan Journal of International Law* 231.

Wilmshurst, E, 'Introduction' in E Wilmshurst (ed), *International Law and the Classification of Conflicts* (Oxford University Press, 2012).

—— 'Conclusions' in E Wilmshurst (ed), *International Law and the Classification of Conflicts* (Oxford University Press, 2012).

Wyatt, J, 'Law-making at the Intersection of International Environmental, Humanitarian and Criminal Law: The Issue of Damage to the Environment in International Armed Conflict' (2010) 92 *International Review of the Red Cross* 593.

Young, M, 'Regime Interaction in Creating, Implementing and Enforcing International Law' in M Young (ed), *Regime Interaction in International Law: Facing Fragmentation* (Cambridge University Press, 2012).

Yuzon, FJ, 'Deliberate Environmental Modification Through the Use of Chemical and Biological Weapons: "Greening" the International Laws of Armed Conflict to Establish an Environmentally Protective Regime' (1996) 11 *American University Journal of International Law and Policy* 793.

Zacharias, D, 'The UNESCO Regime for the Protection of World Heritage as Prototype of an Autonomy-Gaining International Institution' in A von Bogdandy *et al* (eds), *The Exercise of Public Authority by International Institutions* (Springer, 2010).

International Law Commission Documents

Draft Articles on Prevention of Transboundary Harm From Hazardous Activities, Report of the International Law Commission, adopted at the 65th Session (2001) *Yearbook of the International Law Commission*, Volume II, Part Two.

Draft Articles on Responsibility of States for Internationally Wrongful Acts, Report of the International Law Commission, adopted at the 65th Session (2001) *Yearbook of the International Law Commission*, Volume II, Part Two.

Draft Articles on the Effects of Armed Conflicts on Treaties, With Commentaries, adopted at the 63rd Session (2011) *Yearbook of the International Law Commission* Volume II, Part Two.

'Fragmentation of International Law: Difficulties Arising From the Diversification and Expansion of International Law', Report of the Study Group of the International Law Commission, Finalised by Martti Koskenniemi, UN Doc A/CN.4/L.682, 13 April 2006.

'Fragmentation of International Law: Difficulties Arising from the Diversification and Expansion of International Law', Report of the Study Group of the International Law Commission, UN Doc A/CN.4/L.702, 18 July 2006.

International Law Commission, 'Protection of the Environment. Text and Titles of the Draft Principles Provisionally Adopted by the Drafting Committee on First Reading' (Protection of the Environment, First Reading) UN Doc A/CN.4/L.937 (2019).

Protection of the Environment in Relation to Armed Conflict, Text of the Draft Introductory Provisions and Draft Principles Provisionally Adopted so far by the Drafting Committee, UN Doc A/CN.4/L.870, 22 July 2015.

Reservation to Treaties (Continued), Report of the International Law Commission, 63rd Session (26 April–3 June and 4 July–12 August 2011) (2011) *Yearbook of the International Law Commission*, Volume II, Part Two.

Report of the International Law Commission, 58th Session (1 May–9 June and 3 July–11 August 2006) UN Doc A/61/10 (2006) *Yearbook of the International Law Commission*, Volume II, Part Two.

Report of the International Law Commission, 63rd Session (26 April–3 June and 4 July–12 August 2011) *Yearbook of the International Law Commission*, Volume II, Part Two.

Report of the International Law Commission, 65th Session (6 May–7 June and 8 July–9 August 2013) UN Doc A/68/10 (2013) *Yearbook of the International Law Commission*, Volume II, Part Two.

Report of the International Law Commission, 67th Session (4 May–5 June and 6 July–7 August 2015) (2015) *Yearbook of the International Law Commission*, Volume II, Part Two.

Report of the International Law Commission, 68th Session (2 May–10 June and 4 July–12 August 2016) (2016) *Yearbook of the International Law Commission*, Volume II, Part Two.

Report of the International Law Commission on the Work of its 68th Session (2016) Chapter X 'Protection of the environment in Relation to Armed Conflicts' Commentaries to the draft principles provisionally adopted by the Commission.

Report of the International Law Commission, 70th Session (30 April–1 June and 2 July–10 August 2018) (2018) *Yearbook of the International Law Commission* Volume II, Part Two.

Special Rapporteur Jacobsson, Preliminary Report on the Protection of the Environment in Relation to Armed Conflicts, UN Doc A/CN.4/674, 30 May 2014.

Special Rapporteur M Lehto, First Report on the Protection of the Environment in Relation to Armed Conflicts, UN Doc A/CN.4/720, 30 April 2018.

Special Rapporteur M Jacobsson, Second Report on the Protection of the Environment in Relation to Armed Conflicts, UN Doc A/CN.4/685, 28 May 2015.

Special Rapporteur M Lehto, Second Report on the Protection of the Environment in Relation to Armed Conflicts, UN Doc A/CN.4/728, 27 March 2019.

Special Rapporteur M Jacobsson, Third Report on the Protection of the Environment in Relation to Armed Conflicts, UN Doc A/CN.4/700, 3 June 2016.

UNESCO Documents

The Operational Guidelines for Implementation of the WHC (November 2011), available at: whc.unesco.org/archive/opguide11-en.pdf.

UNESCO World Heritage Committee, Monitoring of the State of Conservation of the World Heritage Cultural and Natural Properties, UN Doc WHC-94/CONF.OOJ/6 Paris, 28 October 1994.

UNESCO World Heritage Committee, State of Conservation of the Properties Inscribed on the List of World Heritage in Danger, UN Doc WHC-98/CONF.203/7, 30 September 1998.

UNESCO World Heritage Committee, State of Conservation of the Properties Inscribed on the List of World Heritage in Danger, UN Doc WHC-99/CONF.209/13, 18 October 1999.

UNESCO World Heritage Committee, State of Conservation of the Properties Inscribed on the List of World Heritage in Danger, UN Doc WHC-04/28.COM/15A Rev, 21 June 2004.

UNESCO World Heritage Committee, State of Conservation of the Properties Inscribed on the List of World Heritage in Danger, UN Doc WHC-06/30.COM/7A, 26 May 2006.

UNESCO World Heritage Committee, State of Conservation of the Properties Inscribed on the List of World Heritage in Danger, UN Doc WHC-07/31.COM/7A, 10 May 2007.

UNESCO World Heritage, State of Conservation of the Properties Inscribed on the List of World Heritage in Danger, UN Doc WHC-08/32.COM/7A, 22 May 2008.

UNESCO World Heritage Committee, State of Conservation of the Properties Inscribed on the List of World Heritage in Danger, UN Doc WHC-09/33.COM/7A, 11 May 2009.

UNESCO World Heritage Committee, State of Conservation of the Properties Inscribed on the List of World Heritage in Danger, UN Doc WHC-10/34.COM/7A, 1 June 2010.

UNESCO World Heritage Committee, State of Conservation of the Properties Inscribed on the List of World Heritage in Danger, UN Doc WHC-10/34.COM/7A.Add, 22 June 2010.

UNESCO World Heritage Committee, State of Conservation of the Properties Inscribed on the List of World Heritage in Danger, UN Doc WHC-11/35.COM/7A.Add, 27 May 2011.

UNESCO World Heritage Committee, State of Conservation of the Properties Inscribed on the List of World Heritage in Danger, UN Doc WHC-12/36.COM/7A.Add, 1 June 2012.

UNESCO World Heritage Committee, Legal Considerations Concerning the Inscription of Properties on the List of World Heritage in Danger and the Deletion of Properties From the World Heritage List, UN Doc WHC-02/CONF.202/8, 21 May 2002.

UNESCO World Heritage Committee, Reflection on the Trends of the State of Conservation, UN Doc WHC-12/36.COM/7C, 15 June 2012.

UNESCO World Heritage Committee, Report of the Rapporteur on the 23rd Session of the Bureau of the World Heritage Committee, UN Doc WHC-99/CONF.209/4, 11 October 1999.

UNESCO World Heritage Committee, Report, UN Doc WHC-94/CONF.003/16, 31 January 1995.

UNESCO World Heritage Committee, Report, UN Doc WHC-01/CONF.208/24, 8 February 2002.

World Heritage Papers 17, Proceedings and Preserving Congolese Heritage, Linking Biological and Cultural Diversity/ Promouvoir et Préserver le patrimoine congolais, Lier diversité biologique et culturelle, Proceedings of the Conference and Workshops, UNESCO, 13–17 September 2004, available at: whc.unesco.org/en/documents/6411.

UN Environment Documents

UNEP, 'Environmental Assessment of the Gaza Strip Following the Escalation of Hostilities in December 2008–January 2009' (UNEP, Kenya, 2009).

UNEP, 'Environmental Governance' (2009), available at: www.unep.org/pdf/brochures/EnvironmentalGovernance.pdf.

UNEP, 'From Conflict to Peacebuilding: The Role of Natural Resources and the Environment' (UNEP, Switzerland, 2009).

UNEP, 'Greening the Blue Helmets, Environment, Natural Resources and UN Peacekeeping Operations' (2012) 81–82, available at: postconflict.unep.ch/publications/UNEP_greening_blue_helmets.pdf.

UNEP, 'Lebanon Post-Conflict Assessment' (UNEP, Switzerland, 2007).

UNEP MONUSCO, Final Report From Expert Meeting, 'Background Paper on Illegal Exploitation and Trade in Natural Resources Benefitting Organized Criminal Groups and its Implications on MONUSCO's Role in Fostering Stability and Peace in Eastern DR Congo', Goma, DRC, 21 March 2015, available at: postconflict.unep.ch/publications/UNEP_DRCongo_MONUSCO_OSESG_final_report.pdf.

UNEP, Partow, H, 'The Mesopotamian Marshlands: Demise of an Ecosystem' Division of Early Warning and Assessment (UNEP, Kenya, 2001).

UNEP, 'Protecting the Environment During Armed Conflict: An Inventory and Analysis of International Law' (UNEP, Switzerland, 2009).

UNEP, 'Report of the Working Group of Experts on Liability and Compensation for Environmental Damage Arising from Military Activities, 1996' (1997) 27 *Environmental Policy and Law* 134.

UNEP, 'Sierra Leone, Environment, Conflict and Peacebuilding Assessment, Technical Report' (UNEP, Switzerland, 2010).

UNEP, 'Sudan Post-Conflict Environmental Assessment' (UNEP, Kenya, 2007).

UNEP, 'The Democratic Republic of the Congo Post-Conflict Environmental Assessment United Nations Environment Programme Synthesis for Policy Makers' (UNEP, Kenya, 2011).

UNEP, The Last Stand of the Gorilla, Environmental Crime and Conflict in the Congo Basin (2010), available at: www.unep.org/pdf/GorillaStand_screen.pdf.

UNEP and UNCHS, 'The Kosovo Conflict, Consequences for the Environment and Human Settlements' (UNEP and Habitat, Nairobi, 1999).

Other UN Documents

'A More Secure World: Our Shared Responsibility Report of the High-level Panel on Threats, Challenges and Change' (United Nations, 2004).

Agreement on the Conservation of Gorillas and Their Habitats (Gorilla Agreement) (adopted 26 October 2007, entered into force 1 June 2008) 2545 UNTS 55.

Declaration of the United Nations Conference on the Human Environment, Stockholm, 16 June 1972, 11 ILM 1416.

Declaration of the United Nations Conference on Environment and Development, Rio de Janeiro, 13 June 1992, 31 ILM 874.

Exploitation of the Environment as a Weapon in Times of Armed Conflict and the Taking of Practical Measures to Prevent Such Exploitation, UN Doc A/46/141, 8 July 1991.

FAO, 'Project Resource' (2017), available at: www.fao.org/3/a-i7626e.pdf.

FAO, 'The 2012 crisis in Mali and its implications on resilience and food security' (2017) FAO Agricultural Development Economics Working Paper, available at www.fao.org/3/a-i7560e.pdf.

Final Report of the Groups of Experts on the DRC, Pursuant to Security Council Resolution 1698 (2006), UN Doc S/2007/423, 18 July 2007.

General Assembly, International Institutional Arrangements Related to Environment and Development, UN Doc A/54/468, 15 October 1999.

General Assembly, UN Doc A/49/50, 15 February 1994.

OCHA, Democratic Republic of the Congo Mapping Exercise (2010), available at: www.ohchr.org/Documents/Countries/ZR/DRC_MAPPING_REPORT_FINAL_EN.pdf.

Protection of the Environment in Times of Armed Conflict, General Assembly, UN Doc A/RES/47/37, 25 November 1992.

Report and Recommendations Made by the Panel of Commissioners Concerning the First Instalment of 'F4' Claims, UN Doc S/AC.26/2001/16, 22 June 2001.

Report of the International Commission of Inquiry on Darfur to the Secretary-General, UN Doc S/2005/60, 1 February 2005.

Report of the Secretary General, UN Doc A/49/323, 19 August 1994.

Report of the Secretary-General, 'Assistance in Mine Clearance', UN Doc A/49/357/Add.1, 20 September 1994.

Report of the United Nations Integrated Water Task Force for Iraq, 'Managing Change in the Marshlands: Iraq's Critical Challenge', UN White Paper (2011).

Second Review Conference of the Parties to the ENMOD Convention, held in Geneva, 14–18 September 1992, Final Document, ENMOD/Conf.II/12, 22 September 1992.

Summary Record of 18th Meeting of the Sixth Committee of the General Assembly, held on 22 October 1991, UN Doc A/C.6/46/SR.18.

UNCHR, Environmental Guidelines (Geneva, 2005).

UN Environment Assembly of the UN Environment Programme, adopted Nairobi 23–27 May 2016, UN Doc UNEP/EA.2/Res.15.

UN Office for West Africa and the Sahel (UNOWAS), 'Pastoralism and Security in West Africa and the Sahel – Towards Peaceful Coexistence' UNOWAS Study (2018), available at: unowas.unmissions.org/sites/default/files/rapport_pastoralisme_eng-2.pdf.

UN Security Council, 'Report of the UN Panel of Experts on the Illegal Exploitation of Natural Resources and Other Forms of Wealth of the Democratic Republic of the Congo', UN Doc S/2001/357, 12 April 2001.

United Nations Country Team, 'Gaza in 2020 A liveable place? A Report by the United Nations Country Team in the Occupied Palestinian Territory' (August 2012).

World Bank, Niger River Basin Management Project (P149714), Implementation Status & Results Report, available at documents.worldbank.org/curated/en/911111559857546894/pdf/Disclosable-Version-of-the-ISR-Niger-River-Basin-Management-Project-P149714-Sequence-No-09.pdf.

World Charter for Nature, UN Doc A/Res/37/7, adopted 28 October 1982.

World Health Organization, 'Our Planet, Our Health, Our Future: Human Health and the Rio Conventions: Biological Diversity, Climate Change and Desertification' Discussion Paper (2012) 2, available at: www.who.int/globalchange/publications/reports/health_rioconventions.pdf.

Other Reports and Publications

A Conceptual Framework for the Wise Use of Wetlands and the Maintenance of their Ecological Character, Resolution IX.1 Annex A, adopted by the 9th meeting of COP (2005), Kampala, available at: www.ramsar.org/sites/default/files/documents/pdf/res/key_res_ix_01_annexa_e.pdf.

Afrik21, 'Mali: Close to €11 million to be invested to protect Inner Niger Delta' (20 February 2019), available at: www.afrik21.africa/en/mali-close-to-e11-million-to-be-invested-to-protect-inner-niger-delta/.

Ajayi, OC et al, 'Rapid assessment of the inner Niger Delta of Mali' (2012) World Agroforestry Working Paper, available at: www.worldagroforestry.org/downloads/Publications/PDFS/WP17336.pdf.

Al Jazeera English, 'Syria's forests pay a heavy price' (*YouTube*, 22 October 2012), available at: www.youtube.com/watch?v=mV6apaqmnPw.

Al Jazeera English, 'UN: Syrian fighters burning vital farmland is "weapon of war"' 4 June 2019, available at: www.aljazeera.com/news/2019/06/syrian-fighters-burning-vital-farmland-weapon-war-190604175625835.html.

BBC News, 'Syrian military "burning farmland in rebel-held north"' 29 May 2019, available at: www.bbc.com/news/world-middle-east-48444596.

Bodansky, D., 'Effects of Military Activity on the Environment', Final Report, May 2003, 5 Executive summary, vi.

'Chainsaw Project, An INTERPOL Perspective on Law Enforcement in Illegal Logging', available at: www.illegal-logging.info/sites/default/files/uploads/WorldBankChainsawIllegal LoggingReport.pdf.

Chalmers, P, 'Managing Mali's Wetland Wealth', Wetlands International, available at: archive.wetlands.org/Portals/0/publications/Strategy%20paper/WI_Managing%20Malis%20Wetland%20Wealth_WEB.pdf.

Changwon Declaration, Resolution X.3 adopted by the 10th meeting of COP (2008) 5, available at: www.ramsar.org/sites/default/files/documents/library/cop10_changwon_english.pdf.

Concern Worldwide and Welthungerhilfe, 'Country Case Studies, Coping with armed conflict and hunger Mali and South Sudan' (2015), available at: www.concernusa.org/wp-content/uploads/2015/03/global_hunger_index_2015_-_case_studies.pdf.

Crawford, A and Bernstein, J, *MEAs, Conservation and Conflict: A Case Study of Virunga National Park, DRC* (International Institute for Sustainable Development, Winnipeg, 2008).

Current Issues Briefing held at the United States Institute of Peace, 'Marshland Arabs of Iraq', 12 December 2002, available at: www.usip.org/publications/marshland-arabs-iraq.

Délégation de l'Union Européenne au Mali, 'Révision du profil environnemental du Mali – Rapport final' (2014), available at: eeas.europa.eu/sites/eeas/files/profil_environnemental_du_mali_0.pdf.

Draft Resolution and Report of the 31st International Conference of the Red Cross and Red Crescent held in Geneva, Switzerland 28 November–1 December 2011, 31IC/11/5.1.1.

European Union Training Mission Mali website: eutmmali.eu/en/eutm-mali-mission/.

Factsheet of Inner Niger Delta, Ramsar Convention website, available at: www.ramsar.org/sites/default/files/documents/library/wwd2004_rpt_mali_press_e.pdf.

Ferrini, L and Benavides, L, 'The Inner Niger Delta/Nexus Dynamics at the Heart of the Sahel' (2018) *Nexus – The Water, Energy and Food Security, Resource Platform*, available at: www.water-energy-food.org/resources/resources-detail/the-inner-niger-delta-nexus-dynamics-at-the-heart-of-the-sahel/.

Final Report to the Prosecutor by the Committee Established to Review the NATO Bombing Campaign Against the Federal Republic of Yugoslavia, published 13 June 2000 on ICTY's web page at: www.icty.org/sid/10052 (Review Committee Report for the ICTY Prosecutor).

'Genocide by Other Means: US Army Slaughtered Buffalo in Plains Indian Wars' *Indian Country Today* (24 September 2017), available at: newsmaven.io/indiancountrytoday/archive/genocide-by-other-means-u-s-army-slaughtered-buffalo-in-plains indian-wars-nEWiK2AZık-yWbnFLXOqfw/.

Griffin, P, 'The Ramsar Convention: A New Window for Environmental Diplomacy?' The Institute for Environmental Diplomacy and Security (2013), available at: www.uvm.edu/ieds/sites/default/files/Ramsar_IEDSResearchSeries.pdf.

Grauer's Gorillas and Chimpanzees in Eastern Democratic Republic of Congo (Kahuzi-Biega, Maiko, Tayna and Itombwe Landscape) Conservation Action Plan 2012–2022, available at: www.cms.int/sites/default/files/document/IUCN%20Grauer%E2%80%99s%20Gorillas%20and%20Chimpanzees%20in%20Eastern%20Democratic%20Republic%20of%20Congo_2013.pdf.

Guidelines for Operation of the Montreux Record, adopted by the Conference of the Contracting Parties in Resolution VI.1, Brisbane, 1996, Accompanying the Guidelines for Operation of the Montreux Record.

Guzel, M, 'Syria Crisis: Turkey's Border Fires Were Deliberately Set By Syrian Forces, Say Turkish Officials' (*Huffington Post*, 7 April 2012), available at: www.huffingtonpost.com/2012/07/04/turkey-border-fires-syria-deliberate_n_1649091.html.

Heath, K, 'Virunga Cleared of Rebels Claim' *Wildlife News* (2 March 2015), available at: wildlifenews.co.uk/2015/03/virunga-cleared-of-rebels-claim/.

Hsiao, E, 'Protecting Places For Nature, People, and Peace: A Critical Socio-Legal Review of Transboundary Conservation Areas' (PhD Thesis, University of British Colombia, 2018).

Human Rights Watch report, 'La Paix – Mali Conflict and Aftermath. Compendium of Human Rights Watch Reporting 2012–2017' (2017) 32, 146–47, available at: www.hrw.org/sites/default/files/report_pdf/malicompendium0217.pdf.

Ibrahim, YI and Zapata, M, 'Regions at Risk – Preventing Atrocities in Mali', Early Warning Country Report (2018), the Simon-Skjodt Center for the Prevention of Genocide, available at: www.ushmm.org/m/pdfs/Mali_Report_English_FINAL_April_2018.pdf.

IFAD, Sahelian Areas Development Fund Programme (FODESA) Project Completion Report, Main report, 2013, available at www.thegef.org/sites/default/files/project_documents/GEF%25201152_TER_IFAD_MALI_English%2520Translation_0.pdf.

ILPI 2014, 'Protection of the Natural Environment in Armed Conflict: An Empirical Study', International Law and Policy Institute, Report 12/2014.

Implementation Force Final Factsheet, 2 October 1996, available on NATO's website: www.nato.int/ifor/general/shrp-grd.htm.

International Institute of Humanitarian Law, The Manual on the Law of Non-International Armed Conflict With Commentary, issued by the Drafting Committee consisting of M Schmitt, C Garraway and Y Dinstein (San Remo, 2006) (the IHHL Manual).

International Law Association (ILA), Final Report of the Committee on Formation of General Customary International Law, London Conference (2000).

IUCN, 'Draft International Covenant on Environment and Development – Implementing Sustainability', 5th edn, IUCN Environmental Policy and Law Paper No 31 Rev 4 (IUCN, Gland).

Jeffries, S, 'Isis's destruction of Palmyra: "The heart has been ripped out of the city"' *The Guardian* (2 September 2015), available at: www.theguardian.com/world/2015/sep/02/isis-destruction-of-palmyra-syria-heart-been-ripped-out-of-the-city.

Joint NATO Doctrine for Environmental Protection During NATO-led Military Activities (STANAG 7141/AJEPP-4).

Jones, P, 'Congolese Rebels Cash in on Gorilla Tourism to Fund Insurgency' *The Guardian* (19 October 2012), available at: www.theguardian.com/world/2012/oct/19/congo-rebels-gorilla-tour-insurgency.

Kalpers, J, Overview of the Armed Conflict and Biodiversity in Sub-Saharan Africa: Impact, Mechanisms and Responses (Biodiversity Support Program, Washington DC, 2001).

Klemm, J, 'Lifeline for Over 1 Million in Mali Under Threat by World Bank Dam Plans' (*International Rivers* Blog post), available at: www.internationalrivers.org/blogs/352/lifeline-for-over-1-million-in-mali-under-threat-by-world-bank-dam-plans.

Kortlandth, J, 'An environmental flow for the Inner Niger Delta' (*Wetlands International* Blog post), available at: www.wetlands.org/blog/an-environmental-flow-for-the-inner-niger-delta/.

Leech, TDJ, 'The Final Report of the Project "Seal"', 18 December 1950, available at: www.wanttoknow.info/documents/project_seal.pdf.

Liggitt, B, 'Inner Niger Delta threatened by Fomi Dam construction', The Royal Society for the Protection of Birds (RSPB), available at: community.rspb.org.uk/getinvolved/b/specialplaces/posts/inner-niger-delta-threatened-by-fomi-dam-construction.

List Of Wetlands of International Importance Included in the Montreux Record, 2016, available at: www.ramsar.org/sites/default/files/documents/library/montreux_list_2016_efs.pdf.

'Long Term System for Monitoring the Illegal Killing of Elephants, Phase II Final Evaluation Report', available at: www.cites.org/sites/default/files/common/prog/mike/prog_reports/1309_MIKE_ph2_final_EvaluationReport.pdf.

Lovgren, S, 'Congo Warlord's Arrest Puts Gorillas' Future in Turmoil' *National Geographic News* (23 January 2009), available at: news.nationalgeographic.com/news/2009/01/090123-nkunda-arrested.html.

Mach, K et al, 'Climate as a risk factor for armed conflict' *Nature* (2019), available at: www.nature.com/articles/s41586-019-1300-6.

Maliweb.net, Programme de développement durable du delta intérieur du Niger: Après le succès de la première phase, la seconde lancée' (13 October 2018), available at: www.maliweb.net/economie/programme-de-developpement-durable-du-delta-interieur-du-niger-apres-le-succes-de-la-premiere-phase-la-seconde-lancee-2781498.html.

NATO Military Principles and Policies for Environmental Protection (MC 469/1).

Owen, J, 'Congo Rebels Agree to End the Gorilla Slaughter' *National Geographic News* (25 January 2007), available at: news.nationalgeographic.com/news/2007/01/070125-gorillas-congo.html.

Partow, H, 'Environmental Impact of Wars and Conflicts' in *Future Arab Environmental Challenges* (Arab Forum for Development Report, Lebanon, 2008).

Permanent Forum on Indigenous Issues, 'Who are indigenous peoples?', Fact Sheet, available at: www.un.org/esa/socdev/unpfii/documents/5session_factsheet1.pdf.

Pearlman, J, '"Tsunami bomb" tested off New Zealand coast' *The Telegraph* (1 January 2013), available at: www.telegraph.co.uk/news/worldnews/australiaandthepacific/newzealand/9774217/Tsunami-bomb-tested-off-New-Zealand-coast.html.

Programme for Infrastructure Development in Africa (PIDA), 'Fomi Multi-purpose Dam (Niger River Basin)', available at: www.au-pida.org/view-project/1013/.

Ramsar Advisory Mission No 55: Croatia (2005) 1-2, available at: www.ramsar.org/sites/default/files/documents/library/ram55_croatia_kopacki_rit_2005.pdf.

Ramsar Advisory Mission, Rapport De Mission, Mission de suivi réactif de l'Etat de Conservation du parc national des Virunga, République démocratique du Congo (RDC) (2014) 4–7, available at: www.ramsar.org/sites/default/files/documents/library/ram78_e_drcongo.pdf.

Ramsar Convention, 'Investing in Wetlands' (2014), available at: www.ramsar.org/sites/default/files/documents/library/ramsar_sgf_portfolio_2014_20.pdf.

Ramsar Convention Recommendation 4.7 in 1990.

Ramsar Convention Resolution VII.3 (1999).

Ramsar Convention Recommendation 6.3, 1996; Handbook 7.

Ramsar Convention, Resolution IX.16 (2005).

Ramsar Convention, Resolution IX.1 Annex A, A Conceptual Framework for the Wise Use of Wetlands and the Maintenance of Their Ecological Character. 9th Meeting of the Conference of the Parties, Kampala, Uganda, 8–15 November 2005

Ramsar Convention Secretariat, 'An Introduction to the Ramsar Convention on Wetlands', 5th edn (previously The Ramsar Convention Manual) (2016), Gland, Switzerland.

Recommendation 4.1, Wetland restoration, adopted by the fourth meeting of the COP, Montreux (1990), available at: www.ramsar.org/sites/default/files/documents/library/key_rec_4.01e.pdf.

Rutherford, M, 'German Scientists Developing Green Bombs New Environmental Friendly, Nitrogen-based Explosives Could Deliver More of a Bang While Being Safer to Handle Than Traditional Charges, German Scientists Say' (*Cnet*, 5 June 2008), available at: www.cnet.com/news/german-scientists-developing-green-bombs.

Small Grants Fund (SGF) Operational Guidelines 2019, available at: www.ramsar.org/document/ramsar-small-grants-fund-for-wetland-conservation-and-wise-use-sgf-operational-guidelines-0.

Swedish International Development Cooperation Agency (Sida) website: www.sida.se/English/where-we-work/Africa/Mali/examples-of-results/inner-niger-delta-mali/facts-inner-niger-delta/.

UN News, 'Climate change recognized as "threat multiplier", UN Security Council debates its impact on peace' (25 January 2019), available at: news.un.org/en/story/2019/01/1031322.

UNEP, 'Sudan Post-Conflict Assessment' 105–06, available at: postconflict.unep.ch/publications/sudan/05_displacement.pdf.

United States Institute of Peace, 'Marshland Arabs of Iraq', 12 December 2002, available at: www.usip.org/publications/marshland-arabs-iraq.

van Dam, A, 'Wetlands: Important for Nature and for People', 2019, available at: www.un-ihe.org/stories/world-wetlands-day-2019-ramsar-convention-wetlands-remains-important.

Weir, D, 'The Civilian Health Risks From TNT in Syria's Barrel Bombs' (*Toxic Remnants of War Project Blog*, 27 March 2015), available at: www.toxicremnantsofwar.info/the-civilian-health-risks-from-tnt-in-syrias-barrel-bombs.

Wetlands International, 'Impact of dams on the people of Mali', available at: archive.wetlands.org/Portals/0/publications/Count%20Form/Brochure/WI%20Upper%20Niger%20brochure.pdf.

'What's the environmental impact of modern war?' *The Guardian* (6 November 2014), available at: www.theguardian.com/environment/2014/nov/06/whats-the-environmental-impact-of-modern-war.

World Conservation Congress Resolution 2.97 entitled 'A Martens Clause for environmental protection' (Amman, 4–11 October 2000).

World Food Programme (WPF), Mali, WFP website: www1.wfp.org/countries/mali.

Written statement submitted by the United States to the International Court of Justice in the *Nuclear Weapons* Advisory Opinion. Letter dated 20 June 1995 from the Acting Legal Adviser to the Department of State, together with written statement of the Government of the United States of America, available at: www.icj-cij.org/docket/files/95/8700.pdf.

Index